GCSE in Applied Science

Teachers' File (2nd edition)

Authors: *Colin Bell, David Brodie, Byron Dawson and Ann Tiernan*

Contributors: *Henry Elliott and Mike Tingle*

Editors: *David Brodie and Byron Dawson*

About the authors

The authors

Colin Bell is a former Deputy Head of a comprehensive school. He has been Head of Biology in both grammar and comprehensive schools. Colin now works as a freelance author. He has long experience of working with various awarding bodies as Senior Examiner for GCSE, both in the UK and internationally.

David Brodie has been Head of Science in a Midlands comprehensive school, a Senior Examiner and a Moderator. He has worked for the Nuffield Foundation as editor of GCSE and GNVQ publications, as well as working for the British Association for the Advancement of Science. He is author of a wide range of educational resources across the whole range of the science curriculum.

Byron Dawson is a former Head of Science and is now an Assistant Head Teacher with responsibility for the curriculum in an 11–18 secondary school. He works as a freelance author, and has written science textbooks for several publishers. Byron is also a Senior Examiner, with responsibilities for the assessment of GCSE Science and overseas A level Biology examinations.

Ann Tiernan was for many years Head of Science in an 11–18 secondary school. She now works as a freelance author, producing texts and Internet-based learning materials for use at Key Stages 3 and 4. She also works for awarding bodies as a Senior Examiner, managing the assessment of chemistry and science at GCSE and A level, both in the UK and internationally.

The contributors

Henry Elliott worked in further and higher education for over 30 years, the final 12 of which were as Head of a large Department of Science. He has worked freelance since 1997. He is an experienced Senior Examiner, Verifier and Moderator across GCSE, GNVA and VCE science programmes.

Mike Tingle is a former Head of Chemistry in a 13–18 high school. He now works as a freelance educational consultant and in-service trainer. He is involved with vocational science programmes as a Senior Examiner and Verifier.

How to use the CD-ROM

README-instructions for installing your CD-ROM

- **On a PC**

The installation procedure will automatically copy the PDF files on the CD into a folder on your hard drive called **applsci** (**c:\applsci**).

If you want to put the PDF files somewhere else, e.g. make them available on your server, click **Browse** then find and select the alternative location to which you want the files to be copied. Then press **Next** to continue with the installation procedure.

To access the files once they have been copied, go to **c:\applsci** (or wherever you copied the files to), open the relevant sub folder, select which file you want and double click on it.

- **On a Mac**

Open the CD icon and drag the folder onto the desktop.

Contents

Introduction

About the course

The Folens Applied Science course for GCSE in Applied Science (Double Award) consists of flexible resources that can be applied to, and integrated with, any scheme of work.

The course consists of the Student Book and a Support Pack. The Support Pack has versions developed for particular awarding bodies.

Student Book
In the Student Book, the contents of the specifications are broken down into the following themes:
Theme 1: Introducing scientific skills
Theme 2: Living organisms
Theme 3: Useful chemicals
Theme 4: Energy and devices
Theme 5: The Earth and universe
Theme 6: Science in the workplace

Theme 1 could be useful during induction. Theme 6 will be a useful lead into the assignments relating to science at work and science in the workplace.

The themes are divided into sections. Each section begins with a list of objectives for the student. It also identifies links to assignments for assessment and other practical activities in the Support Pack. Each section is then divided into manageable topics.
Each topic has:

- activities for skill development;
- a case study relating science to everyday life or science at work;
- questions in the text to check understanding;
- differentiation of materials for students working at Higher tier.

There are review questions at the end of each section to check progress and understanding.

Key words are highlighted throughout, and if they are not defined in the text a 'word check box' is used to define the word. Copying and completing key fact boxes with key words will help the students gain the knowledge needed for their Unit 2 test.

By answering the questions throughout the book, students will develop knowledge, skills and understanding required for the course.

Answers to all the questions and key fact boxes in the Student Book are given in Section 2 of the Teachers' File.

The symbol (T) on the pages of the Student Book guides the teacher to associated materials in the Support Pack.

Support Pack
The Support Pack is made up of the Teachers' File and a CD-ROM with a site license. It provides guidance, information and the materials required for delivering the Applied Science course. Everything in the Teachers' File is also provided electronically on the CD-ROM.

The Support Pack provides:

- guidance on portfolio building and assessment;
- a set of assignments with which to deliver the portfolio evidence required;
- a practice test for both Foundation Tier and Higher Tier, with mark schemes;
- practical activities to help with understanding of the topics and to develop skills;
- reference sheets that can be used for producing handouts or OHTs;
- key websites, including those linked to particular topics, and other useful information;
- answers to all the questions and key fact boxes in the Student Book.

Section I
Reference section

This summary table should help you decide when to use these reference sheets.

		Student Book	Practical activities	Assignments
1 Using measuring instruments		1.4 Handling scientific equipment and materials (pages 16–19)	18, 19	5, 6, 13
2 Presenting data		1.5 Recording and analysing scientific data (pages 20–23)	6	3
3 Working with microscopes		2.1 Cells (pages 26–29)	1, 4	2, 3
4 Monitoring living organisms		2.7 Photosynthesis (pages 52–55)	5, 7	2, 3
5 The Mansfield Brewery	OHT	2.14 Fermentation (pages 82–85)		8, 14
6 Aseptic techniques		2.17 Preserving food (pages 94–97)	9, 10	14
7 The Harvard fitness test	OHT	2.24 Oxygen debt (pages 124–127)	6	14
8 Structures and properties		3.10 Splitting the atom (pages 188–191) 3.13 More about molecules (pages 200–203) 3.16 Polymers (pages 214–217)		4, 9, 10, 11
9 Particles in reactions		3.1 Elements from the Earth (pages 146–149)		4, 9, 10, 11
10 Amounts of substance		3.8 Putting numbers into industry (pages 178–181)	16	4, 5, 9, 10, 11
11 The blast furnace	OHT	3.4 Iron and steel (pages 160–163)		8
12 Fractional distillation of crude oil	OHT	3.5 Crude oil to petrol (pages 166–169)		8
13 Comparing materials		3.18 Physical properties (pages 222–225)	19	7
14 Composites		3.18 Physical properties (pages 222–225)		7
15 Energy calculations		4.4 Lighting power (pages 244–247) 4.5 Heating for profit (pages 248–251)	20, 23	12, 13
16 The electromagnetic spectrum		5.4 Waves and communication (pages 298–305)		
17 The Earth and atmosphere		5.1 Our atmosphere (page 287) 5.3 The Earth beneath our feet (pages 294–297)		
18 The universe		5.4 Waves and communication (page 298)		
19 The microscope	OHT		1, 4	2, 3
20 Parts of a light microscope	OHT		1	2, 3
21 Distillation	OHT		13	4, 11
22 Distillation apparatus	OHT		13	11

Using measuring instruments

1. Reading scales

- Check the scale markings. Do they go up in ones, twos or fives?

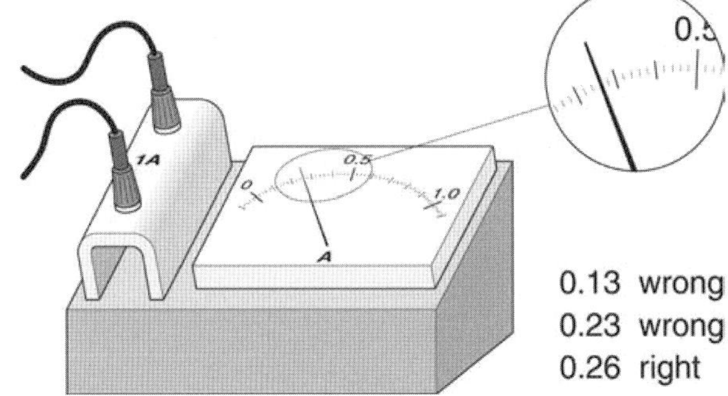

- Make sure that your eye is in the right place.

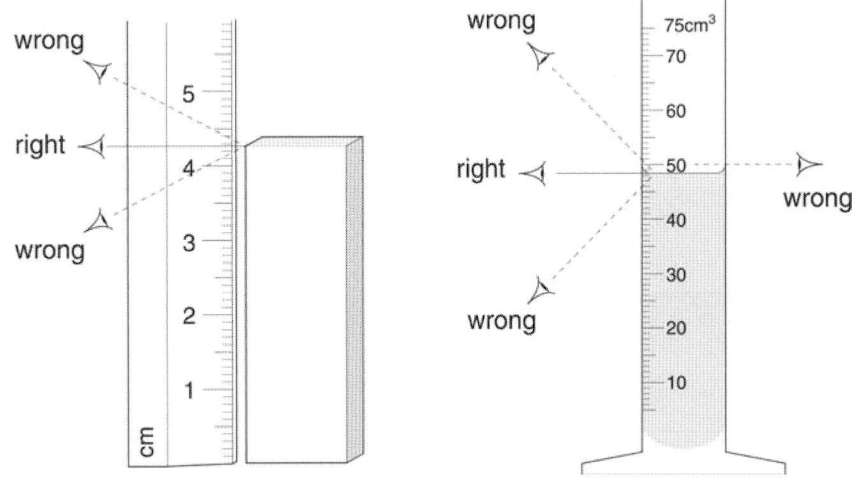

- Check the unit of measurement. For example, is it centimetre or millimetre, or amp or milliamp? What is the abbreviation for the unit – is it cm, mm, A or mA?

2. Uncertainty

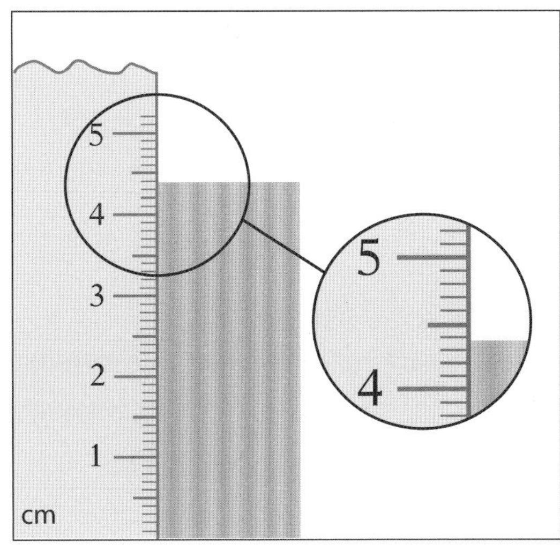

What is this reading?

The reading is 4.4 cm – or is 4.38 cm? We can't be certain. We can only say that the measurement is close to 4.4 cm. It is more than 4.35 cm and less than 4.45 cm. We can write the value as 4.4 ± 0.05 cm. Here the '± 0.05 cm' is the **uncertainty** in our measurement.

Using measuring instruments (continued)

3. Precision instruments

A simple rule

A rule can be used to measure to the nearest 0.1 cm (1 mm).

This measurement is 4.4 cm.

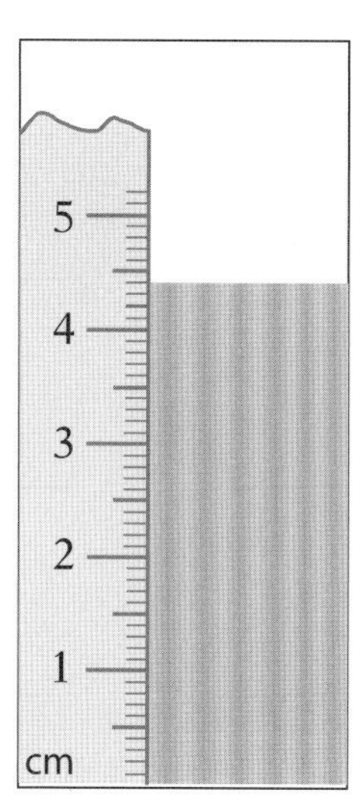

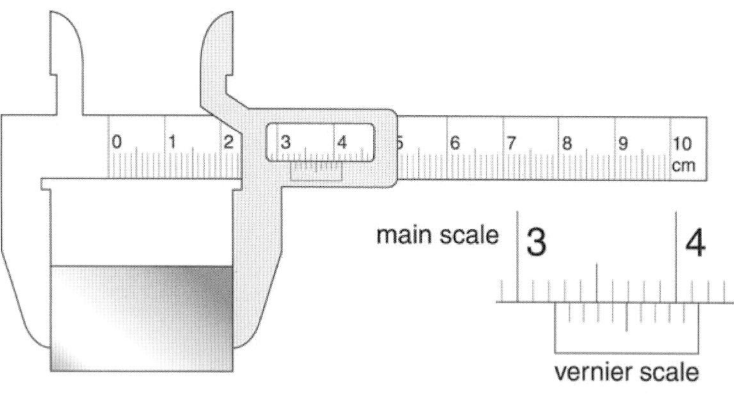

This measurement is 3.24 cm.

Vernier callipers

The start of the sliding vernier scale tells us that the measurement is 3.2? cm.The 4th mark on the vernier scale is the only one that is lined up with a mark on the main scale.The measurement is 3.24 cm.

Micrometer

The main scale on the micrometer tells us that the measurement is more than 0.45 cm. The rotating scale tells us how much to add to 0.45.

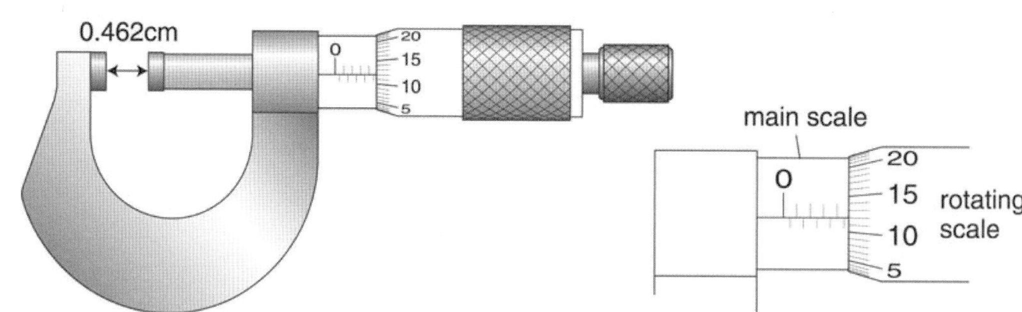

The measurement is: 0.45 (from main scale)
0.012 (from rotating scale)
0.462 cm

Precision

rule measurement = 4.4 cm
vernier calliper measurement = 3.24 cm
micrometer measurement = 0.462 cm

The micrometer gives the highest precision.

Using measuring instruments (continued)

4. High and low range instruments

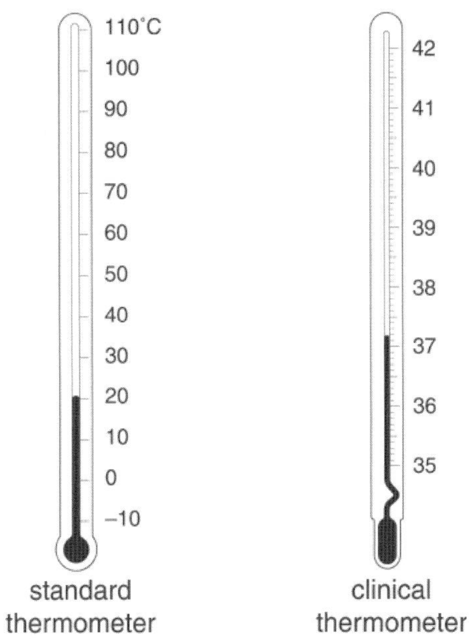

Two thermometers.

- The range of the standard thermometer is from −10°C to 110°C, which is a range of 120°C. It reads to the nearest 1°C.
- The range of the clinical thermometer is from 35°C to 42°C, which is a range of 7°C. It reads to the nearest 0.1°C.

The clinical thermometer has a narrower range but gives the higher precision.

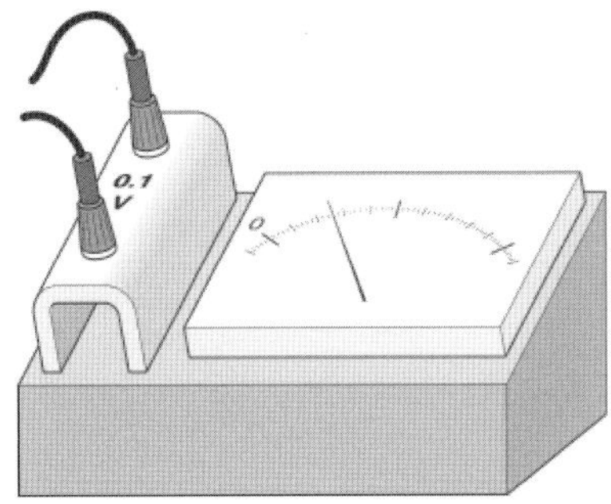

The range is from −0.01 V to 0.1 V.
It reads to the nearest 0.002 V.

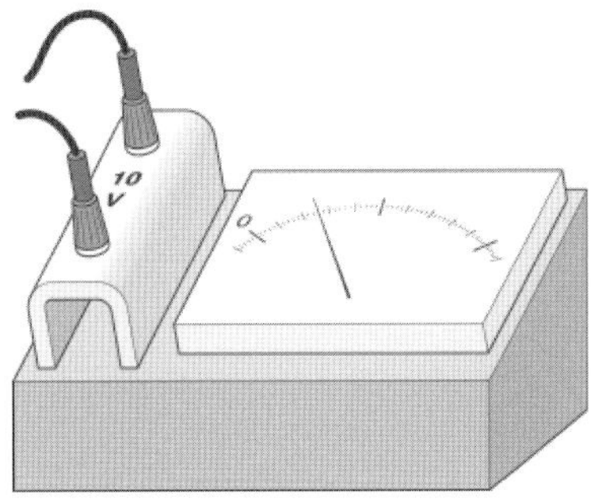

The range is from −1 V to 10 V.
It reads to the nearest 0.2 V.

An analogue meter can be adapted to different ranges and different precisions. Take care to check what these are.

Presenting data

Visual information

Data are collections of information – usually involving quantities. We can often understand the information more quickly when it is visual information.

A **bar chart** has only one numbered axis. It gives us a useful visual comparison of quantities.

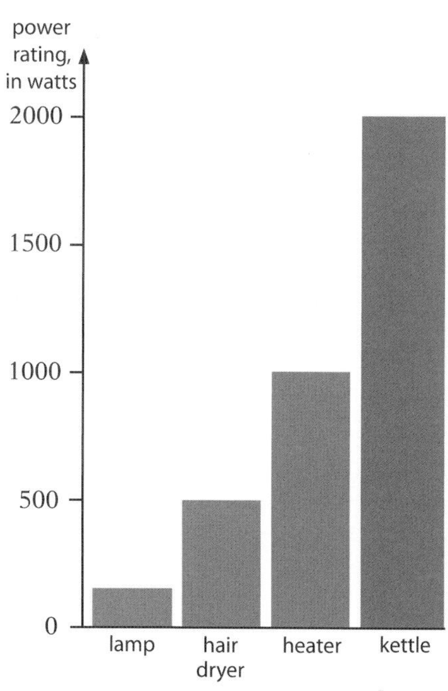

Pie charts provide useful representations of percentages.

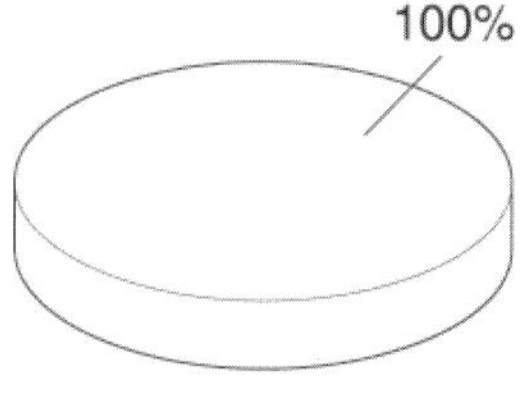

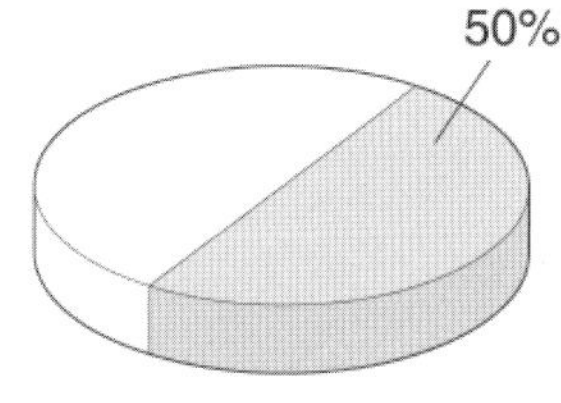

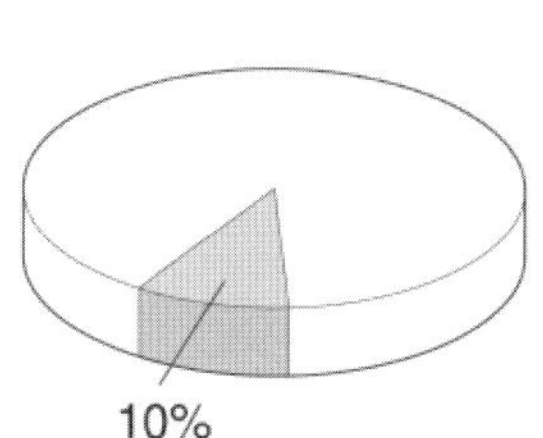

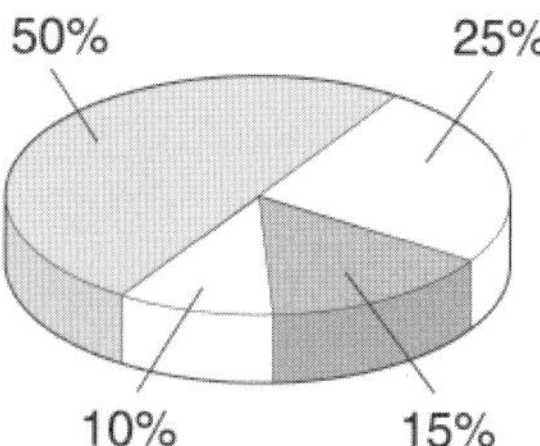

Graphs let us make quick visual comparisons.

Here the vertical axis (sometimes known as the *y*-axis) is 'Cooking time, in minutes'. This is the **output variable** or **independent variable**, the variable that we do not control directly.

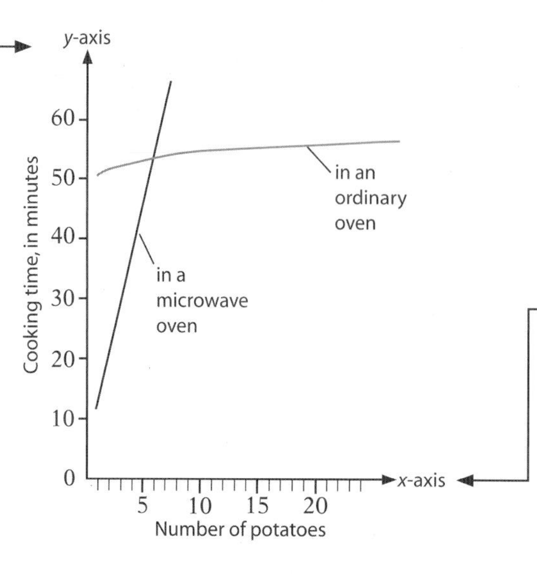

Here the horizontal axis (sometimes known as the *x*-axis) is 'Number of potatoes'. This is the **input variable** or **dependent variable**, the variable that we control directly.

Presenting data (continued)

Graphs from investigations

There is uncertainty in every measurement. This means that the line on this graph does not have to pass through every point. We use judgement to draw the line, guided by the general pattern of the points.

Here, the pattern that we see is that the current decreases as the length increases.

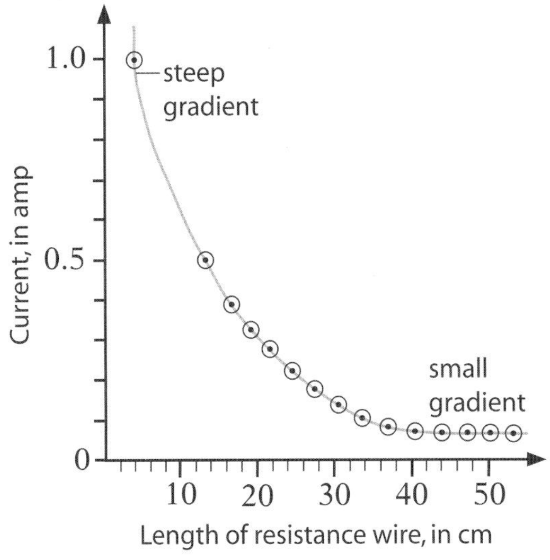

This graph has a simple shape – it is a straight line. It tells us that when we change the voltage, the current changes by the same proportion.

The graph has a constant gradient.

We can work out the gradient by drawing a triangle:

$$\text{gradient} = \frac{\text{change in current}}{\text{change in voltage}}$$

$$= \frac{0.5}{2}$$

$$= 0.25 \text{ amp per volt}$$

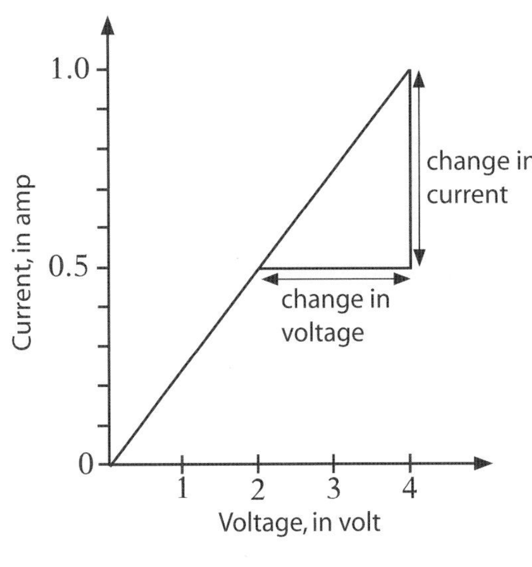

All the triangles that we could draw for this graph will give the same answer for the gradient. The bigger the gradient, the better the wire is at conducting electricity.

Working with microscopes

The microscope

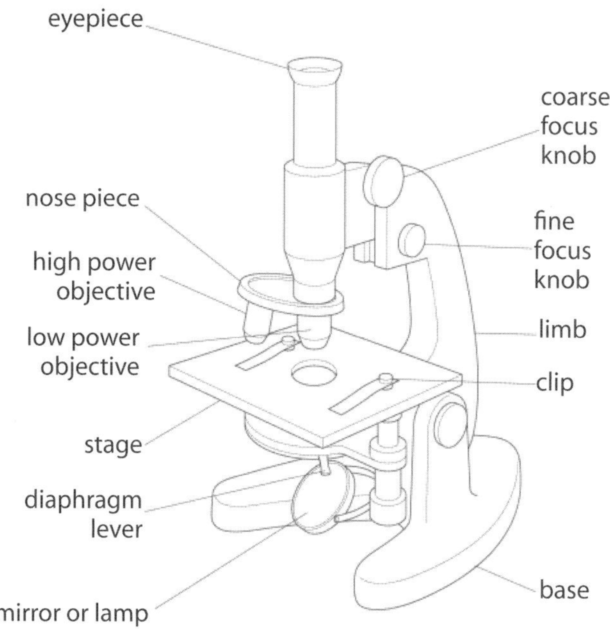

How the light microscope works

The light is focused on the specimen using a mirror or lamp. Light leaving the specimen passes through the transparent objective lens, which magnifies the image of the specimen. The image is further magnified by the eyepiece lens. The image the user sees by looking through the eyepiece is therefore bigger than the specimen.

The overall magnification of the specimen is found by multiplying the magnification of the objective lens by the magnification of the eyepiece lens.

The focus knobs are used to make the image clearer. These change the distance between the specimen and the lens.

Setting up the microscope

1. Place the microscope in the middle of your bench, out of sunlight.
2. Tidy the electric lead and connect it to the electricity supply. Check that the lamp is on. If your microscope does not have a lamp, then you need to adjust the mirror so that it reflects light up through the microscope. Do not focus directly on the Sun.
3. Click the low magnification objective lens, such as ×4, into place.
4. Move the slide so that the specimen is under the lens and the light is shining up through it.
5. Clip the slide onto the stage.
6. Use the coarse focus knob so that the lens is roughly 13 mm above the specimen. You will need to look at the microscope from the side to do this.
7. Look through the eyepiece and adjust the coarse focus knob to make the image sharper.
8. Use the fine focus knob, turning it very slowly, to obtain the sharpest image that you can.
9. Check the image is actually of the specimen by moving the slide around a little. The image should also move.
10. Adjust the diaphragm to control the amount of light to improve the quality of detail that you can see.
11. Now that the microscope is set up at low magnification, you can change the objective lens to highest power, ×40. Take care, because the lens will now be very close to the specimen. You could break the cover slip.
12. The specimen should still be visible. ONLY use the fine focus knob to make the image sharper. (Using the coarse focus knob could break the cover slip.)

Monitoring living organisms

Working with living organisms is not like working with less complicated physical systems. You have to be especially careful about the welfare of the organisms. These are some monitoring guidelines.

Choose an appropriate organism

- If you are monitoring growth, then choose a fast-growing organism, such as broad bean or mustard and cress. This means that you have to complete the monitoring within a few weeks.
- Yeast is used to make beer. Special bacteria are used to make yoghurt. These organisms can be monitored to find the conditions to which the yeast or the bacteria are best suited, so that the maximum amount of product can be made.
- If you are monitoring responses to environment, choose an organism that responds in a clear and simple way to different conditions. Animals such as woodlice are suitable.
- You can measure physical or mental performance in humans. The Harvard fitness test is used to indicate someone's fitness. Some people may have a medical reason that means they should not do the fitness test. The person doing the monitoring needs to be close by to steady any equipment used.

Protect the welfare of the organism

Your investigation must be ethical.

- If you are using animals, such as woodlice, you must make sure that they are not harmed and that you return them to their natural environment when your investigation is complete. Note that woodlice are especially sensitive to bright lights and excess heat. Such conditions must not be continued for more than a few moments with constant observation.
- If you are using a humane small mammal trap to investigate the animals in an area of woodland you need to check the traps every few hours. Small mammals die if they go only a few hours without food. You will need a monitoring schedule for this.

Make a written plan

Your plan should deal with these points.

- What organism will you use?
- What do you hope to find out?
  For example:
  - Does temperature affect the growth of plants?
- If you are using an animal, how will you consider the welfare of the organism?
  - Are there any ethical issues to be considered?
- What conditions will you provide and how will you control them?
  For example:
  - Will you need to water plants?
  - Will they survive over the weekend?
- What will you monitor?
  For example:
  - Will you measure height of seedlings, or dry mass of new growth material?
  - How will you detect the preferences of woodlice?
- What monitoring schedule will you follow?
  For example:
  - For seedlings, a measurement once a day should be enough. But you might need to monitor bacterial growth more frequently.

And then…

Once you have planned and prepared you can then:

- carry out the investigation, recording all relevant data
- analyse your results and explain what they show
- evaluate your investigation.

The Mansfield Brewery

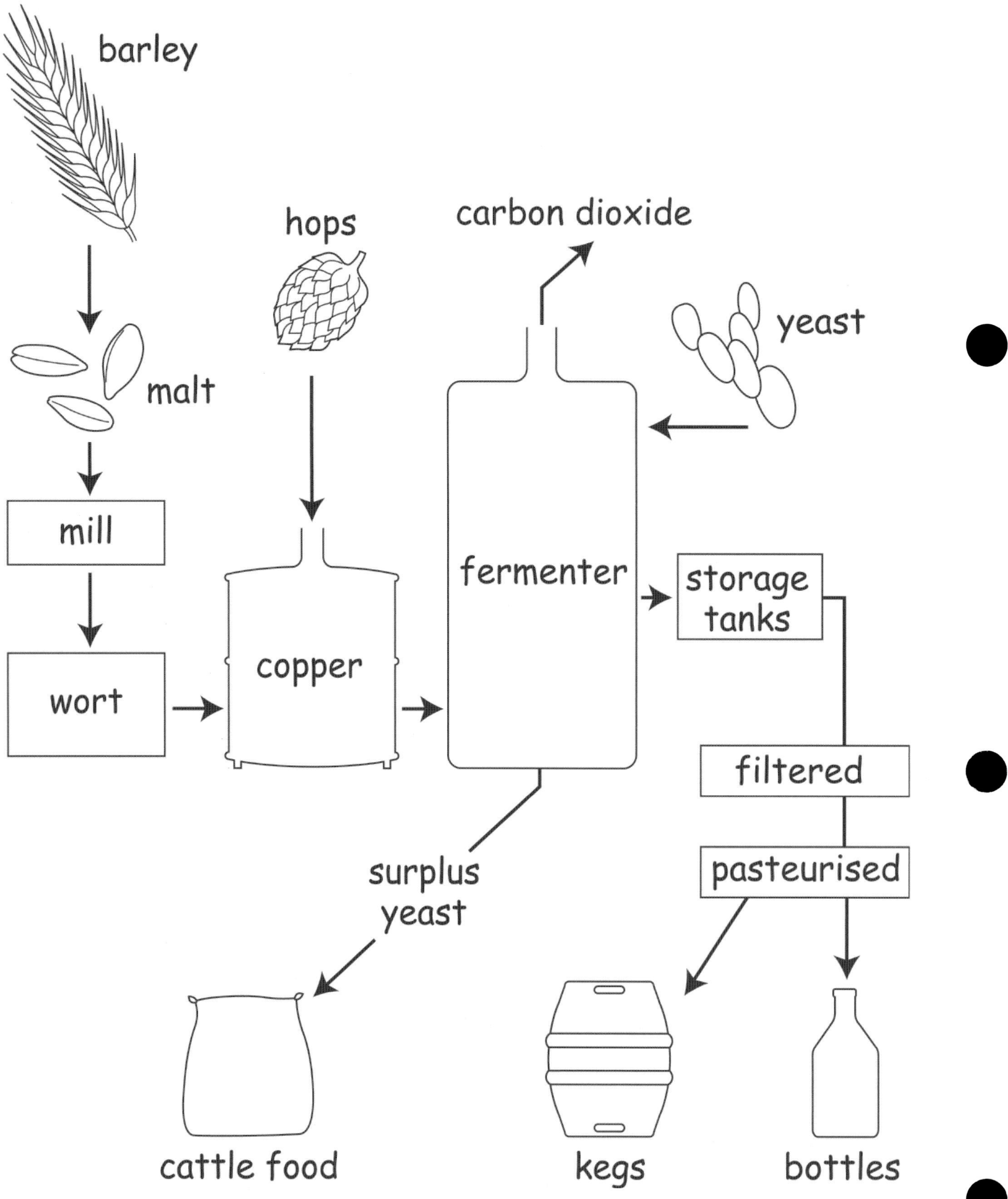

Aseptic techniques

Microorganisms are living things that are too small to see with the eye alone. **Bacteria** are one kind of microorganism. Bacteria are everywhere, though not all bacteria are harmful. Our bodies must defend themselves against infection by harmful sorts of bacteria, all day and every day.

Routes of infection by bacteria

There are many ways that bacteria can infect us:

- through the nose and mouth, carried by air;
- through the mouth, by contact with contaminated food, hands or equipment;
- through broken skin, such as cuts – even old cuts;
- through sexual contact.

All microorganisms should be treated as if they can cause infections and disease.

Studying bacteria

We may want to study bacteria. Technicians in hospital laboratories do this, for example. We can provide the nutrients and the right temperature to encourage bacterial cultures to grow. The nutrient materials on which we grow bacteria are called **media**.

We have to work carefully when we study bacteria, for two reasons:

- contamination by bacteria from sources other than the ones we want to investigate can ruin an experiment;
- bacteria can be dangerous – we must prevent the release of bacteria that have been grown on media.

Sterilisation

Sterilisation is the process that is used to make objects or material sterile. A sterile object or material is one that is free of all living cells.

- All equipment and media must be sterilised before use, so that they do not carry bacteria before we even start our experiment.
- All equipment and media must be sterilised after use so that any bacteria which have grown, including any harmful bacteria, are destroyed.
- Sterilisation can be done by:
  - dry heat, in a hot oven or a Bunsen burner flame;
  - wet heat, by boiling;
  - steam heat, in an autoclave.
- All equipment and material that comes into contact with sterilised items must itself be sterilised.
- Benches must be disinfected.
- The neck of any container must be passed through a Bunsen burner flame when it is opened.
- Wire loops or mounted needles that we use for transferring bacteria must be sterilised before and after use by heating them in a Bunsen burner flame until they are red hot.

Further essential safety rules

Here are some more safety rules:

- keep cuts, grazes or other exposed parts of the body covered by a waterproof dressing;
- use disinfectant to clean all surfaces, before and after working with microorganisms;
- keep your hands away from your mouth – do not drink, eat or lick labels when working with microorganisms;
- do not use mouth pipettes;
- do not squirt liquids which contain microorganisms;
- if you drop a culture of microorganisms, get help straight away;
- do not try to transfer microorganisms from one container to another;
- all media must be kept covered – observe cultures in the sealed containers in which they have been grown;
- dispose of all cultures and equipment by sterile disposal;
- wash and dry your hands thoroughly after working with microorganisms.

The Harvard fitness test

The Harvard fitness test can be used to work out how fit you are.
It works by timing your pulse rate after you have done some exercise.
Look at the safety notes in Optional Practical Activity 6 before you carry out this test.

What to do

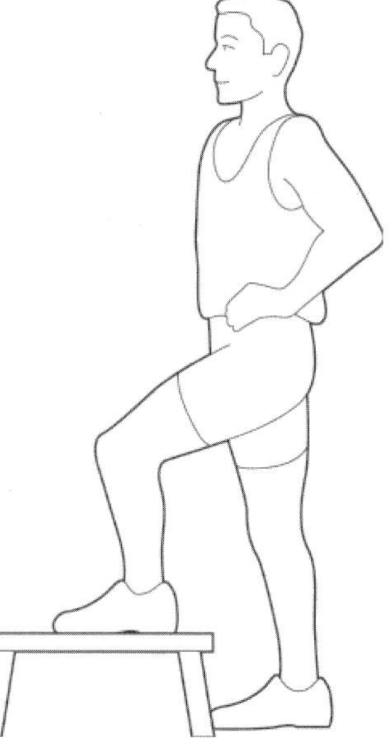

The exercise

The exercise involves stepping up and down on a bench for 300 seconds (5 minutes).

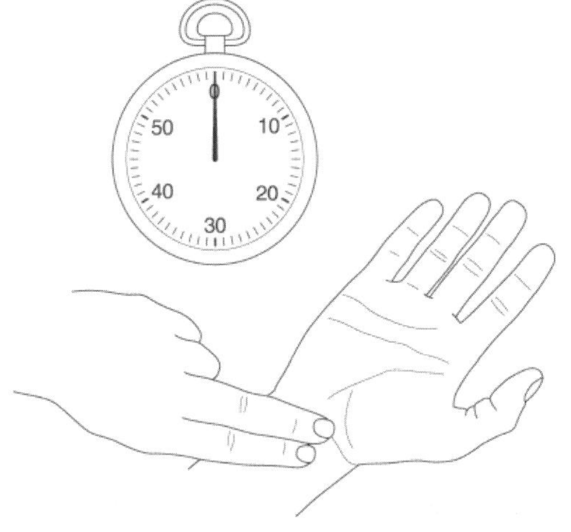

Counting your pulse

After you have finished your exercise, you rest for 60 seconds. Then you count your pulse for 30 seconds, wait for 30 seconds, take your pulse for a further 30 seconds, wait for another 30 seconds and then take a final pulse reading for 30 seconds.

How fit are you?

You work out your fitness level as follows:

$$\frac{\text{time spent on exercise} \times 100}{2 \times (\text{1st} + \text{2nd} + \text{3rd pulse counts})}$$

Compare the value you get with this scale:

more than 90	is super fit
81–90	is very fit
71–80	is fit
60–70	is fair
less than 60	is unfit

Structures and properties

1. Picturing particles

Picturing the particles in all materials is not easy.

We know that atoms can attract each other: 

But when they get too close together they repel each other: 

We can draw springs or sticks to show the attraction and repulsion. A spring can represent attraction or repulsion. A stick is easier to draw than a spring.

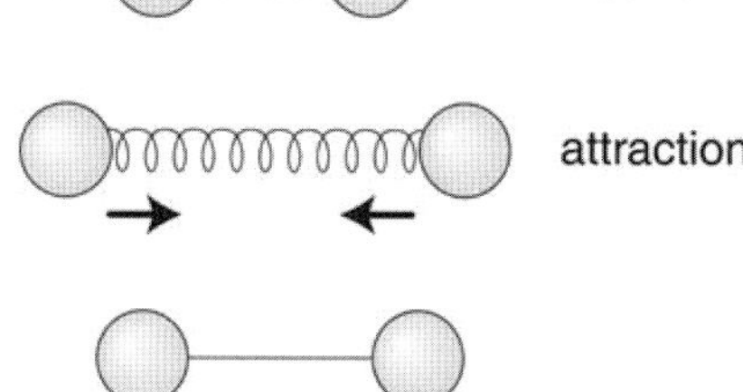

We can draw molecules with and without sticks. These are two ways of showing the same molecule.

without sticks

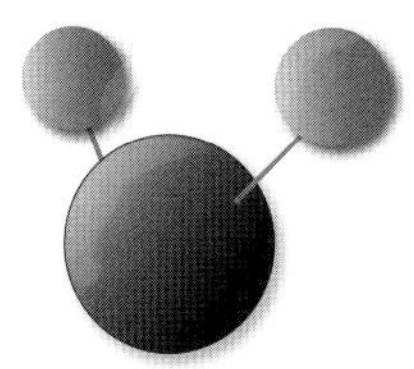
with sticks

2. Predicting behaviour

If you know about particles, then you can <u>predict</u> the behaviour of materials. Here are some examples.

<u>Diamond</u> is hard and strong because its atoms are held strongly in place by the forces between them and their neighbours. In diamond, each atom sits firmly in place between four close neighbours. A diamond has a huge array of atoms (this diagram only shows five).

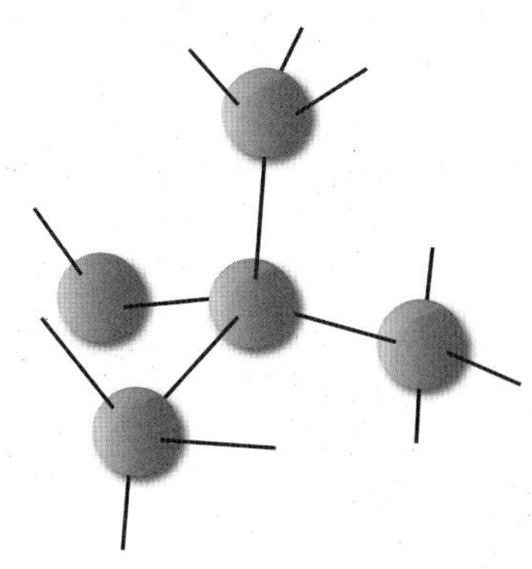

<u>Methane</u> is a gas made of small molecules. Each molecule of methane only has five atoms.

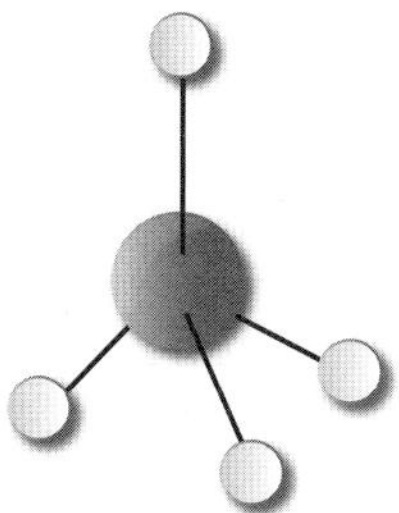

Structures and properties (continued)

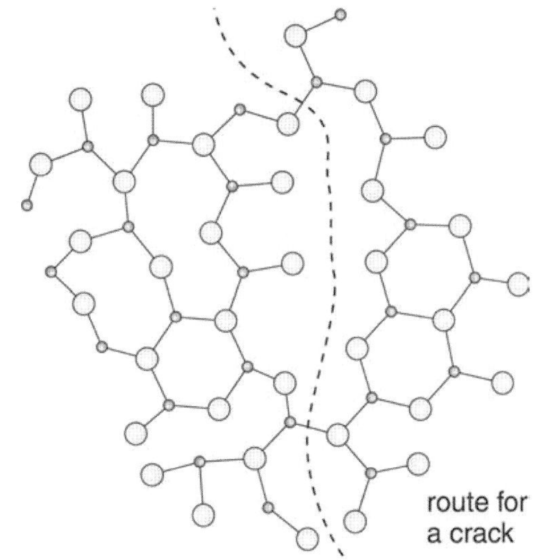

Glass is an unusual material. It has a disordered arrangement of atoms. A crack can work through the material without having to break many bonds between atoms.

3. Electrons and metals

There are electrons in all atoms. They are very, very tiny particles with electric charge.

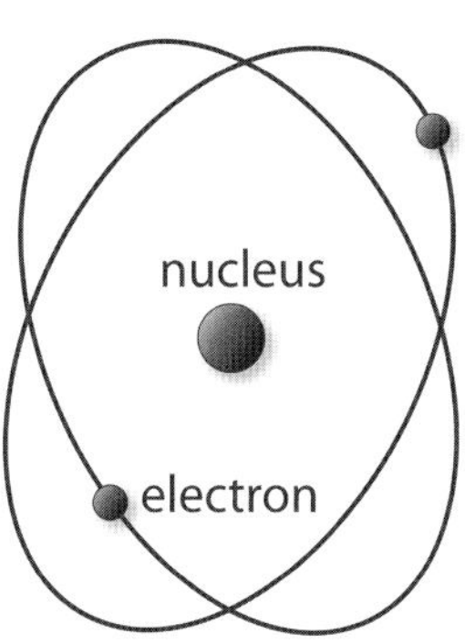

Inside an atom.

Metals have crystals of tightly packed atoms. A special feature of metals is that some of the electrons are not fixed to individual atoms. These electrons can travel around inside the metal.

When you connect a metal to a battery, the free electrons inside start to drift along because of the electric force. Metals conduct electricity.

Electrons can gain energy in one part of a metal and carry the energy through the metal. Metals conduct heat.

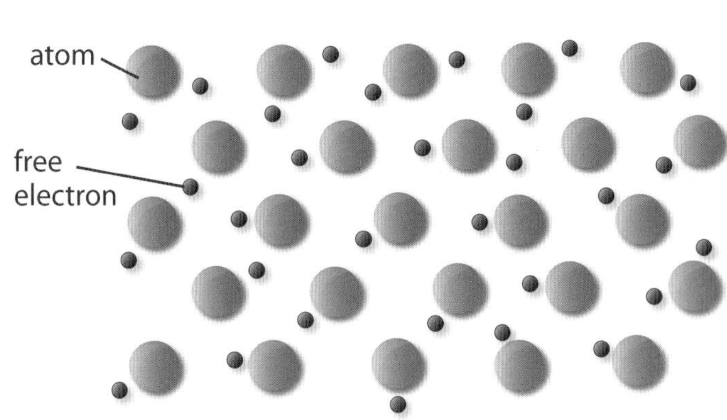

Electrons in a metal.

Particles in reactions

Representing particles

Particles are much too small to see. So we have different ways of 'picturing' them in our heads and on paper and computer screens.

Different ways of picturing atoms

a We can draw atoms as simple dots or
b we can draw the same atoms as balls.

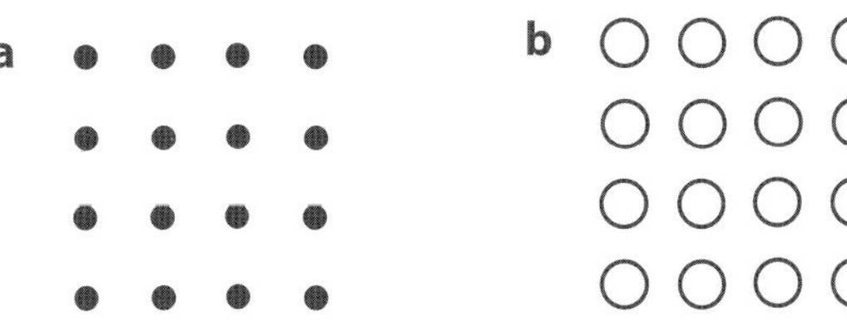

When atoms attract each other together, we can show the strong forces of attraction (or bonds) as sticks.

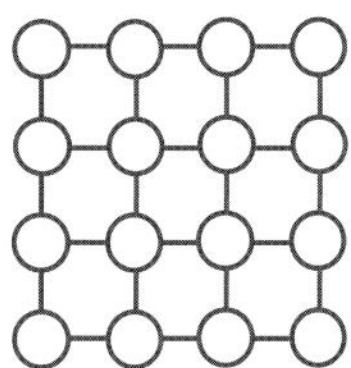

a This is a bigger picture of an atom, but showing no detail.
b This is a picture of the same atom, but this time showing the electrons and the nucleus that contains the protons and neutrons.

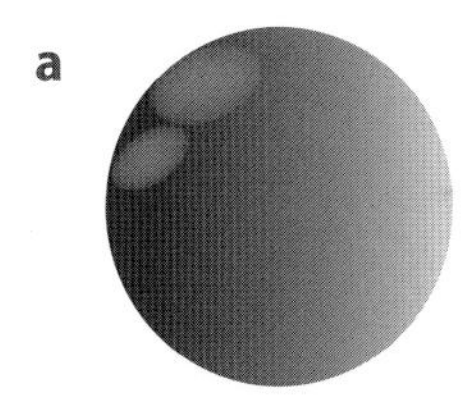

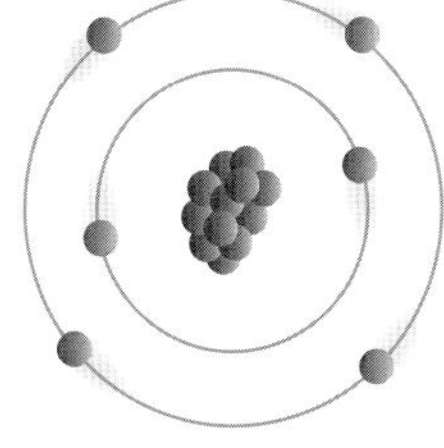

Different ways of picturing molecules

We can draw molecules of gas as simple dots, even though we know that molecules are more complicated than that. It's a useful <u>simple</u> picture.

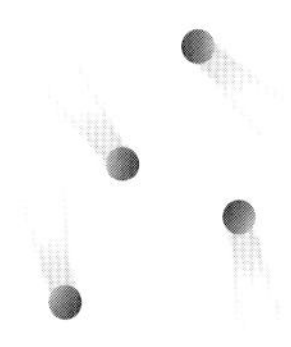

A molecule is a cluster of atoms. We can draw a molecule to show that it is made up of different atoms.

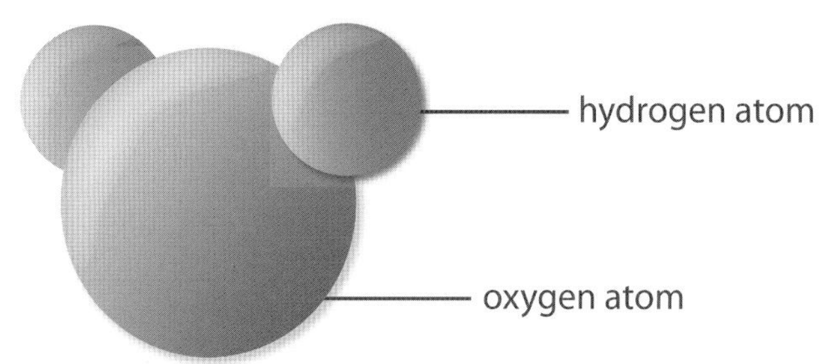

Particles in reactions (continued)

Atoms and chemical changes

In chemical changes, atoms are not created or destroyed. They just arrange themselves differently. Every chemical equation must show that there are exactly the same number of each kind of atom before the change as there are afterwards.

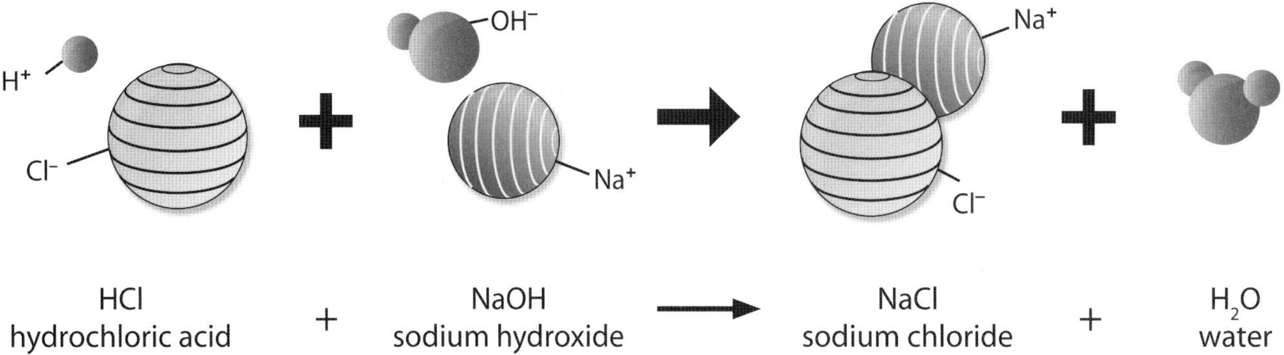

HCl hydrochloric acid	+	NaOH sodium hydroxide	⟶	NaCl sodium chloride	+	H_2O water

Ions

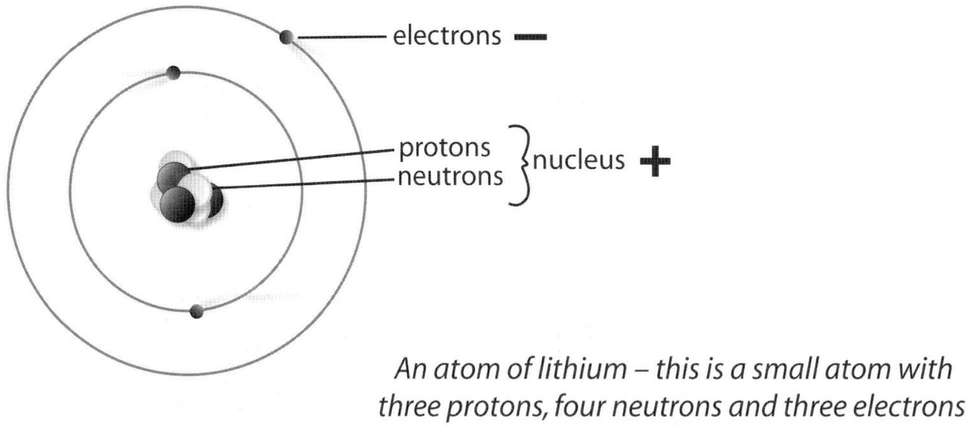

An atom of lithium – this is a small atom with three protons, four neutrons and three electrons.

Nuclei in atoms have positive electric charge, which is carried by the protons. The neutral neutrons in the nucleus add mass to the atom but no charge. All electrons are the same and have negative charge. This diagram shows a lithium atom with three protons and three electrons. In a neutral atom, the number of electrons is exactly the same as the number of protons, so that the negative and positive charges cancel out. (There are neural neutrons in the nucleus too. They add mass to the atom, but not charge.)

Particles in reactions (continued)

If an atom <u>loses</u> an electron (or more than one electron) then it has more positive charge than negative charge. It has become a **positive ion**.

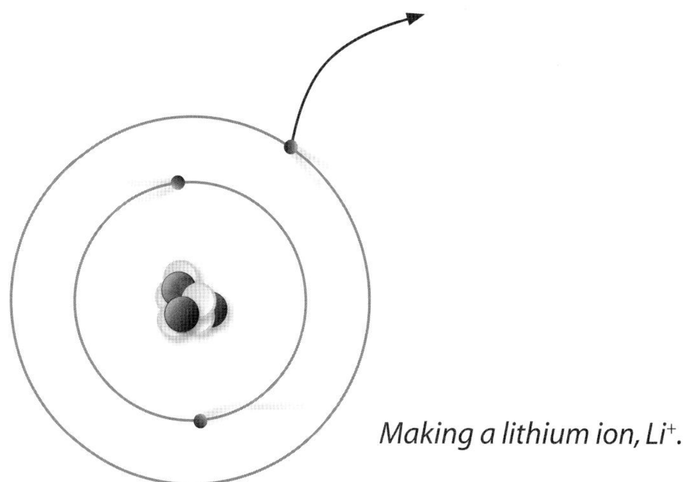

Making a lithium ion, Li^+.

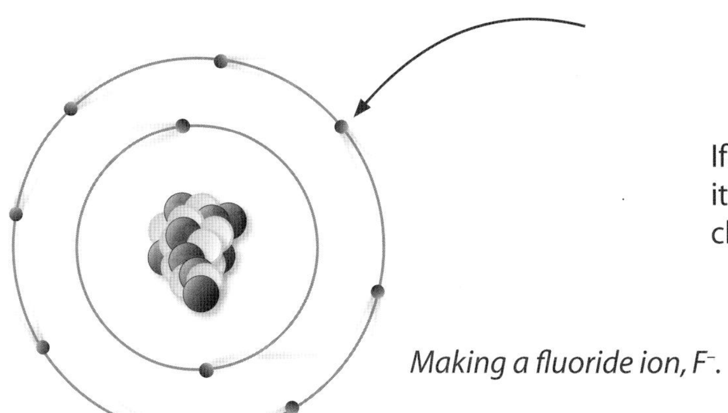

Making a fluoride ion, F^-.

If an atom <u>gains</u> one or more electrons then it has more negative charge than positive charge. It has become a **negative ion**.

Salts are ionic compounds. There are strong electrical forces of attraction between positive ions and negative ions.

Some positive ions	Some negative ions
hydrogen, H^+	fluoride, F^-
lithium, Li^+	chloride, Cl^-
sodium, Na^+	hydroxide, OH^-
ammonium, NH_4^+	oxide, O^{2-}
calcium, Ca^{2+}	nitrate, NO_3^-
copper, Cu^{2+}	sulphate, SO_4^{2-}
iron, Fe^{3+}	carbonate, CO_3^{2-}

Particles in reactions (continued)

Tests for the presence of ions

Flame tests

We can see whether some metal ions are present in a salt by placing a small sample in a flame.

Metal ion	Colour of flame
potassium, K^+	pale mauve
sodium, Na^+	yellow
calcium, Ca^{2+}	orange-red
copper, Cu^{2+}	green-blue

Chemical tests – metal ions

We can add sodium hydroxide solution, drop by drop, to test a salt solution to see what metal ions it contains.

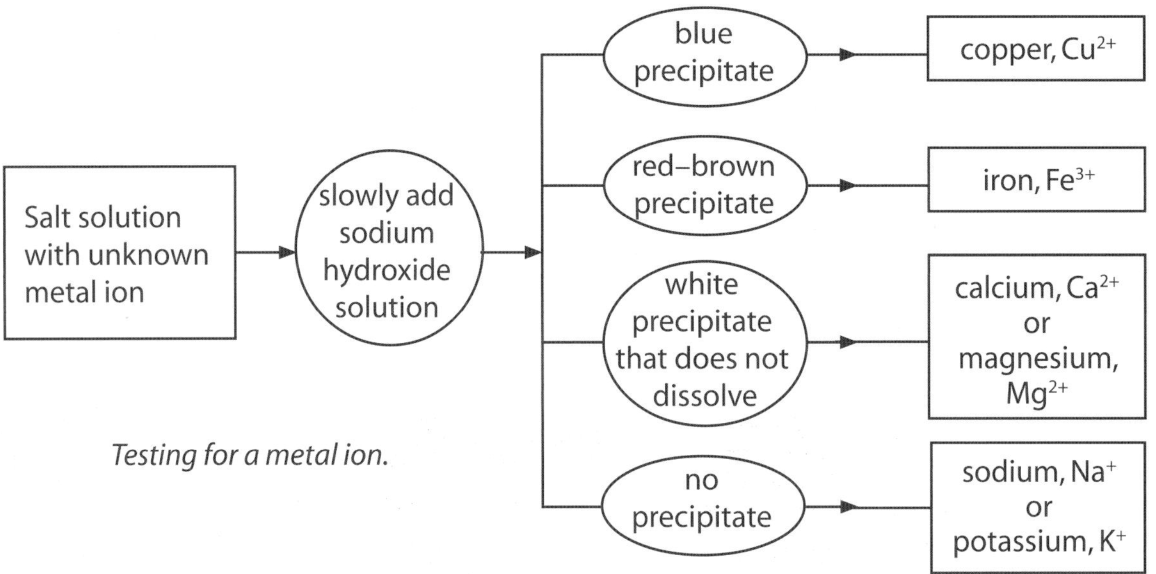

Testing for a metal ion.

Chemical tests – non-metal ions

We can test for non-metal ions in other ways:

Action	Result and conclusion
Add nitric acid to a fresh solution of the salt. Then add a solution of barium nitrate.	If a white precipitate appears then the salt contains sulphate ions.
Add nitric acid to a fresh solution of the salt. Then add a solution of silver nitrate.	If a white precipitate appears then the salt contains chloride ions.
Add dilute hydrochloric acid to the solid salt.	If a gas is given off that turns limewater cloudy then the salt contains carbonate ions.

Amounts of substance

Comparing atoms

The smallest kind of atom is a hydrogen atom. It has a relative atomic mass of one. A carbon atom is 12 times heavier than a hydrogen atom. It has a relative atomic mass of 12.

Moles of substance

We can't count atoms. But we know, from studying chemical changes, how many atoms there are in 12 grams of carbon. There are 600 000 000 000 000 000 000 000.

A **mole** is defined as the amount of substance that contains 600 000 000 000 000 000 000 000 atoms or molecules. To give you an idea, a mole of water is just a saucer-full!

The mass of one mole of atoms in grams is the same as the relative atomic mass.

Element	Relative sizes of atoms	Relative atomic mass	Mass of 1 mole of atoms, in grams
hydrogen	○	1	1
carbon	○	12	12
sodium	○	23	23
aluminium	○	27	27
silicon	○	28	28
sulphur	○	32	32
potassium	○	39	39
calcium	○	40	40
iron	○	56	56
gold	○	197	197

Amounts of substance (continued)

The mass of one mole of a compound is the same as the relative formula mass in grams.

Compound	Relative formula mass	Mass of 1 mole, in grams
carbon dioxide	44	44
sodium hydroxide	40	40
sodium sulphate	142	142
sulphuric acid	98	98
water	18	18

(Note that we can abbreviate mole to mol.)

Concentration

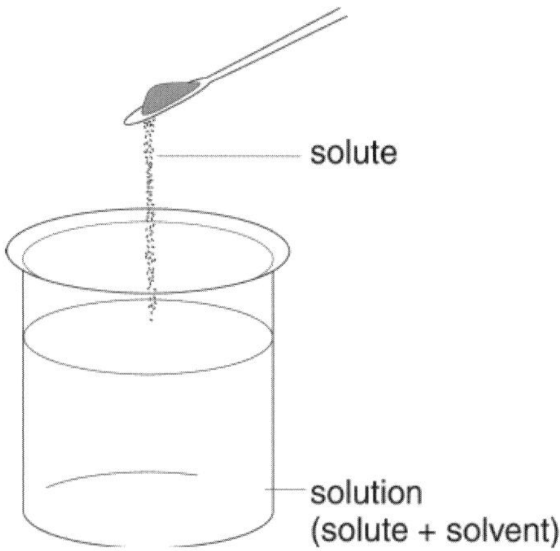

Concentration is a comparison of the amount of solute and the volume of solution.

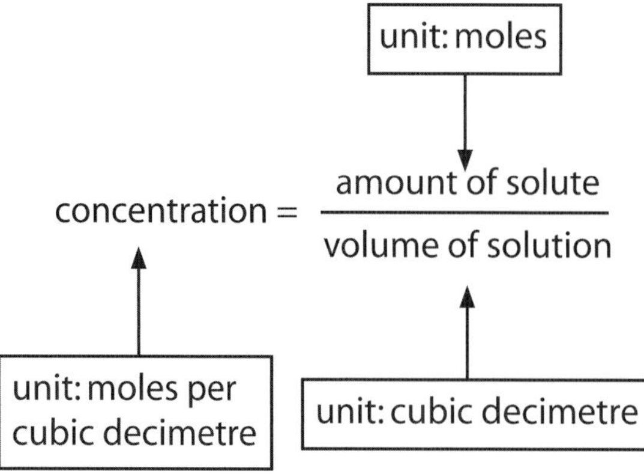

We measure concentration in moles per cubic decimetre (which we can also write as mol dm^{-3}).

Amounts of substance (continued)

Yield

We can write a chemical equation to show reactants and products. For each mole of any one substance, we can see how many moles of the others are involved.

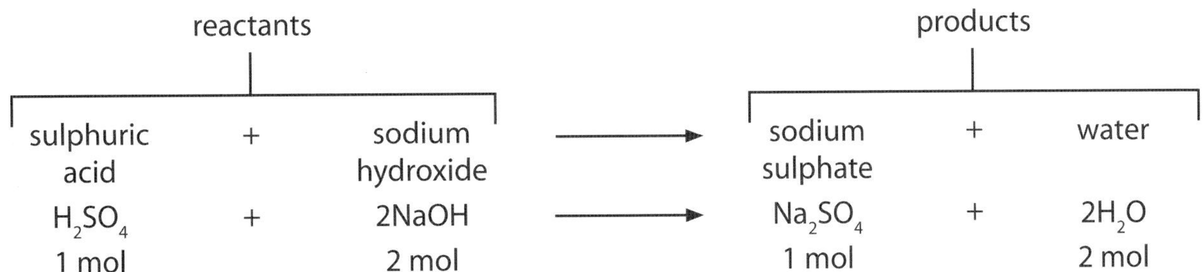

It takes two mol of sodium hydroxide to react with one mol of sulphuric acid. The reaction produces one mol of sodium sulphate and two mol of water.

From the table of relative masses we can see this in terms of masses.

98 grams		2 × 40 grams		142 grams	+	2 × 18 grams
H_2SO_4		2NaOH		Na_2SO_4		$2H_2O$
98 grams		80 grams		142 grams	+	36 grams
	178 grams				178 grams	

The mass of products is the same as the mass of reactants.

For each 98 grams of sulphuric acid we should expect 142 grams of sodium sulphate. But often in reactions we get less of a particular product than we expect. Some product is lost, or some reactants don't actually react. In a company that makes chemicals, this loss is very important.

The **yield** is a comparison of the mass of product we actually get and the mass we expected to get. We compare these masses by doing a division calculation. We multiply our answer by 100 so that we can call it a percentage.

If we only get 120 grams of sodium sulphate then:

$$\text{yield} = \frac{\text{actual mass of product}}{\text{expected mass of product}} \times 100$$

$$= \frac{120}{142} \times 100$$

$$= 0.85 \times 100$$

$$= 85\%$$

The blast furnace

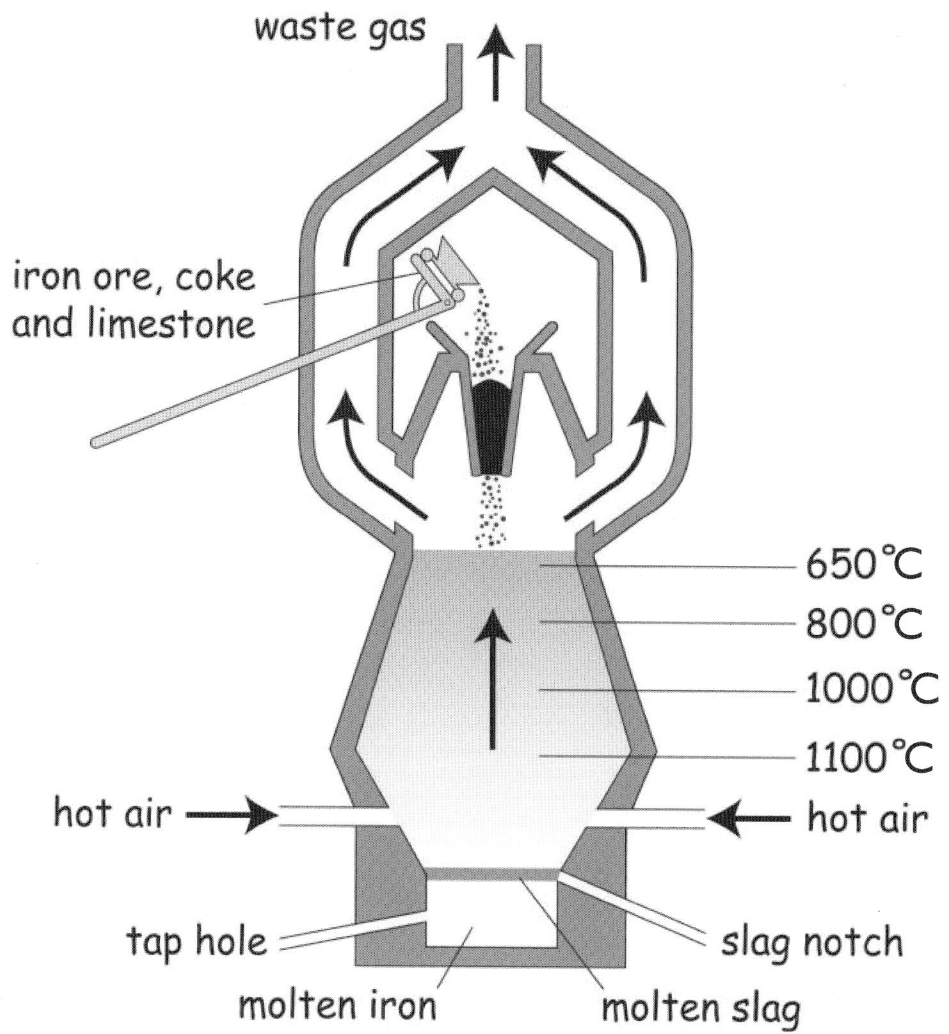

Important equations

Draw lines to link the statements with the correct equations.

Coke burns

Limestone (calcium carbonate)
breaks down

Carbon dioxide reacts to make
carbon monoxide

Iron oxide is reduced to iron

Sand and calcium oxide make slag

Fractional distillation of crude oil

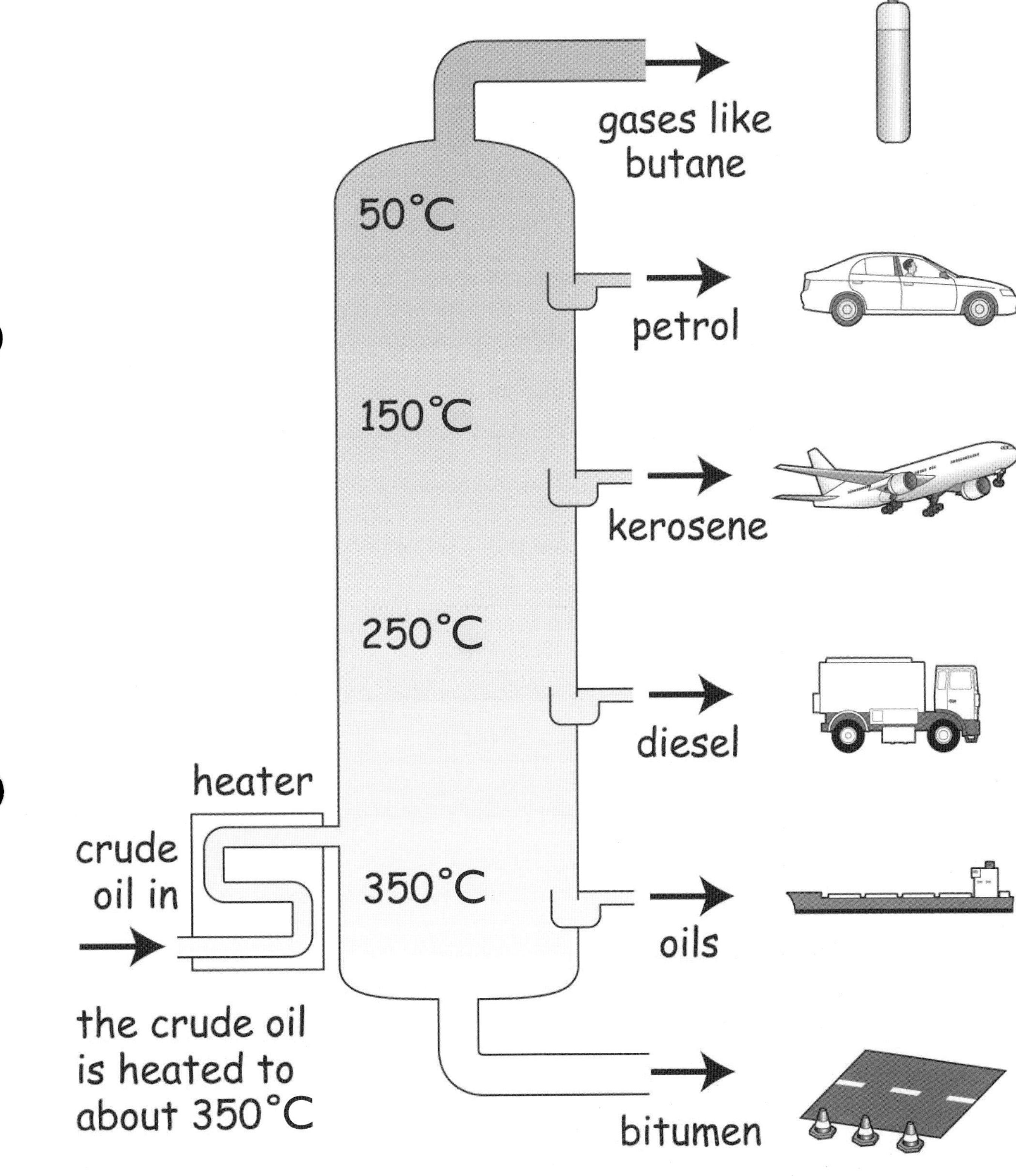

Comparing materials

Density

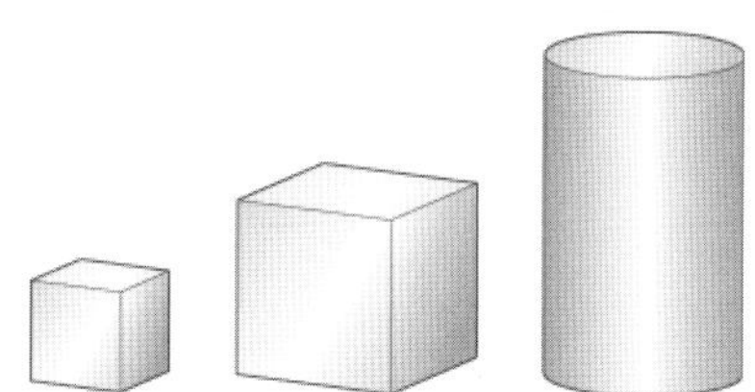

Every sample of a material has a mass and a volume. If the samples are of the same material they will have the same density.

We compare mass and volume by dividing.

We write the division like this:

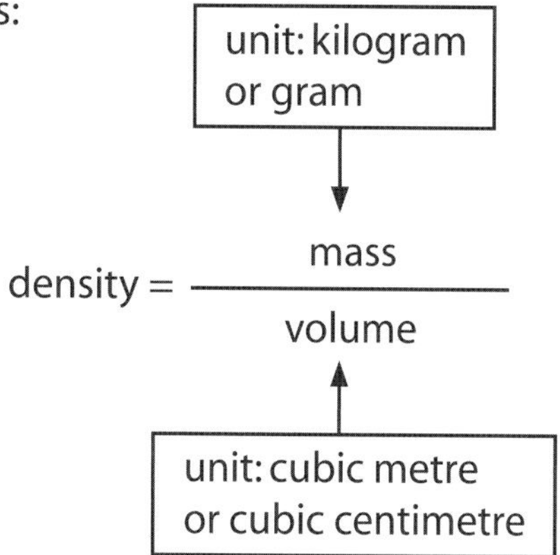

The unit of density can be either kilogram per cubic metre (kg m^{-3}) or gram per cubic centimetre (g cm^{-3}).

Tensile strength

We can compare the **force** that is needed to <u>break</u> a sample of material with its **cross-sectional area**. Different samples of the same material all have the same tensile strength.

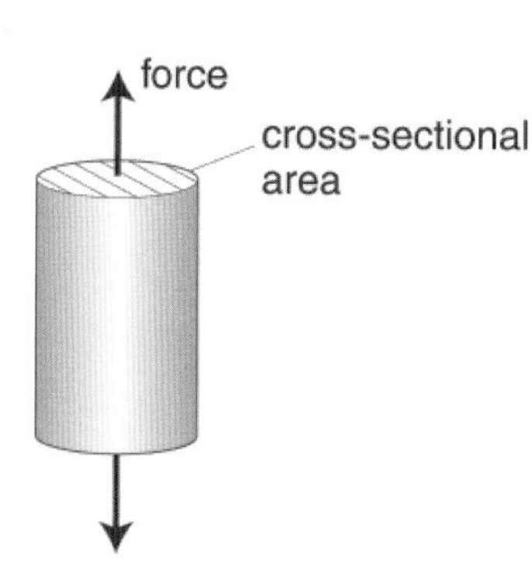

To make the comparison, we divide the force by the cross-sectional area:

$$\text{tensile strength} = \frac{\text{force}}{\text{cross-sectional area}}$$

Comparing materials (continued)

The unit of force is the newton (N). The unit of cross-sectional area is square metre (m^2).

The unit of tensile strength is Newton per square metre (N/m^2).

Opposite properties

We use a lot of different words to describe materials.

Soft	Hard
lead, polythene	steel, diamond
easy to scratch	hard to scratch

Brittle	Tough
concrete, glass	polythene, iron
low tensile strength	high tensile strength

Stiff	Flexible
glass, melamine	rubber, polyethene
hard to change its shape	easy to change its shape

Composites

Concrete is a cheap material that is easy to work with. But it is brittle and it cracks easily when it is stretched. Concrete has a low tensile strength.

Polymers are also usually cheap and easy to work with. But they can be too flexible for many purposes. Polymers can have a low hardness and low stiffness.

Concrete reinforced with steel is much stronger than concrete on its own. Reinforced concrete is a useful **composite** material.

A polymer reinforced with fibres of glass or carbon is much stronger and harder than the polymer on its own. Glass fibre and carbon fibre materials are useful composites.

matrix

fibre

matrix and fibre form a composite material

Many composites have a 'matrix' of material such as concrete or polymer. The matrix is made stronger by fibres. The combined material made from the matrix and the fibres is the composite material.

Many composites, for example laminates, are held together by glue. Scientists are involved in developing, testing and making sure the glues meet the needed specification.

Energy calculations

Energy for heating and working

Heating: one joule of energy can raise the temperature of one kilogram of water by about 0.0002°C.

Working: one joule of energy can allow a body to exert a force of one newton over a distance of one metre.

Efficiencies

For a heater, all of its energy output is heat. All of its energy output is useful. The heater's useful energy output is the same as its energy input.

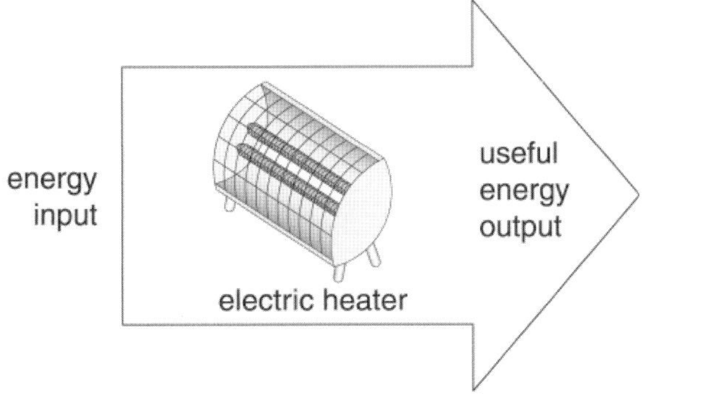

$$\text{efficiency} = \frac{\text{useful energy output}}{\text{energy input}}$$

$$= 100\%$$

A car produces unwanted heating. A car's useful energy output is less than the energy input.

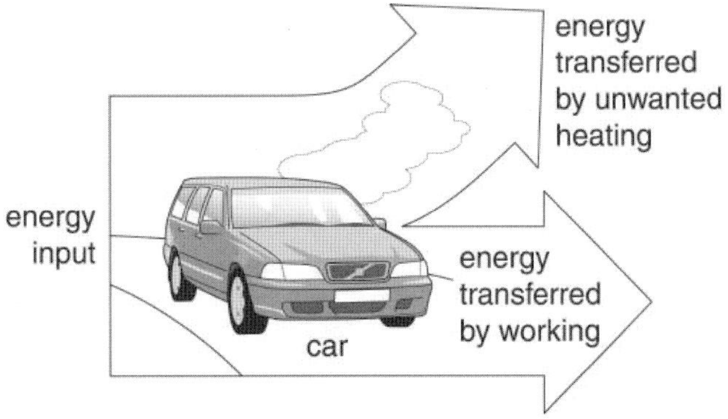

$$\text{efficiency} = \frac{\text{useful energy output}}{\text{energy input}}$$

$$= 40\%$$

Energy calculations (continued)

A pulley system also produces unwanted heating.

energy input = effort × input distance

useful energy output = load × output distance

For a pulley system, the load is bigger than the effort. However, the input distance is bigger than the output distance. Overall, the useful energy output is less than the energy input.

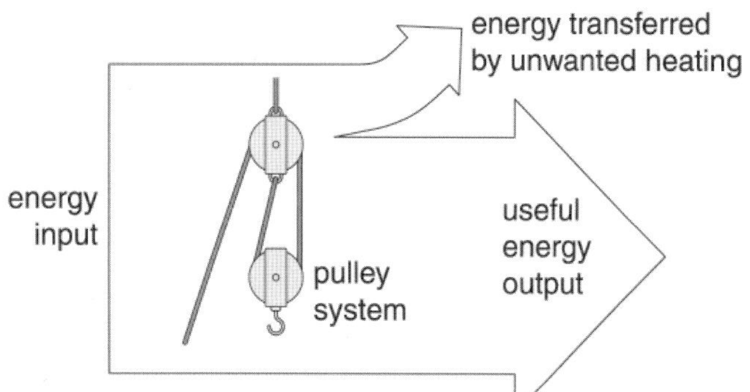

$$\text{efficiency} = \frac{\text{useful energy output}}{\text{energy input}}$$

$$= 90\%$$

Power, energy and cost for electrical appliances

We measure power in watts or kilowatts. A kilowatt is a thousand watts (1 kW = 1000 W).

We can work out the energy that an appliance transfers by multiplying its power by the time for which it is switched on.

energy = power × time

If power is in watts and time is in seconds then energy is in joules. If power is in kilowatts and time is in hours then energy is in kilowatt-hours.

Electricity and gas supply companies prefer to use the kilowatt-hour as their unit of energy, because a joule is a very small amount of energy.

Energy prices (in 2006)

- The typical price for gas is 2.5p per kilowatt-hour.
- Typical price for electricity is 9p per kilowatt-hour.

We can work out the cost of running an electric appliance from this equation:

cost = power in kilowatt × time in hours × price in pence

The electromagnetic spectrum

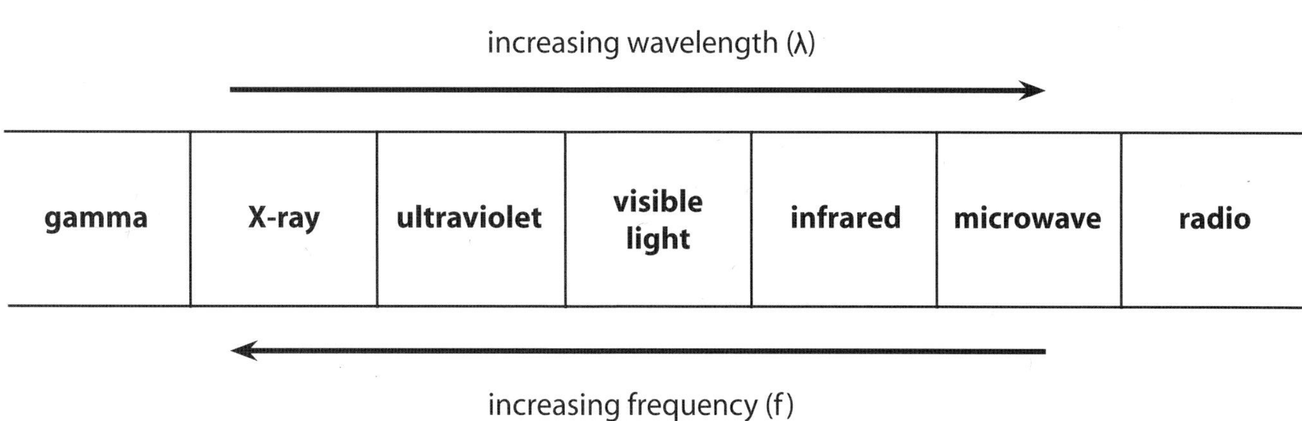

The wave equation:

velocity = frequency x wavelength

$$v = f\lambda$$

Waves are used in communication systems, for example:

electromagnetic wave	communication system
radio	radio and TV
microwaves	mobile phones
infrared	remote controls
visible light	fibre optics

<u>All</u> the parts of the electromagnetic spectrum are used by astronomers to observe the moon, planets, stars and galaxies.

The Earth and atmosphere

The Earth's surface is made of **tectonic plates** which slowly move about.

As the plates move against each other they cause many changes.

slow changes	quick changes
formation of continents	earthquakes
continental drift	tsunami
mountain formation	volcanoes

The quick changes happen so fast they are usually disasters for the people affected.

Gases in the atmosphere

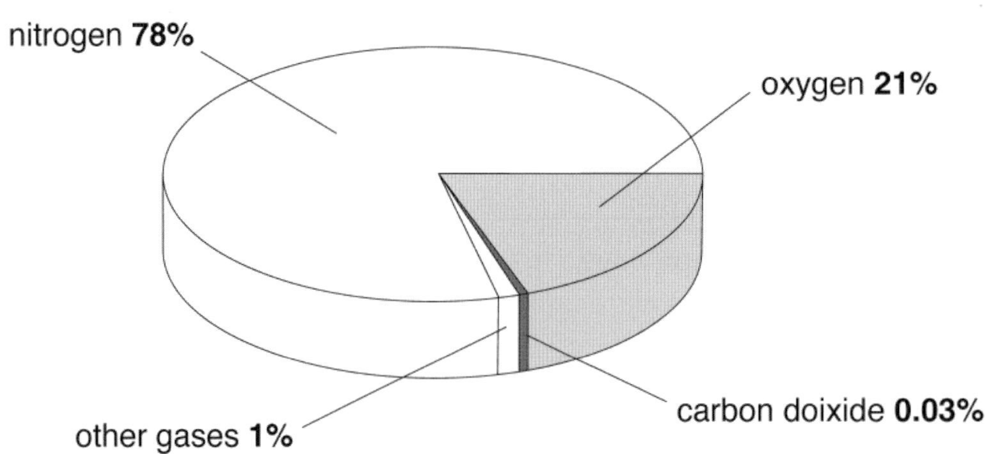

Some gases, like carbon dioxide, cause the **greenhouse effect** which helps to maintain the Earth's surface temperature.

Human activity is changing the amounts of some gases in the atmosphere. Scientists monitor these changes and their effects.

Two example are:

gas	changes	effect
carbon dioxide	increased greenhouse effect	climate change
ozone	more ultraviolet light reaches Earth's surface	increased health risk

The universe

Evidence collected by astronomers and physicists suggests that when the universe started it was very small and very hot. The universe has been expanding and cooling down ever since. This is called the **big bang theory**.

As the universe expanded, atoms formed and then collected together to produce galaxies and stars.

The galaxies are still moving apart as the universe continues to expand.

Galaxies are made up of hundreds of thousands of stars.

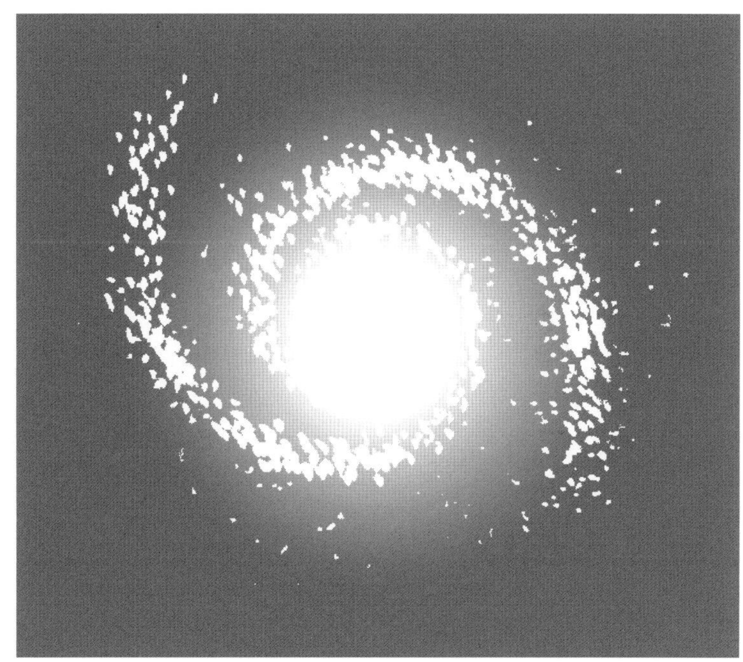

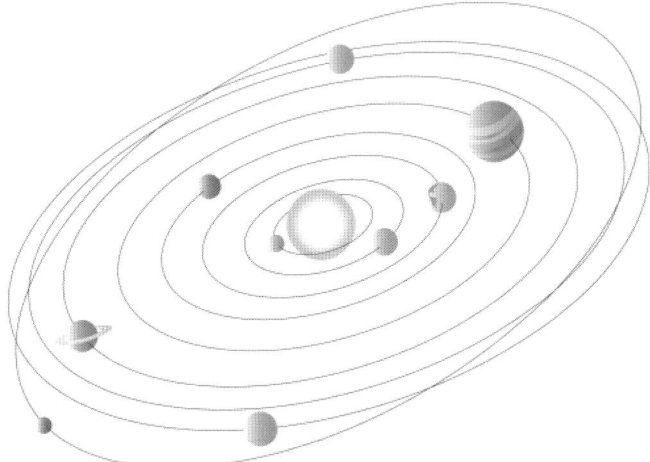

A **solar system** is made up of a **star** orbited by **planets**.

In our solar system the star is our Sun and the Earth is one of the planets orbiting the Sun.

Astronomers have used telescopes to find evidence of that some other stars have planets around them. This means that there are other solar systems.

Distances between stars are very large and are measured in light years. The nearest star is over four light years away. Our galaxy is about 80 000 light years across.

A **light year** is the distance light travels in one year (almost 10 000 000 000 000 km).

The microscope

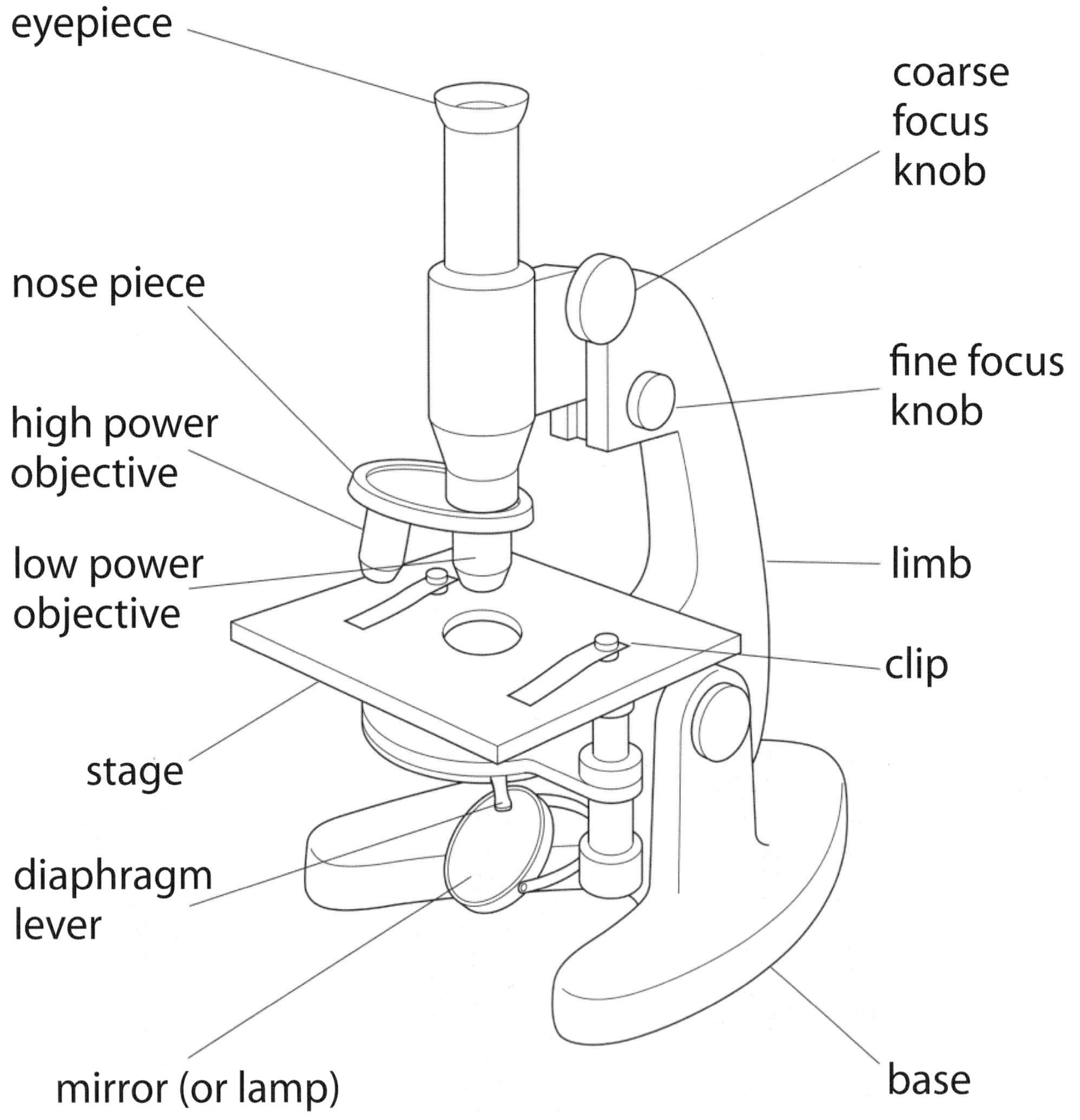

Parts of a light microscope

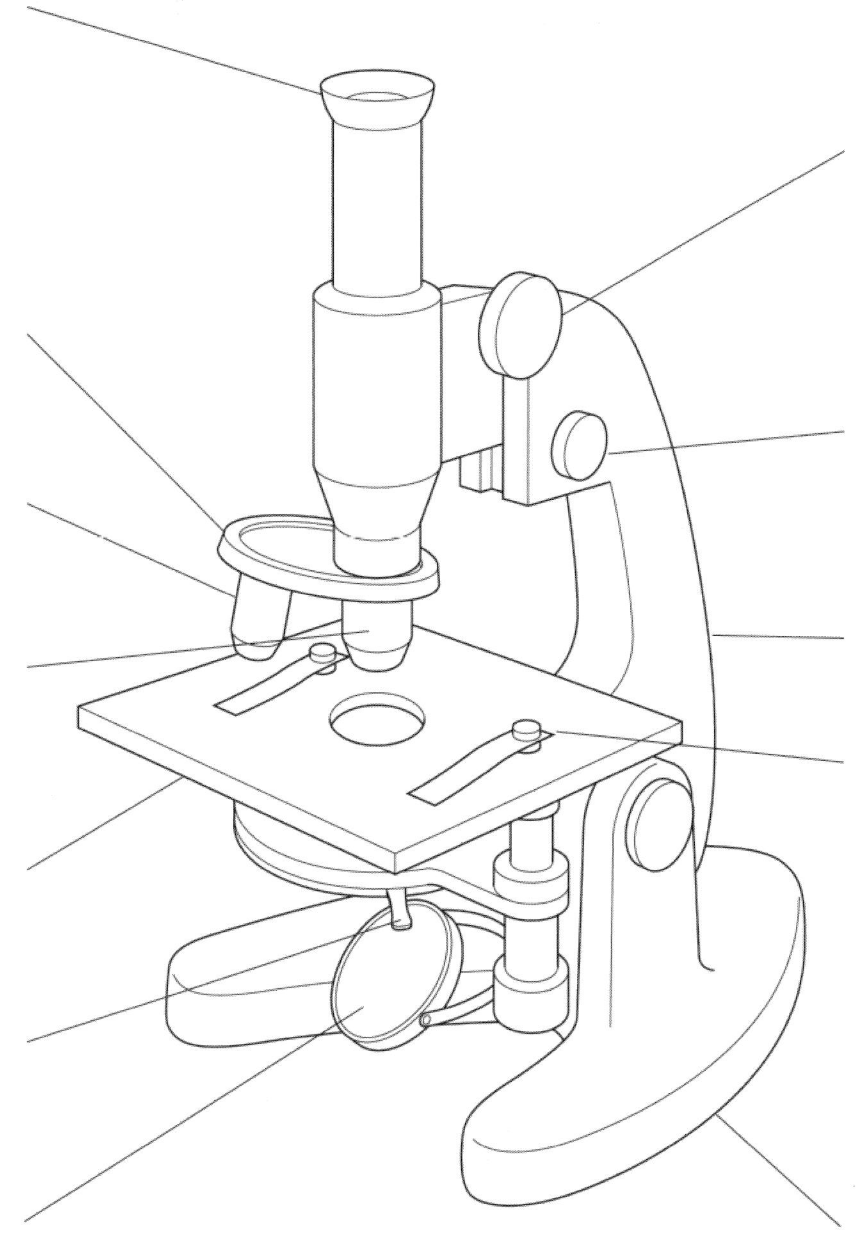

base	high power objective
clip	limb
coarse focus knob	low power objective
diaphragm lever	mirror (or lamp)
eyepiece	nose piece
fine focus knob	stage

Distillation

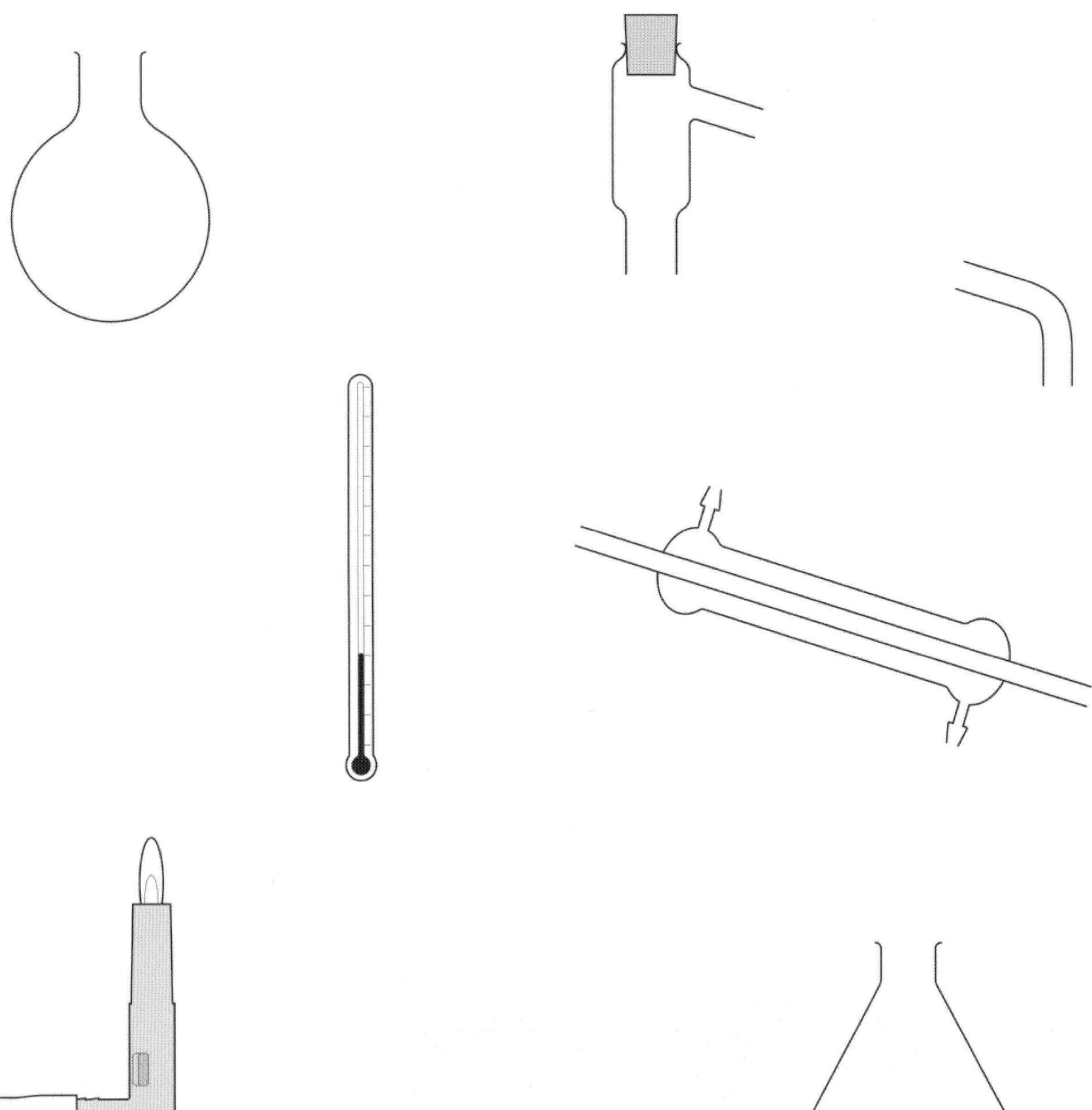

antibumping granules
cold water in here
cold water out here
condenser
distillate (pure water)
heat
seawater
thermometer

Distillation apparatus

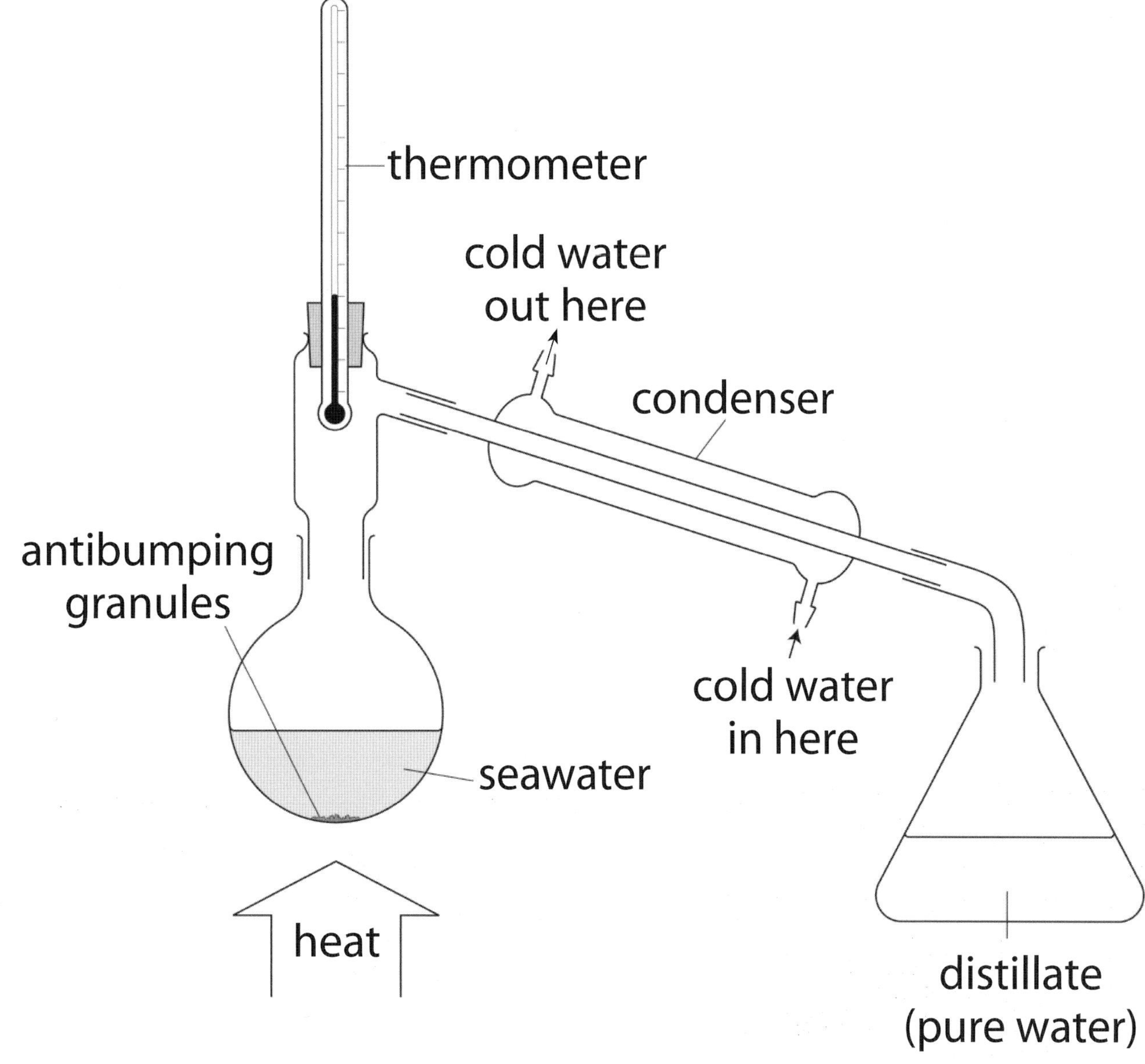

Useful information, addresses and websites

The information in this section is divided into the categories below.

All details are believed to be correct at the time of going to press, but may be subject to updating.

A QCA and Awarding Bodies
Contact details for each organisation

B Learning and Skills Development Agency
Outline of LSDA help available for Applied Science and other vocational courses

C Professional Bodies
Contact details for relevant scientific organisations

D Safety matters
A summary of sources for safety information

E Sources of information and materials
Contact details for companies and organisations publishing relevant resource materials

F Useful topic-related websites
Sites found by the authors to be particularly relevant to specific topics in the Student Book

You can also refer to the resource suggestions given by all the Boards in their Specifications and separate Teachers' Guide/Scheme of Work.

Teachers' evaluations of 25 CD-ROMs and 550 websites for KS4 Science (not specifically Applied Science) are given at http://www.teem.org.uk/findcdorweb

Section A: QCA and Awarding Bodies

QCA
http://www.qca.org.uk
83 Piccadilly, London W1J 8QA
0207 509 5555
Publication orders
0208 867 3333

AQA
http://www.aqa.org.uk
Stag Hill House, Guildford, Surrey GU2 7XJ
01483 506506

Specification at: http://www.aqa.org.uk/qual/appliedgcse/new_sci.html

Specimen assessment material at: http://www.aqa.org.uk/qual/appliedgcse/new_sci_assess.html

OCR
http://www.ocr.org.uk
1 Hills Road, Cambridge CB1 2EU
01223 552552

http://www.ocr.org.uk (Start here and follow the links. Select the 'Qualification Finder' at the top of page. In the two boxes, select 'GCSEs in Vocational Subjects' and 'Sciences'.)

Section B: Learning and Skills Development Agency (LSDA)

Learning and Skills Development Agency (LSDA)
http://www.lsda.org.uk
Regent Arcade House, 19–25 Argyll Street, London W1F 7LS
0207 297 9000

Helpline – for general or specific enquiries, or to order publications
0870 872 8080
enquiries@lsda.org.uk

Increased Flexibility Support Programme
http://www.vocationallearning.org.uk
Support for vocational education at KS4. Includes the resources below, plus a limited amount of in-service training and consultancy for individual schools or consortia.

Industry Information Pack (Science)
A free CD-ROM can be ordered through the Helpline (see above). This contains an eclectic collection of over 400 pages of wide-ranging information. Adaptable for GCSE, GNVQ and VCE. Includes:

- VCE Science Resource Directory compiled by 4Science, RSC & IoP;
- information from National Training Organisations;
- resource materials from specific industries:
  - plastics
  - steel
  - National Radiological Protection Board
  - precious metals
  - Central Laboratory of the Research Councils
  - Miscellaneous (including coatings, aluminium, health and sugar);
- standard operating procedures/worksheets;
- staffing and job descriptions (relating to pharmacy technicians).

Resources for Courses
A free CD-ROM can be ordered through the Helpline (see above). This provides advice on planning and delivering Applied GCSEs (all subjects), with web links to subject-specific resources.

Databank
http://www.vocationallearning.org.uk/databank
Provides teaching resources and training materials reviewed by subject specialists. Includes a directory of approximately 150 scientific organisations, listed by career and occupation.

Local Networks
Links between schools, colleges, LEAs, Education Business Partnerships and training organisations to support increased flexibility at ages 14–16.

Placement Co-ordinators' Network
Designed to provide those aged 14–16 with opportunities for experience beyond school.

Section C: Professional Bodies

The Association of the British Pharmaceutical Industry (ABPI)
http://www.abpi.org.uk
12 Whitehall, London SW1A 2DY
0207 930 3477

Association for Science Education (ASE)
http://www.ase.org.uk
College Lane, Hatfield, Herts AL10 9AA
01707 283000

ASE INSET Services
http://cpd.aseinsetservices.org (registration required)
Unit 2, Barclays Venture Centre, Sir William Lyons Road, Warwick University Science Park, Coventry CV4 7EZ
02476 690053

The Biochemical Society
http://www.biochemistry.org
Third Floor, Eagle House, 1b Procter Street, London WC1V 6NX
0207 280 4100

British Pharmaceutical Society
http://www.bps.ac.uk
16 Angel Gate, City Road, London EC1V 2SG
0207 417 0110

Chemical Industries Association
http://www.cia.org.uk
Kings Buildings, Smith Square, London SW1P 3JJ
0207 834 3399

Crop Protection Association
http://www.cropprotection.org.uk
Units 18 & 20 Evans Business Centre, Culley Court, Bakewell Road, Orton Southgate, Peterborough PE2 6XS
01733 367212

Engineering Council
http://www.engc.org.uk
10 Maltravers Street, London WC2R 3ER
0207 240 7891

Institute of Biology
http://www.iob.org
9 Red Lion Court, London EC4A 3EF
0207 936 5900

Institute of Materials
http://www.materials.org.uk
1 Carlton House Terrace, London SW1Y 5DB
0207 451 7300

Institute of Petroleum
http://www.petroleum.co.uk
61 New Cavendish Street, London W1M 8AR
0207 467 7100

Institute of Physics
http://www.iop.org
76 Portland Place, London W1N 1NT
0207 470 4800

Institution of Chemical Engineers
http://www.icheme.org.uk
Davis Building, 165–189 Railway Terrace, Rugby CV21 3HQ
01788 578214

The Institution of Engineering and Technology
http://www.theiet.org.uk
Savoy Place, London WC2R OBL
0207 240 1871

Royal Society of Chemistry
http://www.rsc.org
Burlington House, Piccadilly, London W1J OBA
0207 437 8656

Section D: Safety matters

CLEAPSS School Science Service
http://www.cleapss.org.uk
Brunel University, Uxbridge UB8 3PH
01895 251496

Health and Safety Executive
See Phone Book for local office
General Enquiries Infoline
0845 345 0055

Health Protection Agency
http://www.hpa.org.uk
7th Floor, Holborn Gate, London WC1V 7PP
0207 759 2700

Safeguards in Science (ASE)
http://www.ase.org.uk
College Lane, Hatfield, Herts AL10 9AA
01707 283000

Scottish Schools Equipment Research Centre (SSERC)
http://www.sserc.org.uk
St Mary's Building, 23 Holyrood Road, Edinburgh EH8 8AE
STS Support Services (Science, Technology & Safety)
0131 558 8180

Section E: Sources of information and materials

AstraZeneca Science Teaching Trust
http://www.azteachscience.co.uk
Yeo Vale, Spreyton, near Crediton, Devon EX17 5AX
01297 24167

BECTA (British Educational Communications & Technology Agency) (formerly National Council for Educational Technology)
http://www.becta.org.uk
Milburn Hill Road, Science Park, Coventry CV4 7JJ
02476 416994

BNFL Education Unit (British Nuclear Fuels)
http://www.bnfl.com
Risley, Warrington, Cheshire WA3 6AS
01925 832826
Publications from: PO Box 10, Wetherby, West Yorkshire LS23 7EL

BP Educational Service
http://www.bpes.com
FREEPOST (SCE 12342), Harrow HA1 2BR
0870 333 0428

British Association for the Advancement of Science
http://www.the-ba.net
Wellcome Wofson Building, 165 Queen's Gate, London SW7 5HD
0807 770 7101

British Nutrition Foundation
http://www.nutrition.org.uk
High Holborn House, 52–54 High Holborn, London WC1V 6RQ
0870 770 7101

British Wind Energy Association
http://www.bwea.com
Renewable Energy House, 1 Aztec Row, Berners Road, London N1 0PW
0207 689 1960

BT Education Services
http://www.bt.com/world/education
BT Centre, 81 Newgate Street, London EC1A 7AJ
0800 622302

Business in the Community
http://www.bitc.org.uk
137 Shepherdess Walk, London N1 7RQ
0870 600 2482

Centre for Alternative Technology
http://www.cat.org.uk
Machynlleth, Powys SY20 9AZ
01654 705983

Chemical Industry Education Centre
http://www.york.ac.uk/org/ciec
University of York, Heslington, York YO1 5DD
01904 432523

Corus Education Service
http://www.coruseducation.com
PO Box 10, Wetherby LS23 7EL
01937 840243

CREATE (Centre for Research Education And Training in Energy)
http://www.create.org.uk
Vermont House, Bradley Lane, Standish, Wigan WN6 0XF
01942 322273

The Easy Learning Company
67 East Knighton, Winfrith, Dorchester, Dorset DT2 8LL
01257 422800

English Nature
http://www.english-nature.org.uk
Northminster House, Peterborough PE1 1UA
01733 455000

Esso Information Service
http://www.exxonmobil.co.uk/UK-English/Responsibility/UK_CR_CL_ED_EducationalResources.asp
PO Box 94, Aldershot, Hampshire GU12 4GJ
01252 669663

The Forensic Science Service
http://www.forensic.gov.uk
Trident Court, 2920 Solihull Parkway, Birmingham Business Park, B37 7YN
0121 329 5250

The Forensic Science Society
http://www.forensicsciencesociety.org.uk
18A Mount Parade, Harrogate, North Yorks HG1 1BX
01423 506068

Hobsons Publishing
http://www.hobsons.co.uk
Bateman Street, Cambridge CB2 1LZ
01223 464334

ICI Group Education Links
http://www.ici.com/ICIPLC/ici-schools/pages/education.htm

Laboratory of the Government Chemist
http://www.lgc.co.uk
Queens Road, Teddington, Middlesex TW11 0LY
0208 943 7457

Medical Research Council
http://www.mrc.ac.uk
20 Park Crescent, London W1B 1AL
0207 636 5422

NCBE (National Centre for Biotechnology Education)
http://www.ncbe.reading.ac.uk
University of Reading, Whiteknights, Reading RG6 2AJ
0118 987 3743

NCET (National Council for Educational Technology)
(see BECTA)

Nuffield Curriculum Projects Centre
http://www.nuffieldfoundation.org
28 Bedford Square, London WC1B 3JS
0207 636 4612

Public Health at NICE (formerly Health Development Agency)
http://www.publichealth.nice.org.uk
See website for addresses of regional offices

Pupil Researcher Initiative
http://www.shu.ac.uk
Centre for Science Education, Sheffield Hallam University, Collegiate Crescent, Sheffield S10 2BP
0114 225 5555

Renewable Energy Enquiries Bureau
http://www.dti.gov.uk/renewable
ETSU, Harwell, Oxfordshire OX11 0RA
01235 432450

Resources Plus Ltd
http://www.resourcesplus.co.uk
Unit 22b, Fareham Enterprise Centre, Hackett Way, Fareham, Hampshire PO14 1TH
01329 825550

Rio Tinto PLC (formerly RTZ)
http://www.riotinto.com
6 St James's Square, London SW1Y 4LD
0207 930 2399

SAPS (Science and Plants for Schools)
http://www-saps.plantsci.cam.ac.uk
(note that this is 'www-' not 'www.')
Homerton College, Cambridge CB2 2PH
01223 507168

SEMTA have a full range of online resources specifically designed for Applied Science GCSE including a topic based list of websites and advice about careers in engineering – useful to support Unit 3. Go to the homepage, (www.semta.org.uk) click on 'Careers Information Advice and Guidance' then 'GCSE resource websites' and finally 'GCSE in Applied Science'.

SETNET (Science, Engineering, Technology & Mathematics Network)
http://www.setnet.org.uk
6th Floor, 10 Maltravers Street, London WC2R 3ER
0207 557 6422
There are also over 50 regional SETPOINTs
SETPOINT Helpline 0800 146415

Transport Research Laboratory
http://www.trl.co.uk
Crowthorne House, Nine Mile Road, Wokingham, Berks RG45 3GA
01344 773131

Unilever Education Liaison
http://www.unilever.co.uk and http://www.unilever.com
PO Box 68 Blackfriars, London EC4P 4BQ
0207 822 5252

Water UK
http://www.water.org.uk
1 Queen Anne's Gate, London SW1H 9BT
0207 344 1844
Materials are also available from regional water companies.

The Wellcome Trust
http://www.wellcome.ac.uk
Gibbs Building, 215 Euston Road, London NW1 2BE
0207 611 8888
Information Service
0207 611 8722

WWF-UK (World Wide Fund for Nature)
http://www.wwf-uk.org
Panda House, Weyside Park, Godalming, Surrey GU7 1XR
01483 426444
Publications from WWF-UK Education Distribution, PO Box 963, Slough SL2 3RS
01753 643104

Section F: Useful topic-related websites

This is a list of sites recommended by the authors as being particularly relevant to specific topics in the Student Book.

General
http://www.howstuffworks.com
Well-illustrated information about the application of all aspects of science to everyday life. The chemistry section includes diamonds, dry cleaning, oil refineries, aerosol cans, hydrogen as a fuel, to name a few.

http://www.schoolscience.co.uk/content/index.asp
Interactive on-line resources produced in association with industries such as BP and Corus. Includes medicine, health, steel-making, oil exploration and refining, audio systems, and much more.

http://micro-magnet.fsu.edu/micro/gallery.html
Electron microscope images, including cells, DNA, drugs, polymers, minerals and so on.

Theme 1: Introducing scientific skills
WORKING SAFELY IN SCIENCE
1.1 Be safe!
http://www.sja.org.uk
http://www.redcross.org
http://www.firstaid.org.uk
First aid information from St John Ambulance, the Red Cross and the St Andrews Ambulance Association.

Theme 2: Living organisms
THE WORKING CELL
2.1 Cells
http://www.sciences.demon.co.uk/whistmic.htm
Brian J Ford website; this page is on the history of the microscope.

http://inventors.about.com/library/inventors/blmicroscope.htm
This site looks at the history of the microscope.

2.2 Diffusion and 2.3 Osmosis
http://www.bbc.co.uk/scotland/education/bitesize/biology/investigating_cells/index.shtml
A BBC site.

2.5 Cells dividing
http://www.cellsalive.com
Includes an animation of mitosis.

2.6 Inheritance
http://www.bbc.co.uk/science/genes
'Genes can tell fascinating stories. And the story of your life is probably the most important of all. Read on…'

http://www.genome.gov
The National Human Genome Research Institute leads the Human Genome Project for the National Institutes of Health in the USA.

http://www.ornl.gov/hgmis/
About the Human Genome Project.

FOOD AND FARMING
http://www.defra.gov.uk
Department for Environment, Food and Rural Affairs.

2.7 Photosynthesis and 2.8 Exchange of gases
http://www.bbc.co.uk/gardening/gardening_with_children/didyouknow_photosynthesis.shtml
The 'Did you know?' section contains information on photosynthesis.

http://www.flyingturtle.org
Explores energy flows, starting with photosynthesis.

2.10 Intensive farming
http://www.planetark.org
'Planet Ark' is 'Your daily guide to helping the planet'.

2.11 Organic farming
http://www.defra.gov.uk/farm
Department for Environment, Food and Rural Affairs.

2.12 Selective breeding
http://www.ciwf.org.uk
Campaigning for farm animals: to end the factory farming and long distance transport of animals.

http://www.dalleywater.freeserve.co.uk
Link via 'Science Pages' and click on the 'Biology' link for information on selective breeding.

http://www.bbc.co.uk/science/genes/gene_safari/index.shtml
A BBC site.

2.13 Genetic engineering
http://www.organicconsumers.org
The Organic Consumers' Association campaigning for justice, health and sustainability.

MICROORGANISMS IN ACTION
2.16 Microorganism spreading
http://www.library.utoronto.ca/spanishflu/project.html
Information about the 1918 Project at Svalbard Cemetery.

2.17 Preserving food
http://www.defra.gov.uk
Department for Environment, Food and Rural Affairs.

HOW YOUR BODY WORKS
2.21 Blood donor
http://www.blood.co.uk
The work of the National Blood Service.

2.25 Keeping warm
http://www.mountainrescue.org.uk
This relates to the case study about the Patterdale Mountain Rescue Team.

Theme 3: Useful chemicals
CHEMICALS FROM THE EARTH
3.1 Elements from the Earth
http://www.9carat.co.uk
http://www.cambriangoldfields.co.uk/authentication.htm
Gold hallmarking and other information about gold.

http://volcano.und.nodak.edu/vwdocs/Parks/hawaii/crater_rim_drive/menu2.html
An on-line drive through a volcano vent. Start the tour at step 2 to see the sulphur.

3.2 Compounds from the Earth
http://www.theimage.com/mineral/
Searchable images and information on minerals including 'iron pyrites' (fool's gold) and 'halite' (sodium chloride).

3.3 Salt from rock salt
http://www.lionsaltworkstrust.co.uk/history_heritage.html
A history of salt-making.

3.4 Iron and steel
http://www.bbc.co.uk/history/games/blast/blast.shtml
An animation of a blast furnace from circa 1709.

http://www.recycle-steel.org/index.html
Recycling steel – scrap cars being processed in a scrapyard.

http://www.schoolscience.co.uk/content/index.asp
Items on 'The chemistry of steel making' and 'Physics in steel making'.

THE CHEMICAL INDUSTRY
3.5 Crude oil to petrol
http://www.schoolscience.co.uk/content/index.asp
This includes items on 'Fossils into fuels' and 'Exploring for oils'; plus 'Virtual visit to Fawley refinery'.

3.6 Bulk and fine chemicals
http://www.chemicals-technology.com/projects/richardsbay/index.html#richardsbay1
Images of fertiliser plant showing the Contact Process towers for sulphuric acid and the phosphoric acid plant.

3.8 Putting numbers into industry
http://www.just4sbm.com/free-resources/review_details.cfm?ID=5922&subcat_title=ICT%20Training:%20Pupil%20Materials&sub_id=26&subcat_id=364
Balancing equations game.

INVESTIGATING CHEMISTRY
3.9 Mixtures everywhere
http://www.schoolscience.co.uk/content/index.asp
Items on 'aerosols' and 'What is a suspension?'

3.10 Splitting the atom
http://www.webelements.com
An interactive Periodic Table, giving details of elements' properties. (Many other sites have similar versions.)

http://www.schoolscience.co.uk/content/index.asp
Contains items on 'A world of atoms' (sub-atomic particles) and 'A world of particles'. The material is beyond the requirements of the specifications, but some higher-level pupils may be interested.

3.13 More about molecules
http://www.nyu.edu/pages/mathmol/library
Images of molecules; excellent for alkanes (click on 'hydrocarbons' option).

http://www.howstuffworks.com
Item on refrigerators includes CFCs.

3.14 Energy and chemical change

http://www.pbs.org/wgbh/nova/kaboom
How fireworks work – an interesting illustration of exothermic reactions.

MATERIALS FOR MAKING THINGS
www.sciencemuseum.org.uk/on-line/challenge/world/index.asp
Materials that changed our lives – an on-line tour of the Science Museum (London) 'Challenge of Materials' gallery. Looks at materials, including polythene, steel, rubber and glass.

3.16 Polymers
http://www.pslc.ws/macrog.htm
The Macrogalleria polymer shopping centre – tour an on-line shopping centre to find out all about polymers.

www.envocare.co.uk/plastics.htm
Information about the labelling system for recycling plastics waste.

Theme 4: Energy and devices
ENERGY
http://www.chpa.co.uk
Lots of links on combined heat and power.

4.3 Nuclear and renewables
http://www.dti.gov.uk/renewables/schools/
Information on each type of renewable energy resource. Contains a separate section for adults, including teachers' notes and worksheets for KS3 and KS4.

http://www.greenenergy.org.uk
A wide-ranging site, containing information promoting renewables.

4.7 Road safety
For information on stopping distances and the effects of alcohol, drugs and tiredness on driving go to
http://www.thinkroadsafety.gov.uk

Theme 5: The Earth and universe
5.2 The Earth and environment
http://www.airquality.co.uk
For air quality data from UK monitoring stations (hourly tables and graphs).

5.3 The Earth beneath our feet
http://www.discoverourearth.org/index.html
For plate tectonics, earthquakes and monitoring systems. Shows global data for mapping of earthquakes and volcanoes all pitched at student level.

http://www.howstuffworks.com
For instructions on how to build model seismographs to monitor Earth movements search for 'seismograph'.

http://earthquake.usgs.gov/learning/kids.php
For accessible earthquake activities.

5.4 Waves and communication
http://www.nasa.gov/home/
NASA – a wide variety of related information.

Theme 6: Science in the workplace
6.1 Working in science
http://www.connexions.gov.uk/occupations/
A searchable database for information about the careers mentioned in the text. Students can use this as an alternative to the Occupations *book for completing the activities. The information covers a description of the responsibilities of each occupation with information about entry qualifications, training and potential career development.*

http://www.cia.org.uk
The Chemical Industries Association - a trade and employer organisation.

http://www.howstuffworks.com
For anyone who wants to know how anything works.

http://www.newscientist.com
The on-line version of the weekly magazine.

http://www.woodland-trust.org.uk
Information about woodland conservation. Students can take part in a national survey (click on 'Phenology' on the drop-down menu) and several areas are aimed at young people (try 'Wild about Woods').

See also Section E for sources of information and materials.

Section II
Answers to questions in the student book

Answers to intext, activity and case study questions

Page	Question number	Answer
1.1 Be safe!		
2	2a	People are more likely to look at pictures than to read words.
	3	Ideas: high benches (for working standing up) and tall stools; floor surface not polished (no slipping) and hard for mopping; bench tops of hardwearing materials; <u>many</u> sinks and gas taps for safe access; position of electrical sockets away from sinks; gas and electrical 'switch off' points for the whole lab; electrical trip switch; fume cupboard; no curtains or carpets to minimise fire risk; location of fire exit and fire extinguisher equipment; advice available on safety notice board; location of Hazcards. Students should be aware that labs are very expensive to set up because of the high specification of the materials to ensure safety.
3	4	Students need to realise the difference between a <u>hazard</u> (for example, flammable) and the <u>action</u> that is needed to prevent accidents (for example, keeping tops on bottles, turning off Bunsens and so on).
	5	Answers might include: separate storage and disposal of organic solvents; and washing less hazardous materials away with lots of water. Could also discuss idea of harm to aquatic life as well as humans from contamination from solvents (at home as well as in school, for example white spirit, oil-based paints and waste motor oil).
	6	Important to distinguish between 'hazard' (for example, flammable); 'risk' (fire); 'safety precautions' (keep tops on bottles, use in small quantities, keep away from flames; and 'in case of accident' (inform teacher and so on).
4	7 a	Answers will vary.
	b	Answers will vary.
5	8	For the first chemical, they would use a fog fire extinguisher; wear full protective clothing, consider evacuation of area, contain the spill using sand bags. Spilled chemical may react violently. For the second chemical, they would use a fog fire extinguisher, wear full protective clothing and wash the spill down drains with lots of water.
	9	Jack says: Really nasty stuff has to be contained – we surround it with sand bags and pump it into containers we seal. The sealed waste gets buried in safe sites. Rest of answer will vary.

Page	Question number	Answer
1.2 Stay safe!		
6	1	So that they are not out of date, to learn new ideas, to check they have not forgotten anything or to make sure that they are not using bad practice.
	2	Burns, breathing in fumes or swallowing chemicals, electric shocks, cuts, damage to the eyes.
7	3	To know what to do if there is an accident.
8	5	Fire alarm will warn others to leave the building as fire spreads.
	6	Fire doors are only effective when shut.
	7	Answers will need to be checked against the fire extinguisher in the lab.
	8	You may get a serious electric shock.
9	9	An injured First Aider is no good to anyone.
	10	Answers will vary but could include electrocution or being knocked down by a car.
	11	Assess a situation quickly. Check safety for yourself, the casualty, any bystanders. Summon appropriate help. Try to identify the injury or the nature of the illness affecting the casualty. Give appropriate and adequate treatment as soon as possible in a sensible order of priority. Arrange for the casualty to be moved to hospital, to the care of a doctor, or to their home. Remain with the casualty until you can hand them over to the care of an appropriate person. Make and pass on a report and give further help if required.
	12	Answers will vary but should include: to avoiding stressing the patient and to reduce shock.

Answers to Review questions, page 10 – Working safely in science

Question number		Answer	Marks
1	a	when filling the backpack she may get spills and splashes on her skin, face and eyes either when putting weedkiller into backpack or when filling it with water; backpack may be dropped or contents may leak during the journey; spray may get onto face, eyes, skin or she may breathe it in	3
	b	all body should be covered with protective, waterproof suit; goggles, gloves; and face mask with filter	3
	c	what symptoms come from contact with the chemical (long-term/short-term); what safety advice the manufacturers give; has a risk assessment been carried out; is all the safety equipment available (any two)	2
2	a	assess a situation quickly and safely and summon appropriate help; protect self, casualty and others at scene from further danger; try to identify the injury or the nature of the illness affecting the casualty; give appropriate and adequate treatment as soon as possible in a sensible order of priority; arrange for the casualty to be moved to hospital, to the care of a doctor, or home; remain with the casualty until you can hand them over to the care of an appropriate person; make and pass on a report and give further help if required (any six)	6
	b	taking care to prevent cross-infection between yourself and the casualty, for example wear rubber gloves; stop flow of blood; raise arm/apply pressure; check for glass in wound; bandage (any four)	4
	c	burns; breathing in fumes or swallowing chemicals; electric shock; cuts; damage to the eyes (any four)	4
	d	St John Ambulance (www.sja.org.uk) or St Andrew's Ambulance Association (www.firstaid.org.uk) or British Red Cross (www.redcross.org)	2
		Total	**24**

Answers to intext, activity and case study questions

Page	Question number	Answer
1.3 Following standard procedures		
14	1	Answers will vary but could include: set the dial to the correct thickness before cutting the slices.
	2	To ensure that the bacon is cut correctly, safely and cleanly, each and every time the bacon slicer is used.
1.4 Handling scientific equipment and materials		
16	1	Answers will vary but should include data logger, temperature probe and thermometer.
17	2	No. Too close together and will produce too many readings. Possibly every five minutes, but answers will vary.
	3	9°C
	4	If she removes the probe from the water it will not be taking the temperature of the water.
18	5	10 cm^3 is more precise. 5 cm^3 pipette is even more precise.
	6	Place jar at the bottom of the pond. Remove top. Allow water in. Replace top. Remove jar from water.
	7	Answers will vary. Part of the risk assessment will relate to the risk of falling in, so should include checks for depth of water, speed of current, life belts available, whether there will be a supervisor, whether someone will have a mobile phone.
	8	Surface water.
	9	Warmed up during the day by the Sun.
19	10	A blood transfusion is sometimes required to replace blood lost during the operation. The blood groups must match to avoid the mixed blood from clotting and blocking blood vessels.
	11	A centrifuge spins at high speed. Particles suspended in a liquid are thrown towards the outside of the container, the heavier the particles the quicker they are deposited at the bottom of the test-tube.
	12	Autoclaving cleans and sterilises equipment by using high temperatures. A school laboratory uses a pressure cooker.
	13	In a biopsy test, small pieces of human tissue are obtained without major surgery. The tissue is quickly prepared for examination under a microscope to look for any damaged, diseased or abnormal cells.

Page	Question number	Answer
	14a	Avoid contanimation/protect hands from bacteria.
	b	Easier to keep clean/free from bacteria. Carpet would quickly become contaminated.
	c	To make sure results are accurate, and prevent mistakes. Pathology work must be accurate because a patient's life may depend on the results.
1.5 Recording and analysing scientific data		
21	1	Answers will vary but could include removing socks to eliminate another variable.
	2	Answers will vary.
	3	6%
23	4	Answers will vary.
	5	Not enough evidence to suggest that vitamins make a difference.
	6	Answers will vary but could include using a standard procedure.
	7	Pupils not standing straight; careless use of measuring equipment.
	8	More reliable results. More reliable because different vitamins may produce different results. Vitamins may affect males and females differently.

Answers to Review questions, page 24 – Carrying out practical tasks

Question number		Answer	Marks
1	a	read the instructions; carry out a health and safety check of the area; carry out a risk assessment; set out the work area and collect the materials and equipment needed; follow the instructions precisely one step at a time; make accurate observations or measurements with correct use of instruments; identify sources of error and repeat the procedure if necessary	7
	b	so everyone who does it knows exactly what to do; always get same quality of result; it's safer (any two)	2
2	a	i needed to know what dyes were in the sweet; so she could compare the other dyes with it ii dyes that she thought might be used to obtain a blue colour and contain the same pigments as the sweet	2 1
	b	B and D	2
	c	any suitable answer, for example wider range of dyes/solvents; control of variables, for example temperature/depth of solvent; repeat the experiment (any two)	2
3	a	i separate bars; at correct heights ii drawings of eyes; correct relative numbers iii pie chart drawn; correctly sized slices	6
	b	10%	1
	c	closest match to colour chart on page 24	1
		Total	**24**

Answers to intext, activity and case study questions

Page	Question number	Answer
2.1 Cells		
26	1	The outer membrane controls what enters and leaves a cell.
	2	The nucleus carries coded information.
	3	Chemical reactions take place in the cytoplasm.
	4	Plant cells have cellulose cell walls, animal cells do not. Plant cells contain green chloroplasts, animal cells do not. Plant cells have large vacuoles, animal cells do not.
	5	The whole plant does not move, so the individual cells do not need to be flexible but they do need to be strong. Plants also make their own food and need special structures called chloroplasts.
27	6	Onion bulb cells do not contain chloroplasts because they grow underground so there is no light for photosynthesis.
	7	Cells are very small and a microscope magnifies them so they are big enough to be seen.
	8	Glass slides and coverslips let light through so the object can be seen clearly.
	9	Stains are used to highlight different structures so we can see them more clearly.
	10	There is a risk of infection, for example from HIV/AIDS and hepatitis, if handling body fluids.
28	12	The wool fibres are loosely spaced; air is trapped in the spaces and warms up.
29	13	A fair test would need strips that are of the same length and width, and the same weights to be used for the same amount of time. Different yarns can be used instead of strips.
	14	Leather stretched the least. Wool stretched the most.
	15	Wool fibres stretch easily and wool is loosely woven or knitted.
	16	Wool fibres are stretchy/elastic and act as good insulators.
	17	It is tough and water resistant.
	18	Repeat the original experiment, but this time apply the same volume of water to materials for the same amount of time at the same temperature.

Page	Question number	Answer
2.2 Diffusion		
30	1	The perfume molecules spread from a high concentration (near the burner) to other parts of the room (low concentration) by diffusion.
	2	The heat makes the molecules move faster and diffusion occurs more quickly. Also, convection currents will speed up diffusion. There is more evaporation of the oil.
	3	The burner could get too hot to touch and cause skin burns. It should not be used when young children are present. It should not be left to burn when no one is in the room. It should not be placed where it could be knocked over or where other things could fall on it to create a fire hazard.
	4	Answers will vary but could include: diffusing perfume could be used in toilets, subways, trains, buses and planes.
31	5	By diffusion.
	6	The strips nearest the ammonia turn blue first.
	7	The speed calculation requires the measurement of the distance travelled by the ammonia from the dish and the time taken to travel this distance.
	8	Leaf D lost the least water because petroleum jelly had blocked both leaf surfaces so that water could not escape.
	9	Leaf A lost the most water because water vapour could diffuse from both leaf surfaces.
	10	Errors could happen if some petroleum jelly was rubbed off when setting up the experiment, or if the petroleum jelly did not cover the leaves completely.
32	11	D A E B C
33	12	On a cold day, the water molecules will be moving slowly; on a wet day, the air will be already saturated with water/high concentration of water molecules so overall diffusion from the cloths will not take place.
	13	An increase in temperature causes the water molecules to move and spread faster.
	14	A tumble drier uses a high temperature and movement of the materials to cause faster evaporation.
	15	Water evaporates into the atmosphere. If the room is cold the water vapour condenses back to water, causing dampness.
	16	The ice cubes cool the hot air. This makes the water vapour condense (change from a gas to a liquid). The liquid stays in the dish, so less moisture escapes into the room.

<table>
<tr><th>Page</th><th>Question number</th><th>Answer</th></tr>
<tr><td colspan="3">2.3 Osmosis</td></tr>
<tr><td>35</td><td>1</td><td>
<table>
<tr><th>Concentration g dm^{-3}</th><th>Original length cm</th><th>Final length cm</th><th>Change in length cm</th></tr>
<tr><td>0</td><td>7.0</td><td>7.8</td><td>+0.8</td></tr>
<tr><td>70</td><td>7.0</td><td>7.4</td><td>+0.4</td></tr>
<tr><td>140</td><td>7.0</td><td>7.0</td><td>0.0</td></tr>
<tr><td>210</td><td>7.0</td><td>6.8</td><td>–0.2</td></tr>
<tr><td>280</td><td>7.0</td><td>6.4</td><td>–0.6</td></tr>
</table>
</td></tr>
<tr><td></td><td>3</td><td>The core in 0 g dm^{-3} (water) increased the most due to the entry of water by osmosis.</td></tr>
<tr><td></td><td>4</td><td>The core in 280 g dm^{-3} decreased the most due to the loss of water by osmosis.</td></tr>
<tr><td></td><td>5</td><td>The core in 140 g dm^{-3} remained the same length. This means that the concentration of dissolved substances inside and outside the potato cells was the same.</td></tr>
<tr><td>36</td><td>6</td><td>The cells would burst.</td></tr>
<tr><td>37</td><td>7</td><td>Portable water purifiers could remove the bacteria and other contaminants, preventing contamination and spread of disease.</td></tr>
<tr><td></td><td>8</td><td>A very high pressure could split the membrane.</td></tr>
<tr><td colspan="3">2.4 Characteristics</td></tr>
<tr><td>38</td><td>1</td><td>Answers will vary, but could include: eye colour, presence of freckles and ear size.</td></tr>
<tr><td></td><td>2a</td><td>Lucy has blond hair, blue eyes, no freckles and large ears.</td></tr>
<tr><td></td><td>b</td><td>Luke has blond hair, green eyes, no freckles and small ears.</td></tr>
<tr><td>39</td><td>3</td><td>Answers will vary, but could include: eye colour, hair colour, hair length and so on.</td></tr>
<tr><td></td><td>4</td><td>Differences could include size, smell, colour, taste, texture, pH, shape, skin, resistance to browning.</td></tr>
<tr><td></td><td>5</td><td>Different varieties mature at different times. Different people like different flavours.</td></tr>
<tr><td></td><td>6</td><td>The two apples would taste very similar but there may be slight differences due to sugar and pH levels caused by the different climates in the two countries and different soils.</td></tr>
<tr><td>40</td><td>7</td><td>Man.</td></tr>
<tr><td></td><td>10</td><td>Men and women compete against each other in events such as show jumping, shooting, and sailing, where skill is more important than strength.</td></tr>
</table>

<table>
<tr><th>Page</th><th>Question number</th><th>Answer</th></tr>
<tr><td colspan="3">2.5 Cells dividing</td></tr>
<tr><td>42</td><td>1</td><td>The biggest height gain in girls is 8.2 cm/year and in boys 9 cm/year.</td></tr>
<tr><td></td><td>2</td><td>Fastest growth occurs in girls at 11/12 years, and in boys at 14/15 years.</td></tr>
<tr><td></td><td>3</td><td>The increase in height could be due to a better diet, better health care and better living conditions.</td></tr>
<tr><td></td><td>4</td><td>Height measurements are two-dimensional. Measurement of mass, which is three-dimensional, would be better. Height is an overall measurement, individual measurements of head size and leg length are important in monitoring a baby's growth.</td></tr>
<tr><td>44</td><td>5</td><td>
<table>
<tr><th>Mitosis</th><th>Meiosis</th></tr>
<tr><td>Takes place to divide normal body cells as part of growth and cell replacement.</td><td>Produces gametes (eggs and sperm in animals).</td></tr>
<tr><td>The cells produced will have the same number of chromosomes as the cell that divided.</td><td>The cells produced will have half the number of chromosomes (two sets in original cell, one set in each new cell).</td></tr>
<tr><td>Two cells are produced from each original cell.</td><td>Four cells are produced from the original cell.</td></tr>
<tr><td>The new cells will have a combination of genes that is identical to the original cell and to each other.</td><td>The new cells will have a different combination of genes from each other and from the original cell.</td></tr>
</table>
</td></tr>
<tr><td colspan="3">2.6 Inheritance</td></tr>
<tr><td>47</td><td>1</td><td>Quick germination requires water and warm conditions (20 to 25°C). Light is not necessary for germination of most seeds.</td></tr>
<tr><td>48</td><td>3</td><td>They carry the dominant allele, G.</td></tr>
</table>

Answers to Key fact boxes

Question	Key word	Question	Key word
2.1 Cells, page 28		**2.2 Diffusion, page 32**	
1	chemical compounds	1	random movements
2	cell	2	high concentration, low concentration, diffusion
3	membrane, cytoplasm		
4	cell wall, vacuole, chloroplast	3	transpiration, stomata
5	leather, wool, silk	4	gaseous exchange
6	cotton, dyes, pharmaceutical products		
2.3 Osmosis, page 36		**2.4 Characteristics, page 41**	
1	osmosis	1	characteristics
2	partially permeable	2	inherited
3	visking tubing	3	environment
4	dialysis	4	nucleus
		5	chromosomes
		6	sex chromosomes
		7	XY, XX
2.5 Cells dividing, page 45		**2.6 Inheritance, page 49**	
1	cell division	1	genes
2	chromosomes, genes	2	genetic code
3	growth, sexual reproduction	3	DNA, double helix
4	replication, spindles	4	alleles
5	gametes, meiosis, mitosis, chromosomes, chromosomes	5	dominant, recessive
		6	homozygous, heterozygous
		7	monohybrid ratio

Answers to Review questions, page 50 – The working cell

Question number		Answer	Marks
1	a	green chloroplasts which photosynthesise; vacuole contains watery sap; cell wall for support (any two)	2
	b	nucleus; cytoplasm; cell membrane (any two)	2
2		diffusion; of molecules; from high to low concentration	3
3	a	water enters; cell swells	2
	b	water leaves; cell not so well supported	2
4	a	partially permeable cell membrane	1
	b	control entry; and exit of materials	2
	c	use glass slide; add water/stain; add glass coverslip	3
5		chromosomes; gametes; XX	4
6	a	mitosis	1
	b	2.1 cm	1
	c	faster growth at higher temperature; because more food/faster photosynthesis/faster flow of materials	2
		Total	**25**

Answers to intext, activity and case study questions

Page	Question number	Answer
2.7 Photosynthesis		
53	1	More chloroplasts would produce more food for the plant, making it bigger and stronger. This would produce a better crop.
	2	Examples of edible plants storing food underground include: swede, turnip, beetroot, carrot, parsnip. Examples of non-edible plants include: crocus corms, dahlia tubers, daffodil bulbs. These contain poisonous or unpleasant flavours.
54	3	No light to make green chloroplasts.
	4	Warm temperature of 25°C.
	5	As paraffin burns, more carbon dioxide is released. This causes faster photosynthesis. A higher temperature also speeds up photosynthesis because it increases enzyme activity. Growth is also speeded up.
55	6	Bunny ears cactus, because it needs plenty of light. Also it does not need much water and is slow growing.
	7	Cast iron plant needs very little water and fertiliser and so can be left for long periods.
	8	Bunny ears cactus has dangerous spikes and Dumb cane can cause painful mouth swellings.
	9	Some plants will need a lot of fertiliser if they are fast growing or producing many flowers and fruits.
	10	Dusting will allow more light to enter the leaves. This will cause more photosynthesis and more food production.

Page	Question number	Answer
2.8 Exchange of gases		
56	1	The air pump will supply more oxygen for respiration. It will also speed up the breakdown of the fish' wastes by bacteria.
	2	Respiration uses oxygen to release energy, water and carbon dioxide from food. Photosynthesis uses light energy from the Sun to combine carbon dioxide and water into food with the release of oxygen. The equation for respiration is the reverse of the equation for photosynthesis
	3	Respiration releases energy, while photosynthesis stores energy in the form of food.
	4	In light, photosynthesis will be taking place at a higher rate than respiration, so the plant needs to take in carbon dioxide and release oxygen.
57	5	Ali uses identical tubes, shone a light on all tubes, kept at the same temperature for the same amount of time, in the same place and used the same volume of distilled water.
	6	The lamp was necessary to make sure there was plenty of light for the plants to photosynthesise.
	7	The cling film prevented anything, for example carbon dioxide entering or leaving the tubes.
	8	The water in tube 3 was the least acidic because any carbon dioxide (which would produce carbonic acid) was used up by the plant.
	9	Tubes 1 and 4 were the same pH because tube 4 contained both plants and animals so the level of carbon dioxide remained the same as the original in tube 1. This was because the animals gave out carbon dioxide and the plants took it in.
58	10	The limiting factor at X is temperature.
	11	The limiting factor at Y could be the level of carbon dioxide.
	12	Plant growth could be limited by the amount of light (if in the shade) or carbon dioxide (if there were few fish).
59	13	Siamese fighting fish need a higher temperature. The males fight each other. Penguin fish eat other small fish like silver hatchet fish which are shy fish.

Page	Question number	Answer
2.9 Minerals		
61	1	Nitrates are required by plants as a source of nitrogen to produce proteins for growth.
	2	He should change the soil in his greenhouse to introduce more minerals, or grow tomatoes using hydroponics (growing them in pots on sand/gravel) or use grow bags. He could grow a different crop such as cucumbers or peppers for one year to avoid pests and diseases building up in his greenhouse.
62	3	If there is a large supply of one mineral, all the carriers might be used up transporting these minerals, which means there are not enough carriers for other minerals.
	4	Human waste could be used as fertiliser.
	5	The algae would produce oxygen from photosynthesis. The astronauts could use this for respiration so they would not need to carry large supplies.
	6	Algae are small, quick growing, do not need much space, can easily be grown in water tanks and do not suffer from many diseases.
	7	Answers will vary. For example, a continuous culture method could be used. In this nutrients are added and algae are harvested at a given steady rate.
63	8	It encourages leaf growth instead of root and potato tuber growth underground.
	9	A control for comparison.
	10	Other factors would include: climatic conditions (temperature, rainfall), soil conditions (pH, drainage), and pests and diseases.
	11	A time line such as: 1600 van Helmont showed minerals required for plant growth 1842 First factory-made fertiliser 1843 Rothamsted Experiment started 1938 Active transport of minerals in plants described 2000+ Space travel ?

Page	Question number	Answer
2.10 Intensive farming		
64	1	Chemical sprays will drift in the wind. May cause side-effects in humans.
65	2	Energy efficiency = 125/3056 x 100 = 0.041%
	3	Protection against wind; less heat lost from cows, so need less food to keep warm, and sheds don't need to be heated; sheds can be insulated to avoid heat loss.
	4	Spread of disease; lack of exercise so poor muscle growth; build up of manure.
66	6	Light, water, temperature, humidity.
67	7	They do not already have good access to the sea for fresh fish as a source of protein.
	8	Feeding and predators of young fish.
	9	A high protein diet can be provided to the fish, ensuring a fast growth rate. Disease and pests can be controlled avoiding heavy losses.
	10	Excess food can decay using up oxygen. More disease in the fish. Cultivated fish could be genetically modified, so if they escape they could successfully compete against the wild fish.
2.11 Organic farming		
68	1	Bees are useful because they pollinate flowers. Pollination results in fertilisation and the production of seeds and fruits.
	2	Answers will vary, for example ladybirds eat aphids which damage plants. Many scavenging beetles help in natural recycling. Locust swarms can completely destroy vast areas of crops.
2.12 Selective breeding		
72	1	Brontosaurus, Dodo, Pterodactyl, Mammoth,
73	2	One year to get average milk yields, one year to get offspring, three or four years to maturity, then the selection process starts again.
	3	A zeedonk from a zebra and a donkey. A tiglon from a tiger and a lion.
75	7	Make it illegal to pick them; build fences/walls to protect them.
	8	Answers will vary, but could include: allow natural evolution and cross-breeding instead of preserving, because their only value is in natural beauty for a few weeks each year.
2.13 Genetic engineering		
76	1	The increase slowed down in 1999 due to public concern over the dangers of GM crops. Some 'direct action' campaign groups damaged some crops.
	2	Industrialised countries developed the techniques of genetic engineering and used them first. So far there has been no public reaction in developing countries about growing GM crops.
79	3	Trees could be weaker and blow down, and could be more easily attacked by pests.
	4	Could cross-pollinate producing weaker trees.

Answers to Key fact boxes

Question	Key word	Question	Key word
2.7 Photosynthesis, page 54		**2.8 Exchange of gases, page 58**	
1	photosynthesis	1	carbon dioxide, oxygen, photosynthesis
2	chloroplasts, pigment, chlorophyll	2	respiration
3	stomata	3	limiting factors
4	xylem		
5	carbon dioxide, enzymes		
2.9 Minerals, page 63		**2.10 Intensive farming, page 67**	
1	minerals, fertilisers	1	intensive farming
2	magnesium, nitrates	2	herbicides, pesticides, fungicides
3	potassium, phosphates	3	energy transfer
4	active transport, energy	4	eutrophication
2.11 Organic farming, page 71		**2.12 Selective breeding, page 74**	
1	organic farming	1	natural selection, variation
2	food chain	2	domesticate
3	biological control	3	selective breeding
4	predator, prey	4	cross breeding
5	compost	5	recessive, variation
6	bacteria, oxygen		
2.13 Genetic engineering, page 79			
1	genetically modified		
2	selection, isolation, replication, insertion		
3	herbicide, insecticides		
4	transgenic		

Answers to Review questions, page 80 – Food and farming

Question number		Answer	Marks
1		photosynthesis; minerals; light; phosphates; magnesium; temperature	6
2	a	limiting factors control the rate of reaction; the reaction will be controlled by the factor which is in the least supply	2
	b	in photosynthesis this is usually light; or temperature being low (rarely the amount of carbon dioxide)	2
3	a	organic farming does not use any extra chemical fertilisers; or use chemical control of pests and diseases	2
	b	they believe this is a natural way, avoiding a chemical build up in soil or food	1
	c	(i) weeds are controlled by hand weeding; (ii) animal pests are controlled by introducing natural predators; (iii) plant pests are controlled by varying planting times/using different varieties of plants	3
4		George; produces better crops; crops are resistant to disease/extremes of climate; can produce medicines; 'cure' genetic disorders; (any two) Neil; not natural; unknown future damage; possible cross breeding of GM plants to produce 'superweeds' (any two)	4
		Total	**20**

Answers to intext, activity and case study questions

Page	Question number	Answer
2.14 Fermentation		
82	1	Beer contains hops that make it taste bitter.
84	2	15°C – takes a long time; 37°C – just right conditions; 65°C – does not work because enzymes are denatured.
	3	The air lock allows carbon dioxide to escape by bubbling through water. Oxygen in the air cannot diffuse back through the water in the air lock.
85	4	When the barley is germinating; starch is converted to maltose; when the yeast is fermenting.
	5	The yeast may continue to ferment and produce carbon dioxide gas. This could cause the keg to explode.
	6	The yeast grows as it ferments and can be used again.
	7	Making food for cattle and foods such as Marmite.
	8	Answers will vary, but may include: movement of large barrels; high levels of carbon dioxide in fermentation vats.
2.15 Types of microorganism		
86	1	Microorganisms are too small to see with the naked eye. They could not be seen until the microscope was invented.
87	2	British meat could not be sold abroad and farmers lost a lot of money.
	3	4 190 319
	4	The deer roam free, so they could spread the disease from farm to farm.
	5	Any other animal that was suspected of being able to spread the disease.
88	6	To stop any infection occurring (for example, athlete's foot).
89	7	To stop the disease spreading to the next farm.
	8	To destroy the virus and stop it spreading.
	9	To destroy any virus on the car tyres.
	10	Birds/soles of boots; any other suitable answer.
	11	To stop the virus being spread by the boots of walkers.

Page	Question number	Answer
2.16 Microorganisms spreading		
90	1	Answers will vary.
	2	They may have had some slight resistance to it because they had already been in contact with an earlier form of the virus.
	3	The virus mutates and changes so the person is not immune to the new form of the virus.
91	4	Refer to atlas.
	5	No. The colour shows the average for the whole country.
	6	The wind is blowing from the sea therefore it will carry fewer viruses.
	7	Hospitals and doctors phone a central data collection point once a week to report the number of cases.
93	8	She did not like desecrating the graves.
	9	To prevent them from catching the flu virus from the dead bodies.
	10	Answers will vary.
	11	When frozen all viral activity stops. The virus would be preserved until it was thawed out again.
2.17 Preserving food		
94	1	The bacteria will grow. The food is not cooked again so the bacteria are not killed and they could cause food poisoning.
	2	To destroy any microorganisms and remove the food that they could grow on.
	3	Answers will vary but could include unwashed hands and contaminated work surfaces.
95	4	68 719 476 736
97	5	To prevent cross-contamination where microorganisms could get onto the cooked meat from the raw meat.
	6	To prevent microorganisms being spread onto food from dirty hands.
	7	Answers will vary.
	8	To stop dirt and microorganisms falling off hair.
	9	Disinfectants are harsher and may damage the skin. Andy could use disinfectants to clean work surfaces and antiseptic handwash to clean his hands.

Page	Question number	Answer
2.18 Immunisation		
98	1	Mumps and measles.
100	2	They might give us the disease.
	3	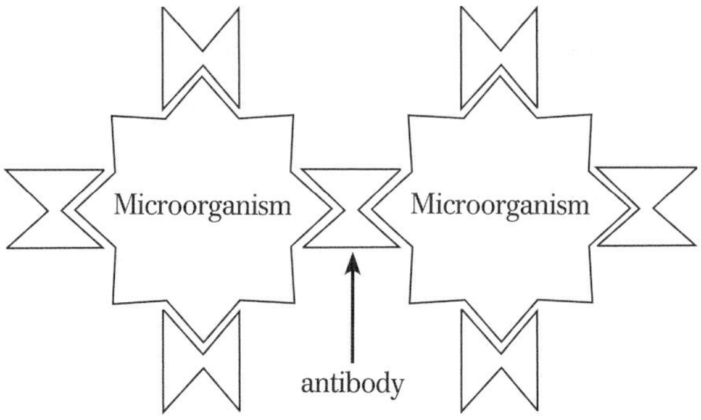 Microorganism Microorganism antibody
101	4	It takes time for us to make the antibodies.
	5	Answers will vary.
	6	Between 1968 and 1972.
	7	It may put pressure on the immune system.
2.19 Antibiotics		
103	1	Graph continues to go up.
	2	It takes time for the antibiotic to kill the microorganism.
104	3	Those caused by bacteria.
105	4	Answers will vary.
	5	The antibiotic will not destroy the virus that causes the cold. However, it may help to make some bacteria that infect humans resistant to the antibiotic.
	6	No, antibiotics kill bacteria not viruses.
	7	Answers will vary, but may include faster growth as an advantage and gut bacteria developing immunity to antibodies as a disadvantage.

Answers to Key fact boxes

Question	Key word	Question	Key word
2.14 Fermentation, page 84		**2.15 Types of microorganisms, page 89**	
1	enzymes	1	fungus
2	catalyst	2	foot and mouth, virus
3	fermentation, maltose, carbon dioxide, alcohol	3	athlete's foot
4	fermentation, temperature	4	bacterium/virus
5	oxygen	5	microorganisms, parasites
		6	DNA
2.16 Microorganisms spreading, page 92		**2.17 Preserving food, page 96**	
1	droplets	1	hygiene, contaminated
2	polio	2	antiseptics, disinfectants
3	epidemic(s), mutation	3	sterilisation
4	tuberculosis, droplets		
5	immune		
2.18 Immunisation, page 101		**2.19 Antibiotics, page 104**	
1	antibody(ies), microorganism(s)	1	tuberculosis, polio
2	immunisation, vaccination, vaccine	2	antibiotics, microorganisms
3	immunised	3	bacteria, virus(es)
4	immunised, MMR	4	antibiotics, viruses

Answers to Review questions, page 106 – Microorganisms in action

Question number	Answer	Marks
1	sugar/malt; water; hops [one mark each]	3
2	please see flow chart on page 85 – Mansfield Brewery [one mark for each correct item up to a maximum of six]	6
3	for example: virus – influenza; fungus – athlete's foot	4
4	a – bacteria; b – virus; c – fungus	3
5	a parasite – lives on or in another organism and gives nothing in return; b epidemic – spread of disease across a country; c pandemic – spread of a disease across the World; d mutation – random change to a gene or chromosome to produce a new strain of the microorganism	4
6	answers will vary but may include touch/contact; contaminated food or water; faeces (for example, polio)	3
7	cooked meats could become contaminated with microorganisms from raw meats; cooked meats will not be cooked again so the microorganisms will not be killed	2
8	keep away from other food; wash hands and work surfaces after preparation; cook well to kill all microorganisms	3
9	bleach – sinks and drains; disinfectants – work surfaces; antiseptics – on skin	3
10	antiseptic is used externally to kill microorganisms; antibiotics are taken internally to kill bacteria	2
11	body reacts to vaccine as if it were a real infection; produces antibodies to fight vaccine; antibodies stay in body ready to attack the live microorganisms	3
	Total	**36**

Answers to intext, activity and case study questions

Page	Question number	Answer
2.20 Heart attack		
109	1	95 is the lower pressure of his blood when the heart is not contracting.
	2	No second peak after the spike.
	3	No.
110	4	If it was blocked before it divided more blood vessels would not receive the blood they need, preventing even more blood getting to the heart muscle – probably a fatal heart attack.
111	5	They were too small for him to see. He did not have a microscope.
	6	Blood is pumped through arteries under pressure. In veins the blood is sluggish. Valves prevent the blood flowing back.
	7	Less fat to prevent blockages to his arteries. More exercise to improve his heart muscle.
	8	Smoking causes clots to form on the walls of blood vessels. If the clot breaks free it could block a small artery leading to the heart, causing a heart attack.
2.21 Blood donor		
114	1	It is an easier and quicker way to get concentrated oxygen-carrying red blood cells into the blood.
115	2	Might be carrying a virus such as hepatitis.
	3	Not enough haemoglobin in the blood.
	4	He will need all the red blood cells for himself. Also the blood will not have enough haemoglobin for a recipient.
	5	They may give the virus to the recipient of the blood.
	6	To get an accurate amount of blood from the donor.
	7	To carry out blood tests, such as the HIV/AIDS test.

Page	Question number	Answer
2.22 Asthma		
116	1	About 4% of the air or 20% of the oxygen.
117	2	Chest = bell jar; lungs = balloons; trachea = glass tube; diaphragm = rubber sheet.
	3	The volume of air is smaller.
	4	The balloons get smaller.
	5	Reduced volume causes increase in pressure in the bell jar, which squashes the balloons.
	6	The volume of air increases.
	7	The balloons get bigger.
	8	There is less pressure in the bell jar than external air pressure, so air enters the balloons from the air outside, through the glass tube, until the pressure is equal.
119	9	To measure how much air Richard can blow out of his lungs in one second.
	10	Patients know when they need to use the medication. Rest of answer will vary.
	11	If Richard cannot breathe he could suffocate and die.
	12	Becotide™ stops the attack from occurring so must be taken regularly. Ventolin™ stops an attack when it is happening so is taken when needed.
	13	His lungs are warmer and more moist than external air.
	14	His airways close up and prevent air entering the lungs.
	15	He knows it is a safe way to take steroids and can save lives.

Page	Question number	Answer
2.23 Aerobics		
121	1	2100 joules or 2.1 kilojoules.
	2	Enclose the heat source so that all the energy is used to warm the water.
	3	Respiration of food/some energy from respiration made into heat energy.
	4	Both use oxygen and produce carbon dioxide and water. Respiration does not produce a flame. It is slower and controlled by enzymes.
122	5	Exercise supplies more oxygen and glucose to the muscles; removes carbon dioxide waste to the lungs.
	6	Respiration uses oxygen and produces carbon dioxide.
	7	4%
	8	Our bodies do not use nitrogen.
123	9	1 dm^3
	10	5 dm^3
	11	15 breaths/min
	12	Breathing rate decreases. Vital capacity increases.
2.24 Oxygen debt		
125	1	Unfit.
	2	Super fit.
126	3	Slowed down.
	4	Speeded up.
127	5	No. Slightly overweight.
	6	Answers will vary
	7	234 000 kJ

Page	Question number	Answer
2.25 Keeping warm		
128	1	Cold and wet.
	2	Waterproofs and warm underclothing.
	3	If it is going to be cold and wet he either does not go or makes sure that he is well equipped.
129	4	They may not both be measured to the same accuracy.
	5	The wet one.
	6	His body would lose heat more quickly. He could get hypothermia.
131	7	Mobile phone; dial 999.
	8	Answers will vary.
	9	Waterproofs; warm suitable clothing; good footwear; first aid kit; food, water and emergency rations; map; compass; whistle; watch; means of shelter.
2.26 Diabetes		
133	1	The body cannot store it/levels in blood too high, so excretes it in his urine.
	2	Yes.
	3	Yes.
	4	Answers will vary.
	5	Answers will vary.
134	6	Insulin would be digested by our digestive system.
	7	Exercise would use up some of the glucose.
	8	Digestion of food such as carbohydrates.
	9	He does not make any insulin of his own, which would lower the level of glucose in his blood.
	10	Water, temperature, or other suitable answer.
	11	Inject insulin. Eat little and often.
135	12	Diabetes can lead to circulatory problems. This can lead to poor circulation in the feet and damage to the retina in the eye.
	13	The blood vessels at the back of the eye get 'leaky'. The patient's doctor should know, so they check if further treatment is required.

Page	Question number	Answer
2.27 Cells and communication		
136	1	Answers will vary but a good reason should be given that relates to the sense chosen, for example eyes so that we can see dangers.
	2	Answers will vary.
137	3	Finger tips because we can feel two points even when they are together, or that is where we do fine manipulation and need the sensitivity.
	4	Finger tips.
138	5	To communicate with different parts of thc body.
	6	Answers will vary but should be less than 0.5 seconds.
139	7	When the nerves that pass through the wrist get compressed and cause tingling and pain.
	8	Phalens test or using special electronic stimulation equipment.
	9	Wrist support, ultrasound or, in severe cases, surgery.
2.28 Drugs and the body		
140	1	Medical drugs are used to treat disease. Recreational drugs are used for pleasure.
	2	Must be tested for both effectiveness and safety.
141	3	Both going down.
	4	Men.
	5	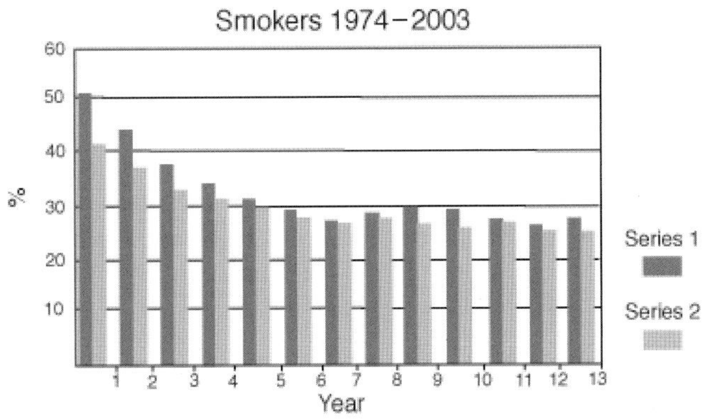
	6	Cigarettes cost relatively more. Better education about health risks.
	7	Answers will vary.
143	8	So the doctor does not influence how the patient feels.
	9	Because both the patients and the doctor do not know who is receiving the drug.
	10	Safety and effectiveness.

Answers to Key fact boxes

Question	Key word
2.20 Heart attack, page 110	
1	arteries
2	capillary(ies), veins
3	circulatory system
4	valves
5	atria, ventricles
6	valve(s)
2.22 Asthma, page 118	
1	thorax
2	ventilation
3	trachea, bronchus, bronchioles
4	alveoli
5	gaseous exchange
6	diaphragm, rib muscles, ribs
7	volume, pressure
8	cartilage
2.24 Oxygen debt, page 126	
1	oxygen
2	anaerobic respiration
3	lactic acid
4	oxygen
5	oxygen debt
6	carbon dioxide
2.26 Diabetes, page 135	
1	glucose
2	insulin, hormone, pancreas
3	diabetes
4	diabetic
5	insulin
6	homeostasis
7	glycogen

Question	Key word
2.21 Blood donor, page 114	
1	fluid, transports
2	plasma
3	red blood cell(s), white blood cell(s), platelets
4	haemoglobin, oxyhaemoglobin
5	anaemic, haemoglobin
2.23 Aerobics, page 122	
1	kilojoules
2	oxygen, glucose
3	aerobic respiration
4	carbon dioxide
5	carbon dioxide, oxygen
6	moisture
2.25 Keeping warm, page 130	
1	temperature
2	respiration
3	shivering
4	evaporation, evaporates
5	vasoconstriction, vasodilation
6	monitors, temperature
7	homeostasis

Question	Key word	Question	Key word
2.27 Cells and communication, page 139		**2.28 Drugs and the body, page 143**	
1	receptors	1	alcohol, nicotine
2	neurone	2	aspirin
3	effector	3	antibiotics
		4	heroin, cocaine, amphetamines, barbiturates
		5	anti-depressants

Answers to Review questions, page 144 – How your body works

Question number		Answer	Marks
1		a artery – carries blood from the heart to the organs; b vein – carries blood to the heart; c capillary – connects arteries to veins and carries blood in the organs to the body.	3
2		150 (mmHg) is pressure of blood when heart is contracting; 95 (mmHg) is pressure of blood between heart beats	2
3	a	blood clot in artery that supplies the heart with blood; stopped blood flowing; heart tissue starved of oxygen and dies	3
	b	stop smoking; exercise; eat less fat	3
4		a – carry oxygen; b – fight disease; c – clot blood; d – carry dissolved food, hormones, carbon dioxide, urea	4
5		muscles in bronchioles contract and tubes narrow; air cannot get through to alveoli	2
6		glucose + oxygen; releases energy during respiration	2
7		vasoconstriction/less blood flow to skin surface to reduce radiated heat loss; hairs erect to provide layer of insulating air; shivering to generate heat by respiration	3
8		a – unable to control the body's blood glucose level; b – Geoff does not make insulin. He needs to inject insulin to keep his blood glucose level down; c – body temperature control	3
		Total	**25**

Answers to intext, activity and case study questions

Page	Question number	Answer
3.1 Elements from the Earth		
147	1a	Below 170°C.
	b	The melting point of gold is very high, so it would stay as a solid/gold mines are deeper.
	2a	1 kg gold costs £10 × 1000 = £10 000 1 kg sulphur costs £90 ÷ 1000 = £0.09
	b	Abundance arguments – more sulphur than gold in crust. Accessibility arguments – mining of sulphur is less costly because the process is simpler; fewer workers or items of machinery are needed; deposits are not so deep. Demand arguments – gold commands high price because everyone wants some. Sulphur commands lower prices.
	3	Many baked goods, for example processed bread, contain sulphur dioxide.
	4	Length of name/space on label; some consumers are put off by seeing chemical names; numbering system helps people know what the chemicals do (for example, preservatives all have numbers E200–E 299) and is can be understood regardless of the local language.
	5	Gold is unreactive so it stays as an element; other metals such as iron react with the soil or air.
149	6	Marking points include: appropriate linear scale chosen for axes; labelling; accuracy of plotting; accuracy of line drawing; labelling of lines.
	7	99%
	8	9 carat (illustrated with reference to prices of gold jewellery from catalogue).

Page	Question number	Answer
3.2 Compounds from the Earth		
150	1	Stones for building, road aggregate.
	2	Answers may include: cement, mortar, concrete, steel (cars and so on) windows, aggregate for road building.
152	3	Mortar contains no stones so it is smoother/easier to work with. Concrete contains gravel so it is harder wearing/doesn't crumble easily.
	4a	Both grow moss/algae over time. Both materials are sandy to the touch. When concrete weathers the small stones in it can be seen. Mortar wears away between the bricks over time.
	b	Mortar eventually needs replacing as it is weathered away (mainly by rain).
153	5	Lowers energy costs and therefore less fuel to buy = cheaper process. Also, less difficult to operate because the machinery does not have to withstand such high temperatures and there are fewer safety hazards.
	6	Below 600°C because it is still liquid when glass leaves the furnace.
	7a	Tin would oxidise to form tin oxide, or may say tin corrodes.
	b	Nitrogen.
	8	Digital photographs could be shown via a projector and students comment on which type of glass is used in which place.
154	9a	CO_2, CaO and NH_3
	b	H_2SO_4 and Na_2CO_3
	c	Cl_2
	d	sodium, carbon and oxygen
	e	H_2SO_4
	f	it contains more than one element chemically bonded together
	g	CaO and CO_2
	10	NH_3 : one nitrogen atom, three hydrogen atoms. CL_2: two chlorine atoms
	11	Answers vary depending on choice.

Page	Question number	Answer
3.3 Salt from rock salt		
156	1	Salt pans use the sun's energy, so no need to buy fuel. Low pressure (means water boils at a lower temperature so less fuel needs to be bought).
157	2a	$\frac{6}{20} \times 100 = 30\%$
	b	More crushing, hotter water, more stirring, more time stirring.
	3	Look for a design that takes into account the need for: dissolving; stirring; filtering; evaporating; removing final salt. Evaporating would use the most energy, also less fuel in crushing/operating machinery.
	4	Setting up: buying machinery, land and buildings. Running costs: rents, taxes (for example, rates), energy/fuel, raw materials, wages.
158	5a	Answers could include: food, dyes, dishwashers, preservatives, bath salts, electrolysis to make hydrogen, chlorine and sodium hydroxide.
	b	Sodium carbonate: making glass, soaps, detergents, paper, dyes. Hydrogen: making margarine, fuel. Sodium hydroxide: paper, soaps, detergents, foods, fibres. Chlorine: sterilising water, making disinfectants, bleaches, solvents.
	6	Look for: correct information (discusses other uses of salt from diagram) and correct style (language appropriate for using to a friend – not merely a list of uses).
	7a	NaCl sodium chloride Na_2CO_3 sodium carbonate H_2 hydrogen Cl_2 chlorine NaOH sodium hydroxide
	b	NaCl compound Na_2CO_c compound H_2 element Cl_2 element NaOH compound
159	8	It takes more salt to melt deep snow than to a thin layer of ice.
	9a	Buying more rock salt. More gritting means more trips in gritter – more wear and tear on machinery, more fuel for gritters and more time needed, so more wages for driver and other workers.
	b	Can be planned – not 'last minute rush'. Roads are kept clear – less chance of traffic hold-ups or accidents, therefore much safer.
	10	Salt would corrode expensive equipment/aeroplanes; liquid can be sprayed on (easier to apply) (students may know that liquid can be sprayed onto planes as well); liquid can be collected from 'gutters' alongside runway to stop environmental damage around runway; no stones/grit.

Page	Question number	Answer
3.4 Iron and steel		
161	1	Iron ore, limestone, coke and air (often forgotten!).
	2a	Rings around formulae for O_2, CO_2 (several times), CO.
	b	Carbon monoxide is toxic. Too much carbon dioxide in the air (not enough oxygen) could suffocate you.
	3	A number above 1540°C (the iron is molten).
	4	Do not have to waste time of workers or equipment (furnace is continually producing iron). Saves fuel (do not have to reheat furnace from cold).
	5	Support activities: ordering raw materials, making sure enough workers are employed and available daily, organising iron to be taken away. Supply to furnace: monitoring input of raw materials in correct quantities. Running furnace: checking temperature, and checking furnace for wear and tear. Maintenance: repairing any damaged components quickly. Emptying furnace: supervising output.
	6	Look for – inclusion of relevant facts about each stage of the process; style (appeal of the cartoon to an audience).
162	7	$2PbO + \underline{\mathbf{C}} \longrightarrow 2Pb + \underline{\mathbf{CO_2}}$
	8	Reduced, reducer, oxidised.
163	9	Less energy is needed, so less fuel must be bought, therefore cheaper. Better for environment: saves resources (fossil fuels) and metal ores, reduces CO_2 emissions.
	10	Seats, carpets, dashboards, bumpers, internal fixtures and fittings.
	11	Re-using – using something again, for example taking an old indicator light from a scrapped car and fitting it to a car still in use. Re-cycling – usually means melting down or processing so that the materials are available to make new goods, for example, melting down scrap steel to make new cars.
	12	Car dealing is more profitable than scrapping. There is a more competitive market.

Answers to Key fact boxes

Question	Key word	Question	Key word
3.1 Elements from the earth, page 149		**3.2 Compounds from the earth, page 155**	
1	element	1	calcium carbonate
2	metal	2	cement
3	non-metal	3	compound
4	gold, sulphur	4	formula
3.3 Salt from rock salt, page 159		**3.4 Iron and steel, page 162**	
1	mixture	1	blast furnace
2	separated, dissolves	2	coke, limestone, ore
3	evaporates	3	haematite
4	chemicals	4	steel
		5	carbon
		6	oxidation
		7	reduction

Answers to Review questions, page 164 – Chemicals from the earth

Question number		Answer	Marks
1	a	appropriate scale chosen for axes; accuracy of plotting and of drawing bars (ruler used); labelling of title and bars	3
	b	making glass and cement = 2 + 58 = 60% (Allow 73% – some students may include 'iron and steel')	1
2	a	sulphur – sulphuric acid; nitrogen – ammonia; sodium chloride – chlorine; hydrocarbons – octane (all 4 correct = 3, 2/3 = 2, 1 = 1)	3
	b	chlorine – sterilising water/making disinfectants; sulphuric acid – making detergents/making paints	2
	c	sulphuric acid – 2 hydrogen atoms; 1 sulphur atom; 4 oxygen atoms; octane – 8 carbon atoms; 18 hydrogen atoms	4
3	a	appropriate scale chosen for axes; accuracy of plotting and of drawing bars (ruler used); labelling of title and bars; (An additional mark is available here for students who draw a single bar with all three values to show that they realise that the UK input is part of the European input, which is part of the World input.)	4
	b	$\frac{13\,700}{75\,000} \times 100 = 18\%$	2
	c	12 000 tonnes per day = 500 tonnes per hour; (or realisation that there is a need to ÷ 24); Severn Bridge = $\frac{4500}{500}$ = 9 hours; Millennium stadium $\frac{11\,000}{500}$ = 22 hours	3
	d	steelmaking still takes place in this country; the uses of steel have changed over time; examples – cars, food or drinks cans	3
		Total	**25**

Answers to intext, activity and case study questions

Page	Question number	Answer
3.5 Crude oil to petrol		
167	1	Appropriate scale chosen for axes; accuracy of plotting and of drawing bars (ruler used); labelling of title and bars.
	2	91% (students may not realise that 'making electricity' involves burning fuel).
	3	Answers may include: alternative energy sources in use, for example hydrogen-powered cars, wind turbines, solar panels on house roofs; problems of supply of chemicals from oil (no shampoos/detergents/paints).
	4	A comparative bar chart; with an appropriate scale chosen for axes; plotted and drawn accurately (ruler used); with labelling of title and bars.
	5	Fuel oil and gasoline. Fuel oil is used for heating homes and factories, gasoline makes petrol.
	6	Kerosene and fuel oil.
	7	Bigger molecules that would go to waste could be 'cracked' to make smaller molecules, such as petrol, which are in high demand.
168	8a	Axes drawn with appropriate scale; correct plotting and drawing of line; correct labelling.
	b	Data book value is 42°C, but allow some variation.
	c	C_4H_{10}
	d	Contain carbon atoms and were formed from the remains of living things.
	e	Strongest is pentane. It has the highest boiling point. Weakest is methane. It has the lowest boiling point.
	f	Pentane; it is a liquid at 20°C.
169	9	oxygen ($S + O_2 \longrightarrow SO_2$) sulphur + oxygen ⟶ sulphur dioxide
	10	Acids react with and dissolve metals, so car parts (in particular the exhaust) will be attacked and will corrode away.
	11	Answers could include: dissolves building materials; makes soil infertile (dead trees, plants); makes lakes toxic (dead aquatic life).
	12	Answers could include: less sulphur dioxide emission; less respiratory irritation; less damage to cars; less acid rain; less damage caused by acid rain. Also look for appropriate style of presentation – is it clear, eye-catching and easily understood?

Page	Question number	Answer
3.6 Bulk and fine chemicals		
170	1	Man-made chemicals are found in fertilisers for growing foods, dyes, paints, pigments, petrol, fuels, plastics, fibres, medicines, perfumes. (Answer should be in a 'chatty' style.)
171	2	Answers will vary. (Look for factual information, content and appropriateness of the style.)
	3	All the sulphuric acid is sold to other chemical companies to make final products such as dyes, and detergents. It is NOT sold directly to the public.
	4a	Main bulk chemicals are inorganics, fertilisers and petrochemicals.
	b	Any chemical that will come into contact with human skin is produced as a fine chemical. Medicines have to be made very accurately so that their contents are exactly known. The quality has to be controlled rigorously – no impurities are allowed. Their manufacture often involves multiple complex stages which would be difficult to manage on a large scale.
172	5	Higher temperature is expensive because of higher energy/fuel costs. Catalysts have a high initial cost, but they are not used up so can be used indefinitely, in other words a low cost over a longer period of time. (Some students may discuss how the surface of catalysts can become fouled so that the catalyst must be regenerated or cleaned periodically.)
173	6	Longer storage time/shelf life; tablets less liable to damage/do not go dusty; patients do not taste unpleasant medicine; easier to swallow; can tell what tablet is because can be printed with name. (Style: appropriate language and style for magazine advert.)
	7	Sterile equipment; materials and tablets tested at each stage; coating is carried out by hand; any imperfect tablets are rejected.
	8	Cost of fuel for rotating drum and heating air.

Page	Question number	Answer
3.7 Making ammonia		
174	1a	i The catalyst speeds the reaction up without being used up, therefore the reaction happens faster, leading to more product made and cheaper fuel bills. ii Powdering will give the catalyst a greater surface area; higher temperatures further increase the rate of reaction.
	b	Each time the mixture passes over the catalyst, more reactions will happen so more ammonia will be made.
175	2	Decreases
	3	Increases
	4	A high pressure and a low temperature (may quote from graph: 400 atm and 0°C).
	5	Higher pressures lead to higher yields, but this would put a strain on the equipment. Breakdowns and repairs are costly; working conditions may be unsafe. 150 atm gives a compromise, allowing reasonable costs and safety standards with reasonable yield. Very low temperatures would give the best yield but the reactions would be too slow. Higher temperatures mean more fuel needs to be bought, so this would be expensive. 400°C is a compromise between yield and rate. (Style: appropriate to a business/scientific memo.)
176	6a	methane + water ⟶ carbon monoxide + hydrogen
	b	3; $CH_4 + H_2O \longrightarrow CO + 3H_2$
	7a	sulphur + oxygen ⟶ sulphur dioxide sulphur dioxide + oxygen ⟶ sulphur trioxide sulphur trioxide + water ⟶ sulphuric acid
	b	$2SO_2 + O_2 \longrightarrow 2SO_3$
	c	The reaction which makes sulphur trioxide is a reversible reaction, so will not make 100% yield.
177	8	A chemist works in a lab and carries out research and experiments on a small scale. A chemical engineer works to scale up reactions so that they can be carried out on a large scale in a chemical plant.
	9	It is a toxic gas (it can kill people) and it is heavier than air. Its density means that it lies on the ground and does not disperse easily.
	10	Answers should include: 1913: First success in converting nitrogen to ammonia. Importance of ammonia as a fertiliser 1918: Nobel Prize 1934 Mentions later uses of ammonia for warfare (Style: appropriate 'diary' style and should show contrasts of views about ammonia with time.)

Page	Question number	Answer
3.8 Putting numbers into industry		
178	1	Ca = 40 O = 16, 40+16 = 56
	2	44
	3	560 tonnes
	4	11 200 tonnes
	5	Limestone isn't pure/is mixed with other rocks or sand; reaction does not go to full completion (for example, not heated long enough).
179	6a	20.0 g
	b	15.0 g
	c	11.2 g
	7	Faster reaction with a larger surface area/limestone will decompose quicker.
	8	Limestone might not be pure.
	9	Heat for longer/crushed limestone. Do several experiments and taking an average. (Some students could be introduced to the idea of heating to constant mass.)
180	10	copper oxide + sulphuric acid ⟶ copper sulphate + water
	11	copper oxide relative mass = 64 +16 = 80 copper sulphate relative mass = 64 + 32 + (4 × 16) = 160
	12	40.0 g
	13	$\frac{36}{40} \times 100 = 90\%$
	14	The copper sulphate may not have been pure; the reaction might not have fully finished; she might have lost some yield in transferring product between containers.
181	15	Iron oxide 2 × 56 + 3 × 16 = 160 Iron 2 × 56 = 112
	16	160 × 100 = 16 000 tonnes
	17	You will need to order more than the minimum.
	18a	Good transport links – road, rail, sea – and access to workforce.
	b	As above, the main link is that they are all ports to take the big tankers.
	c	Iron ore from Australia has a much higher (twice as much) iron content. This will give double the yield, and so make the process much more profitable. This will offset the very high cost of transport. Also this will mean there is less slag and waste to be disposed of (better for the environment). Similarly, the coal from Poland is higher quality, so less needs to be used. (Some students may realise that Polish coal is cheap because labour is cheap in Poland and there are fewer safety and environmental laws governing its extraction.)

Answers to Key fact boxes

Question	Key word	Question	Key word
3.5 Crude oil to petrol, page 169		**3.6 Bulk and fine chemicals, page 173**	
1	organic	1	fine
2	inorganic	2	bulk
3	hydrocarbon(s), boiling points	3	catalyst, rate of reaction
4	fractional distillation	4	temperature, energy
5	hydrocarbons, fractionating column		
3.7 Making ammonia, page 177			
1	ammonia, bulk		
2	balanced		
3	formulae		

Answers to Review questions, page 182 – The chemical industry

Question number		Answer	Marks
1		mark by correct use of the words in correct context, showing understanding of the term. (one mark per word and one mark for appropriate language use – told from the point of view of a molecule)	9
2	a	octane contains carbon (and was originally formed from dead animals and plants)	1
	b	neither contain carbon; although they are involved in reactions in living things they are not a living part of the organism	2
3	a	bulk = ammonia; petrol; fertiliser; fine = food colourings; aspirin (all five correct = two marks; three or four correct = one mark)	2
	b	quality needs to be strictly controlled/many tests carried out; many stages in the manufacturing process; final product must exactly fit specifications; no impurities allowed; not produced in very large quantities (any two)	2
4	a	calcium carbonate + sodium chloride ⟶ calcium chloride + sodium carbonate; lead oxide + carbon monoxide ⟶ lead + carbon dioxide; hydrogen + chlorine ⟶ hydrogen chloride (accept hydrochloric acid)	3
	b	reaction 1	1
	c	reaction 1 should read 2NaCl; reaction 3 should read 2HCl	2
	d	reaction 2	1
5	a	methane; mass 16	2
	b	lead oxide; mass 223	2
	c	sodium hydroxide; mass 40	2
	d	copper carbonate; mass 124	2
	e	potassium nitrate; mass 101	2
	f	sodium sulphate; mass 142	2
6	a	$CuO + CO \longrightarrow Cu + CO_2$ (one mark for at least two formulae fully correct)	2
	b	relative mass of copper oxide is 80; relative mass of copper is 64; theoretical yield of copper is $\frac{64}{4} = 16$ g; percentage yield of copper is $\frac{14}{16} \times 100 = 87.5\%$	4
	c	the copper oxide may not have been pure; the reaction might not have fully finished; he might have lost some yield in transferring product between containers (any two)	2
		Total	**43**

Answers to intext, activity and case study questions

<table>
<tr><th>Page</th><th>Question number</th><th>Answer</th></tr>
<tr><td colspan="3">3.9 Mixtures everywhere</td></tr>
<tr><td>185</td><td>1</td><td>
<table>
<tr><td>Salad dressing</td><td>Oil part</td><td>Water part</td><td>Stops oil from separating</td><td>Makes dressing taste better</td></tr>
<tr><td>French dressing</td><td>walnut oil</td><td>herb vinegar/ lemon juice</td><td>mustard</td><td>sugar
salt
pepper
mustard</td></tr>
<tr><td>Garlic mayonnaise</td><td>olive oil</td><td>lemon juice</td><td>egg yolk</td><td>garlic
salt</td></tr>
</table>
</td></tr>
<tr><td></td><td>2</td><td>Recipe should include: a reduced quantity of oil, an increased ‘water’ phase (for example, vinegar or lemon juice), no eggs, an emulsifier such as mustard, flavourings such as garlic and salt.
Letter should include: factual information to cover comments on less fat and sugar and how the dressing is flavoured. (Style: appropriate to a letter to a friend.)</td></tr>
<tr><td></td><td>3</td><td>
<table>
<tr><td>Type of colloid</td><td>Example</td><td>Dispersed phase (drops)</td><td>Continuous phase</td><td>Colloid contains</td></tr>
<tr><td>Emulsion</td><td>salad dressing</td><td>oil</td><td>water</td><td>liquid/liquid</td></tr>
<tr><td>Foam</td><td>shaving foam</td><td>bubbles of gas</td><td>shaving cream</td><td>gas/liquid</td></tr>
<tr><td>Aerosol</td><td>hairspray</td><td>liquid hairspray</td><td>gas</td><td>liquid/gas</td></tr>
</table>
</td></tr>
<tr><td>186</td><td>4</td><td>
<table>
<tr><td>Emulsions</td><td>face/nappy/medical creams; some hair conditioners; body lotions; hand creams</td></tr>
<tr><td>Foams</td><td>shaving foams; some bath cleaning products; hair mousse</td></tr>
<tr><td>Suspensions</td><td>some medicines, e.g. milk of magnesia; abrasive cream cleaners</td></tr>
<tr><td>Gels</td><td>hair styling gels, lip glosses</td></tr>
</table>
</td></tr>
<tr><td>187</td><td>5</td><td>Hanging basket each $= \frac{24}{12} = £2$
4 litres compost $= \frac{8.00}{25} = £0.32$
6 plants $= \frac{3.60}{8} = £0.45$
Total cost = £2.77
Other costs: hire of stall, cost of van and petrol, Martyn’s time, need for potting shed/ workspace, time spent watering and looking after baskets before sale.
Price £5–£8 seems reasonable.</td></tr>
</table>

Page	Question number	Answer
3.9 Mixtures everywhere (continued)		
	6	£0.10 Yes: because the extra cost is low, and it will save him watering the baskets so much before he sells them. It will also save his customers watering them so much, and may give a better display of flowers for customers who forget to water their baskets regularly.
	7	Gels absorb and release water; diagram of structure of hydrogel; use of gel reduces need for regular watering. (Style appropriate to an advert.)
3.10 Splitting the atom		
188	1a	hydrogen, lithium, carbon
	b	Hydrogen atom drawing shows one proton in nucleus and one electron; lithium atom shows three protons, four neutrons in nucleus and three electrons (at this stage, all electrons will be shown in first shell); carbon atom shows six protons and six neutrons in nucleus and six electrons (accept six in same shell here).
	2	There are over 100 elements so symbols would be very confusing/letters are more familiar or easier to remember and understand/letters give a clue to the name/other reasonable answers possible.
189	3	Correct numbers of each particle; collage has labels or a key to identify the element and which particle is which.
	4	17: 2,8,7
	5	He 2; Ne 8; Ar 8: they all have full outer shells.
190	6	Three electrons around Li in configuration 2,1; nine electrons around F in configuration 2,7. (Look for: different symbols (such as dot and cross) used for each atom; correct electron arrangement shown in ions; charges shown on ions Li^+ and F^-.)
	7a	Mg has a charge of 2^+ and O has a charge of 2^-.
	b	Magnesium and oxide because they have higher charges.
	8	For sodium oxide: 11 electrons around Na in configuration 2,8,1; eight electrons around O in configuration 2,6; (Look for different symbols (such as dot and cross) used for each atom; correct electron arrangement shown in ions; two sodium ions shown for each oxide ion; charges shown on ions Na^+ and O^{2-}.) For magnesium chloride: 12 electrons around Mg in configuration 2,8,2; 17 electrons around Cl in configuration 2,8,7; (Look for different symbols (such as dot and cross) used for each atom; correct electron arrangement shown in ions; two chloride ions shown for each magnesium ion; charges shown on ions Mg^{2+} and Cl^-.)
191	9a	Number 1
	b	Number 3
	c	Number 2

Page	Question number	Answer
3.11 Making salts		
192	1	ammonium nitrate – nitric acid; sodium nitrate – nitric acid; copper sulphate – sulphuric acid; potassium chloride – hydrochloric acid
	2	nitric acid salts – magnesium nitrate; hydrochloric acid salts – sodium chloride and magnesium chloride
	3	Answers will vary.
193	4	It contains an impurity (the indicator).
	5	If you just mix together the two solutions then the quantities may not be exactly right for neutralisation; excess acid or ammonia would be toxic to the plants; the plants will die.
	6	Evaporate; by heating (over a water bath); until about $\frac{1}{3}$ is left; leave to form crystals.
194	7a	Silver nitrate + potassium bromide ⟶ silver bromide + potassium nitrate
	b	Nitrates are made when the silver bromide is made.
	8a	Silver nitrate and potassium chloride.
	b	Silver nitrate and potassium iodide.
	c	silver nitrate + potassium chloride ⟶ silver chloride + potassium nitrate $AgNO_3 + KCl \longrightarrow AgCl + KNO_3$ silver nitrate + potassium iodide ⟶ silver iodide + potassium nitrate $AgNO_3 + KI \longrightarrow AgI + KNO_3$
	9	Silver bromide goes darker when light shines on it. The darkest areas on a negative will be where most light has been shining. The lightest areas will be where least light has been shining.
	10	Need for high purity/rigorous quality control/high specification. Fertilisers do not need to be as pure.
195	11	Lead chromate – colours the markings yellow. Thermoplastic beads – melt when hot so the marking can be poured onto the road; set when cold so that the marking is permanent.
	12	Heating them to soften the plastic (in fact they are burnt off – the fumes are very strong, workers wear breathing protection).
	13	Both lead ions and chromate ions are very toxic. (Some students may give more detail, for example the cumulative nature of lead poisoning). Research for a non-toxic alternative is ongoing.
	14	Look for understanding of the role of the components of road markings, such as lead chromate as pigment, thermoplastic beads form the marking, the filler makes the marking hard wearing. Appreciates specialised, skilled nature of work applying markings, and need for specialised equipment/need to melt markings. Paint is easily applied but will wear off very quickly. Limestone and glass beads are very hard wearing. (Style: letter style with language and approach appropriate from a business to a councillor.)

Page	Question number	Answer
3.12 Chemical analysis		
196	1	Potassium.
197	2	Sample 1: copper; Sample 2: iron; Sample 3: calcium.
	3a	The flame test implies that there is calcium in Sample 2.
	b	A flame spectrometer shows all the colours – our eyes just see the strongest, which can mask the others, so the spectrometer will show all the metals in the sample. Our eyes will only notice the main one.
	4	If it dissolved it would contain lead rather than calcium.
	5	The lead had been collected and sold. Only the unwanted ores are left on the waste heaps.
	6a	Tests have to be very sensitive to identify very dilute solutions – you would not see any results.
	b	By evaporating it.
198	7	A is either sodium or potassium chloride; B is lead carbonate; C is calcium sulphate You would need to flame test A to find out if it contains sodium or potassium. The health and safety inspector should be worried about the lead carbonate because lead is toxic.
199	8	To get the solid crystals from it/to concentrate it.
	9	Look for: a comparative chart drawn (if possible using a spreadsheet); appropriate scale chosen for axes; accurately plotted and drawn (ruler used); labelling of title and bars.
	10	Dead Sea water: 279 g; Atlantic Ocean: 34.7 g.
	11	The Dead Sea contains many more minerals than the Atlantic.
	12a	It contains much more bromine. (Some students can work out it is about 50 times as much.)
	b	More sodium, potassium, magnesium, calcium and chloride ions.
	c	These other elements all occur in lots of places – it is bromine that is rare.

Page	Question number	Answer
3.13 More about molecules		
200	1	$C_2H_3Cl_3$
	2	H │ H—C—H │ H F H │ │ F—C—C—Br │ │ F Cl
201	3	CCl_3F 1 carbon, 3 chlorine, 1 fluorine CCl_2F_2 1 carbon, 2 chlorine, 2 fluorine CCl_2FCClF_2 2 carbon, 3 chlorine, 3 fluorine CF_3Cl 1 carbon, 1 chlorine, 3 fluorine
	4a	Students are not expected to know about ozone depletion for this course, but these are points they might raise from their general knowledge: ozone depletion allows more UV rays to strike Earth's surface; this may result in skin cancer, death of phytoplankton, death to crops, sea life and so on. Customers are more likely to buy a product that is 'ozone friendly'. The law may ban products that contain ozone-depleting substances.
	b	Non-toxic, non-reactive/does not react with polish, does not burn, long shelf life, good solvent/dissolves polish.
202	5	Look for: correct numbers of electrons around each atom; use of different symbols to show electrons of different atoms (such as dot and cross); correct numbers of atoms in the compound; each bond shown as comprising two shared electrons; outer shell totals correct.
	6a	Very high melting points.
	b	They dissolve grease. (Some students may also realise that their low boiling points mean they evaporate off the boards quickly.)
	c	Simple covalent compounds have low melting and boiling points so they are often liquids or gases at room temperature. Ionic compounds have very high melting and boiling points and are usually solids.
203	7	Harmful/irritant.
	8	Filter.
	9	Look for correct use of the terms: cool, heat, condenses, evaporation, pure solvent, waste, separation.

Page	Question number	Answer
3.13 More about molecules (continued)		
	10	Heating the clothes makes any solvents evaporate so that they can be recovered. Otherwise the clothes would be wet with solvents when they came out of the machine, and the solvents would evaporate into the air.
	11a	Some solvent will escape on the clothes that come out of the machine, with the waste from the filter, and by evaporation through any vents and imperfect seals in the machine.
	b	Look for: explanation of the distillation process; discussion of how clothes are heated to drive off solvents. (Style should be appropriate to a magazine letter.)
3.14 Energy and chemical change		
204	1	calcium oxide + water ⟶ calcium hydroxide
	2	Answers will vary. Look for: awareness of corrosive nature of the chemicals, and the exothermic reaction of calcium oxide with water. Designers will have had to make sure the calcium oxide was kept in a sealed, dry container within the can so it did not come into contact with the water in the coffee. The metal chosen for the can would have to be able to withstand the corrosive nature of the chemicals. The designers would need to make sure the chemicals did not enter the coffee.
	3	Keep off skin, for example wear gloves, boots; do not inhale dust; wear goggles when using; wash any splashes off with lots of water; store cement in a very dry place; be aware that mixing the cement with water will generate heat. (Style: should look and read like instructions.)
	4	a; d
205	5a	Same amount of water (some students may mention volume); same start temperature; same amount of chemical (some students should realise this is the same mass).
	b	Instructions should include: measuring a volume of water, for example 50 cm^3; checking the temperature; weighing a sample, for example 2 g; adding to the water and measuring temperature change (either read temperature every few seconds, for example 15s, or read maximum temperature change).
	6	+ 3°C, −2°C, −3°C (signs important)
	7	Ammonium chloride. It has the biggest negative temperature change.
	8	Repeat the experiments to take an average (mean) of readings.
	9	Harmful/irritant
	10	The can should be similar to self-heating can but should show ammonium chloride. In the advert, look for: how the can works; drink examples, for example lemonade. (Style appropriate to an advert.)

Page	Question number	Answer
3.14 Energy and chemical change (continued)		
206	11	Bonds are broken when water and calcium oxide react together, which takes in energy. Bonds are formed when calcium hydroxide is made, giving out energy. More energy is given out than taken in so the reaction is exothermic.
207	12	Very exothermic reaction with oxygen means that energy is given out; ignite means to use a flame/put in energy to start a fire/start an exothermic reaction; combust means to burn.
	13	The hydrogen that powers the fuel cell does not burn, so there is no need for a flame to ignite the stored hydrogen. The reactions take place at a low temperature.
	14	Hydrogen is made by electrolysing brine, which takes a lot of electricity. Electricity is usually generated by burning fossil fuels. So, at the moment, hydrogen powered cars still deplete fossil fuels. Hydrogen is usually stored in pressurised gas canisters. It is explosive, the canisters could be a risk in the filling stations or cars.

Answers to Key fact boxes

Question	Key word	Question	Key word
3.9 Mixtures everywhere, page 186		**3.10 Splitting the atom, page 191**	
1	colloid	1	protons; neutrons
2	dispersed phase, continuous phase	2	electrons; nucleus
3	emulsion	3	ionic
4	suspension; gel	4	shell(s)
5	foam	5	transfer
6	aerosol	6	ion
7	solution		
3.13 More about molecules, page 202		**3.14 Energy and chemical change, page 206**	
1	molecule	1	exothermic
2	covalent	2	endothermic
3	share	3	breaking bonds
4	solvents	4	making bonds
		5	exothermic

Answers to Review questions, page 208 – Investigating chemistry

Question number		Answer	Marks
1		endothermic, because energy is taken in, so pack feels cold	1
2	a	they contain the correct elements	1
	b	the numbers of atoms in the formulae are wrong	1
	c	each bond shown as two shared electrons; N electrons fully correct; H electrons fully correct and different to nitrogen (dot and cross)	3
3	a	potassium chloride – hydrochloric acid; magnesium sulphate – sulphuric acid; calcium sulphate – sulphuric acid	3
	b	need for control of quality/rigorous testing/multi-stage processes (any two)	2
	c	electrons around K shown fully correct; electrons around Cl shown fully correct – dot and cross; charges shown clearly K^+ and Cl^-	3
4	a	add sodium hydroxide solution; to a solution of the samples; add hydrochloric acid; add excess hydrochloric acid to confirm result; test any gases with lime water; written as clear set of instructions	6
	b	sodium hydroxide test – blue precipitate for copper salt; white precipitate for calcium salt; that does not redissolve; both are carbonates that should turn the lime water milky	4
		Total	**21**

Answers to intext, activity and case study questions

Page	Question number	Answer
3.15 Bricks		
210	1a	Water in the brick has evaporated.
	b	In bricks, the cross links make the brick hard and rigid because the layers cannot move. Layers can move over each other in clay, so clay can change shape. [It is important that students can link properties to a molecular explanation in each case.]
	2	Metallic element: aluminium; non-metallic elements: oxygen and silicon.
	3	Bricks do not rot/they are waterproof/do not burn.
211	4a	Wet cloth mass change = +5 g. It has absorbed water. Left to dry mass change = −40 g. Water has evaporated from the clay. Kiln fired mass change = −42 g. Water has evaporated when in the kiln.
	b	$\frac{42}{212} \times 100 = 19.8\%$
	5	When air-dried clay is wet, the water goes back between the layers. There are no crosslinks to stop this from happening.
	6	Look for correct, contextualised use of the terms.
	7	Possible points include: design of roof (materials, angle, overhang of walls, gutters and downpipes); installation of damp proof course.
212	8a	In the solid, **the particles are held together firmly** in a lattice of bonds. **The temperature has to be very high** to provide enough **energy** to **break bonds** in the giant structure. The particles can **then move over each other** and become a liquid. (Some students may realise that only some of the bonds break – if all the bonds break, it would result in atomisation of the sample.)
	b	Melted silicon dioxide contains (clusters of) neutral atoms. Melted aluminium oxide contains ions that can carry electricity because the ions are positively or negatively charged.
	c	The melting point is very high, so a lot of energy is needed to break the bonds.
	d	Aluminium oxide, because it has the higher melting point.
213	9	The larger surface area leads to faster reaction. (Some students may be able to give explanation using collision theory.) Faster burning creates a hotter fire.
	10	Oxygen from the air is needed for burning, otherwise the fire would go out.
	11	Nitrogen comes from the air. It is not involved in the combustion reaction. Carbon dioxide comes from the reaction between the carbon in the coal and oxygen.
	12a	It would evaporate/turn to steam/turn to a gas.
	b	The gas would build up pressure between the layers of clay/inside the bricks leading to explosion.
	13	Computers can monitor the temperature continuously; more accurate readings; people do not have to work near kilns/less dangerous working conditions/more comfortable in office.

Page	Question number	Answer
3.16 Polymers		
214	1	Non-biodegradable polymers have an indefinite life in use. They are very hardwearing, but when they are discarded they do not rot. This creates a long-term litter problem in landfill sites.
	2	Shorter chains will not tangle up so much, so will be easier to pull apart. This means that the plastic will break more easily. (It is important that the students can discuss the properties and how they relate to the structure of the polymer.)
	3	It is a thermoplastic, and so can be melted and shaped when hot.
	4	Milk bottle – does not shatter like glass. Bucket – does not corrode away like metals. Paper bag – stronger and is not affected by water.
215	5	LDPE is cheaper, but HDPE is stronger and more stable to heat. (Note: when a comparison is asked for, students need to discuss both compounds.)
	6	LDPE is suitable for coffee cups because the drinks are unlikely to be at a temperature higher than 90°C, but the cups would melt in the higher temperature of a microwave. HDPE containers are suitable for cooking food at up to 200°C.
	7	Main error to look for here will be drawing the chains getting longer before breaking – this is incorrect. The chains stay the same size, but pull apart, as shown, as the plastic stretches. Notice that the group of chains get both longer and thinner as the plastic stretches.
	8	Both, because they are both less dense than water (density of water is 1 g cm^{-3}).
216	9a	It does not conduct heat like metals do so you don't burn your hand. It does not burn as wood does.
	b	Factual information to cover: meaning of thermoset; diagram to show cross links; linking cross links to resistance to heat. Style: should be appropriate language and style for an advert.
217	10	Costs involved = £250, PET sells for £150, cost to council = £100.
	11	The plastics do not need to be sorted into individual types. (Some students may realise that sorting plastics is very difficult because they all have such similar properties – it is easy, for example, to separate out iron with a magnet, or paper, which can be blown off in an air stream.) Many recycling schemes rely on hand-sorting of waste plastics.
	12	There will be less plastics in landfills, so do not have to find new landfill sites as often. Recycling is good for the council's image – many local people want to see recycling schemes operating.
	13a	Wood and iron.
	b	The benches are made by melting and moulding the waste plastics. Thermoset plastics do not melt and so would not mould successfully.

<table>
<tr><th>Page</th><th>Question number</th><th>Answer</th></tr>
<tr><td colspan="3">3.17 Electrical behaviour</td></tr>
<tr><td>218</td><td>1</td><td><table><tr><th>voltage</th><th>current</th><th>resistance</th></tr><tr><td>volt</td><td>amp</td><td>ohm</td></tr></table></td></tr>
<tr><td>219</td><td>2</td><td>Material of the cable; diameter of the cable. (The distances from power stations to electrical consumers cannot be controlled by the National Grid Company, although they can make sure that their cables take short routes wherever possible.)</td></tr>
<tr><td></td><td>3</td><td>Glass – has high resistance for a given length and thickness.
Lead – has high density and would require many strong pylons to support it.</td></tr>
<tr><td></td><td>4</td><td>A thick wire has less resistance. There is a bigger area for electrons to travel along. In a similar way, water flows more easily along a thick pipe than a thin pipe.</td></tr>
<tr><td></td><td>5a</td><td>It is the shortest, so less cabling and fewer pylons needed.</td></tr>
<tr><td></td><td>b</td><td>Obstacles in the way, for example buildings; scenic considerations; unable to access land.</td></tr>
<tr><td></td><td>6a</td><td>Answers will vary.</td></tr>
<tr><td></td><td>b</td><td>Answers will vary.</td></tr>
<tr><td>220</td><td>7</td><td>Conductors: aluminium, constantan, copper, iron, lead, mild steel, tin.
Insulators: concrete, sheet glass, nylon, polythene.</td></tr>
<tr><td></td><td>8a</td><td>Current changes by the same proportion as voltage.</td></tr>
<tr><td></td><td>b</td><td>The graph is curved which means the ratio of voltage to current is not constant.</td></tr>
<tr><td>221</td><td>9</td><td>$\text{resistance} = \frac{\text{voltage}}{\text{current}} = \frac{12}{2} = 6 \text{ ohm}$</td></tr>
<tr><td></td><td>10a</td><td><table><tr><td>wire</td><td>wire 1</td><td>wire 2</td><td>wire 3</td><td>wire 4</td><td>wire 5</td></tr><tr><td>resistance/ohm</td><td>10.0</td><td>5.0</td><td>2.5</td><td>2.0</td><td>1.7</td></tr></table></td></tr>
<tr><td></td><td>b</td><td>Look for: linear axes, labelled, points plotted, smooth line.</td></tr>
<tr><td></td><td>c</td><td>Resistance</td></tr>
<tr><td></td><td>d</td><td>As resistance increases, current decreases.</td></tr>
<tr><td></td><td>11a</td><td><table><tr><th>material</th><th>resistance of wire 1 metre long and diameter 1 mm</th></tr><tr><td>aluminium</td><td>0.031</td></tr><tr><td>constantan</td><td>0.490</td></tr><tr><td>copper</td><td>0.020</td></tr><tr><td>iron</td><td>0.113</td></tr><tr><td>lead</td><td>0.242</td></tr></table></td></tr>
</table>

(continued)

Page	Question number	Answer
3.17 Electrical behaviour (continued)		
	11b	Look for: bars drawn to single scale, labelled.
	c	So that our comparisons are 'fair tests'.
	12a	Its temperature increases.
	b	The graph is curved. The ratio of voltage to current is not constant.
3.18 Physical properties		
222	1a	$\text{resistance} = \frac{\text{voltage}}{\text{current}}$ $\quad$ $\text{density} = \frac{\text{mass}}{\text{volume}}$
	b	Both are worked out by division. They are ratios.
	2	Increase in temperature. Expansion reduces density.
	3a	Power supply is broken. Loose cable presents a hazard.
	b	Power supply is broken. Broken cable may be difficult, and expensive, to locate.
223	4	Cables must not be allowed to get too hot. Need to allow excess heat to dissipate.
	5a	It is made of more than one material.
	b	Glass and plastic.
	c	It is lightweight and strong, but flexible, and can be moulded. It can be used where either glass or plastic alone would not be suitable.
224	6	$\text{density} = \frac{\text{mass}}{\text{volume}} = \frac{1000}{1}$ = 1000 kilograms per cubic metre (kg m^{-3})
	7	$\text{density} = \frac{\text{mass}}{\text{volume}} = \frac{5000}{2}$ = 2500 kilograms per cubic metre (kg m^{-3})
	8	2500 kilograms per cubic metre
	9a	Copper: 8940 kilograms per cubic metre (kg m^{-3}); aluminium: 2700 kilograms per cubic metre (kg m^{-3}).
	b	Copper: 0.020 ohm; aluminium: 0.031 ohm.
	c	Look for: two bar charts, each with a suitable scale.
	d	Copper is a better electrical conductor (lower resistance of the copper wire) but has higher density, so the wires are heavier. The low density of aluminium makes it suitable for hanging from pylons. Density is less important underground.
	10a	Low density, fairly low resistance of standard wire.
	b	Not strong enough.
	c	Strength.
	d	Steel cables are heavier (more dense) and have more resistance per unit length than aluminium.
	e	Cheaper. (Melting would use a lot of energy.)

(continued)

Page	Question number	Answer
3.18 Physical properties (continued)		
225	11a	Thicker wire has lower resistance.
	b	If it is too thick it will be too heavy.
	12	Overhead.
	13a	Answers will very, but might include: can't route cable through towns, over big hills; should not spoil views of countryside.
	b	Customers want cheap electricity. Power station operators want their electricity to be as cheap as possible.
	c	Residents, tourists, local government.
	14a	Look for correct lables and description of properties.
	b	The inner layer, poly(ethene) must be closest to the liquid for water-proofing. Without this, the carton would not hold the liquid for long. The aluminium needs to be in the middle so it doesn't touch the juice on the inside and get damaged by acids in the juice. It also needs protection from damage on the outside. The cardboard protects the carton. It is light and flexible, but strong enough too.
	c	The poly(ethene) acts as a water-proof layer in both.

Answers to Key fact boxes

Question	Key word	Question	Key word
3.15 Bricks, page 213		**3.16 Polymers, page 216**	
1	ceramics	1	polymer
2	cross links	2	thermoplastic
3	giant structure	3	cross links
4	covalent	4	thermosetting
5	ionic	5	side groups
		6	plasticisers, composite
3.17 Electrical behaviour, page 221		**3.18 Physical properties, page 224**	
1	conductors	1	hardness
		2	malleability
		3	composite(s)
		4	strength
		5	alloy

Answers to Review questions, page 226 – Materials for making things

Question number		Answer	Marks
1	a	giant structure – **many atoms bonded** together; in a **lattice/three-dimensional arrangement**; covalently bonded – have bonds made by **shared electrons**	3
	b	i the atoms are held together very firmly; in a lattice/by strong bonds/in a 3-D arrangement	2
		ii the bonds are very strong	1
2	a	carries out an accurate calculation to give prices for the **same weight** of clay (for example, works out that 12.5 kg air dry clay costs £62.38); makes a relevant comparison statement (for example, air dry is much more expensive than fresh clay) [must mention BOTH]	2
	b	schools will buy fresh clay **because** [must have reason for mark] it is cheaper, schools buy large amounts and they will have the kilns to fire it; people who make small items for a hobby will buy air dry because they only need small amounts and will not have access to kilns	2
	c	factual information: air dried clay will soften when wet; fired clay is permanently hard/not affected by water; [some students should be encouraged to give answers using structures of un-fired and fired clays]; language and style appropriate for a leaflet for art supply customers	3
3	a	any suitable example, for example any practical situation such as long distance transmission; further explanation, for example high resistance increases heating effect	2
	b	current; 230; ohm	3
4	a	so the filament glows white hot	1
	b	graph with voltage on the horizontal axis; line is curved; with decreasing gradient	3
	c	straight line (with same initial gradient as the curve)	1
5	a	(see table below) the densities are all the same; because the samples are all of the same material	6
	b	strength	1
		Total	**30**

Table for 5a:

sample	1	2	3	4
density/g cm^{-3}	4.8	4.8	4.8	4.8

Answers to intext, activity and case study questions

Page	Question number	Answer
4.1 Fuels and generators		
229	1	Burning fossil fuels produces carbon dioxide, which is a greenhouse gas (and other pollutants that cause, for example acid rain, smog).
	2	The price will increase.
	3	Some of it is used for useful work. It dissipates as heat, just like the energy output from a power station.
231	4a	It dissipates.
	b	No
	c	Useful energy output is less than the energy input.
	5a	Fuel (such as coal, nuclear fuel).
	b	Electricity
	c	The power station does not have an efficiency of 100%. Energy is lost from the hot boiler to the surroundings, and from the cooling steam to the surroundings.
	6a	Small
	b	Energy input, 100, 2.
232	7	They will fall.
	8	The level of known reserves does not fall so quickly (and can, temporarily, increase).
	9	Use of fossil fuels continues to increase but they cannot go on forever.
	10	Answers may include: more industry around the world; wealthier people consuming more goods; energy resources around the world.
	11	Concern about the effects of climate change; concern about the use of limited resources; taxes and laws that make fuel more expensive to purchase.
	12a	$\text{efficiency} = \dfrac{\text{useful energy output}}{\text{energy input}}$
	b	$\text{efficiency} = \dfrac{2000}{5000} \times 100$
	c	40%
	d	3000 megajoule
233	13	It uses fossil fuel. This is non-renewable. Carbon dioxide is produced.
	14a	List or table to show: type of fuel, form of energy output, material output (in other words, products of combustion).
	b	The CHP unit is smaller, close to where people live, and its waste energy can be used for heating, so it is more efficient overall.
	c	Answers could include: CHP unit provides heating as well as electricity. Less energy dissipates, to (wastefully) heat the surroundings. Unit is close to where heating is needed (such as homes).

(continued)

Page	Question number	Answer
4.1 Fuels and generators (continued)		
	15a	A storage heater is an electric heater that contains a large block of material. The block is heated up at night and releases energy (heat) slowly for several hours.
	b	Electricity is cheaper at night. By making use of an electricity meter with a timer.
	c	The storage heaters did not provide enough heat by the evening. Other heaters were needed, and these were expensive to run.
	16	Sankey diagram showing 80% useful transfer, 20% loss.
	17a	During the practical investigation students will discover that the same mass of water cools more quickly in several small containers than in one large one.
	b	Energy dissipates more rapidly from several small power stations than one large one. This is the reason for building large power stations. However, small power stations (such as CHP units) can be close to places where heating is needed, so that use can be made of their waste energy.
4.2 Looking inside the body		
234	1	Advantage is that it will show damage to tissue such as bone. Disadvantage is that X-rays are ionising and the energy released can damage cells.
	2	Dense bone stops X-rays so film does not expose, in other words it turns white when developed. Soft tissue allows X-rays through, so film exposed turns black when developed.
235	3	Buildings.
	4	Twice as much.
	5	Food.
	6	It is at a very low level so does little damage to our body.
236	7	Consists of relatively large particles that are stopped by other particles.
	8	Is just electromagnet energy so can pass through materials easier than particles.
237	9	All will let through some gamma rays but lead will stop all of the rest. Paper will let some alpha rays through and all of the rest.
	10	Part covered by paper and aluminium.
4.3 Nuclear and renewables		
238	1	The nucleus is a part of the atom. Its size is small compared with the size of the whole atom, but it has most of the mass of an atom. It is the atom's biggest single part, the other parts are the electrons.
239	2	The explanation should include ideas about: the atom, the nucleus, radioactivity and fission. Both involve the nucleus. Radioactivity is an ejection of a particle or of energy in the form of radiation that is similar to X-rays. This can cause change (ionisation) in surroundings materials. Fission is the break-up of a nucleus to make two smaller ones. This process releases a lot of energy, and is used as an energy resource in power stations.

<table>
<tr><th>Page</th><th>Question number</th><th>Answer</th></tr>
<tr><td colspan="3">4.3 Nuclear and renewables (continued)</td></tr>
<tr><td></td><td>3</td><td>Fossil fuels are a non-renewable resource. When they burn, they release carbon dioxide and other pollutants. Nuclear fuel is a non-renewable resource. The reaction produces radioactive waste products. Rest of answer will vary.</td></tr>
<tr><td>241</td><td>4</td><td>Solar, wind, waves.</td></tr>
<tr><td></td><td>5a</td><td>Problems of storm damage.</td></tr>
<tr><td></td><td>b</td><td>Expense of solar panels, uncertainty of weather.</td></tr>
<tr><td></td><td>c</td><td>Can cause drastic environmental changes to places where they are built.</td></tr>
<tr><td>243</td><td>6</td><td>Ideas such as: solar panels on roof, wind generator.</td></tr>
<tr><td></td><td>7</td><td>Ideas such as: once installed, the only costs are maintenance costs; maintenance costs are very low for solar panels, and low for wind generators; the school energy bill could be reduced; it gives students an opportunity to study energy resources and energy issues directly; it is environmentally friendly; it provides good publicity for the school.</td></tr>
<tr><td></td><td>8</td><td>Ideas such as: other schools don't do it; how do we know that it will save money; how do we know what the maintenance costs will be.</td></tr>
<tr><td colspan="3">4.4 Lighting power</td></tr>
<tr><td>244</td><td>1</td><td>They provide a lot of heat, which is not a useful energy output in this case.</td></tr>
<tr><td></td><td>2</td><td><table>
<tr><th></th><th>filament lamp</th><th>fluorescent lamp</th></tr>
<tr><td>energy input/joule</td><td>1.00</td><td>1.00</td></tr>
<tr><td>transferred usefully/joule</td><td>0.02</td><td>0.20</td></tr>
<tr><td>wasted/joule</td><td>0.98</td><td>0.80</td></tr>
<tr><td>efficiency %</td><td>2.00</td><td>20.00</td></tr>
</table></td></tr>
<tr><td></td><td>3a</td><td>60 watt filament lamp</td></tr>
<tr><td></td><td>b</td><td>100 watt filament lamp</td></tr>
<tr><td></td><td>c</td><td>10 watt fluorescent lamp</td></tr>
<tr><td>245</td><td>4</td><td>1 kilowatt = 1000 watt   2.5 kilowatt = 2500 watt</td></tr>
<tr><td></td><td>5a</td><td>2 kW</td></tr>
<tr><td></td><td>b</td><td>2 kW</td></tr>
<tr><td></td><td>c</td><td>4 kW</td></tr>
<tr><td>246</td><td>6</td><td><table>
<tr><th>units of energy</th><th>units of power</th></tr>
<tr><td>joule</td><td>watt</td></tr>
<tr><td>kilowatt-hour</td><td>kilowatt</td></tr>
</table></td></tr>
</table>

Page	Question number	Answer
4.4 Lighting power (continued)		
	7	Power measures how quickly energy is transferred.
	8	100 joule per second
	9	zzz = energy input, 10, 20
	10a	i 2 kilowatt-hour ii 0.2 kilowatt-hour iii 20 kilowatt-hour
	b	i 16p ii 1.6p iii 160p = £1.60
	c	For 1 hour, energy transferred is 0.1 kilowatt-hour, cost is 0.8p; for 6 minutes, energy transferred is 0.01 kilowatt-hour, cost is 0.08p; for ten hours, energy transferred is 1 kilowatt-hour, cost is 8p.
247	11	Low efficiency results in unwanted heating, and increased cost.
	12	Replacement cost, running cost, compact size, brightness.
	13a	4000 joule every second
	b	4 kilowatt
	c	4 kilowatt-hour
	d	32p
	e	£25.60
4.5 Heating for profit		
249	1a	Conduction
	b	Radiation
	c	Convection
	2	They have fibres that trap air. This prevents convection currents. Air is a very poor conductor.
	3	It could be uncomfortable or dangerous to touch if hot. It will lose heat to the surroundings more rapidly if it is hot.
	4	The house has cavity walls with insulation, and loft insulation. The oven also has insulating material between its inner and outer walls. The oven has only one door; a house has doors and windows where heat can escape.
	5	Hot air escapes through gaps around the door; the atoms of this air have higher energy which they transfer to external air atoms. Heat will radiate from oven surfaces. Also, there will be conduction through the walls of the oven, with energy passing from particle to particle.
250	6	Mains electricity
	7	Convenience, flexibility (available at all fixed venues), safety (no explosion or naked flame hazards), cost (comparable with mains gas, cheaper than bottled gas).

Page	Question number	Answer
4.5 Heating for profit (continued)		
	8a	Ideas such as: use a vehicle battery, with the engine running if necessary, or bottled gas.
	b	Ideas such as: bottled gas or electrical generator.
	c	Mains gas.
	9	Answers will vary.
	10	More.
	11	zzzz = current, 230, 2300
	12	zzzz = 3, 3, 8, 24
	13	It's a small proportion – many potatoes can be cooked in one hour.
251	14	There is no need to connect to a mains gas supply. It is easy to install and remove if potatoes don't sell well. The unit can be moved around.
	15a	Less.
	b	Energy costs are a small proportion of total costs, so any cost difference between gas and electricity is not too important.
	16	Thermal insulation reduces the rate of energy transfer through the oven wall into the room, so the oven is more efficient (costs less to run).
4.6 Cooling systems		
252	1a	It increases.
	b	It decreases.
253	2a	Prototype – a single vehicle built to test the design before any more vehicles are made.
	b	Specification – detailed description, usually with drawings, of how something is to be made.
	c	Dissipation – transfer of energy wastefully as heat into the surroundings.
	3	The engine is working hard. There is a high rate of energy transfer, and a high rate of heating.
	4a	It is cheaper and more convenient to test prototypes in test chambers with the required conditions (for example, of high or low temperature) than to test in distant places.
	b	The test chambers might not provide perfect simulations of real outdoor conditions.
254	5a	The water could freeze, and expand, cracking the radiator or even the engine.
	b	The water could boil.
	6	Look for: particles shown slightly **closer together** in water (liquid) than in ice (solid), moving more chaotically in liquid, vibrating about fixed positions in the solid. When water freezes it expands (due to inter-particle distance increase). This can damage the radiator and engine, so water must not be allowed to freeze.

<table>
<tr><th>Page</th><th>Question number</th><th>Answer</th></tr>
<tr><td colspan="3">4.6 Cooling systems (continued)</td></tr>
<tr><td>255</td><td>7</td><td>The higher the proportion of antifreeze the lower the freezing point.</td></tr>
<tr><td></td><td>8</td><td>Temperatures as low as –20°C are very rare, so 50% mixture is adequate.</td></tr>
<tr><td></td><td>9</td><td>
<table>
<tr><td>mass and temperature increase</td><td>1 kilogram 1°C</td><td>2 kilograms 1°C</td><td>1 kilogram 2°C</td><td>2 kilograms 2°C</td></tr>
<tr><td>water</td><td>4180</td><td>8360</td><td>8360</td><td>16720</td></tr>
<tr><td>antifreeze</td><td>2420</td><td>4840</td><td>4840</td><td>9680</td></tr>
</table>
</td></tr>
<tr><td></td><td>10</td><td>Extra energy in joules; mass in kilograms; temperature rise in °C.</td></tr>
<tr><td></td><td>11</td><td>Extra energy stored = 4180 × mass × temp rise = 4180 × 0.6 × 70 = 175 560 joule</td></tr>
<tr><td></td><td>12</td><td>Mains electricity, which comes from the power station, which is powered by fossil fuel.</td></tr>
<tr><td></td><td>13</td><td>It would heat water too slowly, because its power is low.</td></tr>
<tr><td colspan="3">4.7 Road safety</td></tr>
<tr><td>256</td><td>1a</td><td>Thinking distance against speed gives a straight line – more able students may use the term ‘directly proportional’ but all students should realise that if the speed is doubled, the thinking distance doubles.</td></tr>
<tr><td></td><td>b</td><td>Braking distance against speed gives a curve – if speed is doubled, the braking distance more than doubles.</td></tr>
<tr><td></td><td>c</td><td>23 m and 73 m, when speed doubles, stopping distance almost triples.</td></tr>
<tr><td></td><td>2</td><td>Fewer accidents because cars can stop in time. Accidents are less serious because collisions are less violent at lower speeds.</td></tr>
<tr><td>257</td><td>3</td><td>Students should find that their reaction times are much longer when they are distracted, particularly if they are not watching the ruler.</td></tr>
<tr><td></td><td>4</td><td>Different people have very different reaction times.</td></tr>
<tr><td></td><td>5a</td><td>Drivers differ in their thinking distance, for example reaction speeds due to age, eyesight, concentration, tiredness and so on.</td></tr>
<tr><td></td><td>b</td><td>Any distraction will increase reaction time, braking distance and hence stopping distance.</td></tr>
<tr><td></td><td>6</td><td>Don’t drive after drinking/take rests/no drugs when driving.</td></tr>
<tr><td>258</td><td>7</td><td>1200/80 = 15 m/s</td></tr>
<tr><td></td><td>8a</td><td>One minute</td></tr>
<tr><td></td><td>b</td><td>20 m/s</td></tr>
<tr><td></td><td>9</td><td>3/5 = 0.6 m/s^2</td></tr>
</table>

Page	Question number	Answer
4.7 Road safety (continued)		
	10a	A fine, points on licence (possibly increasing insurance premiums) act as speeding deterrents. They also run courses to discourage drivers from speeding by showing them what accidents can happen.
	b	Police check that the driver has a licence and that the car is roadworthy by having a current MOT, and that cars are fully insured.

Answers to Key fact boxes

Question	Key word	Question	Key word
4.1 Fuels and generators, page 231		**4.2 Looking inside the body, page 237**	
1	fossil fuels, non-renewable	1	X-rays
2	fossil fuels, turbine, generator	2	radiation
3	dissipates, dissipates	3	gamma
4	efficiency	4	alpha
		5	beta
4.3 Nuclear and renewables, page 243		**4.4 Lighting power, page 247**	
1	renewable	1	joule
2	fission	2	kilowatt-hour
3	fission, radioactive	3	watt
4	ionisation	4	power
5	ionisation, high level nuclear waste		
4.5 Heating for profit, page 251		**4.6 Cooling systems, page 254**	
1	convection	1	heat exchanger
2	conduction	2	coolant
3	radiation	3	heat capacity
4	insulating material, thermal insulator		
4.7 Road safety, page 259			
1	braking distance		
2	reaction time		
3	ice, friction		
4	velocity		
5	acceleration		

Answers to Review questions, page 260 – Energy

Question number		Answer	Marks
1	a	the car engine's energy comes from fossil fuel (petrol or diesel, from oil); the coal-fired power station gets its energy from fossil fuel (coal)	2
	b	the car's useful energy output is movement against resistance; the coal-fired power station's useful energy output is electricity for work and heating	2
	c	the car's coolant is water/antifreeze mix; the coal-fired power station's coolant is water	2
	d	the car engine produces carbon dioxide and other pollutants; the coal-fired power station produces carbon dioxide and other pollutants	2
2	a	(see table below)	7
	b	conduction	1
	c	energy transfers through the metal radiator by conduction; energy transfers out to the surroundings by radiation; movement of air (convection) transfers energy away from the radiator	3
3	a	kilowatt; 5; 10	3
	b	80p	1
4		transfers energy from hot water to heat water in a separate system	1
		Total	**24**

Question 2 a:

	solid	**liquid**	**gas**
radiation	radiation is quickly absorbed by solid so it can't penetrate through	liquids absorb (soak up) most radiation so the radiation can't travel far	radiation can usually pass easily through gases without being absorbed
convection	can't take place because solids can't flow	convection currents can take place in liquids	convection currents can take place in gases
conduction	solids are quite good conductors because energy can easily pass from particle to particle; metals are excellent conductors because energy can pass very easily from particle to particle	liquids are usually quite poor conductors because energy can't easily pass from particle to particle	takes places very slowly because particles are too far apart to influence each other enough

Answers to intext, activity and case study questions

Page	Question number	Answer
4.8 Electronic life support		
263	1a	It monitors temperature.
	b	It uses a thermistor. The resistance of the thermister changes.
	c	It changes the variable with a heater.
265	2a	$V_1 = V_2$
	b	V_2 is bigger than V_1.
	c	V_2 is smaller than V_1.
	3a	R_t increases, so V_2 increases.
	b	R_t decreases, so V_2 decreases.
	c	R_v increases, so V_1 increases, so V_2 decreases.
	d	R_v decreases, so V_1 decreases, so V_2 increases.
	4	The answers are all reversed. The bigger resistance always has the bigger share of the voltage (in either arrangement).
	5a	$\frac{R_t}{R_v} = \frac{8}{4} = 2$
	b	$R_t = 1600$ ohm
	c	$\frac{R_t}{R_v} = \frac{3000}{1000} = 3$ $\frac{V_2}{V_1} = 3$ and $V_2 + V_1 = 12$ $V_2 = 9$ volt, $V_1 = 3$ volt
	6	Resistance opposes current.
	7	They would then be on all of the time, and would not be operated by the processor.
266	8	The block diagram should show power supply, input components, processor, and output components.
	9	The input component is the movement detector. The output components are the buzzer and LED.
	10	No movement.

Page	Question number	Answer
4.9 Movement under control		
267	1a	The thermistor is a device for which resistance decreases as temperature increases. It can be used as a temperature sensor.
	b	In series means components are connected in a single line, with no parallel sections or loops.
	c	A voltage divider is a pair of resistors, connected in series, which share the voltage. The bigger resistor has the bigger voltage.
268	2a	Input voltage must be between 0 volt and 6 volt.
	b	Output voltage must be between 0 volt and 6 volt.
	3	An electronic switch has no moving parts, is usually quicker in operating, is part of the electrical circuit, and can be controlled directly by input voltages.
	4a	Input components of many electronic circuits change when their environment changes. This means they can be used as sensors. Output components then actively cause change in the environment.
	b	A processor provides outputs which depend on the inputs it receives.
269	5	When light is bright, LDR resistance is low, so it takes a lower share of the voltage. When the input voltage to the transistor is high, the transistor has low resistance, and it takes a lower share of the voltage. When the output voltage from the transistor is low, the LED is off.
	6a	The output from the transistor cannot supply enough current to drive a motor.
	b	The circuit should include an LDR as the input and a relay switch to drive the motor/output component.
	7	A transistor acts as a resistor in a voltage divider system. Its resistance changes when the input voltage changes, so then its share of the supply voltage changes.
	8	Look for: thermistor, in series with fixed or variable resistor. Thermistor voltage is the processor input voltage.
	9	Look for: LDR, in series with fixed or variable resistor. Fixed or variable resistor voltage is the processor input voltage.
	10	The output from a processor usually cannot supply enough current to drive a motor, so the motor needs its own power supply. That's why it is in a separate circuit that is switched on and off by a relay.

Page	Question number	Answer
4.10 Digital information		
270	1	An LDR.
	2	Optical fibres can carry information more rapidly.
272	3	An LED/a laser diode.
	4	Information can be carried for long distances by the optical fibres.
	5	Any suitable application involving transfer of information from remote site to processor (for example, a burglar alarm that has a movement detector connected to a remote processor unit).
	6	Answers will vary.
	7a	0
	b	1
	8	Column (including first digit) reads: 0, 0, 1, 0, 1, 0, 1, 0
273	9	LDRs can detect light to create input voltages.
	10	Motors (with relay system or other system to drive motors).
	11	Look for: diagram with two LDRs providing input which is used by processor to control motors. Systems may be simple block diagrams or sophisticated diagrams showing details of appropriate components.
	12	Digital – presentation system that uses codes for 'on' and 'off' (1 and 0). Voltage divider – a pair of resistors in series sharing the total applied voltage. Input components – components (for example, resistor or sensor) that apply voltage to a processor. Resistance – a measure of how much a wire opposes the flow of current when it is connected to a source of voltage, measured by dividing voltage by current.
	13	Answers will vary.

Page	Question number	Answer
4.11 Lifting		
275	1a	More than 1
	b	1
	c	Less than 1
	2	1
276	3	10 000 newton
	4	100 newton
	5	Yes
	6	More than 1
	7	Velocity ratio is much less than 1. The extra distance moved by the effort must compensate for the extra load.
	8	Load; 10 (newton); 10.
	9	Distance moved by load; 50 (centimetres); 10.
277	10	Yes. The load is bigger than the effort.
	11	Pulleys are machines with mechanical advantage more than 1. They can be used to lift loads that are bigger than the efforts.
	12	If mechanical advantage is more than 1 then the velocity ratio must be less than 1. The energy output of a machine cannot be bigger than the energy input.
	13	Answers will vary.

Page	Question number	Answer
4.12 Gears		
278	1	The output force/load is bigger than the input force/effort.
279	2a	The output distance is bigger.
	b	The velocity ratio is less than 1.
	3a	By using rubber tyres, with grip, and by having a rough road surface.
	b	By using oil, and ball bearings.
280	4	(see table below)
281	5	Distance multiplier – distance moved by load/output distance is bigger than distance moved by effort/input distance, in the same time. Friction – opposition to relative motion/sliding of two surfaces. Efficient – giving an energy ouput that is as big as possible when compared with the energy input.
	6a	From the rider.
	b	The worn surfaces were rubbing more, getting hotter.
	7	To reduce friction between wheel and axle.
	8	'Work' in science means 'force × distance'.
	9a	Look for: sketch showing system with effort smaller than load.
	b	It will feel as if you are in very, very low gear – you'd have to pedal fast but not go very far.

Question 4 (page 280):

Effort/Newton	50	50	50
Load/Newton	200	100	40
Mechanical advantage	4	2	0.8
Distance moved by effort/metres	5	3	1
Distance moved by load/metres	1	1	1
Velocity ratio	5	3	1
Force multiplier or distance multiplier?	force multiplier	force multiplier	neither
Energy input/joule	250	150	50
Useful energy output/ joule	200	100	40
Efficiency	80%	67%	80%

Answers to Review questions, page 282 – Devices at work

Question number		Answer	Marks
1	a	blocks showing: power supply; input components; processor; output components.	4
	b	thermistor; heater	2
2	a	LDR	1
	b	LDR symbol; resistor symbol; in series; connect to power supply; voltage applied to processor taken from the centre of the system	5
	c	the bigger of the two resistors; takes a bigger share of the voltage; the input voltage to the power supply is the voltage across one of the resistors	3
3		examples: light intensity – to monitor and control room lighting, tanning lamps; heart rate – to monitor people while exercising	2
4	a	a machine is a device with an input force/effort and an output force/load	2
	b	i at edge of tin ii at handle iii under lip of lid	3
	c	the load	1
	d	more than 1	1
	e	the effort	1
	f	force multiplier	1
5		such a machine would have an energy output that is bigger than the energy input; which is impossible (increase in force must be compensated for by reduction in distance, and vice versa)	2
6	a	$\text{MA} = \frac{\text{load}}{\text{effort}}; = \frac{1200}{100}; = 12$	3
	b	$\text{VR} = \frac{\text{distance moved by effort}}{\text{distance moved by load}}; = \frac{30}{2}; = 15$	3
	c	work done by effort = $F \times d$; = 100×30; = 3000; joule	4
	d	work done by load = $F \times d$; = 1200×2; = 2400; joule	4
	e	energy is lost/dissipated by the machine; due to friction	2
	f	$\text{efficiency} = \frac{\text{work done on load}}{\text{work done by effort}} \times \frac{100}{1}; = \frac{2400}{3000} \times \frac{100}{1}; = 80\%$	4
		Total	**48**

Answers to intext, activity and case study questions

<table>
<tr><th>Page</th><th>Question number</th><th>Answer</th></tr>
<tr><td colspan="3">5.1 Our atmosphere</td></tr>
<tr><td>284</td><td>1</td><td>Planting trees increases the amount of photosynthesis, which removes CO_2 from the atmosphere, and would counteract the increase due to burning fossil fuels. Students should realise, however, that it is not possible to plant enough trees to counteract the very large quantities of fossil fuels we burn daily.</td></tr>
<tr><td>285</td><td>2</td><td>Oil used for petrol for cars and other fuels for vehicles such as lorrys, trains, aeroplanes and so on. Gas and coal used to generate electricity in power stations and for domestic and industrial heating.</td></tr>
<tr><td></td><td>3</td><td>Less able students may copy out the points without further evaluation. Look for integration of the two points of view in better answers, and original evaluative comments.</td></tr>
<tr><td></td><td>4</td><td>Possible illustrations/photos of: conditions at – 33°C (Antarctic), lifeless planets/ surface of the moon compared with lush life on Earth, floods, severe weather, famine, crop failure and so on.</td></tr>
<tr><td>286</td><td>5a</td><td>N_2 increased, O_2 increased, CO_2, water vapour and SO_2 decreased</td></tr>
<tr><td></td><td>b</td><td>More is continually added by volcanic activity. Due to its unreactivity it stays in the atmosphere (more able candidates may comment on some fixing of nitrogen in the nitrogen cycle).</td></tr>
<tr><td></td><td>c</td><td>
<table>
<tr><th>gas</th><th>reason for change</th></tr>
<tr><td>nitrogen</td><td>more produced by volcanoes</td></tr>
<tr><td>oxygen</td><td>produced by photosynthesis in plants</td></tr>
<tr><td>carbon dioxide</td><td>used in photosynthesis in plants dissolves in seas</td></tr>
<tr><td>water vapour</td><td>condensed out as Earth cooled</td></tr>
<tr><td>sulphur dioxide</td><td>dissolved in seas</td></tr>
</table>
</td></tr>
<tr><td>287</td><td>6</td><td>The deeper layers are older because the ice is formed one layer at a time over the years.</td></tr>
<tr><td></td><td>7a</td><td>The ‘troughs’ on the temperature graph show periods when the Earth was much colder than today.</td></tr>
<tr><td></td><td>b</td><td>When the amount of carbon dioxide is high, the surface temperature is high, when it is low, the temperature is low. Both graphs show the same pattern.</td></tr>
<tr><td colspan="3">5.2 The Earth and the environment</td></tr>
<tr><td>288</td><td>1a</td><td>Examples: household rubbish: glass, plastics, paper, food, garden waste, toilet waste. Remind students that this is just household rubbish – more waste will have been produced in factories and shops to provide the goods for each household.</td></tr>
<tr><td></td><td>b</td><td>Ideas: burn flammable waste, bury or compost biodegradable, re-use containers, non-biodegradable more difficult to dispose of – bury but it will not rot. Problems: idea of disease, smell, flies, volume of waste difficult to handle, non-biodegradable waste would pile up.</td></tr>
</table>

<table>
<tr><th>Page</th><th>Question number</th><th>Answer</th></tr>
<tr><td colspan="3">5.2 The Earth and the environment (continued)</td></tr>
<tr><td></td><td>c</td><td>All waste was biodegradable. No disposable packaging used. Much smaller population.</td></tr>
<tr><td>289</td><td>2</td><td>Sources of information to use include books, CD-ROMS and websites. If PC access is limited, a 'pack' of suitable websites could be printed for each group in advance. Students could do their presentations using posters of cuttings, electronic slide shows or OHTs of spider diagrams or bullet points.</td></tr>
<tr><td>290</td><td>3</td><td>Example table:
<table>
<tr><th>gas</th><th>problem</th><th>solution</th></tr>
<tr><td>unburnt petrol (hydrocarbons)</td><td>smog</td><td>catalytic converter</td></tr>
<tr><td>carbon dioxide CO_2</td><td>greenhouse effect / climate change</td><td>more efficient engines, use less fuel, use alternative fuel</td></tr>
<tr><td>carbon monoxide CO</td><td>toxic</td><td>catalytic converter</td></tr>
<tr><td>nitrogen oxides NO and NO_2</td><td>acid rain and smog</td><td>catalytic converter</td></tr>
<tr><td>sulphur dioxide SO_2</td><td>acid rain and smog</td><td>low sulphur petrol</td></tr>
</table></td></tr>
<tr><td>291</td><td>4</td><td>Asthmatics can plan and take extra care if they are in danger of more attacks. You can check air quality for where you live (or buying a house!) and, if necessary, campaign for action if you are worried.</td></tr>
<tr><td></td><td>5a</td><td>Where there are high levels of pollutants, road layouts can be changed to help.</td></tr>
<tr><td></td><td>b</td><td>Cars are not stopping, starting or sitting in traffic jams. This reduces the pollutants produced.</td></tr>
<tr><td></td><td>c</td><td>More able candidates may address each pollutant that the station will test for and explain why this is necessary.</td></tr>
<tr><td>292</td><td>7a</td><td>Diesel as it needs the smallest volume to go 100 km.</td></tr>
<tr><td></td><td>b</td><td>Statement 1 – true. Statement 2 – false, diesel has most C but does not have the highest emission of CO_2 per litre. Statement 3 – true.</td></tr>
<tr><td></td><td>8a</td><td>Petrol 7 x 0.91 = £6.97; Diesel 4.8 x 0.95 = £4.56; LPG 9.3 x 0.42 = £3.91.</td></tr>
<tr><td></td><td>b</td><td>You would also need to know how much the cars cost and the cost of servicing.</td></tr>
<tr><td></td><td>c</td><td>People are worried about the environmental effects of CO_2 on the environment – the greenhouse effect could lead to global warming and climate change (more able students may add detail about the outcomes of climate change).</td></tr>
</table>

Page	Question number	Answer
293	9	Unburnt petrol causes smog; carbon monoxide is toxic. Also they are both caused by incomplete combustion, showing that the fuel is not burning efficiently in the car, leading to wasted fuel (and expense) and reduced efficiency (fewer MPG).
	10a	Unburnt petol has not burned at all. Carbon monoxide and soot are both formed when the petrol burns in too little oxygen.
	b	Yes, all readings are below the limits.
5.3 The Earth beneath our feet		
294	1	We are on different tectonic plate to North America but on the same plate as Europe.
	2	We are in the middle of a plate. Earthquakes and volcanoes happen near the edges.
295	3a	Until 100 MYA the rock layers and fossils were identical, after that there are different layers and the fossils are different.
	b	The development of mountains could have happened by shrinking, but this does not explain continental drift, earthquakes, volcanoes or how new rock is formed.
	4a and b	Students should see that Africa and South America fit easily together. Earthquakes and volcanoes follow the lines of the plate boundaries.
296	5	Rock comes up from the mantle and solidifies as it cools. Over millions of years, the rock is pushed towards the edge of the plate. When the plates are pushed together, it is either pushed up to form mountains or sinks, remelts and rejoins the mantle.
297	6	p waves travel faster. The closer the two waves are together, the nearer the quake.
	7	Scientists are trying to predict when the quake will happen to allow evacuation. Buildings and bridges are being made on shock-absorbing foundations and more flexible so that they will not collapse. Gas, electricity and water mains will be shut off so that there is no risk of fire or electrocution. No building is allowed on the fault line where there is likely to be most damage.
5.4 Waves and communication		
298	1	Radio longest, light for eyes shortest.
299	2	It was closer to epicentre.
	3	The energy in the wave was spread out over a larger area.
	4	Shallower seabed forced wave upwards.
	5	Less depth more height.
300	6	0.4 m/s
301	7	TV remote
	8	Wave spreads out and has little energy.
	9	Fibre optics
	10	Microwaves travel in straight lines so will not go around corners.

Page	Question number	Answer
5.4 Waves and communication (continued)		
	11	TV and radio
302	12	42 750 000 000 000 km
303	13	The milky way
	14	Venus 44.22 m Earth 61.38 m Mars 93.72 m Jupiter 319.44 m Saturn 586.08 m Uranus 1.177 km Neptune 1.847 km Pluto 2425 km
	15	Answers may vary.
	16	26 564 000 000 000
304	17	Blue
305	18	Tombaugh
	19	Charon
	20	Pluto's orbit is tilted to other planets, its rotation matches its moon so the moons appears in the same part of the sky all the time, its poles face east and west compared to other planets.
	21	Answers will vary but should include dark and cold.

Answers to Key fact boxes

Question	Key word	Question	Key word
5.1 Our atmosphere, page 287		**5.2 The Earth and the environment, page 293**	
1	photosynthesis	1	volcanoes
2	respiration	2	soot (carbon), carbon monoxide, incomplete combustion
3	combustion, fossil fuels		
4	greenhouse effect	3	gasohol, hydrogen
5.3 The Earth beneath our feet, page 296		**5.4 Waves and communication, page 301**	
1	tectonic plates	1	electromagnetic spectrum
2	continental drift	2	frequency, waves
3	mountains	3	amplitude
4	volcanoes/earthquakes	4	energy
		5	wavelength
5.4 Waves and communication, page 305			
1	Pluto		
2	solar system		
3	galaxy		
4	star		
5	universe		

Answers to Review questions, page 306 – The Earth and the universe

Question number	Answer
1a	look for: axes labelled with time along the x axis; points correctly plotted; smooth curve drawn through points
b i	appearance of plants and animals marked correctly on graph
ii	the percentage of oxygen increased after plants appeared: due to photosynthesis producing oxygen; the percentage became stable after animals appeared; because it is used for respiration
2a	labelled diagram showing these gases and their effects: CO_2; greenhouse effect causes global warming (may give additional details); CO: toxic/inhibits oxygen transport by blocking haemoglobin; NOx (nitrogen oxides): cause respiratory difficulties/cancers/acid rain (may give additional details); SO_2: acid rain (may give additional details); unburnt hydrocarbons: cause smog / breathing difficulties
b	answers will vary, possible points include the following. Advantages: will raise money; will encourage people to use public transport; fewer cars will be in city; less atmospheric pollution (possible details as in (a); less fuel used; idea that many people on a bus or tube use less fuel than the same number of people in private cars. Disadvantages: inconvenient to people; may discourage tourists; people who depend on tourism for income may make less money; not fair because rich people will be unaffected; poorer people will not be able to afford to take their cars to work
3a	Main points: p waves arrive first in every case. A: p and a waves close together. B: s waves further away from p waves. C: largest gap between the two. Explanation: p waves travel faster than s waves. The gaps between the arrival of the waves at each monitoring station get longer the further away the station is from the quake.
b	the Mercalli scale is based on eyewitness accounts, the Richter scale measures the speed of the moving rocks. Advantages of Mercalli: allows earthquakes to be classified without specialist equipment (for example, in poor countries, from historical accounts or where an earthquake is very unexpected). The Richter scale is much more reliable and accurate as it relies of numerical data
4	Answers will vary. Suggested photos should contain earthquakes, volcanoes, mountains and some evidence for continental drift. Bullets should show how each feature relates to the movement of tectonic plates.
5a	330 m/s
b	increases

Answers to intext, activity and case study questions

Page	Question number	Answer
6.1 Working in science		
308	1a	National
	b	Local
	c	International
	d	International
	2	Nurse (NHS): knowledge: human biology/physiology/drugs/medicines. Skills: following procedures, measurement of temperature/volumes. Nurse (private home): knowledge: human biology/physiology/drugs/medicines. Skills: following procedures, measurement of temperature/volumes. Car design engineer: knowledge: physics of machines and levers, fuel, energy, friction. Skills: calculations, predicting, planning, measurement. Fertiliser sales rep: knowledge: plant biology/chemistry of soils and fertilisers. Skills: explaining science to people, decision making, calculating quantities.
309	3a	Possible ideas: road/rail/sea access is limited; transport not easy. Space is available for buildings and carparks; but planning permission difficult due to environmental objections. Fewer people for workforce or customers; land and rents cheaper.
	b	More difficult to make a company profitable in rural areas/explained as in (a) above, therefore fewer companies and jobs in rural areas.
	4	Look for evidence that student has thought about access and transport, workforce, customers, availability of land and buildings, rent costs.
	5	Look for evidence as in (5).

Answers to Review questions, page 312 – Working in science

<table>
<tr><th>Question number</th><th></th><th>Answer</th></tr>
<tr><td>1</td><td></td><td>Possible ideas covered.
<table>
<tr><th>Case study</th><th>Qualifications and training</th><th>Science skills used at work</th><th>Services given</th><th>Products made</th></tr>
<tr><td>Dental nurse</td><td>GCSEs, NCDN, on-the-job training</td><td>organising work area, following standard procedures, sterilising, handling equipment, recording information</td><td>health care for people's teeth</td><td>none directly, may mention dentures or fillings</td></tr>
<tr><td>Woodland officer</td><td>A levels; on-the-job experience and training; HND in forestry; degree in forestry</td><td>measuring, applying knowledge of trees, soils, chemical pesticides, environmental knowledge, using equipment</td><td>maintenance of woodlands for recreation for local people</td><td>wood and chippings for building trade</td></tr>
</table>
</td></tr>
<tr><td>2</td><td>a</td><td>
<table>
<tr><th>Name of job</th><th>Qualifications needed to start</th><th>Do you need experience/ further training?</th><th>Example of daily task that uses science</th></tr>
<tr><td>Dental hygienist</td><td>five GCSEs; two A levels; two years dental experience</td><td>yes (diploma in dental hygiene)</td><td>wide range possible</td></tr>
<tr><td>Electrician</td><td>GCSEs</td><td>yes (modern apprenticeship programme)</td><td>wide range possible</td></tr>
<tr><td>Sound technician</td><td>none</td><td>yes (list of possibilities given in reference)</td><td>wide range possible</td></tr>
<tr><td>Vet</td><td>A levels; degree in veterinary science</td><td>yes – degree and practical experience</td><td>wide range possible</td></tr>
</table>
</td></tr>
<tr><td></td><td>b</td><td>start following exams: electrician and sound technician
training: dental hygienist and vet</td></tr>
<tr><td></td><td>c</td><td>wait until you have two years' experience and go for a diploma in dental hygiene</td></tr>
<tr><td></td><td>d</td><td>look for awareness of scientific knowledge and skills in the workplace</td></tr>
<tr><td>3</td><td></td><td>answers should include qualifications, training and experience, as well as some mention of personal skills and attributes</td></tr>
<tr><td>4</td><td>a–d</td><td>variable, depending on the person chosen [answers should include description of science used, health and safety, and location of company]</td></tr>
</table>

Section III Optional practical activities

	Student Sheets	Teacher and Technician Sheets
1 Using a light microscope	III:5	III:62
2 Osmosis in living tissue	III:8	III:62
3 Starch in leaves	III:10	III:63
4 Looking at chromosomes	III:12	III:64
5 Plants, animals and their environment	III:14	III:65
6 Exercise and recovery rates	III:16	III:66
7 Racing mustard and cress	III:18	III:66
8 Long live cabbage	III:20	III:67
9 Microorganisms, milk and yoghurt	III:22	III:67
10 Investigating the action of antibiotics	III:24	III:68
11 Elements, compounds and mixtures	III:27	III:69
12 Making saline solutions	III:30	III:70
13 Setting up a distillation apparatus	III:33	III:70
14 Investigating dyes	III:34	III:71
15 Investigating rates of reaction	III:36	III:71
16 Finding the concentration of an acid	III:40	III:72
17 Making ammonium sulphate	III:44	III:73
18 Investigating resistance	III:47	III:73
19 Measuring density	III:49	III:74
20 Energy transfers	III:52	III:74
21 Investigating electricity generation	III:55	III:75
22 Constructing an electronic system	III:57	III:75
23 Investigating a lever	III:59	III:76

Introduction

These practical activities, each with its own 'Teacher and Technician Information' sheet, can be used in conjunction with the topics in the Student Book, to help the students' understanding of the topics. For each practical activity, there is an indication of the related topic or topics in the Student Book. Some of the questions at the end of each practical activity will give students the opportunity to link the practical activity with the science that is carried out in a variety of settings.

These practicals also offer opportunities for developing the skills students will require to carry out their assessment activities (assignments) for portfolio development. The skills opportunities for each practical are indicated on the practical skills mapping grid on page III:3.

In their present form the practicals have not been written to be used for collecting portfolio evidence. Some of the practical activities could be developed further to give assessment opportunities for Units 1 and 3, but you will need to refer to the assessment evidence grid for your awarding body to enable you to do this. Please note that the Health and Safety advice will need to be adjusted accordingly.

A full set of assessment activities (assignments) for your awarding body are provided in Section IV of the Teachers' File and also on the CD-ROM.

Health and safety

Health and safety guidance and information

The following publications give advice on health and safety. The students need to have access to copies of 'Student Safety Sheets' throughout the course; a set of these should be available for student reference. 'Hazcards' are not intended for student use.

Student Safety Sheets	CLEAPSS School Science Service, 1997
Topics in Safety	ASE, 3rd edition, 2001
Hazcards	CLEAPSS School Science Service, 1995 and later updates
Handbook	Laboratory handbook, CLEAPSS School Science Service, 2001
Haz Man	Hazardous Chemicals Interactive Manual (CD-ROM), SSERC, 2002
Safety in Science Education	DfEE, HMSO, 1996

The CLEAPSS publications, '*Hazcards*' and '*Handbook*' have been produced on CD-ROM (2002). '*Safety in Science Education*' is also available, with permission, on the Members' Section of the ASE website (http://www.ase.org.uk).

ASE and DfEE publications are available from:
ASE (Association for Science Education), Tel: 01707 283000, www.ase.org.uk

CLEAPSS publications are only available to members.
CLEAPSS School Science Service, Tel: 01895 251496, www.cleapss.org.uk

Teacher responsibility

In the practical activities which follow, all hazardous substances and operations are indicated and appropriate precautions are suggested. Nevertheless, you should be aware of your obligations under the Health and Safety at Work Act, the Control of Substances Hazardous to Health (COSHH) Regulations and the Management of Health and Safety at Work Regulations. In this respect you should, at all times, follow the requirements of your management and employers. There is a legal requirement that you keep yourself informed of current advice from professional bodies. In order to fulfil these obligations, you need to familiarise yourself with any safety advice or requirements issued by your employer.

Students' risk assessments and safety

Students should be encouraged to carry out a risk assessment when carrying out any practical activities. They should be able to identify hazards and suggest suitable ways of reducing the risks from them. A copiable Risk Assessment Form is provided for this purpose (page III:4). When completed, each form must be checked by a teacher. Students will need access to the 'Student Safety Sheets' or the relevant safety reference books.

However, the responsibility for health and safety lies with the teacher. You need to carry out your own risk assessment for each activity, and check students' risk assessments before any practical work takes place. You need to take account of the maturity and likely behaviour of the class, the number of students in the class and the nature of the room where the practical work will take place. You need to make sure they follow your health and safety guidance, for example wearing eye protection and adhering to laboratory rules.

You should make sure that all students are aware of all health and safety issues involved in a practical before they start working. Students need to know what to do in the event of a spillage or an accident. They must also know what to do in an emergency, such as a fire.

Mapping skill areas to the optional practical activities

Practical Activity	Following standard procedures							Handling scientific equipment and materials			Recording and analysing scientific data			
	Read procedure, check anything you do not understand.	Carry out a health and safety check of working area.	Carry out a risk assessment.	Set out work area.	Follow instructions one step at a time.	Make observations/measurements, selecting appropriate instruments.	Identify possible sources of error and repeat, when necessary.	Recognise and use equipment provided.	Select/prepare equipment.	Calibrate instruments.	Present data (tables, graphs, etc).	Carry out simple numerical calculations.	Analyse and interpret results.	Evaluate investigation/suggest improvements.
1 Using a light microscope	✓			✓	✓	✓						✓		
2 Osmosis in living tissue	✓				✓	✓		✓					✓	✓
3 Starch in leaves	✓		✓		✓	✓		✓			✓		✓	
4 Looking at chromosomes	✓				✓	✓		✓						
5 Plants, animals and their environment	✓			✓	✓	✓		✓	✓		✓		✓	
6 Exercise and recovery rates	✓				✓	✓			✓		✓		✓	
7 Racing mustard and cress	✓			✓	✓	✓					✓		✓	✓
8 Long live cabbage	✓	✓	✓	✓	✓	✓					✓		✓	
9 Microorganisms, milk and yoghurt	✓	✓		✓	✓	✓							✓	
10 Investigating the action of antibiotics	✓	✓	✓	✓	✓	✓		✓					✓	
11 Elements, compounds and mixtures	✓		✓	✓	✓	✓		✓			✓		✓	
12 Making saline solutions	✓			✓	✓	✓	✓	✓	✓	✓	✓	✓	✓	✓
13 Setting up a distillation apparatus	✓				✓	✓		✓						
14 Investigating dyes	✓			✓	✓	✓		✓	✓		✓	✓	✓	
15 Investigating rates of reaction	✓		✓	✓	✓	✓		✓	✓	✓	✓		✓	
16 Finding the concentration of an acid	✓		✓	✓	✓	✓		✓	✓	✓	✓	✓	✓	✓
17 Making ammonium sulphate	✓		✓	✓	✓	✓	✓	✓	✓		✓	✓	✓	
18 Investigating resistance	✓	✓	✓	✓	✓	✓	✓	✓	✓		✓	✓	✓	
19 Measuring density	✓	✓	✓	✓	✓	✓	✓	✓	✓		✓	✓	✓	
20 Energy transfers	✓	✓	✓	✓	✓	✓							✓	
21 Investigating electricity generation	✓	✓	✓	✓	✓	✓		✓					✓	
22 Constructing an electronic system	✓	✓	✓	✓	✓			✓	✓					✓
23 Investigating a lever	✓	✓	✓	✓	✓	✓	✓				✓	✓	✓	

Risk Assessment Form

Name of student: ______________________ Class/set: ______________________ Date: ______________

Title of practical: ______________________ Checked by: ______________________ Date: ______________

Material/procedure	**Hazard**	**What could go wrong?**	**Safety precautions**	**What to do in case of accident**	**Risk:** low; medium; high

Name ______________________ Date ______________

Practical activity 1

Using a light microscope

See 'Cells' on pages 26–29 in your student book.

Aim

You are going to identify the parts of a light microscope. You will then use a light microscope to examine a variety of specimens. You will gain an understanding of magnification when you use different lenses.

Introduction

If you need to examine cells or very small plants or very small animals, then you cannot use your ordinary eyesight. You need to use a light microscope. A light microscope is an important and expensive piece of equipment. You need to practise if you are going to use a light microscope effectively.

A light microscope has two lenses – an eyepiece lens and an objective lens. Together, these two lenses magnify and focus so you see a much more detailed image.

Health and safety

You must handle light microscopes with care.
You must use the main limb to move or carry a light microscope.
You must be careful when using the high power objective lens because it will be very close to the glass slide.
If you break a glass slide or cover slip, tell your teacher immediately so the glass fragments can be disposed of quickly and safely.
You must be careful when using iodine solution because it stains skin and clothes and is irritating to the eyes.

What you need

- goggles
- light microscope
- diagram of light microscope
- lamp, if required
- transparent plastic ruler
- slides and cover slips
- dropping pipette
- mounted needle
- pond water containing algae
- iodine solution
- variety of prepared slides

What you do

1. Look at your microscope and identify all the parts listed on the reference sheet 'Parts of a light microscope'. Label the diagram.
2. If you are using a built-in or extra lamp, switch it on. If not, adjust the mirror so that light is reflected through the microscope. ***Do not focus directly on the Sun.***
3. Turn the microscope nose piece round so that the smaller (lower power) objective lens is in line with the rest of the microscope. The objective lens will probably have ×4 marked on it. Look at the eyepiece lens. The eyepiece lens will probably have ×6 marked on it. However, your microscope may have different markings.
4. Does your microscope have an adjustable diaphragm? If it does, then turn the lever so that the view down the microscope is not too bright.

Using a light microscope (continued)

5. Place the plastic transparent ruler on the microscope stage. Keep the ruler in place with the clips. Look down the eyepiece. Turn the large coarse focus knob to focus what you see. You may find it easier to close your other eye. Use your left eye to look down the microscope if you are right handed or your right eye if you are left handed. This will make it easier for you when you are drawing what you see.
6. Move the ruler around until you can see the divisions on the ruler. The smaller fine focus knob can be used to get a clear sharp image.
7. Draw a circle on a piece of paper and mark how many millimetre divisions on the ruler you can see.
8. Pull a hair from your head and place it on a glass slide. Add a drop of water to keep the hair in position. Lower a cover slip onto the hair using the mounted needle – this method avoids large air bubbles. The diagram shows you how to do this.

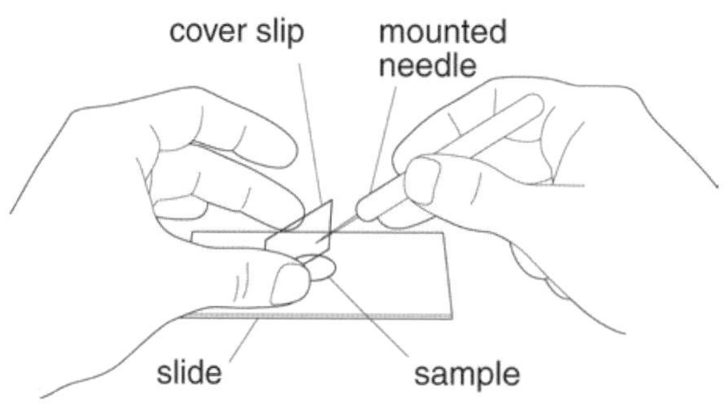

Applying a cover slip.

9. Compare the view of your hair with the view of the millimetre marks on the ruler. Estimate how many hairs would fit into one millimetre.
10. Once the hair is in focus at low magnification, the high power objective lens can be used. The high power lens is usually ×10, ×20 or ×40. The image should still be in focus. If not, you must use only the fine focus knob to focus. If you use the coarse focus knob, you will probably break the cover slip and the slide and damage the expensive objective lens.
11. Look at the lenses you are using. You can work out the overall magnification by multiplying the two numbers together.
12. Some examples are given here:

eyepiece lens	objective lens	magnification
x6	x4	24
x6	x10	60
x10	x10	100
x10	x20	200

Using a light microscope (continued)

13. Place a small piece of green algae on a glass slide. Add two drops of water using a pipette. Lower a cover slip onto the algae using the mounted needle. ***Wash your hands if you contaminate them with pond water.***
14. Examine the slide using a low magnification. Move the slide around to select the best view. You will be able to see plant cells. You may also be able to see small animals moving around in the water.
15. ***Wear eye protection while transferring iodine solution.*** Remove the cover slip and add two drops of iodine solution. Replace the cover slip.
16. Examine the slide again, first using a low magnification and then a high magnification. Parts of the cells will be stained black. What does this show?
17. Draw a diagram of what you see. Only draw two cells in detail. Label the cell wall, the nucleus, a chloroplast and the cytoplasm. Write down the magnification you used.
18. Wash the slides carefully. Return them to your teacher.
19. Examine some prepared slides provided by your teacher.

Questions

Q1 A different type of microscope called the electron microscope is used by universities, hospitals, research centres and various industries.
Carry out some research on electron microscopes to find out:

- **a** who invented them
- **b** how they work (in outline only)
- **c** how they differ from light microscopes
- **d** their range of magnification
- **e** what the image is like, compared to that from a light microscope.

Q2 Light microscopes are used in many different places.

- **a** Find out five different places that use light microscopes.
- **b** Find out what light microscopes are used for in these five places.

Practical activity 2

Name ______________________________ Date ______________

Osmosis in living tissue

See 'Diffusion' on pages 30–33 and 'Osmosis' on pages 34–37 in your student book.

Aim

You will use a potato to investigate whether water is passed on from cell to cell by osmosis. A boiled potato will be used for comparison.

Introduction

Living cells are in a balanced state with their surroundings. The cytoplasm of a cell contains many chemicals dissolved in water. The cytoplasm is then surrounded by a partially permeable membrane. Water will pass through this membrane, entering or leaving the cell by osmosis.

The sugar solution you will use in this experiment has a high concentration of sugar. The sugar solution is more concentrated than the solution inside the potato cells.

Health and safety

You must be careful when you use the knife and cork borer. Return them immediately after you have used them. You must be careful when the water is being boiled.

What you need

- 1 potato
- kitchen knife
- cork borer
- beaker
- Bunsen burner, tripod, gauze and heatproof mat
- 2 Petri dishes
- 5 cm^3 syringe
- strong sugar solution

What you do

1. Cut the potato in half using a knife.
2. Peel off a band of potato skin from the cut end of each potato half.
3. Insert a cork borer into the uncut ends of the potato halves. Take care not to force the borer through to the cut edge of the potato. Move the borer from side to side to loosen a plug of potato. Then remove the plug, leaving a pit.

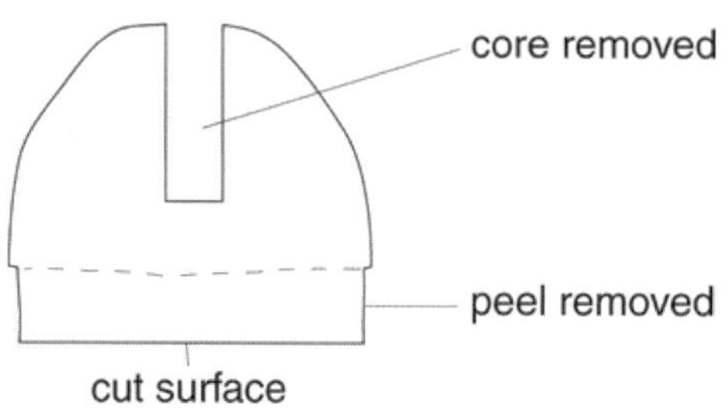

Each half of your potato should look like this.

Osmosis in living tissue (continued)

4. Put one potato half into a beaker of water and boil it for about 10 minutes, or less if it starts to crumble.
5. Remove the cooked potato from the water using tongs.
6. Place each potato half in a Petri dish and add water around the potato.
7. Add sugar solution to each pit using the syringe. Half fill each pit. Mark the level of the sugar solution in each pit.

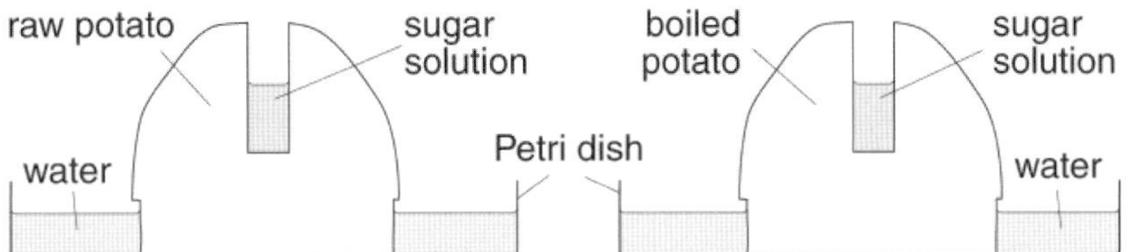

8. Leave your potatoes overnight.
9. Examine the results of your experiment.
10. Write down what happened to the level of sugar solution in:
    - **a** the raw potato
    - **b** the boiled potato.
11. Write down which half of the potato showed osmosis.
12. Suggest what happened to the cells of the boiled potato.
13. Dispose of the pieces of potato in the appropriate bin. Wash the Petri dishes.

Questions

Q1 This experiment could be improved by taking some measurements. Describe what measurements could be taken.

Q2 A fishmonger sells both freshwater fish, such as trout, and seawater fish, such as plaice. Explain what would happen to the cells of the fish if:

a the trout was kept in seawater by mistake

b the plaice was kept in freshwater by mistake.

Practical activity 3

Name ______________________ Date ______________

Starch in leaves

See 'Photosynthesis' on pages 52–55 and 'Exchange of gases' on pages 56–59 in your student book.

Aim

You are going to test some geranium leaves for the presence of starch. The leaves have been kept in different conditions. You will find out about the conditions plants need in order to make starch.

Introduction

Plants make their own food by the process of photosynthesis. Simple sugars, such as glucose, are formed. Some of the glucose is used for energy and some of the glucose is changed into starch for storage. Starch is used for storage because it is insoluble.

Health and safety

You must be careful when using ethanol because it is highly flammable.
All Bunsen burners must be turned off before ethanol is used.
You must return the used ethanol at the end of the activity. You must not pour ethanol down the sink.
You must be careful when using iodine solution because it stains skin and clothes and is irritating to the eyes.

What you need

- a geranium leaf with parts covered in cooking foil kept in place by tape (1)
- a variegated leaf from a geranium plant (2)
- a geranium leaf which has been kept without carbon dioxide (3)
- a geranium leaf that has been exposed to light and carbon dioxide (4)

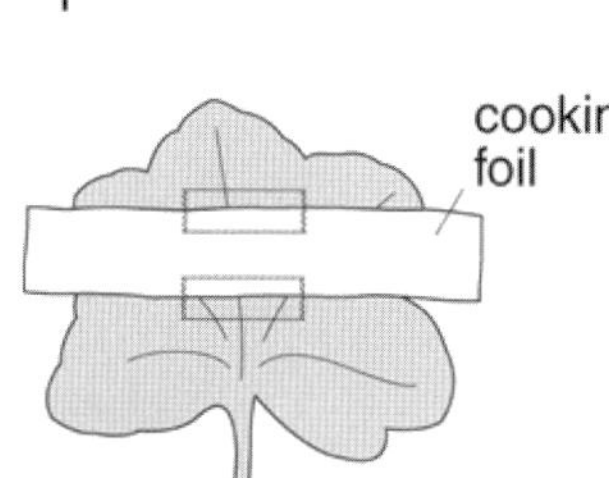

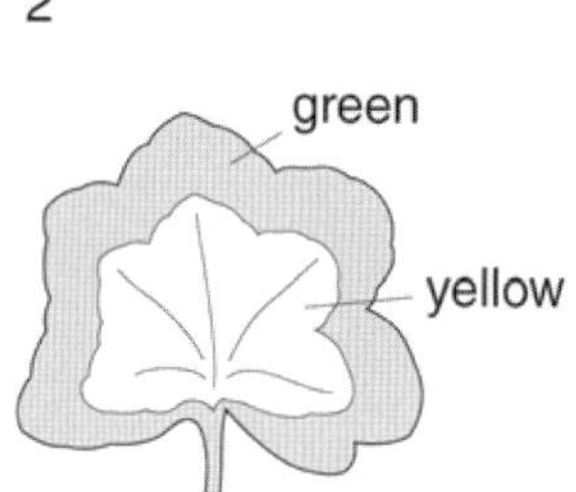

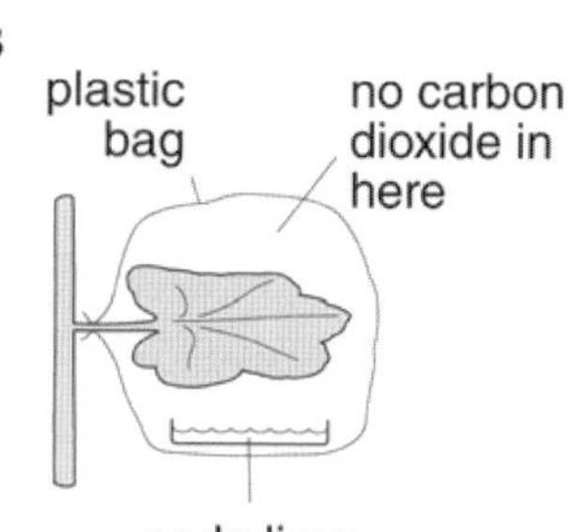

The leaves have been kept under four different conditions.

- goggles
- large beaker
- Bunsen burner, tripod, gauze and heatproof mat
- ethanol
- forceps and tongs
- small beaker to fit inside the large beaker
- white tile
- iodine solution in a dropping bottle

What you do

1. Look at the leaf that has been partly covered by cooking foil. Draw the leaf outline accurately. Shade in the covered areas that did not get any light.
2. Look at the variegated leaf. Draw the leaf outline accurately. Shade in and label the areas that are not green and so do not contain chlorophyll.

Starch in leaves (continued)

3. Identify the four leaves by altering the length of the leaf stalks. Make a note of what you have done so you can identify the leaves later.
4. ***Wear eye protection from now on.*** Set up the large beaker, Bunsen burner, tripod, gauze and heatproof mat. Add water to the large beaker, light the Bunsen burner and wait until the water is boiling.
5. Place all four leaves in the beaker of boiling water for about one minute.
6. Turn off the Bunsen burner.
7. When the whole class is ready, your teacher will give you some ethanol. Pour the ethanol into the small beaker.

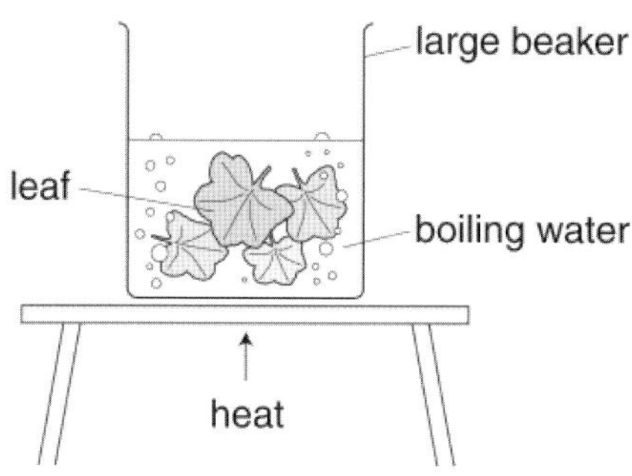

Heating the leaves in water.

8. Use tongs to remove the leaves from the water. Now place the leaves in the small beaker. Make sure that there is enough ethanol to cover the leaves.
9. Place the small beaker inside the large beaker containing the hot water. The boiling point of ethanol is lower than the boiling point of water, so the ethanol will boil.

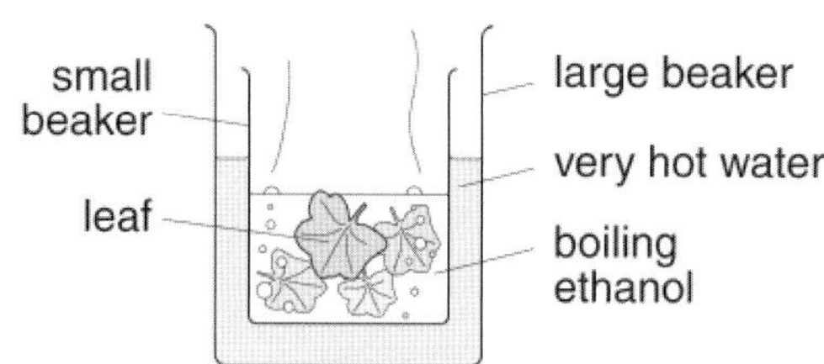

Heating the leaves in ethanol.

10. Observe what happens to the colour of the leaves and the colour of the ethanol. Write down an explanation.
11. Remove the leaves, using forceps, after about five minutes.
12. Place the leaves on a white tile and identify which leaf is which. Add a few drops of iodine solution to each leaf. Iodine solution stains starch a blue/black colour.
13. Observe any colour changes.
14. Draw the outline of the leaf which had been partly covered by cooking foil. Shade in the areas that contain starch.
15. Draw the outline of the variegated leaf. Shade in the areas that contain starch.
16. Compare these new drawings with your original drawings.
17. Compare the results of the leaf kept in normal conditions with the leaf kept in low carbon dioxide conditions.
18. Use all your results to decide what plants need to make starch.

Questions

Q1 Explain why it is necessary to place the leaves in boiling water first.

Q2 A market gardener uses large greenhouses to grow plants. Explain why the plants should be kept:

a with plenty of water
b at a temperature of about 20°C
c in plenty of sunlight
d with the windows open during daytime.

Name ______________________ Date ______________

Looking at chromosomes

See 'Cells dividing' on pages 42–45 and 'Inheritance' on pages 46–49 in your student book.

Aim

You are going to stain the cell contents of root cells and examine the cells with a light microscope. You will try to identify chromosomes in cells that are dividing by mitosis. Mitosis is a type of cell division used in growth. You will then draw and label the chromosomes to show the different stages in mitosis.

Introduction

All living things grow. To do this, cells divide by a process called mitosis. An identical copy of the original cell is produced. Chromosomes, which are inside the nucleus of a cell, carry genetic information. The chromosomes go through a sequence of stages to produce a new set of chromosomes. The new chromosomes contain the same genetic information as the original chromosomes. Once the chromosomes have been copied, the cell divides.

Health and safety

The acetic orcein stain/hydrochloric acid mixture is corrosive. You must take extreme care when using it. Wear eye protection.
You must take care when handling the scalpel and forceps. Return them immediately after use.
You must handle light microscopes with care. You must use the main limb to move or carry a light microscope.
You must be careful when using the high power objective lens because it will be very close to the glass slide.
If you break a glass slide or cover slip, tell your teacher immediately so the glass fragments can be disposed of quickly and safely.

What you need

- goggles
- a growing root from a broad bean or an onion
- tile
- scalpel
- watch-glass
- acetic orcein stain mixed with hydrochloric acid (corrosive)
- oven or hot plate or Bunsen burner, tripod, gauze and heatproof mat
- forceps
- 2 glass slides and 1 cover slip
- glass rod
- filter paper
- light microscope

What you do

1. Place a side branch of a root on the tile.
2. Use the scalpel to cut off the end 0.5 cm. This is the root tip.

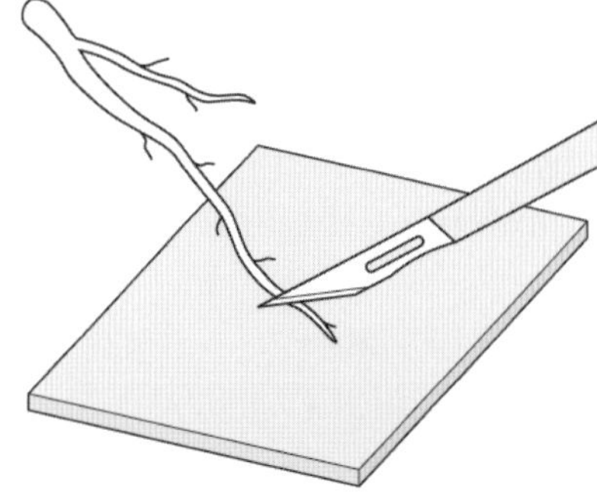

Looking at chromosomes (continued)

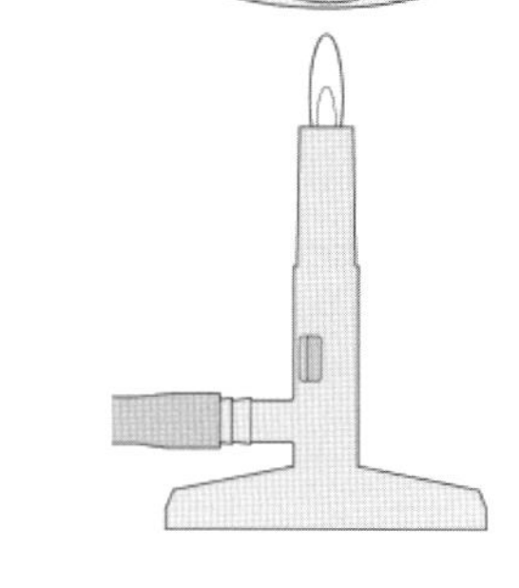

3. Add 10 cm^3 of the acetic orcein stain/hydrochloric acid mixture to the watch-glass. Place the root tip in the watch-glass. ***Wear goggles when using the stain.***
4. Gently warm the watch-glass for a few seconds. Use a very low, but not yellow, Bunsen burner flame or a hot plate or an oven set at about 40°C. You must not let the solution boil.

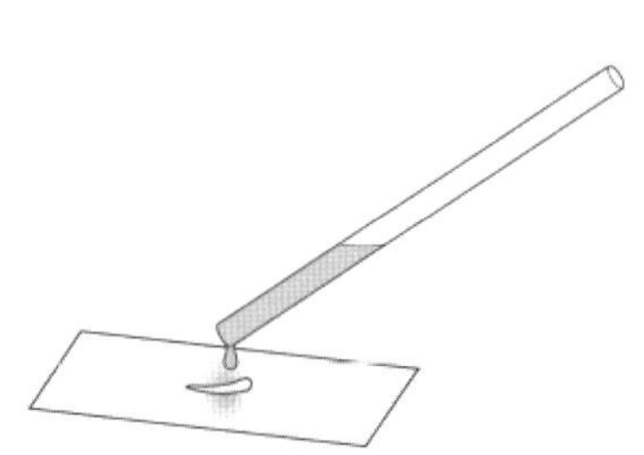

5. Put the root tip on a glass slide using forceps.
6. Add two drops of acetic orcein stain using the glass rod. ***Wear goggles when using the stain.***

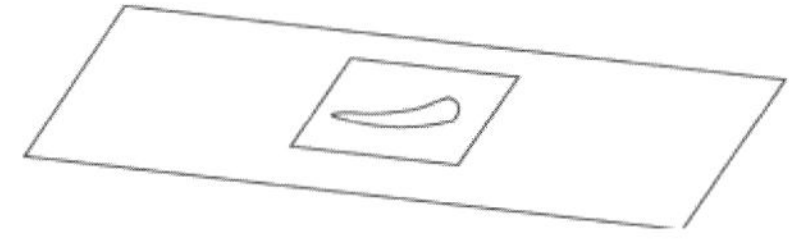

7. Squash the root tip using the flat part of the scalpel blade.
8. Place a cover slip over the squashed root tip.

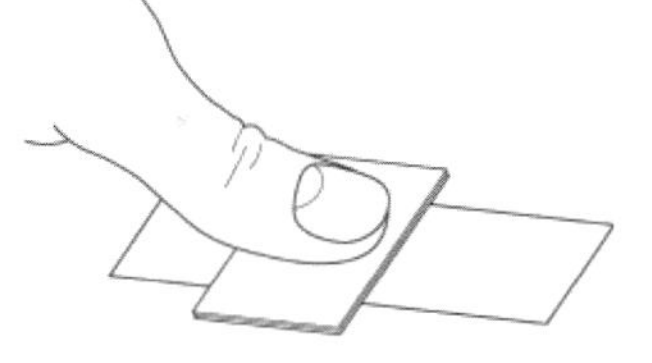

9. Place a folded filter paper over the cover slip, then place another glass slide on the top.
10. Using your thumb, push downwards (not sideways) to squash the root tip even more.
11. Remove the top glass slide and the filter paper.
12. Examine the remaining slide using a light microscope with a low power lens.
13. You will need to move the slide around under the microscope to find the area of dividing cells.
14. Now use a high power lens to look at the cells in more detail.
15. Look for cells showing stained chromosomes. Some of these cells will show stages of mitosis. Look at page 43 in your student book to see some of these stages.
16. Draw any stages you recognise. Write down what is happening to the chromosomes at each stage.

Questions

Q1 The hydrochloric acid softens the cell walls. Why is this step in the experiment necessary?

Q2 The cells that are dividing by mitosis are found near the tips of roots. Why is this?

Q3 Scientists sometimes study sets of chromosomes from an unborn baby. Suggest why they do this.

Practical activity 5

Name ______ Date ______

Plants, animals and their environment

Aim

See 'Photosynthesis' on pages 52–55, 'Exchange of gases' on pages 56–59 and 'Aerobics' on pages 120–123 in your student book.

You are going to find out how plants and animals affect the levels of carbon dioxide in their surroundings.

Introduction

Plants respire in order to release energy from food. Carbon dioxide is produced during respiration. If the plant is under water, some of the carbon dioxide will react with water to produce a weak acid solution.

Green plants also carry out photosynthesis in the light, which is how they make their food. Carbon dioxide is used up during photosynthesis. If the plant is underwater, the water will become less acidic.

Health and safety

You must wash your hands after handling the plants and animals.
If a lamp is used, you must be aware that it will become hot during use and should not be touched.

What you need

- 100 cm^3 measuring cylinder
- supply of distilled water
- rack to hold the boiling tubes
- 8 boiling tubes, labelled A, B, C, E, F, G and H
- water snails, or other pond animals
- *Elodea*, or other pond plants
- 8 rubber bungs to fit the boiling tubes
- lamp
- 2 cm^3 disposable syringe
- bromothymol blue indicator
- boiling tube rack

What you do

It will be more convenient if one group of students sets up tubes A, B, C and D and another group sets up tubes E, F, G and H.

1. Measure out 50 cm^3 distilled water into each boiling tube using the measuring cylinder.
2. Add an equal number of snails to tubes A, C, E and G. Three snails per tube is suggested.
3. Add an equal amount of *Elodea* to tubes B, C, F and G. Two strands per tube is suggested.
4. Nothing is added to tubes D and H.
5. Place tubes A, B, C and D in a rack. Put them in sunlight or shine a bright light on them.
6. Place tubes E, F, G and H in a rack. Put them in a dark cupboard.

Plants, animals and their environment (continued)

7. Leave all tubes for no longer than 48 hours.

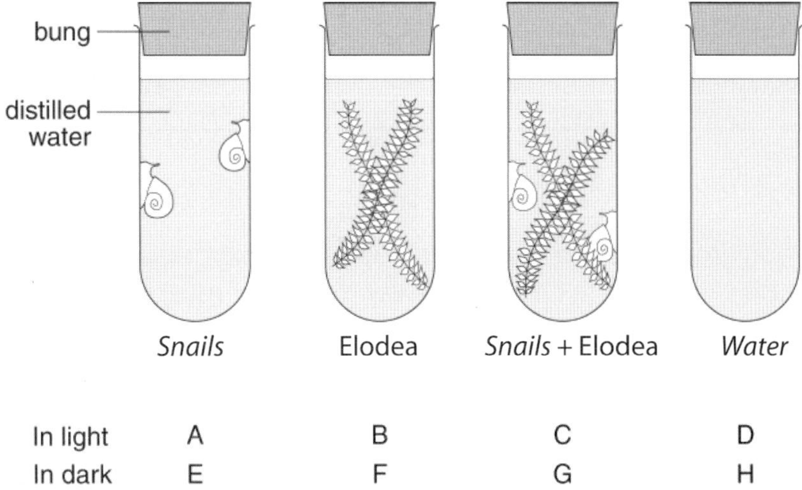

8. Create a results table to show the contents of each tube and where they were kept (in the dark or in the light). You will complete the 'Observations' column later. Use these column headings.

Tube	Dark or light?	*Elodea* present?	Animals present?	Observations
A				

9. Remove the rubber bung of boiling tube A. Add 2 cm^3 of bromothymol blue quickly, using the syringe, and replace the rubber bung immediately. Repeat this with boiling tubes B–H. Do not breath out over the tubes when you are setting them up, as this would affect the indicator.

10. Record the colour changes of each tube in the 'Observations' column of your table.

11. Bromothymol blue is an indicator:
- it is yellow in acidic conditions
- it is green in neutral conditions
- it is blue in alkaline conditions.

Decide whether the water in each tube is acidic, alkaline or neutral. Add this information to the 'Observations' column of your table.

12. Suggest explanations for your results. What are your conclusions?

13. Empty the boiling tubes and return the plants and animals to your teacher.

Questions

Q1 Explain why tubes D and H were set up without plants or animals.

Q2 Scientists often carry out surveys on lakes to find out whether the water is acidic or alkaline. Suggest why their work is important.

Practical activity 6

Name ______________________ Date ____________

Exercise and recovery rates

See 'Asthma' on pages 116–119 and 'Aerobics' on pages 120–123 in your student book.

Aim

You are going to measure pulse rates before and after exercise. You will use your results to find out how long it takes your pulse rate to return to normal. You can then compare your results to those of other students.

Introduction

Your heart pumps blood around your body. Your blood carries oxygen and dissolved food to your muscles. Your blood also carries waste chemicals away from your muscles. Your heart's pumping action can be felt in your arteries as a pulse. You can feel your pulse in various parts of your body, such as your wrist, neck and ear lobe.

Health and safety

You need to tell your teacher if you are usually excused from PE because these exercises may be unsuitable.
If you are asthmatic, you should ensure you have your inhaler in case you need it.
Steady exercise is required to alter your pulse rate. However, the exercise must not be violent or competitive and must be carried out safely.

What you need

- stopwatch or stopclock
- low chair, stool, step or exercise bike
- computer and data logging software, if available
- pulse sensor and interface unit, if available
- graph paper

What you do

1. Use your finger to find your partner's pulse on the inside of their wrist, just below their thumb. Do not use your thumb for this.

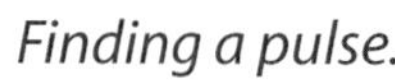

Finding a pulse.

2. Count your partner's pulse each minute for three minutes.
3. If their pulse rate varies by more than five beats per minute, then continue counting for another three minutes. This should allow their pulse rate to reach a normal resting rate.

Exercise and recovery rates (continued)

4. Your partner then carries out exercises. An example is stepping on and off a step fairly vigorously for five minutes. If an exercise bike, computer and pulse sensor set-up is available, pulse recordings can be taken during the exercise.

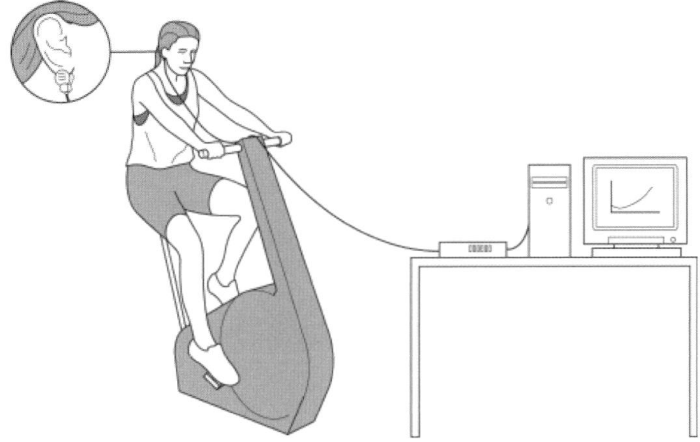

5. Take your partner's pulse for one minute immediately after exercise, and continue for about 10 minutes. This will allow their pulse rate to return to normal.
6. Record all your results in a table.
7. You can repeat the investigation by doing the exercise yourself.
8. Reference sheet 2 'Presenting data' will be useful here. This describes how to plot graphs. Plot and draw a line graph of your results. You need to plot time in minutes on the horizontal axis and beats/minute on the vertical axis.
9. Write down an explanation of why the pulse rate was higher during and immediately after exercise.
10. Use your graph to find out how long it took for your pulse rate to return to normal. This is an indication of how fit you are. The fitter you are, the more quickly your pulse returns to normal. Compare your results with those of your partner and other students in your class.
11. Your results may include an 'anomalous result'. This is a result which does not fit into the general pattern. Such a result will show up when you draw your graph.
    - **a** How could an anomalous result happen?
    - **b** What should you do if you discover an anomalous result?

Questions

Q1 An athlete decides to monitor her fitness levels. During her training sessions she records her recovery time. Explain why these times should decrease over a few weeks.

Q2 The athlete decides to change her event from the 100 metres sprint to the pole vault. She changes her training programme. Explain why her recovery times will change.

Name ______________________ Date ______________

Racing mustard and cress

See 'Photosynthesis' on pages 52–55 in your student book.

Aim

You will find out how long it takes for mustard and cress seeds to germinate at different temperatures. You will then plan a method to produce mustard and cress seedlings to be ready for a set date.

Introduction

You have been asked to produce mustard and cress seedlings for sandwiches on the school Open Day.

The requirements are:

- the seedlings must all be ready for a set date
- the seedlings of both the mustard and the cress must be about 4 cm tall so they can be cut.

Some additional information:

- seeds need both oxygen from the air and water to germinate
- the packets of mustard and cress seeds tell you that mustard seeds germinate faster than cress seeds
- temperature affects the rate of germination.

Health and safety

You must not eat any food prepared in a laboratory.
The aim of this activity is to prepare a plan of how mustard and cress seedlings can be made ready for a set date.
You are not actually producing the seedlings to eat.

What you need

- 6 boiling tubes labelled A, B, C, D, E and F
- boiling tube rack
- measuring cylinder or syringe to measure out 5 cm^3 of water
- cotton wool
- mustard seeds
- cress seeds
- access to a refrigerator
- thermometer
- access to an oven, incubator or water bath

Racing mustard and cress (continued)

What you do

1. Pour about 5 cm^3 of water into each boiling tube.
2. Take a small portion of cotton wool and push it down a boiling tube until the cotton wool touches the water. Do this for all six boiling tubes.
3. Add enough mustard seeds to cover the cotton wool in tubes A, B and C.
4. Add enough cress seeds to cover the cotton wool in tubes D, E and F.
5. Place another piece of cotton wool in the mouth of each boiling tube. Why is this necessary?

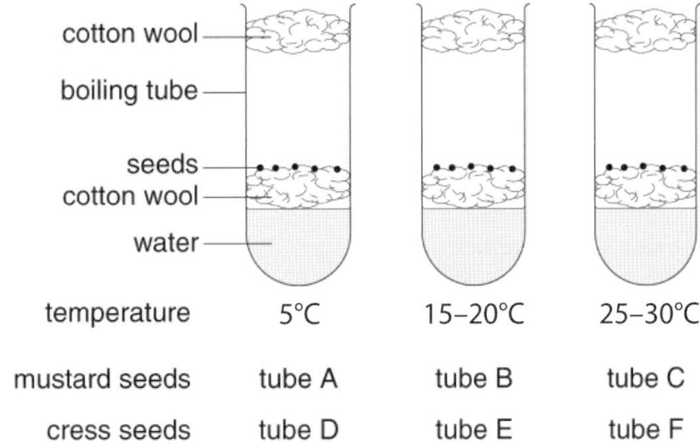

6. Label all the tubes with your name and the seeds used.
7. Measure and record the temperature of the refrigerator. Place tubes A and D in the refrigerator.
8. Tubes B and E will be kept at 15–20°C, in a cool room. Record the actual temperature of the room.
9. Set up an oven, incubator or water bath at a higher temperature of 25–30°C. Tubes C and F will be kept at 25–30°C. Record the actual temperature used.
10. Draw a table to show the contents of each tube and temperature they are kept at.
11. Examine the seeds every day for the next two weeks, or until the seedlings reach the required height. Record the heights of the seedlings in your table each time you measure them.
12. Work out from your results how long mustard seeds and cress seeds take to germinate and reach the required height at each of the three temperatures.
13. You want to start growing the two types of seeds on the same day. Work out from your results the different temperatures required to produce both mustard seedlings and cress seedlings of the required height on a set date.
14. Dispose of the seedlings safely so they cannot be eaten by anyone.

Questions

Q1 Describe how a small business could safely prepare mustard and cress seedlings to eat.

Q2 Investigate the Health and Safety regulations concerning the sale of sandwiches by visiting local shops or your school canteen.

Practical activity 8

Name ____________________ Date ____________

Long live cabbage

See 'Fermentation' on pages 82–85 in your student book.

Aim

You are going to investigate the fermentation of cabbage. This produces sauerkraut. You will then prepare cabbage that will keep for a long time.

Introduction

Modern refrigerators and freezers can keep food safe for a long time. Your grandparents may remember times when refrigerators and freezers were not available. In the past, people had to rely on fruit and vegetables from their own area. If fruit and vegetables were kept too long they would rot. Many methods of food preservation were developed to prevent food from rotting. Some people still use these methods because they prefer the flavours, textures or appearance.

Health and safety

You must not eat food that has been made in a laboratory.
You must wash your hands when you have finished setting up this activity.

What you need

- about half a small cabbage
- kitchen knife
- chopping board
- salt
- balance (to weigh cabbage and salt)
- 2 large beakers
- spatula
- cling film
- pH indicator paper

What you do

1. Cut your portion of cabbage in two.
2. Weigh one portion of your cabbage.
3. Weigh out 3 g of salt for every 100 g of cabbage.
4. Use the kitchen knife and chopping board to chop up this portion of cabbage into small pieces.
5. Put the pieces of cabbage into a large beaker and add the salt. Use a spatula to mix the cabbage and salt well. Cover the beaker with cling film. Salted cabbage is called sauerkraut.
6. Chop up the other portion of cabbage and put the pieces into the other large beaker. Cover the beaker with cling film.
7. Label the two beakers so you know which contains the salted cabbage.
8. Return the kitchen knife to your teacher.
9. Wash your hands.

Long live cabbage (continued)

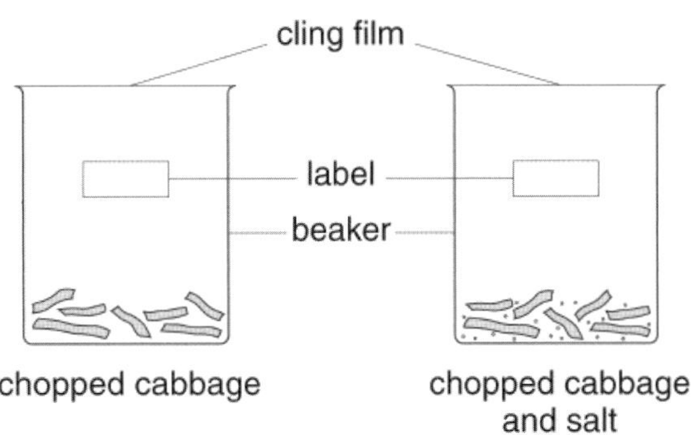

10. Remove the cling film after five minutes. Write down the colour, texture, smell and pH of both portions of cabbage. Replace the cling film.
11. Leave your investigation for a few days and then repeat your recordings.
12. Write down all your results in a table.
13. Explain any differences between the two portions of cabbage.
14. Dispose of the cabbage portions safely.

Questions

Q1 Explain why you must not eat any food prepared in a laboratory.

Q2 Julie's fridge-freezer has broken down. Suggest what she can do to the following foods to keep them safe to eat for a short time:

- **a** plums
- **b** eggs
- **c** milk.

Practical activity 9

Name ____________________ Date ____________

Microorganisms, milk and yoghurt

See 'Types of microorganism' on pages 86–89 and 'Preserving food' on pages 94–97 in your student book.

Aim

You are going to use a dye called resazurin to show microbial activity in milk and yoghurt.

Introduction

Fresh milk contains microorganisms, such as bacteria. Some bacteria cause milk to go bad, but other bacteria can help to preserve food. Yoghurt was first made in hot countries as a way of keeping milk safe over longer periods.

In this experiment you will use:

- UHT (ultra heat treated) milk; this has been heated to 132°C for two seconds
- sterilised milk; this has been heated to 121°C for three minutes
- fresh yoghurt
- boiled yoghurt.

Resazurin dye is a blue solution which changes colour through lilac to pinky mauve to pink to colourless with increasing microbial activity.

blue ⟶ lilac ⟶ pinky mauve ⟶ pink ⟶ colourless

no microbial activity ⟶ high microbial activity

Health and safety

Although you are not using bacterial cultures, you should follow all the guidelines for the use of bacteria.
Wash your hands before and after this activity.
Do not taste the milk or yoghurt samples.
Return the test-tubes to your teacher at the end of the activity for safe disposal.

What you need

- 4 sterile test tubes labelled A, B, C and D
- test tube rack
- sterile syringes or sterile pipettes
- sample of UHT milk
- sample of sterilised milk
- sample of fresh yoghurt
- sample of boiled yoghurt
- resazurin dye
- cling film
- water bath or oven or incubator

Microorganisms, milk and yoghurt (continued)

What you do

1. Put the four labelled sterile test tubes in a test tube rack.
2. Using separate syringes or pipettes, put 5 cm^3 of UHT milk, sterilised milk, fresh yoghurt and boiled yoghurt into separate test tubes and label each test tube.
3. Using a different syringe or pipette, add 1 cm^3 of resazurin dye solution to each test tube. Shake each test tube, then cover it with cling film.
4. Record the colours of the contents of each test tube.
5. Place the four test tubes in the water bath or oven or incubator at 30°C.
6. Examine and record the colours after a day or so.

Questions

Q1 You are preparing a Health and Safety report on milk and yoghurt. Which of the test tubes contained **a** the most and **b** the least microbial activity? Explain your answer.

Q2 Suggest how fresh milk can be kept so it lasts a little longer before it goes bad.

Practical activity 10

Name ______________________ Date ______________

Investigating the action of antibiotics

See 'Antibiotics' on pages 102–105 in your student book.

Aim

You will use a bacterium called *Escherichia coli* (*E. coli*). You will expose *E. coli* to a number of antibiotics, to see which ones have an effect on it.

Introduction

Some bacteria cause disease. Antibiotics can kill bacteria. This means that antibiotics can control some diseases.

The bacterium *E. coli* lives in our gut. Some strains of *E. coli* are harmless, but some do cause diseases.

You will use a 'mast ring' in this experiment. A mast ring is a paper ring with eight projecting arms. Each arm contains a different antibiotic.

Health and safety

You must follow the instructions carefully to ensure you do not spread or catch any bacterial infection.
You will use sterile equipment; you must clean your work area with a disinfectant before and after the experiment.
Your must wash your hands with soap and water after any activity involving bacteria.

What you need

- disinfectant
- Universal bottle containing nutrient agar
- water bath, set at 95°C
- tongs
- heatproof mat
- inoculating loop
- Bunsen burner
- culture of *E. coli*
- sterile Petri dish
- forceps
- mast ring
- sticky tape
- marker pen
- incubator or oven, set at 30°C

What you do

The following instructions are for a right-handed student. The instructions may need adjusting if you are left-handed.

1. Wipe down your work area with disinfectant.
2. Place the Universal bottle containing nutrient agar into the water bath (approximately 95°C). This will melt the agar.
3. When the agar has melted, lift out the Universal bottle, using the tongs, and place it on the heatproof mat to cool down. After 15 minutes or so, the bottle should be cool enough to touch but the agar should still be liquid.

Investigating the action of antibiotics (continued)

4. Hold the inoculating loop in your right hand. Pass the inoculating loop through a Bunsen burner flame to sterilise it. Do not put the tip of the loop straight into the flame. Instead, put the middle of the handle into the flame and slowly move the handle through the flame until the loop is heated. Keep holding the sterile inoculating loop in your right hand.

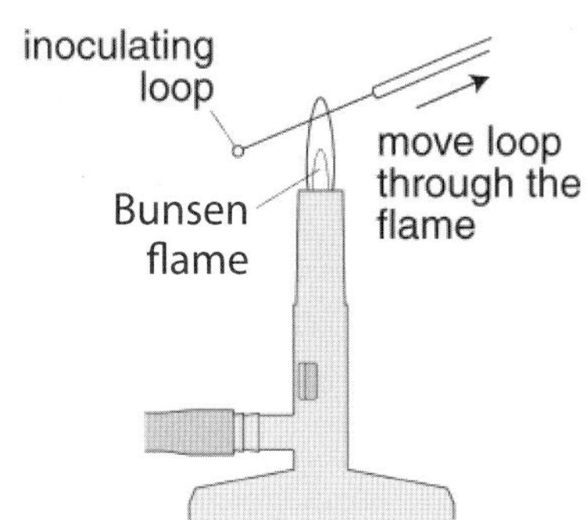

5. Hold the bottle of *E. coli* culture in your left hand. Use the little finger and palm of your right hand to unscrew the top of this bottle. Hold the bottle at an angle to prevent airborne contamination. Hold the neck of the bottle in a Bunsen burner flame for a few seconds. Work close to the Bunsen burner. The neck of the bottle is passed through the flame to create a convection current away from the open bottle.

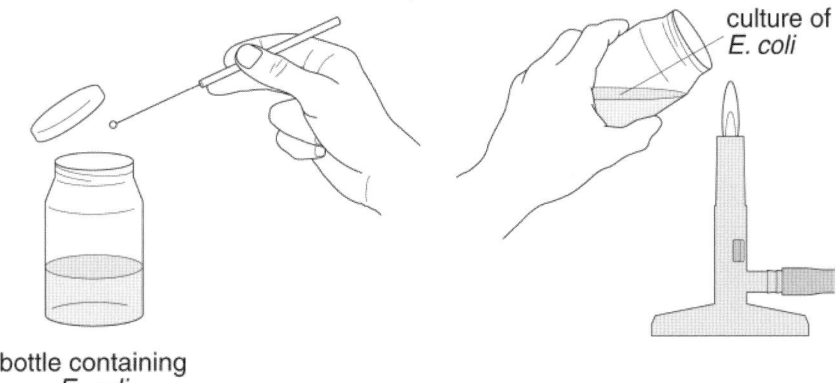

6. Dip the sterile inoculating loop, which you are holding in your right hand, into the bottle of *E. coli* culture, which you are holding in your left hand. Remove the inoculating loop from the bottle. Flame the neck of the bottle again. Screw the top back onto the bottle. You can now put the culture bottle down, but keep holding the inoculating loop in your right hand.

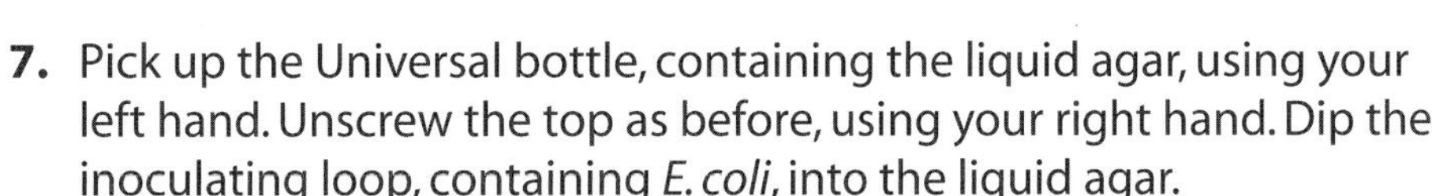

7. Pick up the Universal bottle, containing the liquid agar, using your left hand. Unscrew the top as before, using your right hand. Dip the inoculating loop, containing *E. coli*, into the liquid agar.

8. Remove the inoculating loop and hold it in a Bunsen burner flame to sterilise it. You can now put the inoculating loop down on the heatproof mat. Transfer the Universal bottle to your right hand. Flame the neck of the Universal bottle again.

Investigating the action of antibiotics (continued)

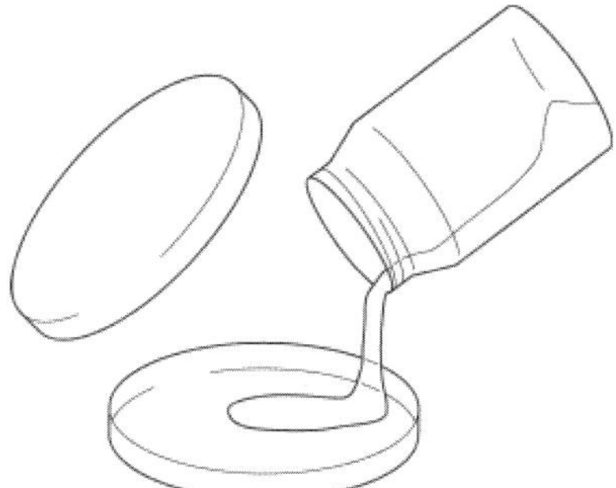

9. Tilt the Petri dish cover with your left hand, so the Petri dish is slightly open, and pour in the liquid agar. Replace the cover of the Petri dish.
10. Gently move the Petri dish around to make sure that the agar is spread evenly. The agar will set in a few minutes.
11. Wait until the agar is set. Pick up a mast ring using sterile forceps (or forceps sterilised in a flame). Tilt the Petri dish cover, as before, and place the mast ring on the surface of the agar. Replace the cover of the Petri dish. If the forceps touch the agar, they must be flamed again.
12. Tape the Petri dish shut with sticky tape. Use two pieces of tape, on opposite sides. Do not seal the Petri dish completely or anaerobic bacteria may grow.
13. Turn the Petri dish upside down and write your name and the date on it using a marker pen. Make your labels small.
14. Draw a circle approximately the same size as the Petri dish on a sheet of paper. Draw in the shape of the mast ring.
15. Put the Petri dish, upside down, in an incubator or oven at 30°C for a few days.
16. Clean your work surface with disinfectant.
17. Wash your hands with soap and water.
18. Examine your Petri dish after a few days. On your diagram, shade in the areas of bacterial growth on the agar. Clear zones around a ring show that the antibiotic has restricted or killed the bacteria. Decide which antibiotics are the most effective. You could use a ruler to measure the diameter of the clear zones.
19. Return your Petri dish to your teacher for safe disposal.
20. Wash your hands with soap and water.

Questions

Q1 You have used the same techniques as those that are used in a pathology laboratory. Explain why:

- **a** the equipment used in this activity is sterile
- **b** the Petri dish cover is tilted open but not completely removed
- **c** the Petri dish cover is taped down.

Q2 What are the possible consequences if the nutrient agar in a pathology laboratory is contaminated?

Name ______________________ Date ______________

Practical activity 11

Elements, compounds and mixtures

See 'Elements from the Earth' on pages 146–149 and 'Compounds from the Earth' on pages 150–155 in your student book.

Aim

You are going to investigate two elements: iron and sulphur. You will find out what happens when they are mixed together. You will also find out how they change when they combine together to make a compound.

Introduction

'Fool's gold' is a mineral ore – you might be able to find some next time you visit a beach. It is called fool's gold because it looks like gold, but it is actually a compound of iron, copper and sulphur. Its formula is $CuFeS_2$. If you'd thought you'd found treasure you'd be disappointed!

In this activity you are going to investigate two of the elements in fool's gold – iron and sulphur.

Health and safety

You need to wear eye protection when you are using acids and when you heat the mixture.
You need to follow the usual laboratory rules for using your Bunsen burner.
Your teacher may ask you to carry out your own risk assessment. You will need to check all the chemicals on 'Student Safety Sheets' and fill in a risk assessment form. Your teacher will need to check your risk assessment form before you start your experiment.
If you get any splashes of acid on your skin, wash under the tap straight away with lots of water, and send a friend to make sure your teacher knows.
Do not breathe in any fumes. Sulphur dioxide is toxic and can trigger asthma attacks.

What you need

- eye protection
- iron filings
- sulphur
- 3 Petri dishes with lids
- hand lens or magnifying glass
- magnet wrapped in cling film (keep the cling film on while you work!)
- 3 test tubes and test tube rack
- beaker of water (labelled)
- bottle of dilute hydrochloric acid (labelled)
- heatproof test tube and holder
- mineral wool
- Bunsen burner and heatproof mat
- spatulas, glass rods and dropping pipettes

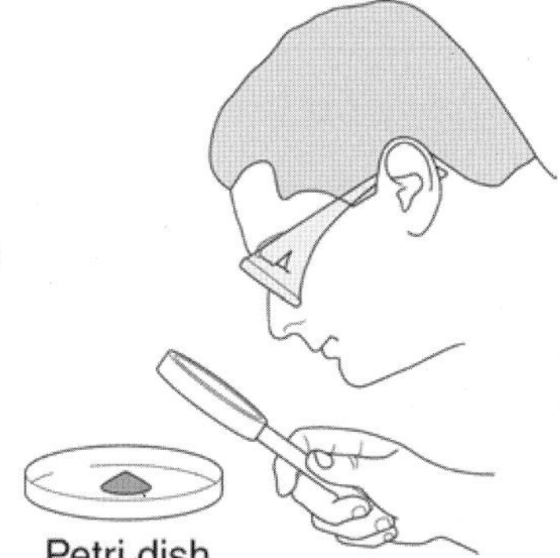

Just looking ...

What you do

1. Put small amounts of iron filings and sulphur into two separate Petri dishes.
2. Look at the iron and sulphur using a hand lens or magnifying glass. Look for the state (solid, liquid or gas), the colour, the size of the grains and if it is shiny or dull.

Elements, compounds and mixtures (continued)

3. Put the lids on the Petri dishes. See if the substances are attracted to the magnet (keep the lid on the Petri dish and keep the cling film around the magnet).

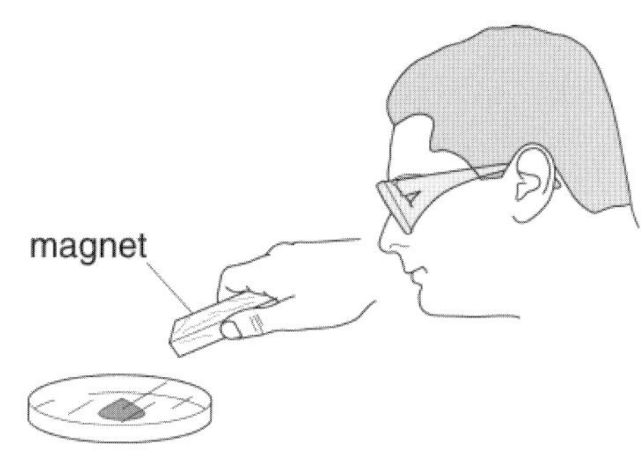

Testing with a magnet.

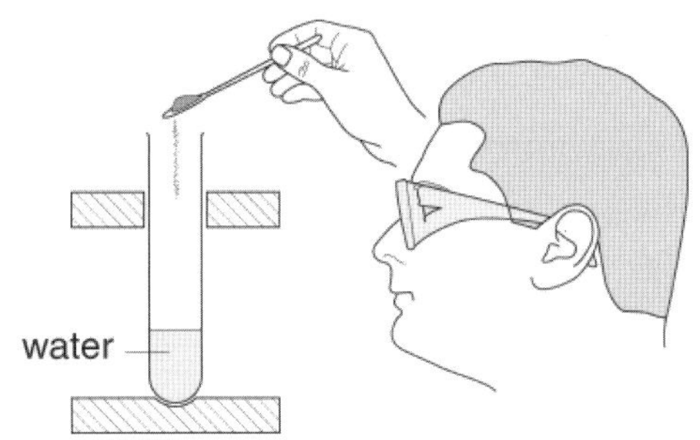

Adding the solid to water.

4. Put some water in a test tube, until the test tube is about a quarter full. Add a small amount of iron to the water. Does it sink or float? Repeat with another test tube, some water and a small amount of sulphur.

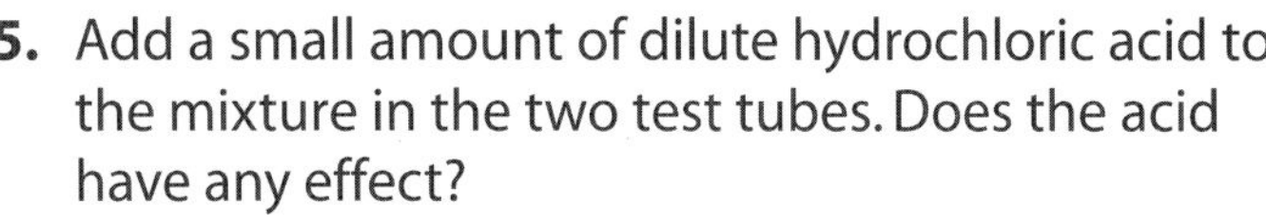

5. Add a small amount of dilute hydrochloric acid to the mixture in the two test tubes. Does the acid have any effect?

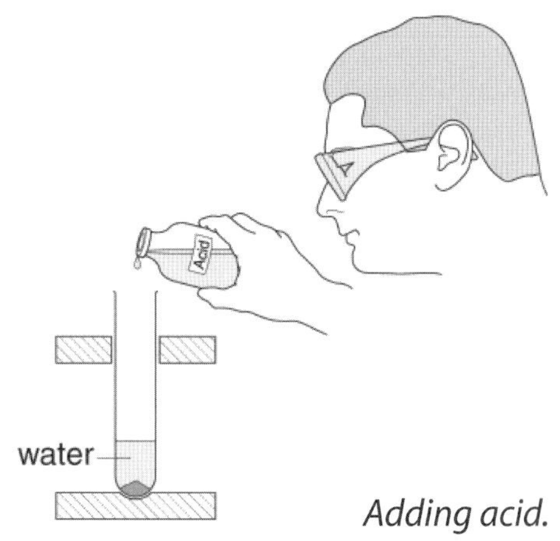

Adding acid.

6. Record your results in a table.

Substance	Appearance	Magnet test	Water test	Acid test
iron				
sulphur				
mixture				
compound				

So far you have tested iron and sulphur – these are both **elements**. The next step is to see whether mixing the two elements together to make a **mixture** makes any difference.

7. Mix a small amount of iron and sulphur together and repeat the four tests. Record your results in the next row of your table.

Elements, compounds and mixtures (continued)

Now, you need to make a **compound** of iron and sulphur. Remember that in a compound the atoms of iron and sulphur will join together. The compound you make is called iron sulphide.

8. Mix a small amount of iron and sulphur together in a small heatproof test tube. Put a mineral wool plug in the test tube.

9. Heat the mixture in a Bunsen flame until the mixture glows red. You may notice it keeps glowing after you take it out of the flame – the reaction continues by itself. Take care when heating the iron/sulphur mixture. If the mixture does ignite then sulphur dioxide will be formed. Sulphur dioxide is toxic and corrosive. Take care not to inhale. Extinguish at once with a damp cloth.

10. Leave the test tube to cool. Then tip the iron sulphide out onto a heatproof mat. Be careful! – the iron sulphide will stay hot for a while.

Making iron sulphide.

11. When the compound is cool, carry out the four tests again. Record your results in the last row of your table. When you add acid to iron sulphide, a toxic gas is formed. When you have detected it, pour the contents of the test tube into the sink and rinse with plenty of water.

12. Put ticks in the table to show which statements are true for compounds and which are true for mixtures. Some statements may be true for both compounds and mixtures.

Statement	Compounds	Mixtures
Contain more than one type of atom		
Can be easily separated		
Atoms are chemically bonded		
Making this is a reversible change		
Making this is a permanent change		
Can be found in the Earth's crust		

Questions

Q1 How can you separate a mixture of iron and sulphur?

Q2 Has mixing the elements together changed how they behave?

Q3 Can you separate the iron and sulphur after you have made iron sulphide?

Q4 In what ways is the compound different from the mixture?

Q5 Use ideas from this activity to explain:

- **a** why iron cans are separated from other rubbish for recycling using an electromagnet
- **b** why iron cannot be separated from fool's gold using a magnet
- **c** why car bodywork parts are sometimes dipped in acid to give a clean surface before they are painted.

Practical activity 12

Name ______________________ Date ______________

Making saline solutions

See 'Salt from rock salt' on pages 156–159 in your student book.

Aim

You are going to learn how to accurately make up saline solutions of known concentrations.

Introduction

Saline solution is a mixture of salt dissolved in water. Saline solution has important medical uses. Many 'drips' in hospitals have the drugs dissolved in saline solution. Contact lens wearers use saline solution to soak, store and clean their lenses.

It is very important that the concentration of the salt in the water is exactly correct. A wrong concentration could make your body tissues swell or dry out, or could even be fatal!

In this activity you are going to learn how to make a saline solution of exact concentration. When you have made your saline solution, you will act as a Quality Controller. You are going to check that another group of students has made their saline solution up accurately.

Health and safety

You need to wear eye protection.
You need to follow the usual laboratory rules for using your Bunsen burner.

What you need

This activity has two parts. You will only need the equipment for Experiment 1 to start with.

- eye protection

Experiment 1

- watch-glass
- salt (sodium chloride)
- weighing balance
- 2 beakers
- water
- 100 cm^3 measuring cylinder
- dropping pipette
- glass rod
- distilled water in a wash bottle

Experiment 2

- measuring cylinder
- evaporating basin
- weighing balance
- Bunsen burner, tripod, gauze, heatproof mat

What you do

Experiment 1: Making a saline solution

1. Read up to instruction number 5 before you start carrying out any experimental work. You are going to think about and suggest improvements to these outline instructions. You will be carrying out your own 'improved' instructions.
2. You are going to make up a solution of 3 g of salt in 100 cm^3 of water. Look at the diagrams to see what you will do.

Making saline solutions (continued)

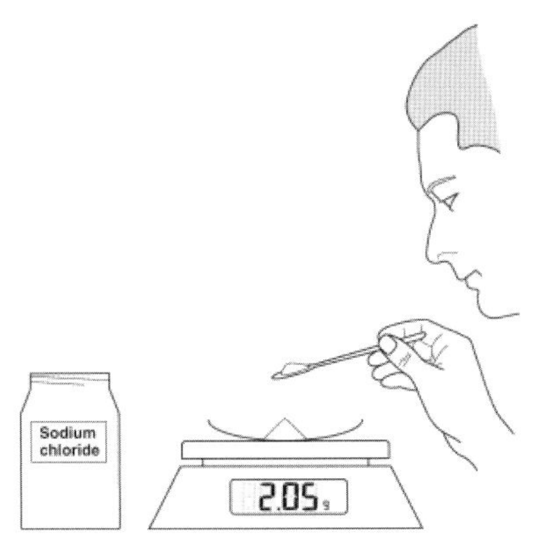

A. *Weigh a watch-glass. Now accurately weigh out 3 g of salt on your watch-glass.*

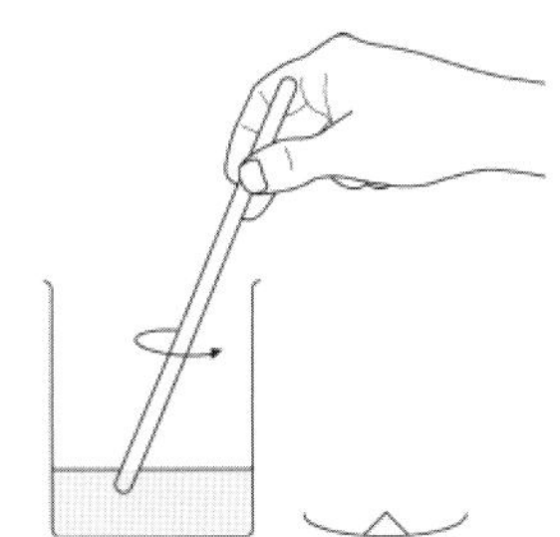

B. *Put the salt in a beaker and dissolve it in water. About 30 cm³ of water will do. You don't need to measure this amount out accurately.*

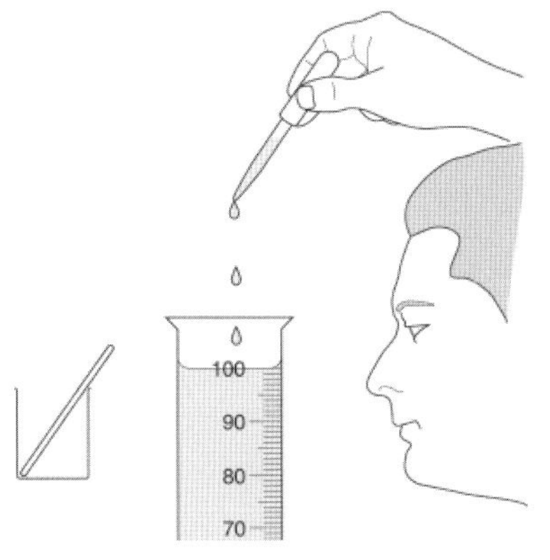

C. *Pour your salt solution into a measuring cylinder. Fill the measuring cylinder so it exactly reads 100 cm³. You can use a dropping pipette to fill the last few drops. You need to make sure the bottom of the meniscus of water is on the 100 cm³ line.*

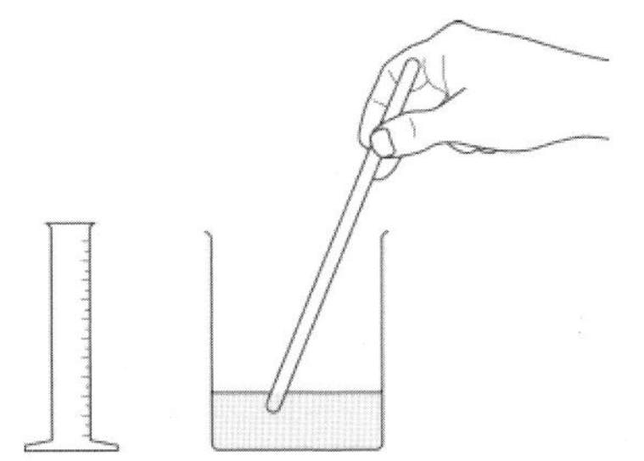

D. *Pour your solution into a clean beaker and stir it to make sure it is well mixed.*

3. Look at the instructions. Think about where you might lose salt after you accurately weighed it. On the diagrams, put a cross on every piece of equipment that will have traces of salt on it. If you are making saline solution for medical use, it must be exactly right. Any 'lost' salt will mean that the final concentration is wrong.
4. 'Washing' involves rinsing equipment with distilled water and adding the 'rinsings' to the measuring cylinder so no salt is lost. Which pieces of equipment would be worth 'washing'? At which stage of the experiment should this be done? Add instructions to the diagrams to show when you will 'wash'.
5. Check your ideas with your teacher and then carry out your experiment.

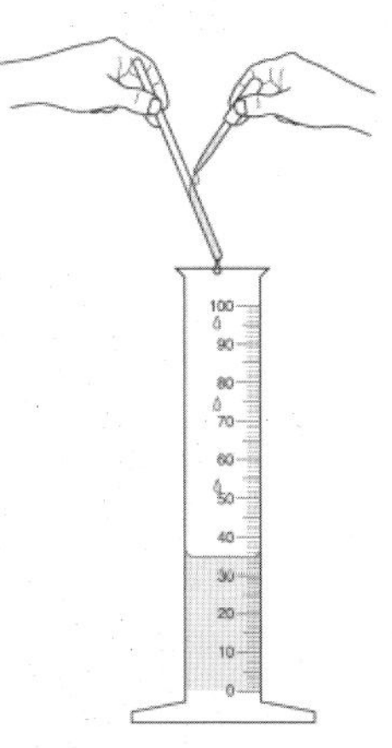

'I'm washing the glass rod.'

Making saline solutions (continued)

If you were making saline solution for medical use or contact lenses, the final solution would have to be sterile. This means that the solution would contain no harmful bacteria or microbes.

6. Look again at the instructions for the experiment. Put a cross on every possible source of harmful bacteria (use a different colour).

Experiment 2: Quality control of a saline solution

Companies who make saline solutions have people working in Quality Control labs. They check the finished saline solutions to make sure the concentration is correct.

Swap saline solutions with another group. You can quality control each others' work. Read these instructions and then carry out Experiment 2.

7. ***Wear eye protection.*** Accurately measure a 10 cm^3 sample of the saline solution. Make sure you choose the most accurate size measuring cylinder to do this.
8. Weigh an evaporating basin and write down the mass.
9. Pour the 10 cm^3 sample of the saline solution into the evaporating basin.

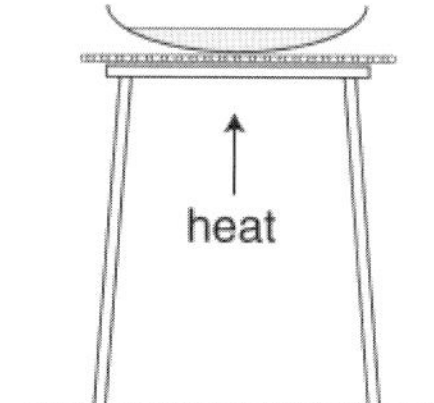

10. Evaporate the sample of saline solution to get the salt back. Turn the heat off when there is still some water left or the solution will spit at you.
11. Re-weigh the evaporating basin when it is cool.
12. a What is the mass of salt in your 10 cm^3 sample?
    b What mass of salt is in 100 cm^3 of the saline solution you are testing?
    c Would this saline solution 'pass' quality control?

Questions

Q1 Making sterile saline solutions involves using steam-sterilised equipment and sterile distilled water. Why are sterile saline solutions expensive, even though salt and water are very cheap?

Q2 The solution you have made contains 3 g of salt in 100 cm^3 of salt solution. Concentrations are usually given in g dm^{-3} (grams per decimetre cubed), where 1 dm^3 = 1000 cm^3. What is the concentration of your saline solution in g dm^{-3}?

Q3 Your saline solution is too concentrated to be used for medical uses. A diarrhoea medicine for babies contains saline of concentration 3 g dm^{-3}. Produce a method to show how you could dilute your saline solution accurately, so that it could be used in the diarrhoea medicine.

Q4 Even accurately made saline solutions can give 'wrong' results in Experiment 2. What are the 'sources of error' in this method?

Q5 What other tests do you think a Quality Control department would carry out on saline solution for medical use?

Name ______________________ Date ______________

Practical activity 13

Setting up a distillation apparatus

See 'Crude oil to petrol' on pages 166–169 and 'More about molecules' on pages 200–203 in your student book.

Aim

You are going to learn how to set up a distillation apparatus. This apparatus will be used to separate pure water from a mixture. Your teacher will demonstrate how the distillation apparatus works. You will then make a poster of the equipment in a 'cut and stick' activity.

Introduction

You are going to see how water free from salt can be made from seawater. The impurities in the water get left behind when the water boils to make steam. The steam can be cooled and collected. The process is called **distillation**.

Distilled water is used whenever it is important that the water has no impurities. It is used in medicines and scientific experiments, and also for irons and for topping up car batteries. The salts dissolved in ordinary tap water could block up irons and batteries.

Your science department prep room probably has a large distillation apparatus or 'still' for making distilled water for the school labs. You may be able to go and look at it.

What you need

- eye protection
- scissors and glue
- photocopy of 'Distillation' sheet
- A3 paper to make a poster

What you do

1. Watch the demonstration of the distillation of seawater.
2. Cut out the pieces of apparatus from the 'Distillation' sheet. Stick them onto your sheet of A3 paper, to show how the distillation apparatus is set up.
3. Cut out the labels from the bottom of the 'Distillation' sheet. Stick the labels on your poster. Draw arrows to show clearly which part is which.

Questions

Q1 How can you prove that the distilled water is now free from salt?

Q2 What impurities will be left in the flask?

Q3 Why is this method of making pure water from seawater too expensive to use on a large scale?

Q4 Your lab may have a 'still' for making distilled water. Find out what happens to the impurities left behind in your lab 'still'.

Practical activity 14

Name ______________________ Date ______________

Investigating dyes

See 'Bulk and fine chemicals' on pages 170–173 in your student book.

Aim

You are going to investigate the dyes used to colour foods.

Introduction

Dyes are manufactured as **fine chemicals**. This activity involves using techniques that are used to check the quality of fine chemicals.

Many food manufacturers use a small number of dyes to make foods of many different colours. They mix the dyes to make the range of colours they need. You are going to use chromatography to find out how many dyes have been used in the food colourings found in some cakes and sweets.

Health and safety

You must not eat food that has been in a laboratory.

What you need

- filter paper
- pencil
- ruler
- capillary tubes
- samples of food dyes
- water
- beakers
- spills
- paper clips
- hairdryer
- small paintbrushes
- coloured sweets

What you do

1. Draw a pencil line about 2 cm from the bottom of your filter paper.
2. Label your line with initials for the food colours you will use.
3. Use the capillary tube to put dots of the food colours on the line. You can do several coats, letting each coat dry to get a strong colour.

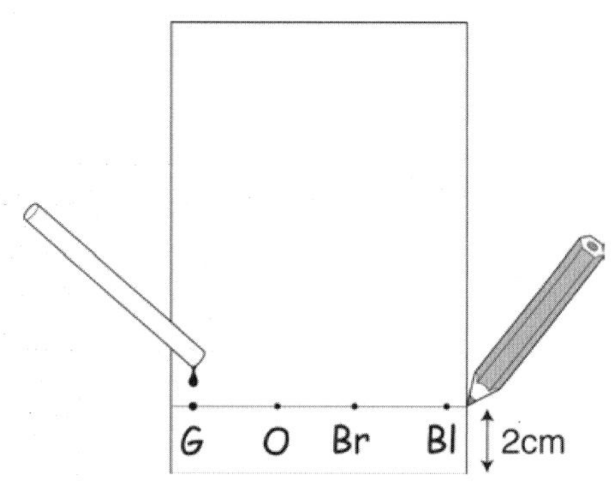

4. Put a 1 cm depth of water in a beaker.
5. Put your filter paper in your beaker. Do not let your dots touch the water. Do not let your paper touch the sides of the beaker. You can use a spill and paper clips to hold your paper up.

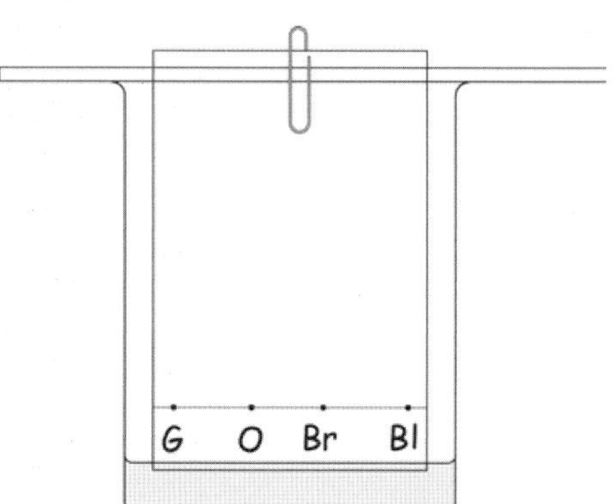

Investigating dyes (continued)

6. Leave your filter paper until the dots have moved up the paper. The water will drag the dyes up as it soaks upwards.
7. Take the paper out when the water is nearly at the top. Mark how far the water has reached.
8. Leave the finished chromatogram to dry. A hairdryer speeds up the drying. When your chromatogram is dry, you can paste it onto your report as evidence.
9. How many dyes have been used to make each food colouring?

Further work

You can use chromatography to investigate the dyes used on sweets.

Make a chromatogram by using a wet paintbrush to make dots of sweet dyes on a pencil line. Use as little water as possible to ensure the greatest concentration of dye.

Run your chromatogram and compare it to your first one.

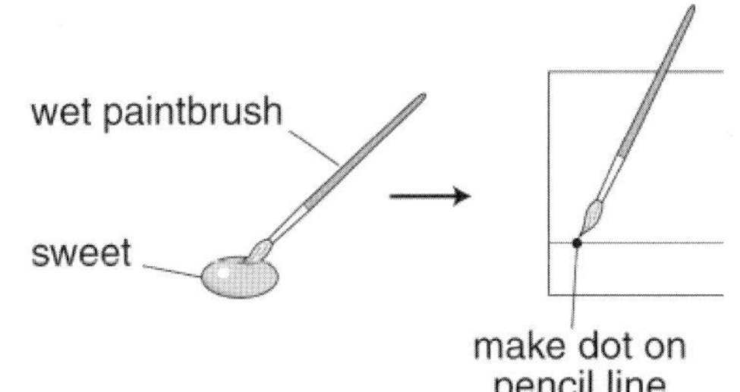

Questions

Q1 Look at this drawing of a chromatogram.

- **a** How many dyes have been used to make the blue dye?
- **b** Which dyes contain some red dye?
- **c** Which two dyes could be mixed together to make the green dye?

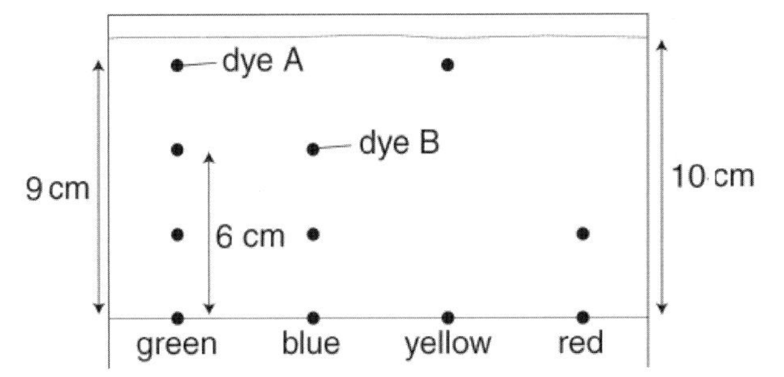

The chromatogram for Q1.

Q2 The R_f values of dyes are worked out using this formula: $R_f \text{ value} = \dfrac{\text{distance travelled by dye}}{\text{distance travelled by water}}$

For dye A, the R_f value is $= \frac{9}{10} = 0.9$ Work out the R_f value for dye B.

Q3 Write a report on your findings from your first chromatogram. Your report should show:

- **a** how many dyes have been used in each food colouring
- **b** the R_f values of each dye
- **c** whether the same dye has been used in more than one colouring.

Q4 (To be answered if you carried out the 'Further work'.)

- **a** How many dyes have been used in the food colourings for each sweet?
- **b** Are any of the dyes the same as those from the food colourings you tested in the first chromatogram?

Q5 Chromatography can be used by people working in Public Health Laboratories, to make sure that banned dyes are not used in foods. Explain how you could use chromatography to find out if a banned food colouring had been used in a food.

Practical activity 15

Name ______________________ Date ______________

Investigating rates of reaction

See 'Bulk and fine chemicals' on pages 170–173 in your student book.

Aim

You are going to investigate how changing the conditions in a reaction affects the rate of reaction.

Introduction

In industry, it is very important to make your product as fast as possible. This will save you money and mean that you need less equipment.

In this activity you are going to investigate the reaction between limestone chips (calcium carbonate) and hydrochloric acid. The equation for the reaction is:

calcium carbonate + hydrochloric acid → calcium chloride + carbon dioxide + water

$$CaCO_3 + 2HCl \rightarrow CaCl_2 + CO_2 + H_2O$$

The carbon dioxide gas can be collected. It is easy to see how fast the reaction is happening by looking at how quickly the carbon dioxide gas is being made.

You are going to find out the best conditions for making the reaction happen as quickly as possible. You will be investigating how concentration of acid, temperature and surface area of limestone affect the rate.

Health and safety

You need to wear eye protection throughout the activity.
Your teacher may ask you to carry out your own risk assessment. You will need to check all the chemicals on 'Student Safety Sheets' and fill in a risk assessment form. Your teacher will need to check your risk assessment before you start your experiment.
If you get any splashes of acid on your skin, wash under the tap straight away with lots of water, and send a friend to make sure your teacher knows.

What you need

This activity is in three parts.

Experiment 1

- eye protection
- limestone chips
- balance
- conical flask with delivery tube
- 100 cm^3 measuring cylinder
- trough or large beaker
- 2.0 mol dm^{-3} hydrochloric acid in a labelled bottle (irritant)
- stopwatch or stopclock
- plastic sieve
- graph paper

Experiments 2 and 3

As for Experiment 1, plus

- ice
- water bath at 40°C
- small limestone chips
- powdered limestone

Investigating rates of reaction (continued)

What you do

1. Weigh out 10 g of limestone chips.
2. Set up your equipment as shown in the diagram.

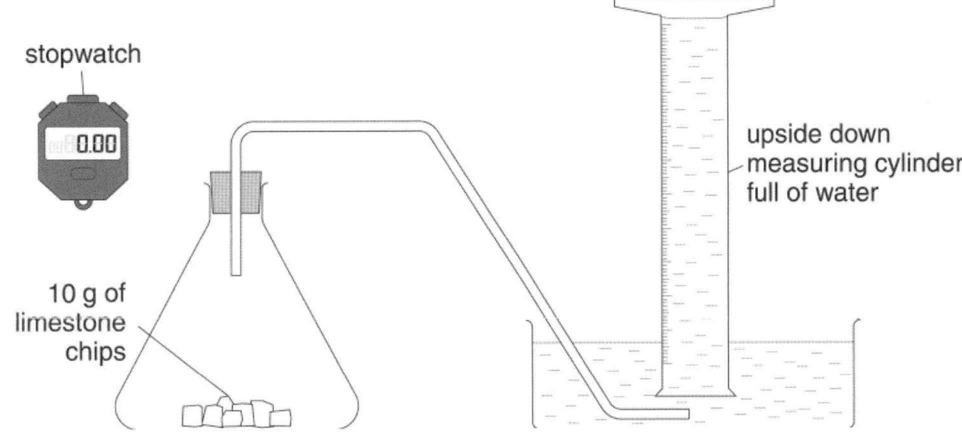

Don't add the acid yet.

3. Measure out 20 cm^3 of 2.0 mol dm^{-3} hydrochloric acid using a measuring cylinder.
4. Make a copy of this table ready to record your results.

Time/sec	**Experiment 1a** (2.0 mol dm^{-3} hydrochloric acid) Volume of gas/cm^3	**Experiment 1b** (1.0 mol dm^{-3} hydrochloric acid) Volume of gas/cm^3	**Experiment 1c** (0.5 mol dm^{-3} hydrochloric acid) Volume of gas/cm^3
15			
30			
45			
60			
75			
90			
105			
120			

You need to leave plenty of space, in case you need to add more rows to your table.

Investigating rates of reaction (continued)

5. Now you need to:
   a take the bung out of the conical flask
   b add the acid to the limestone chips
   c put the bung back on
   d start the stopwatch.
   Do these steps as quickly as possible.
6. Record in your table how much gas has been given off every 15 seconds. Continue until you can see no more change, or until your measuring cylinder is full (you may need to add more rows to your table).
7. Save your limestone chips by pouring the contents of the conical flask through a plastic sieve and rinsing the acid off under a tap.
8. Use your results to draw a graph. You need to choose the scale so that all your results fit on the graph. Join your points using a line of best fit. Your finished graph should look like this.

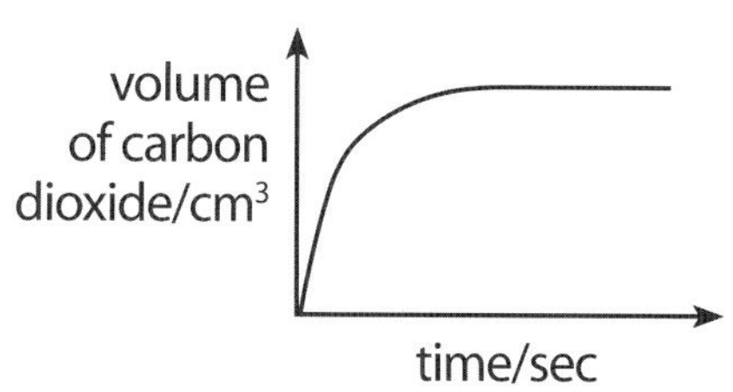

9. a Which part of the curve on the graph shows the fastest reaction?
   b Which part of the curve shows where the reaction has stopped?
   c What happens to the gradient (the steepness) of the graph line as the reaction slows down?

Experiments 1b and 1c

You are going to repeat Experiment 1a using different concentrations of acid.

- In Experiment 1b you will use 1.0 mol dm^{-3} hydrochloric acid.
- In Experiment 1c you will use 0.5 mol dm^{-3} hydrochloric acid.

10. You used 2.0 mol dm^{-3} hydrochloric acid in Experiment 1a. How will you dilute this acid to make 20 cm^3 of:
    a 1.0 mol dm^{-3} hydrochloric acid?
    b 0.5 mol dm^{-3} hydrochloric acid?
11. Make up 20 cm^3 of each concentration of acid. Use the diluted acids to carry out the experiment twice more. You can use the same chips each time – if you look at them you will see very little limestone has dissolved away.
12. Record your results in your table.
13. Draw these results onto your graph. You can put all three curves on the same graph. Make sure you label your curves.
14. a Which concentration of acid reacts the fastest?
    b Which concentration of acid reacts the slowest?
    c Write a sentence to explain what this experiment tells you about the effect of acid concentration on the rate of reaction.

Investigating rates of reaction (continued)

Further work

You can adapt this method to investigate the effect that temperature and surface area of limestone has on the rate of reaction.

Temperature: Use an ice bath and a water bath at 40°C to change the temperature of the acid.

15. Carry out the experiments again to compare the rate of reaction using:
- **a** 20 cm^3 of 2.0 mol dm^{-3} hydrochloric acid at 0°C
- **b** 20 cm^3 of 2.0 mol dm^{-3} hydrochloric acid at room temperature (about 20°C – you can use your results for Experiment 1a here)
- **c** 20 cm^3 of 2.0 mol dm^{-3} hydrochloric acid at 40°C.

16. Plot these results on a new graph.

17. What effect does increasing the temperature have on the rate of reaction?

Surface area: Use limestone in different-sized pieces.

18. Carry out the experiments again, using 2.0 mol dm^{-3} hydrochloric acid with:
- **a** 10 g of large limestone chips (you can use your results for Experiment 1a here)
- **b** 10 g of small limestone chips
- **c** 10 g of powdered limestone chips.

19. Plot these results on a new graph.

20. **a** Which limestone sample has the biggest surface area?
- **b** What effect does increasing the surface area have on the rate of reaction?

Questions

Q1 Why does increasing the temperature cost money when reactions are carried out on a large industrial scale?

Q2 Calcium carbonate is a compound in cement. 'Brick Acid' is used to dissolve cement off old bricks so that they can be re-sold as 'Reclaimed Building Materials'.
- **a** What advice would you give to brick reclaimers to make the 'Brick Acid' work as quickly as possible?
- **b** What safety precautions would the reclaimers need to consider?

Practical activity 16

Name ______________________ Date ____________

Finding the concentration of an acid

See 'Putting numbers into industry' on pages 178–181 in your student book.

Aim

You are going to learn how to carry out a titration.

Introduction

You have been learning about sulphuric acid. Sulphuric acid is used in battery acid. Your teacher will give you some diluted battery acid. Battery acid is too concentrated to work with – we will come back to this point later. You are going to find out exactly what the concentration of the dilute sulphuric acid is. To measure the concentration of an acid, we find out exactly how much alkali we need to use to neutralise the acid. If we know the concentration of alkali we use, we can work out how much acid we must have started with. In this activity you will be using sodium hydroxide solution to neutralise the dilute sulphuric acid. One skill when carrying out titrations is to take all your measurements as accurately as possible.

Chemists working in Quality Control laboratories often use titrations to find out concentrations of acids.

Health and safety

You need to wear goggles throughout the activity.
Your teacher may ask you to carry out your own risk assessment. You will need to check all the chemicals on 'Student Safety Sheets' and fill in a risk assessment form. Your teacher will need to check your risk assessment before you start your experiment.
Acids and alkalis can damage your eyes and skin. If you get any splashes on your skin, wash under the tap straight away with lots of water, and send a friend to make sure your teacher knows.
Put your burette stand on the floor when you fill your burette.

What you need

- goggles
- measuring cylinder (you need to choose which one is best)
- labelled bottle of 1.0 mol dm^{-3} sodium hydroxide solution (corrosive)
- 2 conical flasks
- bottle of litmus indicator
- burette in a clamp stand
- labelled bottle of 'unknown' dilute sulphuric acid (irritant)
- funnel
- white tile

What you do

1. Look up the chemicals you will be using on 'Student Safety Sheets'. What are the main hazards of sodium hydroxide solution and dilute sulphuric acid? What should you do if there is a spillage?
2. Measure out 25 cm^3 of the sodium hydroxide solution. You need to choose which is the best measuring cylinder to use to get the most accurate measurement. Make sure the bottom of the meniscus is on the '25' line.

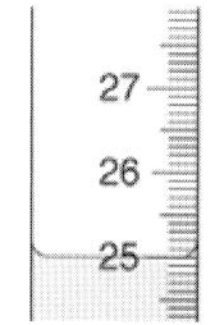

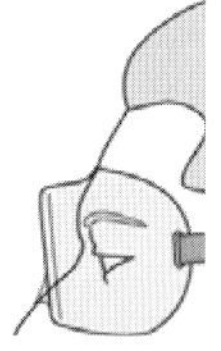

25 cm^3 of sodium hydroxide solution.

Finding the concentration of an acid (continued)

3. Pour the sodium hydroxide solution carefully into the conical flask. Add a few drops of litmus to the sodium hydroxide solution. The solution will go blue because sodium hydroxide is an alkali.

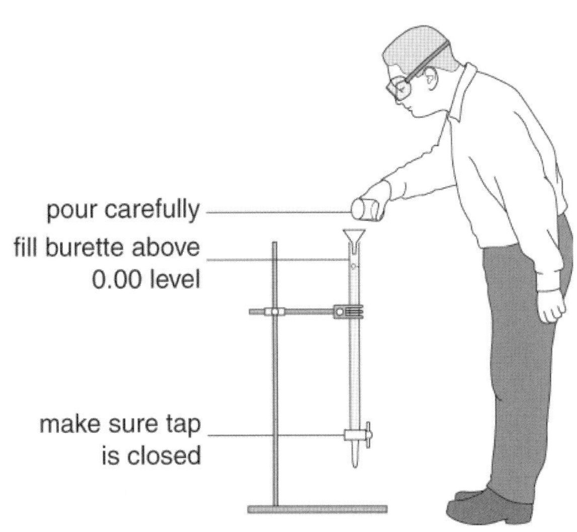

Filling your burette.

4. Stand the burette on the floor and fill it with the dilute sulphuric acid to above the '0.00 cm^3' reading.

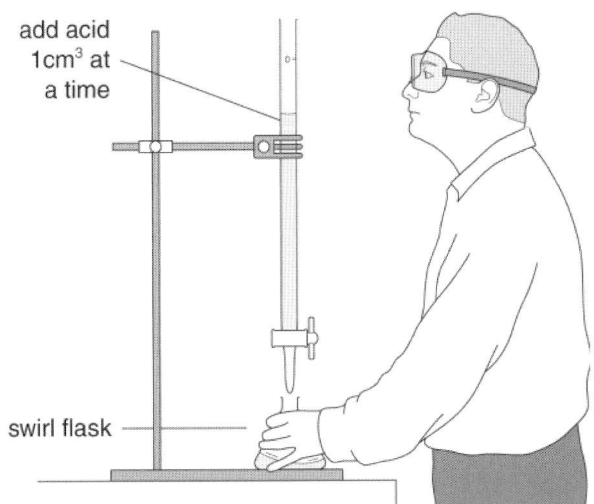

Carrying out the titration.

5. Stand your burette on the bench. Put your beaker of dilute sulphuric acid under the tap of the burette. Turn on the tap and let the dilute sulphuric acid run down until the meniscus is on 0.00 cm^3. The tap at the bottom should now be full of dilute sulphuric acid.
6. You're ready to start titrating! Stand your conical flask of sodium hydroxide solution on a white tile under your burette. Add your dilute sulphuric acid to the flask 1.00 cm^3 at a time and swirl the flask around.
7. Stop adding dilute sulphuric acid when the litmus in the flask turns red. You have now added just slightly too much dilute sulphuric acid, and you have neutralised all your sodium hydroxide solution.
8. Copy this table and fill in the first column.

	First rough try	**Accurate 1**	**Accurate 2**	**Average**
Burette reading at end/cm^3				
Burette reading at start/cm^3				
Amount of acid used/cm^3				

9. Wash out the conical flask, and do the whole titration again (if there is plenty of dilute sulphuric acid left in your burette, you needn't fill it up to the top again). This time, when you get close to the amount of dilute sulphuric acid you used the first time, start adding the dilute sulphuric acid dropwise. This will give you an accurate reading. If you have time, you can do more than one accurate reading and take an average.

Finding the concentration of an acid (continued)

10. You can work out the concentration of the dilute sulphuric acid now. You need to use the equation for the reaction:

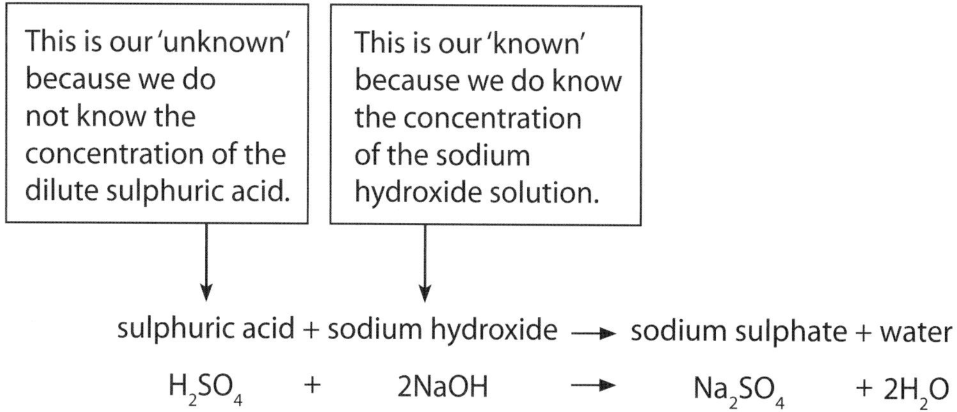

sulphuric acid + sodium hydroxide → sodium sulphate + water

$$H_2SO_4 + 2NaOH \rightarrow Na_2SO_4 + 2H_2O$$

To work out the concentration of our 'unknown' you need to use this formula:

$$C_u = \frac{C_k \times V_k \times N_u}{V_u \times N_k} \text{ mol dm}^{-3}$$

Where:

C_u = concentration of the 'unknown' (in this activity, dilute sulphuric acid) (in mol dm^{-3})
C_k = concentration of the 'known' (in this activity sodium hydroxide solution) (in mol dm^{-3})
V_k = volume of 'known' (you used 25 cm^3 of sodium hydroxide solution)
N_u = number in the equation of 'unknown' (in the equation there is only one H_2SO_4, so this is 1)
V_u = volume of 'unknown' (you need to put in your accurate reading for the dilute sulphuric acid)
N_k = number in the equation of 'known' (there is a '2' before NaOH in the equation, so this is 2)

11. Finish your calculation.

Further work

Sometimes you might need to convert concentrations from mol dm^{-3} (moles per decimetre cubed) to g dm^{-3} (grams per decimetre cubed).

You need to remember that one mole of a substance has the same mass as the relative mass in grams. So, what is the mass of one mole of sodium hydroxide?

formula = NaOH
relative mass = 23 + 16 + 1 = 40
1 mole of sodium hydroxide has a mass of 40 g.

In your experiment, you used a 1.0 mol dm^{-3} sodium hydroxide solution, which is the same as a 40 g dm^{-3} sodium hydroxide solution.

Finding the concentration of an acid (continued)

12. What is the concentration, in g dm^{-3}, of a 0.5 mol dm^{-3} sodium hydroxide solution?

13. a Do a similar calculation to work out the mass of one mole of sulphuric acid.

b What is the concentration, in g dm^{-3}, of 2.0 mol dm^{-3} sulphuric acid?

Questions

Q1 Why do you think battery acid is diluted before titration?

Q2 What information would you need to know before you could work out the concentration of the original battery acid?

Q3 A chemist in a Quality Control laboratory carried out the same experiment for different samples of sulphuric acid. Here are his results.

Volume of 1.0 mol dm^{-3} sodium hydroxide solution used was 25 cm^3.

Sample	Volume of sulphuric acid used/cm^3
1	6.25
2	25.0
3	50.0
4	37.5

Work out the concentrations of each of the acid samples.

Q4 Much more quality control testing of this type is carried out for fine chemicals than for bulk chemicals. Explain why this type of testing adds to the cost of fine chemicals.

Practical activity 17

Name ______________________ Date ______________

Making ammonium sulphate

See 'Making salts' on pages 192–195 in your student book.

Aim

You are going to make a solid sample of ammonium sulphate fertiliser.

Introduction

Ammonium salts are used to make fertilisers because they contain nitrogen. Nitrogen compounds make crops grow bigger and faster. In this activity you will be using dilute sulphuric acid and ammonia solution to make the salt, ammonium sulphate. It is important that the finished salt does not contain acid or ammonia because these are toxic to plants.

This is the equation for the reaction.

ammonia + sulphuric acid → ammonium sulphate

$$2NH_3 + H_2SO_4 \rightarrow (NH_4)_2SO_4$$

You are going to use a titration to make sure you mix the ammonia and sulphuric acid in exactly correct amounts (see Practical Activity 16). You will then make solid ammonium sulphate by evaporating water from the solution you make.

Health and safety

You need to wear eye protection throughout this activity.
Your teacher may ask you to carry out your own risk assessment. You will need to check all the chemicals on 'Student Safety Sheets' and fill in a risk assessment form. Your teacher will need to check your risk assessment before you start your experiment.
Acid and ammonia solution will damage your eyes and skin. If you get any splashes on your skin, wash straight away with lots of water under the tap and send a friend to make sure your teacher knows.

What you need

- eye protection
- 2.0 mol dm^{-3} ammonia solution
- 100 cm^3 measuring cylinder
- conical flask
- litmus indicator solution
- burette and stand
- 1.0 mol dm^{-3} dilute sulphuric acid (irritant)
- beakers and labels
- white tile
- evaporating basin
- balance
- Bunsen burner, tripod, gauze and heatproof mat
- filter paper
- dessicator

What you do

1. Measure out 25 cm^3 of dilute sulphuric acid using the measuring cylinder. Pour the dilute sulphuric acid into the conical flask.
2. Add a few drops of litmus. The acid will turn the litmus red.

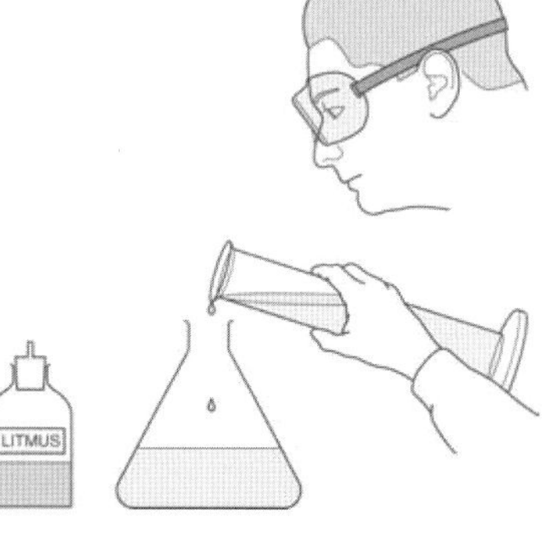

Making ammonium sulphate (continued)

3. Fill your burette with ammonia solution to above the '0.00' line. Remember to put your burette on the floor and make sure the tap is closed.
4. Run some ammonia solution back into the beaker until the meniscus is exactly on the '0.00' line. The bottom of your burette should be full of ammonia solution now.

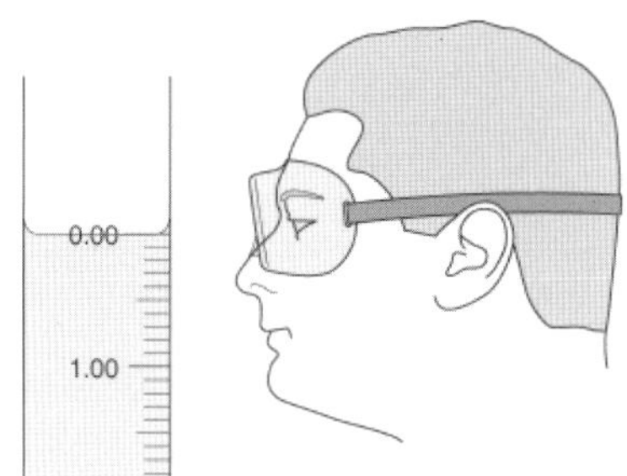

5. Add the ammonia solution to the conical flask, 1 cm^3 at a time, shaking the flask gently. Stop adding the ammonia solution when the litmus goes blue – you have added a little too much now!
6. Write down how much ammonia solution you have used.
7. Now repeat the whole experiment, but this time leave the litmus out. You need to add the same volume of ammonia solution. You have just found out that this is about the right amount to neutralise the acid. (The small amount of extra ammonia will leave the solution as a gas when you heat it in step 9.) You now have a solution of ammonium sulphate in water. You need to evaporate most of the water away and leave your solution to make crystals.

Making solid crystals

8. Weigh an empty evaporating basin. Write down the reading.
9. Pour your solution into the evaporating basin. Evaporate your solution.
   Stop heating when about one-third is left. (Heating dry crystals would damage your fertiliser and produce very dangerous fumes.)
10. Now cover the evaporating basin with a clean filter paper. Leave your solution to stand until your next lesson to form crystals. Your teacher will dry a sample of crystals in a desiccator to show you what effect drying has on the final yield.
11. When your crystals have formed, you need to re-weigh your evaporating basin. Write down the reading.

Working out the yield

12. Now you can work out your 'actual yield' of ammonium sulphate. The 'actual yield' is how much you have made.
13. Look again at the equation for the reaction. You need to use the equation to work out the 'theoretical yield'. The 'theoretical yield' is how much you could have made.

ammonia + sulphuric acid ⟶ ammonium sulphate

$$2NH_3 \quad + \quad H_2SO_4 \quad \longrightarrow \quad (NH_4)_2SO_4$$

Remember that one mole (mol) of a compound is its relative mass in grams. 1 dm^3 = 1000 cm^3.

Making ammonium sulphate (continued)

a Work out the mass of dilute sulphuric acid you started with.
You started with 25 cm^3 of 1.0 mol dm^{-3} sulphuric acid.
1.0 mol of sulphuric acid is the same as the relative mass of sulphuric acid in grams:
$= (2 \times 1) + 32 + (4 \times 16) = 98$
There are 98 g of sulphuric acid in 1 dm^3, so there must be

$$\frac{25}{1000} \times 98 \text{ g in } 25 \text{ cm}^3 = 2.45 \text{ g in } 25 \text{ cm}^3$$

b The relative mass of ammonium sulphate is:
$2 \times \{14 + (4 \times 1)\} + 32 + (4 \times 16) = 132$
From the equation you know that:
1 mol of sulphuric acid makes 1 mol of ammonium sulphate
98 g of sulphuric acid make 132 g of ammonium sulphate
1 g of sulphuric acid makes $\frac{132}{98}$ g of ammonium sulphate

c Finish the calculation to work out your theoretical yield of ammonium sulphate.
2.45 g of sulphuric acid makes $2.45 \times \frac{132}{98}$ g of ammonium sulphate.

14. Work out your percentage yield by using this formula:

$$\text{percentage yield} = \frac{\text{actual yield}}{\text{theoretical yield}} \times 100\%$$

Questions

Q1 **a** Give reasons why your percentage yield is not 100%.
b Your teacher may have dried some ammonium sulphate crystals in a desiccator to remove all the water. What effect will this have on your actual yield?
c Which actual yield value is the most accurate?

Q2 Your teacher will tell you the costs of 1 dm^3 of dilute sulphuric acid and of 1 dm^3 of ammonia solution.
a Work out the cost of making your ammonium sulphate.
b What was the theoretical yield of ammonium sulphate in your experiment?
c Fertilisers are sold in large bags. In theory, how much would 3.3 kg of ammonium sulphate cost?
d What other costs are involved in your experiment that would add to the cost of making ammonium sulphate fertiliser?

Q3 Ammonium sulphate is made on a very large scale. Suggest two ways the reaction to make the salt could be made faster on a large scale.

Name ______________________ Date ______________

Practical activity 18

Investigating resistance

See 'Electrical behaviour' on pages 218–221 in your student book.

Aim

You will gain experience of recording and analysing electrical measurements. You will use your data to plot graphs and describe how variables affect each other.

Introduction

The National Grid Company operates the power lines that supply your electricity. The wires in the power lines are heated as the electricity flows along the wires. This wastes energy. The bigger the resistance of the wires, the more they are heated and the more energy is wasted. Engineers in the National Grid Company need to know about resistance.

Health and safety

You should consider the hazards of using electrical equipment, of working with lengths of wire, including hazards from wires which may be hot when carrying electric current.
You must take action to reduce risk to the minimum possible level.

What you need

- low-voltage d.c. power supply
- ammeter
- connecting wires
- crocodile clips for making connections to wires
- length, about 1 metre, of resistance wire
- metre rule for measuring lengths
- lengths of resistance wire of different diameters
- micrometer for measuring diameters

What you do

1. Set up a circuit like this:

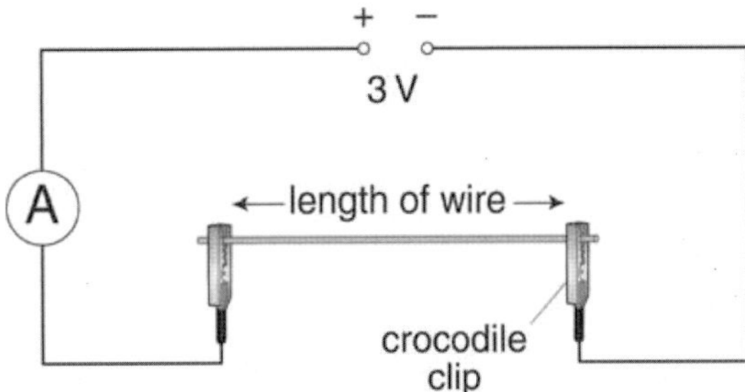

2. Connect a resistance wire between the crocodile clips and measure the length between the crocodile clips. For your first measurement, use a short length of wire (about 10 cm). Do not let the current exceed 1 A.
3. Record the length of wire and the current in a table. Take at least six pairs of measurements, increasing the length of the wire by 10 to 15 cm between each pair of measurements.

Length of wire (cm)	Current (A)

Investigating resistance (continued)

4. Plot a graph with length on the horizontal axis (as the input variable) and current on the vertical axis (as the output variable).
5. a Describe what happens to the current when the length of the wire increases.
   b What happens to the resistance of the wire when its length increases?

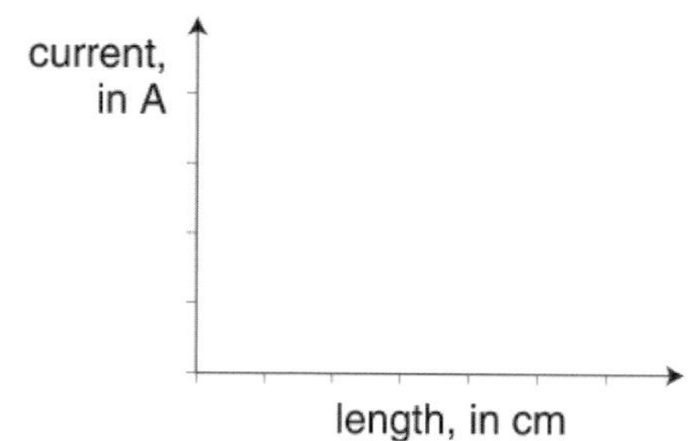

6. a Explain which of the possible variables you kept constant when you were making your measurements. These are some variables to choose from:
   current diameter length material of wire voltage
   b Explain why keeping these constant was important for reaching a reliable conclusion.

7. Repeat the experiment using wires of the same length but different diameters. Measure the diameter of the wires using a micrometer.

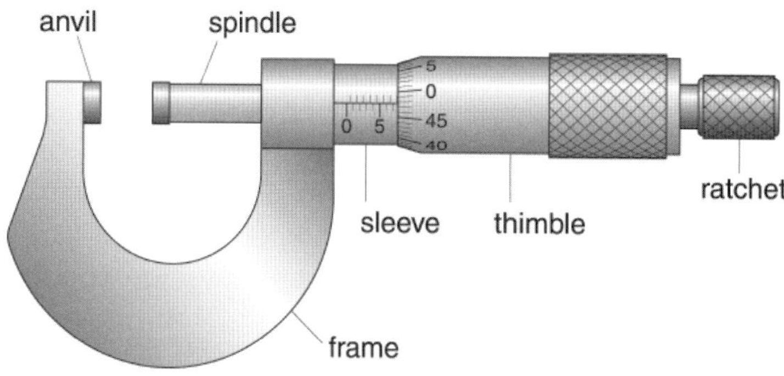

8. Record your results in a new table.
9. Plot a graph with diameter on the horizontal axis and current on the vertical axis.
   a What happens to the current as the diameter of the wire increases?
   b What happens to the resistance of the wire as its diameter increases?

Questions

Q1 Which variable can the National Grid Company control more easily when designing power lines – the length or the diameter of the wire?

Q2 Would you advise the National Grid Company to use cables of large or small diameter?

Q3 Why doesn't the National Grid Company use cables that have:
- a a very small diameter (for example, less than 1 mm)
- b a very large diameter (for example, more than 10 cm)?

Q4 We use a micrometer to make precise measurements. Describe a professional activity for which very precise measurements are important.

Name ________________________________ Date ________________

Practical activity 19

Measuring density

See 'Physical properties' on pages 222–225 in your student book.

Aim

You will gain practice at measurement and at dealing with a range of materials and objects. You will apply ideas about density and will calculate density from your measurements. You will then present your results in a visually attractive and useful way.

Introduction

The electricity cables that run between electricity pylons are just bare wire. The cables must not touch the metal pylons. Insulators are used to hang the cables from the pylons. To the National Grid Company, the density of materials they use for making the cables and the insulators is very important.

$$\text{density} = \frac{\text{mass}}{\text{volume}}$$

We can measure density using the international system of units:

- kilogram for mass (kg)
- cubic metre for volume (m^3)
- kilogram per cubic metre for density ($kg\ m^{-3}$).

However, a cubic metre is a very large volume. In most working situations it is easier to use these units:

- gram for mass (g)
- cubic centimetre for volume (cm^3)
- gram per cubic centimetre for density ($g\ cm^{-3}$).

Health and safety

What hazards are present in this investigation? How will you reduce the risk to a minimum?
You may think that this is a very low hazard activity, but glass should always be handled with care. The sudden snapping of a glass rod, for example, is a well-known cause of cuts to the hand.

What you need

- a selection of glass objects (rod, stopper, microscope slide)
- a selection of copper objects (wire, large washer, length of rod)
- a balance measuring in grams to 1 decimal place (or better)
- ruler
- vernier callipers
- micrometer
- a range of measuring cylinders
- a plastic object used for electrical insulation (for example, part of a plug casing)

Measuring density (continued)

What you do

1. Start with either the glass objects or the copper objects. Measure their masses and record them in a table. Leave space in the table for volume measurements. Also leave space for values of density.
2. You will need to decide which method to use to measure volume. These are your alternatives:

a ruler and calculation

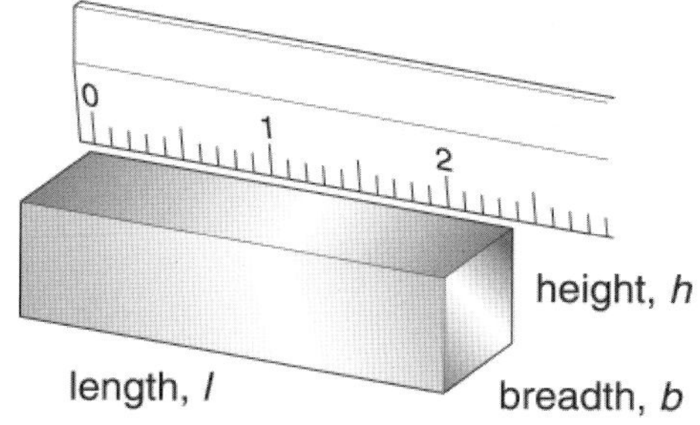

volume = length x breadth x height

volume = $l \times b \times h$

l	=	length
b	=	breadth
h	=	height
r	=	radius

b vernier callipers and calculation: volume = $l \times b \times h$

c micrometer and calculation

volume = π x (radius)^2 x length

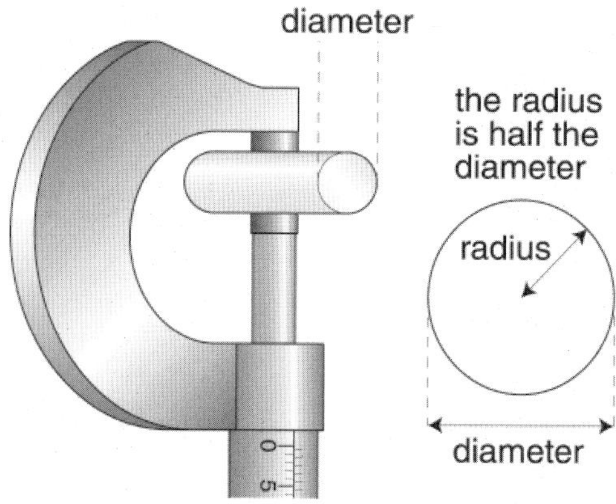

volume = $\pi r^2 \times l$

d measuring cylinder and water

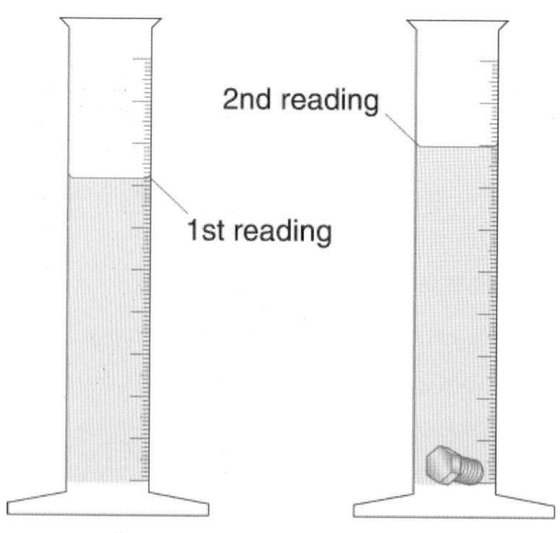

volume = 2nd reading – 1st reading

(remember that 1 ml ≡ 1 cm^3)

Measuring density (continued)

3. Measure the volumes and write them in your table.
4. Calculate the densities and write them in your table.
5. Repeat steps 1 to 4 for the other material (copper or glass). Enter your measurements and density values in a new table.
6. Make a visual presentation of your findings. Use a computer if possible. You should decide whether to use bar charts or another presentation format.
7. Write a summary of your findings. Include an assessment of whether your measurements were always accurate. This is your conclusion.

Further work

8. As an extra challenge, measure the density of a plastic object. Draw sketches to make a storyboard of how you do this. List your measurements carefully so that they are easy for another person to understand.

Questions

Q1 Insulators for hanging cables can be made of glass.

- **a** What is the density of glass in g cm^{-3}, to one decimal place?
- **b** There are different kinds of glass. Did your glass objects all have exactly the same density? Were they made of the same kind of glass?
- **c** What is the density of glass in kg m^{-3}, to the nearest one hundred. (Multiply your answer to part **a** by 1000.)
- **d** Do you think that a pylon would be able to support a cubic metre of glass?
- **e** Do you think that the total volume of the glass insulators that hang from a typical pylon is much less than a cubic metre, about a cubic metre, or much more than a cubic metre?

Q2

- **a** Why doesn't the National Grid Company use copper as the main material for overhead cables?
- **b** Find out what they use instead.

Q3 Use your measurements to say what the density is of:

- **a** a small copper stud
- **b** a length of thick underground cable made of copper.

Q4 All wires have resistance. Do all copper wires have the same resistance?

Practical activity 20

Name ______________________ Date ______________

Energy transfers

Aim

See 'Fuels and generators' on pages 228–233 and 'Cooling systems' on pages 252–255 in your student book.

You will see processes involving transfer, storage and dissipation of energy. You will investigate the amounts of energy that are transferred by heating and by doing work.

Introduction

In most power stations and in CHP (combined heat and power) units like that at Stanhope Street (see pages 228–233 in your student book), hot steam expands and turns turbines. There is a source of energy, there are energy transfers, energy is stored by hot water, the expanding steam does work to turn turbines and energy dissipates to the surroundings.

In a car engine, a gas mixture of air and fuel gains heat energy (from burning) and it expands. This expanding gas pushes pistons to drive the car (see pages 252–255 in your student book).

In both power stations and car engines, we use heated material to provide force.

Health and safety

You will be working with glassware, with clamps that can topple, and with hot water. Assess the hazards and decide what must be done to minimise risk.

What you need

- a plastic syringe with a free-moving plunger (lubricated with petroleum jelly) but with its nozzle blocked with set adhesive
- a clamp to hold the plunger
- a beaker
- a supply of water at room temperature (such as tap water that has been allowed to stand)
- a supply of hot water
- a thermometer
- a rule
- a forcemeter

What you do

This activity is about principles of energy transfers. It involves estimation and comparison. Precise measurements are not needed.

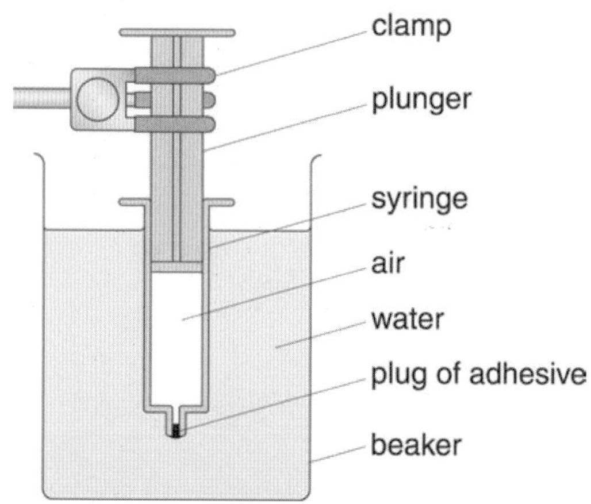

1. Put equal masses of hot water and cool water into two beakers. You need not measure the masses with precision. If you know the volume of the water in cubic centimetres (cm^3) or millilitres (ml) then its mass is the same value in grams (g).

Energy transfers (continued)

2. These are the first measurements you will need to make:

temperature of cool water	=		°C
temperature of hot water	=		°C
temperature difference between hot water and cool water	=		°C
mass of water in either beaker	=		g

energy difference between hot water and cool water = 4.2 × mass (in grams) × temperature difference (in °C)

= .... × ....

= .... J

This is the amount of energy that you would have to give to the cool water to heat it to the temperature of the hot water. It is also the amount of energy that the hot water loses as it cools down to the same temperature as the cool water.

3. Hold the plunger of the syringe in the clamp. Put the lower part of the syringe in the cool water. Leave it there for about one minute. Note the position of the plunger and the cylinder of the syringe.
4. Now transfer the lower part of the syringe to the hot water. Watch carefully what happens. Note the new position of the plunger and the cylinder of the syringe.
5. Estimate the following:

distance moved by plunger/syringe in hot water	=		cm
(you need to divide by 100)	=		m
average force to move plunger/syringe (use the forcemeter to help you to estimate this)	=		N

energy transferred by the air to the plunger/syringe to cause the movement

= work done

= force (in N) × distance (in m)

= .... × ....

= .... J

The energy came from the hot water, was transferred to the air in the syringe and then to the plunger of the syringe.

Energy transfers (continued)

6. Answer these points, to create a 'conclusion' to the activity.
- Some energy from the hot water was used to do work on the plunger/syringe.
- As the hot water cools down, its energy dissipates in the surroundings.

a Write down which one of your energy measurements matches each of these two processes.
b Are your two energy measurements nearly the same, or are they very different? Explain your answer.
c Draw a labelled Sankey diagram to compare your two energy measurements.

Questions

Q1 Hot water holds more energy than cold water.
- **a** What do you use to transfer energy to cold water to make it hot:
  - i) in the lab?
  - ii) at home?
- **b** Water that is hotter than its surroundings cools down. What happens to the extra energy in the hot water?

Q2 In a car engine, an expanding gas does work.
- **a** What makes the gas expand?
- **b** What does the gas push so that the car moves?
- **c** Does all of the energy in the fuel provide useful work?
- **d** What else happens to this energy?
- **e** Why must a car have a cooling system?
- **f** How does the cooling system carry energy away from the engine?

Q3 These questions are about a power station that burns fuel.
- **a** What does the expanding steam push so that the generator moves?
- **b** Does all of the energy of the fuel provide useful work?
- **c** What else happens to this energy?
- **d** How is energy carried from the boiler to the turbines?

Q4 Some power stations do not burn fuel and do not use hot steam. What is it that makes the turbines turn in a hydroelectric power station?

Q5 Explain how heat exchangers are used in:
- **a** combined heat and power units such as that at Stanhope Street
- **b** car passenger heating systems.

Name ______________________ Date ______________

Practical activity 21

Investigating electricity generation

See 'Fuels and generators' on pages 228–233 and 'Nuclear and renewables' on pages 238–243 in your student book.

Aim

You will see how to generate electricity and you will investigate how to make a good generator. You will also compare the inputs and outputs of a working dynamo.

Introduction

All power stations use generators. The coils in a generator turn in a magnetic field.

Health and safety

Consider the equipment you will use and what you will do. Make a list of possible hazards and the actions you will take to minimise risk of harm.

What you need

- a pair of ceramic magnets and U-shaped holder *or* other stong magnet
- lengths of insulated wire with bared ends
- an analogue (needle) centre-zero ammeter with a sensitive scale
- crocodile clips and connecting wires
- a dynamo connected to a lamp

What you do

Firstly you will see if you can use a single wire to generate a current and make the ammeter needle move.

1. Put the magnets into the U-shaped holder with two attracting sides (opposite poles) facing each other.
2. Connect a single wire to the ammeter.
3. Move the wire up and down between the magnets. Watch out for the response of the ammeter.

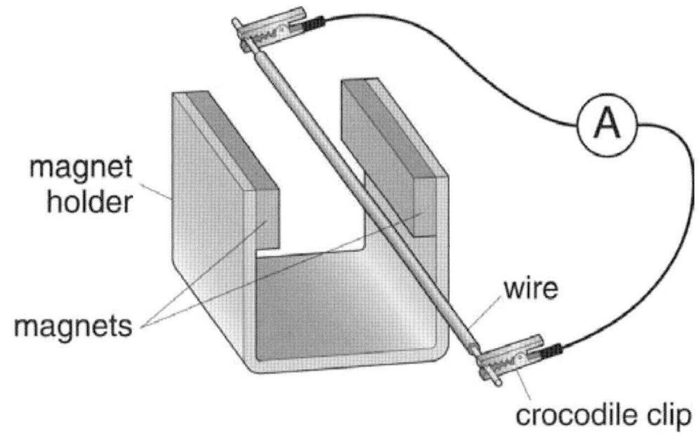

Investigating electricity generation (continued)

4. Use a much longer length of wire to make a 'coil' that will fit over one magnet. Part of the coil needs to be between the magnets. The coil should have at least 20 turns.
5. Move the coil up and down in the magnetic field.
6. Draw the two arrangements. Write down what you saw on the ammeter for each arrangement.

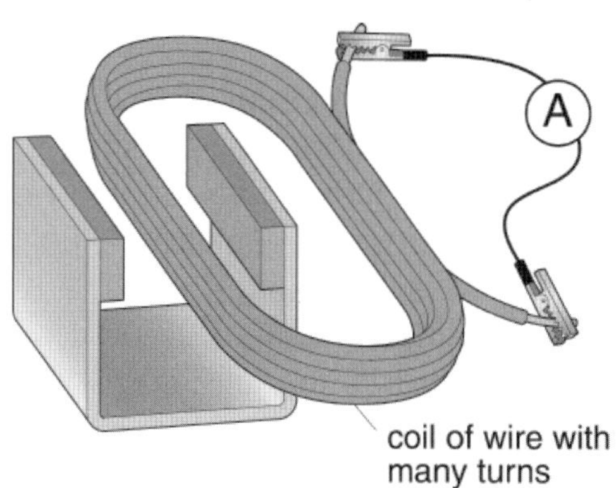

7. Investigate how the direction of movement affects the ammeter response. Write down what you find out.
8. Investigate how the speed of movement affects the ammeter response. Write down what you find out.
9. Try turning a dynamo to create an electrical output. Answer the following questions:
   - what is the source of energy for this electrical generator?
   - what form of energy output does the generator supply?
   - how does energy spread from the system into the surroundings?
   - is this an efficient system?

Questions

Q1 Draw a Sankey diagram for your activity with the dynamo (step 9). Compare this with Sankey diagrams for power stations.

Q2 Describe two ways in which the dynamo transfers energy.

Q3 **a** Explain why, even if we could make a dynamo that could turn without friction, we would still have to supply energy to it to make it generate electricity and light a lamp.

b If we connected several lamps in parallel so that they all lit up brightly, then the dynamo would become harder to turn at speed. Explain why.

Q4 Why would a dynamo which experienced a lot of friction be less efficient than a low-friction dynamo?

Name ______________________________ Date ______________

Practical activity 22

Constructing an electronic system

Aim

See 'Electronic life support' on pages 262–266 and 'Digital information' on pages 270–273 in your student book.

You will follow a standard circuit diagram to construct a simple electronic monitoring system. You will then be offered the challenge of designing and constructing your own system.

Introduction

Electronic systems can monitor many kinds of physical conditions, including temperature, light intensity, pressure and movement. Electronic monitoring and control of physical conditions is useful in many areas of work, including healthcare, horticulture, security and manufacturing production.

Health and safety

Identify the hazards associated with practical work with electronic circuits, and take action to minimise risk. Care is needed when using boiling water.

What you need

- 6 V power supply
- connecting wires
- a selection of resistors
- red LED
- thermistor
- transistor
- test tube and beaker

What you do

1. Set up a circuit using a thermistor, voltage divider, transistor and LED, using resistors as shown.
2. Note the effect on the LED of setting the variable resistor to its different settings.
3. Set the variable resistor so that the LED is *just* on. Now place the thermistor in a test tube and fill the test tube with boiling water. Note what happens to the LED.
4. Draw a large circuit diagram. Show and label the power supply, the input components, the processor and the output components.
5. Write an explanation of how the circuit responds to its surroundings. What could you use the circuit for?

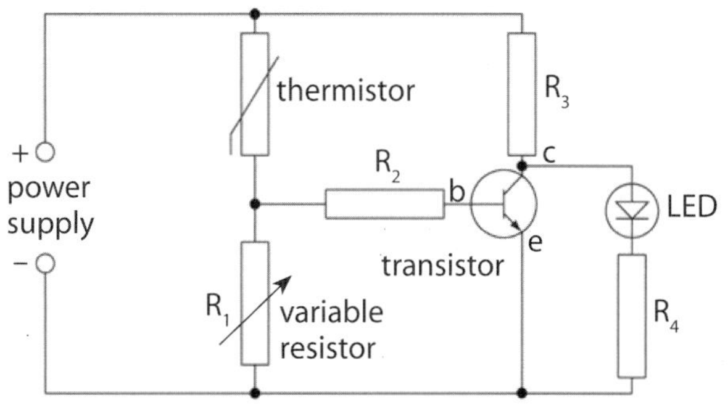

resistor values: R_1 = 0–10kΩ
R_2 = 1kΩ
R_3 = 100Ω
R_4 = 220Ω

Constructing an electronic system (continued)

6. Use your knowledge and experience to think of a working situation where people want to use an electronic system to monitor and control physical conditions. You will find some ideas in the student book. Choose one kind of system. Decide what components you would use for monitoring the physical conditions.
7. Decide what components you would use for controlling the physical conditions.
8. A block diagram shows simple blocks or boxes, and can be used in the place of a detailed circuit diagram. Draw a block diagram, with blocks showing each of power supply, input components, processor and output components. Add notes to describe each of the four blocks in more detail.
9. Write an advertising leaflet directed at the people who might want to use an electronic system like yours. Use a computer to create a two-sided leaflet with a professional appearance.

Questions

Q1 Describe a use for electronic monitoring and control in:

- **a** healthcare
- **b** horticulture
- **c** security
- **d** manufacturing production.

Q2 **a** Why does a voltage divider need two resistors?

- **b** In a monitoring circuit, what must at least one of the resistors do?

Name ______________________ Date ______________

Practical activity 23

Investigating a lever

See 'Lifting' on pages 274–277 and 'Gears' on pages 278–281 in your student book.

Aim

You will make a practical exploration of the behaviour of a simple machine, comparing the inputs with the outputs.

Introduction

Machines, such as bikes, pulleys for lifting and simple levers, all have 'inputs' and 'outputs'. They have input and output forces, input and output distances (or velocities), and input and output energy.

We make comparisons of inputs and outputs by division calculations:

	Input	Output	Output/input
Force	effort	load	mechanical advantage $= \frac{\text{load}}{\text{effort}}$
Distance	input distance	output distance	velocity ratio $= \frac{\text{output distance}}{\text{input distance}}$
Energy	energy input	useful energy output	efficiency $= \frac{\text{useful energy output}}{\text{energy input}}$

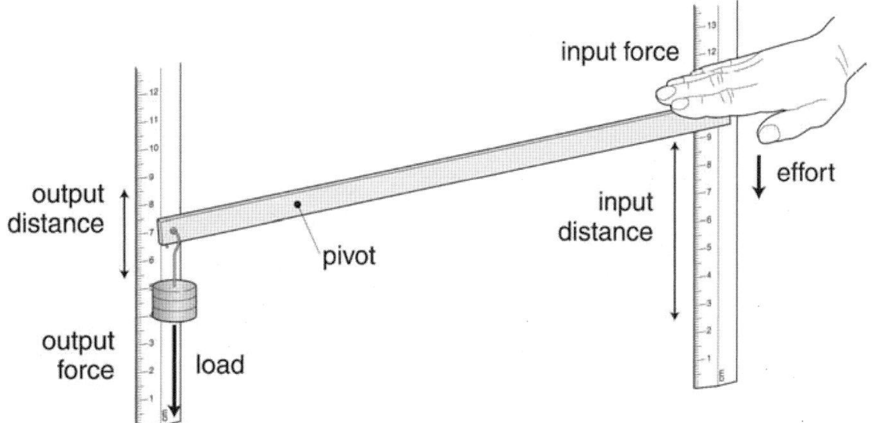

You can apply force to a lever using a forcemeter. The forcemeter then measures the size of the effort for you. You can lift different loads. The force needed to lift a 100 gram mass (100 g) is about 1 newton (1 N).

Health and safety

If using a clamped nail as a pivot, then its point must be covered by a cork to prevent accidental injury.
Clamp stands can topple when carrying significant weight. You must clamp the base to the bench.
Carry out a formal risk assessment, listing the hazards and the action you will take to minimise risk of harm.

Practical activity 23

Investigating a lever (continued)

What you need

- metre rule to act as a lever
- pivot, with clamp stand if necessary
- a G-clamp to fix the clamp stand to the bench
- masses, for use as loads, up to 800 g
- hanger with hook or other suitable means to hang loads from the lever
- forcemeter
- two metre rules to measure distances

What you do

1. You might find it useful to make a mass-force conversion table. 100 g ≡ 1 N, 200 g ≡ 2 N, 300 g ≡ 3 N, and so on …
2. Set up your lever. Try some different arrangements of efforts and loads acting on your lever.
3. Make a sketch to show the lever arrangement when it is acting as a force multiplier. Show the positions of the pivot, load and effort. (A lever acts as a force multiplier when the load is bigger than the effort.)
4. Make a sketch to show the lever arrangement when it is acting as a distance multiplier. Show the positions of the pivot, load and effort. (A lever is acting as a distance multiplier when the distance moved by the load is bigger than the distance moved by the effort in the same time.)
5. Make measurements of the sizes of loads and efforts, using the forcemeter. Also measure the distances they move. Write your measurements in a table like this:

Effort, in N						
Load, in N						
Mechanical advantage = $\frac{\text{load}}{\text{effort}}$						
Input distance, in cm (distance moved by effort)						
Output distance, in cm (distance moved by load in the same time)						
Velocity ratio = $\frac{\text{output distance}}{\text{input distance}}$						
Energy input = effort × input distance						
Useful energy output = load × output distance						
Efficiency = $\frac{\text{useful energy output}}{\text{energy input}} \times 100\%$						

6. Which arrangement of the lever gives the bigger mechanical advantage?
   Which arrangement of the lever gives the bigger velocity ratio?
   Write a conclusion to explain your answers.

Investigating a lever (continued)

Further work

You could repeat your experiments using a pulley system. If you do this, your conclusion should explain why the efficiency is lower than for a simple lever.

Questions

Q1 How are levers used in:

- **a** a car 'tyre and exhaust' centre
- **b** a kitchen
- **c** an office?

Discuss your answers and give at least one example of use of levers.

Q2 Why aren't levers used in place of cranes at construction sites?

Q3
- **a** Why is a lever very efficient?
- **b** What factors affect the efficiency of a machine such as a crane or a bicycle?

Q4
- **a** What was the relationship between mechanical advantage and velocity ratio in your investigation? (In what way does one of them change when the other one changes?)
- **b** Would you expect to see this same relationship in other machines?

Using a light microscope

See 'Cells' on pages 26–29 in the student book.

Background This is a good practical to do after you have studied Topic 2.1 'Cells' in the student book, early in the course. It also covers the microscopy needed for Unit 1. This practical gives practice in the use of the microscope, which would be useful before doing the Unit 1 assessment in Assignment 2 'Microscopy'.

Health and safety
A risk assessment has to be carried out for each practical (see page III:2).
Students should be instructed to carry the microscope only by the main limb.
Students should wash their hands immediately after preparing the slide if pond water is used.
Teachers should be aware that pond water may carry Weil's disease.
Broken cover slips and slides must be removed immediately as they can easily cause cuts.
Iodine solution can stain skin and clothes and is irritating to the eyes.
If you choose to use daylight as the light source, students must not focus directly on the Sun.

Skills See the summary tick list on page III:3.

Materials Although this practical activity is best carried out by individual students, the number of available microscopes will determine the number of groups. The materials listed here are for one group of students.

- eye protection
- light microscope
- printed diagram of microscope (copied from Reference sheet 20 'Parts of a light microscope' (page I:33)
- lamp, if required
- transparent plastic ruler
- slides and cover slips
- dropping pipette
- mounted needle
- pond water containing algae
- iodine solution
- variety of prepared slides

Notes
- Teachers should be aware that there are many different types of light microscopes. Instructions on their use may differ slightly to those on the student sheet.
- It is a good idea to have the microscopes placed around the laboratory before the start of the lesson, as this will avoid students carrying them.
- At the end of the lesson the microscopes should be examined. The removable lenses have been known to disappear ...
- Teachers may wish to lead their students through a structured lesson; microscope instructions can otherwise be rather long-winded.
- Reference sheet 3 'Working with microscopes' (page I:8) and Reference sheet 19 'The microscope' (an OHT, page I:32) are available.
- Most schools have been provided with a video set-up for a microscope. This would be an ideal time to use it.

Answers
Q1 Information on electron microscopes can easily be found in on-line encyclopaedias.
Q2 Students may suggest:
- hospitals, to examine blood
- brewing industry, to examine yeast cultures
- public health laboratories, to examine life in water supplies
- food industries, to look for contamination
- police, to look at information from crime scenes.

Osmosis in living tissue

See 'Diffusion' on pages 30–33 and 'Osmosis' on pages 34–37 in the student book.

Background Students should have a basic understanding of diffusion and osmosis. In particular, they need to know that small water molecules will pass through the partially permeable membranes of living cells, but larger sugar molecules will not.

Health and safety
A risk assessment has to be carried out for each practical (see page III:2).
Students need to take care when using knives, cork borers and syringes. Count them all out and count them back in again.
Avoid too much movement of students when the water is being boiled.

Skills See the summary tick list on page III:3.

Materials The materials listed are for one group of students.

- 1 potato
- kitchen knife
- cork borer
- beaker
- Bunsen burner, tripod, gauze, heatproof mat
- 2 Petri dishes
- 5 cm^3 syringe
- strong sugar solution (about 100 cm^3 will be enough for a whole class)

Notes
- Medium-sized hard potatoes work best. Have extra potatoes available since pupils often push the cork borer completely through the potato. The sugar solution will then leak out.
- A sucrose solution containing 342 g dm^{-3} will be satisfactory, although any strong sugar solution will produce good results.
- Experiments need to be kept in a safe place overnight and labelled with the student's name or group number.

Results The level of the sugar solution in the pit of the living (raw) potato will rise. Sometimes the sugar solution overflows. The level of the sugar solution in the pit of the boiled potato will drop as the sugar solution seeps away. The living half of the potato shows osmosis, while the boiled half will not because the cell membranes have been destroyed.

Osmosis occurs because there is a difference in sugar concentration between the sugar solution and the cell contents, as well as between the cell contents and the surrounding water. Water enters the outer layer of potato cells by osmosis. These cells then become more dilute than the next cells, so water passes from cell to cell. On reaching the pit, the water passes through the cell membranes, leaving the potato cells, and goes into the sugar solution.

Answers
Q1 The depth of the pit or the volume of sugar solution in each pit could be measured before and after the experiment. A very large potato and a narrow deep pit should be used.
- A very strong sugar concentration (golden syrup) would speed up the experiment.
- The time taken to double or halve the depth of sugar solution could be recorded. (Ask students to find a sugar concentration that would give good results in 24 hours.)

Q2 **a** The cells of the trout would lose water by osmosis, causing them to shrink and collapse. The body of the fish would become soft.
b The cells of the plaice would gain water by osmosis, causing them to swell and burst. The body of the fish would swell up. If the fish were alive when placed in the wrong surroundings, they would both die quickly.

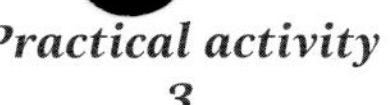

Starch in leaves

See 'Photosynthesis' on pages 52–55 and 'Exchange of gases' on pages 56–59 in the student book.

Background Some teachers may prefer to use this activity before studying the topics on photosynthesis. It may be helpful to demonstrate the action of iodine solution on starch before the students carry out the activity.

Health and safety
A risk assessment has to be carried out for each practical activity (see page III:2).
All Bunsen burners must be turned off before the ethanol is issued to students.
Care must be taken when boiling water. Some teachers may prefer to use a water bath.
Ethanol must not be poured down the sink.
Iodine solution can stain skin and clothes and is irritating to the eyes.

Skills See the summary tick list on page III:3.

Materials The materials listed are for one group of students.

- eye protection
- a geranium leaf with parts covered in cooking foil kept in place by tape
- a variegated leaf from a geranium plant
- a geranium leaf which has been kept without carbon dioxide
- a geranium leaf that has been exposed to light and carbon dioxide
- large beaker
- Bunsen burner, tripod, gauze and heatproof mat
- ethanol (each group needs about 20 cm^3 of ethanol)
- forceps and tongs
- small beaker to fit inside the large beaker
- white tile
- iodine solution in a dropping bottle

Notes

- The geranium plants must be prepared at least one week prior to the activity.
- *Plant 1*: part of a leaf is covered with cooking foil held in place by tape. The leaf may need support from a clamp stand.
- *Plant 2*: a variegated geranium plant.
- *Plant 3*: one leaf is inserted into a flask containing soda lime, which absorbs carbon dioxide. Sode lime is corrosive. Avoid skin contact. Do not create any inhalable dust when pouring out the chemical.
- *Plant 4*: a geranium leaf that will act as a control.
- Teachers may wish each group to have a complete set or they may distribute the different leaves to different groups and collate the final results.
- The geranium plants should be well watered and kept in direct sunlight for good results.

Starch in leaves (continued)

Results After adding iodine solution, the results and conclusions should be as follows:

Treatment	Result	Conclusion
partly covered leaf	shaded parts, no change exposed parts, black colour	starch production needs light
variegated leaf	original green areas, black colour original yellow/white areas, no change	starch production needs green colour (chlorophyll)
leaf without carbon dioxide	whole leaf, no change	starch production needs presence of carbon dioxide
light and carbon dioxide	whole leaf, black colour	used as a control

Answers

Q1 Boiling bursts the cells that contain the starch grains, otherwise the iodine solution will not be in contact with the starch.

Q2 Plants need light and water for photosynthesis. Lack of water will also cause wilting (see 'Osmosis' on pages 34–37 of the student book). Photosynthesis involves enzyme action with an optimum temperature of about 20 to 25°C. Open windows allows good air circulation, with plenty of carbon dioxide for photosynthesis, and prevents overheating.

Looking at chromosomes

See 'Cells dividing' on pages 42–45 and 'Inheritance' on pages 46–49 in the student book.

Background It would be best to do this activity after the pupils have done Practical activity 1 'Using a light microscope'. This activity needs light microscopes fitted with low and high power objective lenses. This is another practical that uses a light microscope and so links with Unit 1, Assignment 2 'Microscopy'. Note that mitosis and meiosis are only needed for Higher Tier.

Health and safety *A risk assessment has to be carried out for each practical activity (see page III:2).*
Care is required when students are using the corrosive acetic orcein stain and hydrochloric acid. Goggles (not safety glasses) should be worn when handling the stain. Teachers may prefer to provide the watch-glass already containing these chemicals.
Care is required when using a scalpel; count them out and count them in.
If you use daylight as the light source for the microscopes, students must not focus directly on the Sun.

Skills See the summary tick list on page III:3.

Materials The materials listed are for one group of students.

- goggles
- a growing root from a broad bean or an onion
- tile
- scalpel
- watch-glass
- acetic orcein stain mixed with hydrochloric acid (corrosive)
- oven or hot plate or Bunsen burner, tripod, gauze and heatproof mat
- forceps
- 2 glass slides and 1 cover slip
- glass rod
- filter paper
- light microscope

Notes

- Broad beans can be grown in a peat-type compost or in a beaker containing sawdust. You may need to start growing the beans about four weeks before the activity.

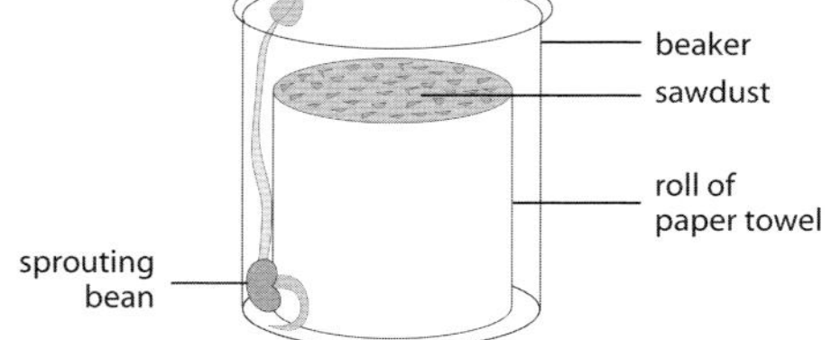

Looking at chromosomes (continued)

- Most schools have been provided with a video set-up for a light microscope. This is an activity where it would be extremely useful, since some pupils find it difficult to use a high power lens without breaking the cover slip.
- A pre-prepared slide that shows chromosomes could be shown to pupils before they start their attempt.
- Some teachers may prefer to first demonstrate the whole procedure to their class.

Answers

Q1 The chromosomes are inside nuclei inside cells. Breaking the cell walls with hydrochloric acid will make the chromosomes easier to see.

Q2 If the dividing cells were further away from the root tip, the delicate root hairs would be torn off as the tip and root hairs just behind it were forced through the soil.

Q3 The examination of chromosomes would show whether the baby was a boy or girl. It would also show chromosome abnormalities, such as Down's syndrome.

Plants, animals and their environment

See 'Photosynthesis' on pages 52–55, 'Exchange of gases' on pages 56–59 and 'Aerobics' on pages 120–123 in the student book.

Background

This is a simple activity, but it requires a good understanding of both photosynthesis and respiration. Teachers may prefer to do it after both topics have been covered. This practical could be a useful introduction to using living organisms. Reference sheet 4 'Monitoring living organisms' (page I:9) reminds students of the care needed when using animals for practical activities.

Health and safety

A risk assessment has to be carried out for each practical activity (see page III:2).
If plant and animal material has been obtained from a pond or lake, it is important that students wash their hands after using this material. Teachers should be aware that pond water may carry Weil's disease.
Care must be taken if lamps are used since they will become hot during use.

Skills

See the summary tick list on page III:3.

Materials

The materials listed are for one group of students. Because of the number of tubes that need to be set up, groups of three or even four students could work together.

- 100 cm³ measuring cylinder
- supply of distilled water
- rack to hold the boiling tubes
- 8 boiling tubes, labelled A, B, C, D, E, F, G and H
- water snails, or other pond animals
- *Elodea*, or other pond plants
- 8 rubber bungs to fit the boiling tubes
- lamp
- 2 cm³ disposable syringe
- bromothymol blue indicator
- boiling tube rack

Notes

- Any pond animals, such as *Asellus* or *Gammarus*, can be used instead of snails.
- It may be helpful to have two sets of groups, with one group setting up the 'light' experiments and the other group setting up the 'dark' experiments.
- Teachers may wish to demonstrate the colour changes of bromothymol blue before the students use it. It is important to stress that the students should be looking at comparisons between results.
- Students must not breathe out over the tubes when they are setting them up. The indicator is very sensitive to carbon dioxide.
- Students may need assistance in interpreting their results.

Plants, animals and their environment (continued)

Results

Tube A: yellow, acidic, snails producing carbon dioxide
Tube B: green/blue, neutral or slightly alkaline, plants using up carbon dioxide
Tube C: yellow/green, slightly acidic, plants using up carbon dioxide but animals producing some

Tube D: no change in colour, no plants or animals present
Tube E: yellow, acidic, snails producing carbon dioxide
Tube F: green/yellow (different from B), slightly acidic, plants not using up carbon dioxide
Tube G: yellow (different from C), acidic, both plants and animals producing carbon dioxide
Tube H: no change in colour, no plants or animals present

A number of conclusions are possible:
- animals give out carbon dioxide in both light and dark conditions
- plants produce carbon dioxide in the dark
- overall, plants do not produce carbon dioxide in the light (they use up the carbon dioxide they produce)
- when plants and animals are together in the light, the carbon dioxide produced by the animals is used by the plants.

This activity can be adapted if pH meters or a dissolved oxygen meter is available.

Answers

Q1 Tubes D and H are set up without plants or animals to act as controls for comparison. They show that neither the indicator nor distilled water are affected by light or dark conditions.

Q2 High acidic or alkaline conditions would kill most plants and animals. They would indicate an imbalance between plants and animals or acid rain pollution.

Exercise and recovery rates

See 'Asthma' on pages 116–119 and 'Aerobics' on pages 120–123 in the student book.

Background Pulse recordings may have been taken at Key Stage 3. This activity uses the same technique to look at recovery rates, which indicate fitness levels. This is a useful practical, relating 'How your body works' to Unit 3 'Monitoring living organisms'. The assessment for this section of the specifications is provided in Unit 3, Assignment 14 'The production of yoghurt from milk'.

Health and safety
A risk assessment has to be carried out for each practical activity (see page III:2).
Teachers can check the medical history of students prior to the lesson via school records, Form Tutors or the PE department. Be tactful!
Care is required when students are exercising. The recording partner should be close by, to steady the exerciser and/or equipment if necessary.
No violent, aggressive or competitive exercises should be undertaken.

Skills See the summary tick list on page III:3.

Materials The materials listed are for one group of students.

- stopwatch or stopclock
- low chair, stool, step or exercise bike
- computer and data logging software, if available
- pulse sensor and interface unit, if available
- graph paper

Notes

- Students may need guidance about how to use a stopwatch.
- A group of two, one recording and one exercising, usually works well since those students with a medical history (or just lethargic) can still take part by recording the data.
- A joint lesson with the PE department could work well.
- A set of good results will show the over-compensation of pulse rate by initially returning to below the normal rate before returning to normal. This can be discussed with the students.
- The experiment can lead to further discussions about what is meant by fitness, and other ways of measuring it.
- Reference sheet 2 'Presenting data' (page I:6) contains information on plotting graphs.
- An anomalous result could happen by mis-counting the pulse or mis-timing through incorrect use of the stopwatch. The result is ignored when the graph is plotted. It would not be feasible to repeat a single recording, the whole investigation may need repeating.
- Reference sheet 7 'The Harvard fitness test' (page I:12) could be used to see how fit students are.

Answers

Q1 Her heart muscles become more powerful, so the pulse becomes stronger. The heart rate (and pulse rate) can then decrease since more oxygen and food are being supplied to muscles.

Q2 Different muscles are being used for different purposes. Therefore, recovery rates will at first be longer.

Racing mustard and cress

See 'Photosynthesis' on pages 52–55 in the student book.

Background Students will have some basic information about seed germination from Key Stage 3. This practical builds on this information, in order to plan a procedure to harvest seedlings. It provides an ideal introduction for students to understand what is required for 'Monitoring living organisms' in Unit 3. Assignment 14 'The production of yoghurt from milk' is provided to assess this part of the specification.

Health and safety
A risk assessment has to be carried out for each practical activity (see page III:2).
Students must be instructed not to eat any material prepared in a laboratory. It is also a good idea to have notices, with this information, prominently displayed for this lesson.

Skills See the summary tick list on page III:3.

Materials The materials listed are for one group of students.

- 6 boiling tubes labelled A, B, C, D, E and F
- boiling tube rack
- measuring cylinder or syringe to measure out 5 cm^3 of water
- cotton wool
- mustard seeds
- cress seeds
- access to a refrigerator
- thermometer
- access to an oven, incubator or water bath

Notes

- Reference sheet 4 'Monitoring living organisms' (page I:9) could be a useful introduction.
- There are many different varieties of mustard and cress seeds on sale, so an exact answer cannot be provided. There is at least one variety of cress seeds which specifically states that it has the same germination time as mustard seeds, so avoid these!
- Some seeds are treated with a fungicide so that they do not start to decay when planted. Although the seedlings are not meant to be eaten, it would be better to ensure that the seeds are not coated with fungicide. They will be safer for students to handle.
- Students may be surprised at the temperature of the refrigerator, they often believe it should be 0°C.
- Make sure that the water bath is at least 10°C warmer than the temperature of the cool room.
- Students may also note that the seedlings in the refrigerator will eventually grow tall and yellow due to lack of light.
- To avoid repetition, teachers may find it easier to arrange that half the class groups use cress seeds and the other half use mustard seeds.
- Students may find it difficult to plan to an exact day because only three temperatures are investigated. This gives an opportunity for them to suggest improvements.
- The cotton wool in the mouth of the boiling tubes will prevent the seeds from drying out, as well as preventing contamination.

Answers

Q1 A small business will probably buy in the seedlings. To prepare them for sandwiches, sterile equipment and work surfaces are required. Precautions, such as washing hands, special clothing and hair coverings, handling food with disposable gloves/tongs, must also be followed.

Q2 The full Health and Safety regulations can be found when visiting local shops or the school canteen.

Long live cabbage

See 'Fermentation' on pages 82–85 in the student book.

Background

This is a good activity to encourage accurate observations. Students also need to construct a table to record their results. This activity can be used to trigger off a class discussion about food preservation.

Health and safety

A risk assessment has to be carried out for each practical activity (see page III:2).
Students must be instructed not to eat any material prepared in a laboratory. It is also a good idea to have notices, with this information, prominently displayed for this lesson.
Kitchen knives can be sharp. Students should be warned about their use.
Teachers may wish to demonstrate the safe use of knives in chopping material such as cabbage. The knives should be returned immediately after use. Count the knives out and count them in.

Skills

See the summary tick list on page III:3.

Materials

The materials listed are for one group of students.

- about half a small cabbage
- kitchen knife
- chopping board
- salt
- balance (to weigh cabbage and salt)
- 2 large beakers
- spatula
- cling film
- pH indicator paper

Notes

- This activity could be carried out in the Technology department, using their kitchen knives and chopping boards. If kitchen knives and chopping boards are borrowed from the Technology department and used in a Science laboratory, care must be taken to follow Health and Safety guidelines before the equipment is used again for food use.
- Students may not immediately realise what caused the lowered (acidic) pH. The salt will cause juices to be released from the cabbage. These juices will contain some sugars. Lactic acid bacteria will very quickly convert these sugars into acids, preserving the cabbage. This alters the texture, colour and smell of the cabbage. The salt also prevents the growth of other bacteria, so the cabbage does not rot.
- This activity can be extended by placing a piece of both samples of cabbage onto agar in sterile Petri dishes. The dishes are taped down and incubated at 22°C for three days. The agar from the salted cabbage will show little bacterial activity, the other cabbage will show a lot.

Answers

Q1 The equipment used in a school laboratory will not be sterile and so the food samples can easily be contaminated during preparation and during the investigation. Strict rules and regulations exist for anyone preparing food for sale. Students can further extend this activity by visiting a food factory or shop preparing and selling food to discover these rules and regulations.

Q2 **a** Plums can be bottled in a sugary solution.
b Eggs can be boiled and then pickled in vinegar.
c Milk can be boiled or turned into yoghurt.

Microorganisms, milk and yoghurt

See 'Types of microorganism' on pages 86–89 and 'Preserving food' on pages 94–97 in the student book.

Background

This simple activity would be an ideal introduction to investigating bacterial activity. It could be used as a lead up to Practical activity 10 'Investigating the action of antibiotics' and Unit 3, Assignment 13 'The production of yoghurt from milk'.

Health and safety

A risk assessment has to be carried out for each practical activity (see page III:2).
All Health and Safety guidelines for experiments involving bacteria should be followed. For more information, see the 'Safety' section in Practical activity 10 'Investigating the action of antibiotics'.
Work surfaces must be cleaned with disinfectant after use.
Students must wash their hands with soap and water before and after the activity.
Students must not taste the milk or yoghurt used in this activity.
Reference sheet 6 'Aseptic techniques' (page I:11) will alert students to the precautions needed when handling microorganisms in the laboratory, which they will need for practical activities and assignments where bacterial cultures are used.

Skills

See the summary tick list on page III:3.

Materials

The materials listed are for one group of students.

- 4 sterile test tubes and labels
- test tube rack
- sterile syringes or sterile pipettes
- sample of UHT milk
- sample of sterilised milk
- sample of fresh yoghurt
- sample of boiled yoghurt
- resazurin dye
- cling film
- water bath or oven or incubator

Notes

- Reference sheet 6 'Aseptic techniques' (page I:11) is available to use with students.
- Since colour changes are involved, the results are somewhat subjective.
- After use, the equipment should be sterilised using autoclavable bags in an autoclave. Disposable items, still in their bag, can then be disposed of in a dust bin. Liquids can be flushed down a toilet.

Answers

Q1 **a** Fresh yoghurt will show the greatest microbial activity.
b Sterilised milk will show the least.

Q2 The easiest way to prolong the life of fresh milk is to keep it cool in a refrigerator. It can be boiled, but this alters the taste.

Investigating the action of antibiotics

See 'Antibiotics' on pages 102–105 in the student book.

Background

This activity requires good manual dexterity and the ability to follow instructions exactly, so it would be a good idea to leave it until students have carried out a range of other activities. The safe culture of microorganisms will be needed for Unit 1, Assignment 3 'Investigating microorganisms'.

Safety is paramount when using bacteria cultures. Teachers should first read all the instructions, and then carry out the activity themselves to ensure they understand the techniques.

Health and safety

A risk assessment has to be carried out for each practical activity (see page III:2).
Equipment suppliers usually supply guidelines with their products, for example Philip Harris supplies 'Safe handling of micro-organisms'.
Work surfaces should be disinfected after use.
Students must wash their hands with soap and water after using bacteria cultures.
Bunsen burners should be turned off immediately after use.
After use, the Petri dishes, Universal bottles and inoculating loops must be dealt with safely. Autoclavable bags can be used to hold the equipment during sterilisation by autoclaving. Any disposable equipment, in a separate bag, can then be disposed of in a dustbin.

Skills

See the summary tick list on page III:3.

Materials

The materials listed are for one group of students.

- disinfectant
- Universal bottle containing nutrient agar
- water bath, set at 95°C
- tongs
- heatproof mat
- inoculating loop
- Bunsen burner
- culture of *E. coli*
- sterile Petri dish
- forceps
- mast ring
- sticky tape
- marker pen
- incubator or oven, set at 30°C

Notes

- Reference sheet 6 'Aseptic techniques' (page I:11) is available to use with students.
- The Universal bottles, nutrient agar, sterile Petri dishes, inoculating loops, *E. coli* cultures and mast rings can be obtained from scientific suppliers such as Philip Harris. The Universal bottles can be supplied complete with 15 cm^3 nutrient agar. If preferred, teachers can make up their own, using an autoclave or pressure cooker.
- Teachers are strongly advised to first demonstrate the procedure to their students. The students should then carry out a dummy run using ordinary bottles and water for practice.
- The method on the 'Student Sheets' teaches the techniques for transferring bacteria. However, only a small number of *E.coli* will be transferred to the agar. You may wish to demonstrate and teach the use of an inoculating loop, but then pour at least 1 cm^3 of *E.coli* broth culture into a Petri dish, then pour in the agar and mix together. This will ensure that sufficient bacteria are transferred.
- Students must follow the instructions in point 4 very closely. Heating the tip of the inoculating loop first will cause any liquid to splutter and bacteria may be spread around the lab. This technique also needs to be followed in point 8.

Investigating the action of antibiotics (continued)

Answers

Q1 **a** The equipment must be sterile to avoid contamination of the nutrient agar and the growth of other bacteria.
b The tilted Petri dish cover allows space to pour the agar in, but prevents airborne contamination.
c The taped down Petri dish cover also prevents contamination. More importantly, it prevents the accidental removal of the cover and escape of the bacteria.

Q2 Contamination would lead to incorrect results, and possibly to wrong treatment of the patient. It could cause delays in treatment since the tests would have to be repeated.

Elements, compounds and mixtures

See 'Elements from the Earth' on pages 146–149 and 'Compounds from the Earth' on pages 150–155 in the student book.

Background

This experiment is designed to reinforce ideas about elements, compounds and mixtures that the students have covered in the student book. Some students may have carried out similar experiments at Key Stage 3, but these ideas are central to the course, and so bear repetition.

Health and safety

A risk assessment has to be carried out for each practical (see page III:2).
Eye protection needs to be enforced.
The usual precautions of working with dilute acids and Bunsen burners need to be considered. When the iron/sulphur mixture is heated, there is a risk of the sulphur vapourising and igniting at the mouth of the tube. Toxic and corrosive sulphur dioxide would be formed. To minimise this risk, insert a plug of mineral wool in the mouth of the tube. Sulphur dioxide can also trigger asthma attacks.
Adding acid to iron sulphide gives off hydrogen sulphide gas. Students need to be asked to put their test tubes of acid and iron sulphide to stand in a fume cupboard or they need to be told to empty them quickly through a sieve into a sink to stop the reaction.

Skills

See the summary tick list on page III:3.

Materials

The materials listed are for one group of students.

- eye protection
- iron filings
- sulphur
- 3 Petri dishes with lids
- hand lens or magnifying glass
- magnet wrapped in cling film (keep the cling film on during the experiment)
- 3 test tubes and test tube rack
- beaker of water (labelled)
- bottle of dilute hydrochloric acid (labelled) (0.4 mol dm^{-3})
- heatproof test tube and holder
- mineral wool
- Bunsen burner and heatproof mat
- spatulas, glass rods and dropping pipettes
- Student Safety Sheets

Notes

- Samples of fool's gold would provide stimulus for the early discussion. Images of fool's gold and samples of the elements copper, iron and sulphur can be used at the end of the lesson to discuss the ideas learned. You could also use samples of minerals and the elements they contain.
- Wrapping the magnets in cling film stops them becoming fouled with iron filings.

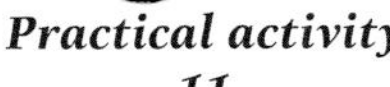

Elements, compounds and mixtures (continued)

The main ideas to reinforce are:
a elements contain only one type of atom
b mixtures can be separated
c compounds contain atoms of two or more elements chemically bonded together
d elements cannot be easily separated out from compounds – chemical reactions are needed to do this, it is not possible to use simple physical methods (discuss electrolysis and the energy needed in a blast furnace)
e reactions that result in compounds being made are not easily reversed.

Answers

Statement	Compounds	Mixtures
Contain more than one type of atom	✓	✓
Can be easily separated		✓
Atoms are chemically bonded	✓	
Making this is a reversible change		✓
Making this is a permanent change	✓	
Can be found in the Earth's crust	✓	✓

Q1 Separation by magnet or by using difference in densities.
Q2 No, the properties of the elements are not affected.
Q3 No, they are permanently bonded together. (Small amounts of un-reacted iron filings sometimes separate off – this should be explained to the students.)
Q4 Appearance – no separate grains of grey and yellow
magnet – not possible to separate iron by magnet
water – all sinks
acid – bubbles of very foul smelling gas
Q5 **a** Iron is attracted to a magnet, other substances are not.
b Fool's gold is a compound – the atoms are bonded together and cannot be separated.
c Iron dissolves in acid – the surface dissolves away leaving a clean surface underneath.

Making saline solutions

See 'Salt from rock salt' on pages 156–159 in the student book.

Background

These experiments are designed to give students an early taste of quantitative work in chemistry. They will need these skills later when they carry out titrations and measure yields accurately. Students make and test an accurate concentration of salt solution. This supports the specification for Unit 1 for working with known concentrations of solutions.

Health and safety

A risk assessment has to be carried out for each practical (see page III:2).
Eye protection needs to be worn.
The usual precautions of working with Bunsen burners need to be considered.
Do not allow students to heat the solution to dryness, or the salt crystals will spit.

Skills

See the summary tick list on page III:3.

Materials

The materials listed are for one group of students.

- eye protection

Experiment 1

- photocopies of instructions that the students can write on
- watch-glass
- salt (sodium chloride)
- weighing balance
- 2 beakers
- water
- 100 cm^3 measuring cylinder
- dropping pipette
- glass rod
- distilled water in a wash bottle

Experiment 2

- measuring cylinder
- evaporating basin
- weighing balance
- Bunsen burner, tripod, gauze, heatproof mat

Notes

- The most important skill being practised here is accurate working.
- The technique of 'washing' will probably be best demonstrated. The early work adapting the experiment for accuracy could be carried out as a class discussion.
- It would be interesting for the students to see some examples of commercial saline solutions, for example contact lens aerosol saline, diarrhoea remedies ('Dioralyte' sachets have accurate values for sodium chloride on the back, with instructions for dilution 'in cooled boiled water' which might stimulate interesting discussion).

Answers

Q1 Costs involved: energy for heating to make steam, to boil or distil water; training people and paying wages; specialised equipment needed.
Q2 3 g in 100 cm^3 = 30 g dm^{-3}.
Q3 Dilute 10 times by measuring 100 cm^3 and accurately diluting to 1 dm^3 (or measuring 10 cm^3 and diluting to 100 cm^3).
Q4 The main reason is moisture content. The original salt used to make the saline solution probably contains moisture. The evaporated salt may well be drier, so will weigh 'lighter'. If the evaporating basins are left for a few days and re-weighed, the mass may be different.
Q5 Sterility will be checked (possibly by culture growth on agar plates).

Setting up a distillation apparatus

See 'Crude oil to petrol' on pages 166–169 and 'More about molecules' on pages 200–203 in the student book.

Background

Students need to know about distillation to fulfil the requirements of Unit 1. This activity is designed to be covered as a demonstration and a 'cut and stick' activity. This is based on the assumption that there may not be enough apparatus available for all students to carry out the distillation themselves.

This demonstration covers simple distillation, for Unit 1. If there is time, the fractional distillation of crude oil could be demonstrated separately.

Health and safety

A risk assessment has to be carried out for each practical (see page III:2).
Eye protection should be worn by the teacher and by students during the demonstration.

Skills

See the summary tick list on page III:3.

Materials

For the demonstration:

- eye protection
- 'seawater' (can be made by shaking tap water with sand and salt)
- Bunsen burner (and matches)
- round-bottomed flask with thermometer
- condenser
- conical flask
- anti-bumping granules

For students:
The materials listed are for one group of students.

- scissors and glue
- photocopy of Reference sheet 21 'Distillation' (page I:34)
- A3 paper to make a poster

Notes

- Reference sheet 22 'Distillation apparatus' (page I:35) shows the assembled apparatus, with the parts labelled.
- Bring to the attention of the students:
  a the seawater boils and the steam is pure water; other impurities are left in the flask
  b the thermometer shows a temperature of 100°C; this is the boiling point of water, and shows that the steam entering the condenser is pure water
  c the cooling water flowing through the condenser flows in at the bottom and out at the top to make sure the condenser is full of water
  d the steam condenses in the condenser and pure water drips out of the end.

Answers

Q1 Boiling point should be 100°C.
Q2 Salt/sodium chloride and sand, traces of seaweed and so on.
Q3 Too expensive due to cost of energy.
Q4 Depends on design of still.

Investigating dyes

See 'Bulk and fine chemicals' on pages 170–173 in the student book.

Background Chromatography is one of the separating techniques needed for Unit 1. This practical activity should also raise awareness about the detail and care needed for handling fine chemicals.

Health and safety *A risk assessment has to be carried out for each practical (see page III:2).*
The students should be discouraged from eating the sweets.

Skills See the summary tick list on page III:3.

Materials The materials listed are for one group of students.

- filter paper
- pencil
- ruler
- capillary tubes
- samples of food dyes
- water
- beakers
- spills
- paper clips
- hairdryer
- small paintbrushes
- coloured sweets

Notes

- Food dyes should be 'bottled' supermarket food dyes, preferably several different colours from the same manufacturer. Note that darker colours work best.
- The coloured sweets can be 'Smarties' or 'Minstrels' or similar sugar-coated sweets. Again, darker colours work best.
- It is probably a good idea to demonstrate how to set up the chromatogram.
- The rectangles of filter paper need to be wide enough to put several spots on and tall enough so they extend above the beaker. The filter paper should be able to either be clipped to a spill or curled into a tube without touching the sides of the beaker.
- The beakers need to be 50, 100 or 250 cm^3, depending on the size of paper used.
- The hairdryer will need to have passed the portable electrical appliance test, especially if brought in from home.

Answers

Q1 **a** 2
b Green, blue (and red).
c Blue and yellow.
Q2 $R_f = \frac{6}{10} = 0.6$
Q3, Q4 Answers depend on students' own results.
Q5 Run a chromatogram using known banned dye. Run a chromatogram of the food colouring. Compare R_f values or compare positions to identify banned dye.

Investigating rates of reaction

See 'Bulk and fine chemicals' on pages 170–173 in the student book.

Background This practical activity reinforces ideas met in the student book. It also prepares students for the chemical discussion they will need to include in their preparation work for Unit 3. It leads to Unit 3, Assignments 9, 10 and 11.

Health and safety *A risk assessment has to be carried out for each practical (see page III:2).*
Eye protection needs to be worn.
The usual precautions of working with dilute acids need to be considered.

Skills See the summary tick list on page III:3.

Materials The materials listed are for one group of students.
This practical activity is in three parts.

Experiment 1

- eye protection
- limestone chips
- balance
- conical flask with delivery tube
- 100 cm^3 measuring cylinder
- trough or large beaker
- 2.0 mol dm^{-3} hydrochloric acid in a labelled bottle (irritant)
- stopwatch or stopclock
- plastic sieve
- graph paper

Experiments 2 and 3
As for Experiment 1, plus

- ice
- water bath at 40°C
- small limestone chips
- powdered limestone

Notes

- Students will need help in managing the apparatus.
- If possible, a 'trial run' should be carried out before the students carry out their experiment. A 250 cm^3 measuring cylinder is recommended for use to collect the gas, but this should be checked. Different grades of calcium carbonate chips react very differently. It is strongly recommended that the gas collection apparatus is demonstrated by the teacher first.
- The technique of warming to constant temperature in a water bath will also need to be shown. A boiling tube will be fine for holding the acid in the water bath.
- If time is short, the different variables can be investigated by different groups of students. The results can then be collated on OHTs to share for graph purposes.

Answers

Q1 Cost of energy/fuel.
Q2 **a** Use hot, concentrated acid. Could crush the cement before treating the bricks.
b Workers need to wear protective gloves, boots and goggles. They need to beware of acid spills on skin. Any spills should be cleaned up by diluting with lots of water.

Finding the concentration of an acid

See 'Putting numbers into industry' on pages 178–181 in the student book.

Background Students will need to have studied the section 'How much cement can we make?' in Topic 3.8 'Putting numbers into industry' (pages 168–171 in the student book) for practice at calculations before trying this experiment. Students may also need reminding of Key Stage 3 information about acids and alkalis. This practical uses titration procedures and leads to Unit 1, Assignment 5 'Quantitative analysis'.

Health and safety *A risk assessment has to be carried out for each practical (see page III:2).*
The alkali used is corrosive, so goggles (not safety glasses) should be worn.
Students must rinse any splashes or spillages immediately.
Students need to be told to fill burettes below eye level.

Skills See the summary tick list on page III:3.

Materials The materials listed are for one group of students.

- goggles
- measuring cylinders (students will need to choose which one is best)
- labelled bottle of 1.0 mol dm^{-3} sodium hydroxide solution (corrosive)
- 2 conical flasks
- bottle of litmus indicator
- burette in a clamp stand
- labelled bottle of 'unknown' dilute sulphuric acid (this should be 1.0 mol dm^{-3} but the concentration must not be known by the students) (irritant)
- funnel
- white tile
- Student Safety Sheets for sodium hydroxide and sulphuric acid

Notes

- Part of Reference sheet 10 'Amounts of substance' (page I:20) will be of use in explaining concentration.
- The sodium hydroxide solution does not need to be accurately assayed. If possible, a trial run of the titration should be carried out first. This should give a burette reading of close to 12.5 cm^3 for the 'unknown' sulphuric acid.
- Put out a range of measuring cylinders, from 10 cm^3 to as big as possible. The students are asked to choose which one is best.
- The student sheet details the procedures. Students will need to have the titration techniques demonstrated first and will need support with first attempts at calculations.

Finding the concentration of an acid (continued)

Answers

Student Safety Sheets: 1 mol dm^{-3} sodium hydroxide is corrosive; 1 mol dm^{-3} sulphuric acid is irritant. Spillages should be cleaned by rinsing with lots of water.

Titration calculation: This will depend on the student's own titration result, but should give a value close to 1.0 mol dm^{-3}. (Students may be interested to consider that half the volume of acid was needed because of the ratio of reacting quantities in the equation – sulphuric acid is a dibasic acid.)

Q1 Safety ideas: less harm to people or less potential damage to the equipment. Accuracy ideas: need too much sodium hydroxide and so on.

Q2 You would need to know the dilution factor, for example how much acid and how much water were mixed.

Q3

Sample	Volume/cm^3	Concentration of sulphuric acid/mol dm^{-3}
1	6.25	2
2	25.0	0.5
3	50.0	0.25
4	37.5	0.33

Q4 Costs involved include: training of staff, wages of staff (quality control testing is time-consuming), need to provide labs and equipment, cost of rejected batches.

Making ammonium sulphate

See 'Making salts' on pages 192–195 in the student book.

Background This experiment closely follows the activity in 'Making salts' (pages 192–195 in the student book), and leads to Unit 3, Assignment 10 'The production of a fertiliser'.
Students need to be reminded about how to carry out titrations – this is probably best demonstrated. The mathematics involved in calculating theoretical yields is very complex – students will need a lot of support with this.
You will also be using ideas from the following topics in the student book: 'Bulk and fine chemicals' (pages 170–173), 'Making ammonia' (pages 174–177) and 'Putting numbers into industry' (pages 178–181).

Health and safety
A risk assessment has to be carried out for each practical (see page III:2).
Eye protection should be worn throughout.
Students need to be reminded to fill burettes below eye level.
The usual procedures for the safe handling of acids and alkalis should be followed.
If students use more than a tiny excess of ammonia when they start to evaporate the solution, the lab will fill with pungent ammonia fumes. Be vigilant for this and stop heating at once.
Make sure students do not heat the solution to dryness, as the crystals will decompose to give toxic and corrosive fumes.

Skills See the summary tick list on page III:3.

Materials The materials listed are for one group of students.

- eye protection
- 2.0 mol dm^{-3} ammonia solution
- 100 cm^3 measuring cylinder
- conical flask
- litmus indicator solution
- burette and stand
- 1.0 mol dm^{-3} dilute sulphuric acid (irritant)
- beakers and labels
- white tile
- evaporating basin
- balance
- Bunsen burner, tripod, gauze and heatproof mat
- filter paper
- desiccator

Notes

- Titration techniques, including safe burette filling, should be demonstrated.
- Students will need support with carrying out the calculations.
- Students will need a safe place to store their samples until the next lesson.
- At least one sample should be dried in a desiccator, to compare dried and damp crystals. The main reason for odd actual yields here is due to water in the final product.

Answers

Q1 **a** Concentrations may not be exactly accurate, loss of product during transfer between conical flask and evaporating basin, water content of crystals may give falsely high actual yield.
b Actual yield will appear lower.
c The dried crystals give a more accurate value.
Q2 **a** Costs will depend on values used. Ask your technician for current prices.
b 3.3 g
c 1000 × answer to part **a**.
d Energy costs for evaporation process, labour costs, equipment costs.
Q3 Use higher concentrations of reactants, use a higher temperature.

Investigating resistance

See 'Electrical behaviour' on pages 218–221 in the student book.

Background The specifications require that students investigate, quantitatively where possible, the factors which affect the resistance of a particular wire. This activity provides step-by-step guidance for an investigation involving length. The activity then leaves students to follow the same pattern themselves for an investigation involving diameter. Instruction is provided on the specific skill of measurement of small distances. This practical leads to Unit 1 assessment in Assignment 6 'Electrical properties'.

Health and safety
A risk assessment has to be carried out for each practical (see page III:2).
Low-voltage power units are safe if correctly maintained and checked before use.
Loose wire ends can present an eye hazard. Eye protection may be needed.
Wires may become hot. Minor burns are possible if student procedures do not take account of this.

Skills See the summary tick list on page III:3.

Materials The materials listed are for one group of students.

- low-voltage d.c. power supply (3 V)
- ammeter, 0–1 A
- connecting wires
- crocodile clips for making connections to wires
- about 1 metre of 0.27 mm diameter constantan wire
- metre rule for measuring lengths
- lengths of constantan resistance wire of different diameters (for example, 0.56 mm, 0.38 mm, 0.19 mm)
- micrometer for measuring diameters

Notes

- This activity provides an opportunity for considering issues of precision of measurement, fair tests, and the validity of conclusions for given experimental results.
- Reference sheet 1 'Using measuring instruments' (page I:3) will be of use in this activity.

Answers

Q1 Diameter
Q2 Large
Q3 **a** Very thin wires would have high resistance and would snap easily.
b Very thick wires would be too heavy to support on pylons.
Q4 Mechanical engineering where mechanical components must fit tightly together, or other examples.

Measuring density

See 'Physical properties' on pages 222–225 in the student book.

Background Students have compared wires by measurement of resistance. They now compare objects by measurement of density. They learn that all objects of the same material have the same density. That is, density is a property of a material, whereas resistance is a property only of a particular sample. This practical leads to Unit 1 assessment in Assignment 7 'Physical properties'.

Health and safety *A risk assessment has to be carried out for each practical (see page III:2). This is an opportunity to tutor students on safe handling of glassware, including how to deal with broken glass.*

Skills See the summary tick list on page III:3.

Materials The materials listed are for one group of students.

- a selection of glass objects (rod, stopper, microscope slide)
- a selection of copper objects (wire, large washer, length of rod)
- a balance measuring in grams to 1 decimal place (or better)
- ruler
- vernier callipers
- micrometer
- a range of measuring cylinders
- a plastic object used for electrical insulation (for example, part of a plug casing)

Notes

- In this work, students are given responsibility for their own layout of data. Some students will need more coaching than others on this. Reference sheets 1 'Using measuring instruments' (page I:3), 2 'Presenting data' (page I:6) and 13 'Comparing materials' (page I:24) will be of use here.
- Able students are given the opportunity to solve problems associated with finding the density of an irregular object that is less dense than water.
- The questions deal with ideas suitable for all students. However, there are also opportunities for able students to discuss uncertainties of practical measurement and relevance of these to reliable conclusions, for example in deciding whether the glass objects are all made of the same kind of material.

Answers

Q1 **a** 2.5 (± 0.1) g cm^{-3}.
b Students need to decide whether any differences in their density values are due to experimental error or to real density differences. Teacher guidance and discussion will be valuable here.
c 2500 (± 100) kg m^{-3}.
d A cubic metre of glass has a mass of about 2500 kg, or 2.5 tonne. (Weight is 25 000 N; there is no need to introduce this complication here but the word 'weight' should not be used for measurements in grams, kilograms or tonnes.) A pylon could probably support this, but there would be problems in windy weather…
e Less than a cubic metre.
Q2 **a** Copper is dense and too soft. Long, heavy lengths of cable would stretch due to their own weight.
b Aluminium is much less dense and is used instead, wrapped round a steel core.
Q3 **a** 8.9 g cm^{-3}
b 8.9 g cm^{-3}
Q4 No. Resistance, unlike density, is a property of a particular sample, not a property of a material.

Energy transfers

See 'Fuels and generators' on pages 228–233 and 'Cooling systems' on pages 252–255 in the student book.

Background 'Source', 'transfer', 'storage' and 'dissipation' are key language in understanding energy and energy issues. This practical activity provides experience of observing the related processes and applying the language.

Health and safety *A risk assessment has to be carried out for each practical (see page III:2). Apart from the adapted syringe, materials used are standard laboratory items.*

Skills See the summary tick list on page III:3.

Materials The materials listed are for one group of students.

- a plastic syringe with a free-moving plunger (lubricated with petroleum jelly) but with its nozzle blocked with set adhesive
- a clamp to hold the plunger
- a beaker
- a supply of water at room temperature (such as tap water that has been allowed to stand)
- a supply of hot water
- a thermometer
- a rule
- a forcemeter

Notes

- A 10 ml syringe will show significant expansion if well lubricated. Individual syringes should be tested for freedom of movement before students make their observations. It may be that your plastic syringes will not work well in this experiment. Proper gas syringes will work well, but may need more care when they are used.
- Students must realise that precise measurement of quantities, such as average force acting during expansion, may be very difficult, and in such cases estimates are useful.
- The syringe nozzles must be blocked by Araldite well in advance of the lesson. Ensure that the plunger is at a point in the syringe so that there is enough trapped air for a significant expansion. The plunger should be lubricated with petroleum jelly.
- Blocking the nozzle with sufficient Araldite also acts to discourage abuse of the syringes. The length of the nozzle should be reduced, such as to prevent fitting of needles.
- It is suggested that the plunger is held in the clamp so that the syringe itself is free to move. It is the relative motion that is important.

Answers

Q1 **a** i) Bunsen burner or electric heater. ii) Kettle or cooker.
b The energy spreads into the surroundings. It dissipates.
Q2 **a** The exploding fuel, the sudden heating.
b A piston.
c No.
d It causes heating, the energy dissipates.
e To carry away excess energy, so that the engine temperature is not too high.
f Water is heated in the engine, travels to the radiator, where some of its energy passes to the air around, so that it cools down. The water then returns to the engine.
Q3 **a** Turbine blades.
b No.
c It causes heating, the energy dissipates.
d Water is heated by the boiler, it travels to the turbines as steam.
Q4 Moving water.
Q5 **a** To transfer energy from the hot water (that needs to be cooled down) to a local system of water in pipes that provides hot water and heating to houses.
b To transfer energy from hot water in the engine cooling system to air that can flow through the passenger compartment.

Investigating electricity generation

See 'Fuels and generators' on pages 228–233 and 'Nuclear and renewables' on pages 238–243 in the student book.

Background This activity gives students the opportunity to investigate the generation of electricity. The emphasis is on issues of energy input and energy output, which are applicable to all generators.

Health and safety *A risk assessment has to be carried out for each practical (see page III:2), although the risks are minimal in this activity.*

Skills See the summary tick list on page III:3.

Materials The materials listed are for one group of students.

- a pair of ceramic magnets and U-shaped holder *or* other strong magnet
- lengths of insulated wire with bared ends
- an analogue (needle) centre-zero ammeter with a sensitive scale
- crocodile clips and connecting wires
- centre-zero galvanometer (for demonstration)
- a dynamo connected to a lamp

Notes

- The response of an ordinary ammeter may be too small to see when using ceramic magnets and a single wire. A centre-reading galvanometer might need to be used in a follow-up demonstration.
- Lengths of wire should be cut and stripped at their ends ready for student use.
- As an additional activity, students could construct a 'Westminster motor' and observe its behaviour as a simple generator.

Answers

Q1 Sankey diagram showing input and outputs. For dynamo input is movement, output is electrical. For power station input is thermal, output is electrical.
Q2 Electrically – to the lamp, thermally – friction.
Q3 **a** Energy must be supplied to the dynamo to match the energy that the dynamo supplies to the lamp.
b The energy output is bigger, so the energy input must also be bigger.
Q4 A dynamo with a lot of friction wastes more energy, which it transfers thermally to its surroundings; the energy dissipates.

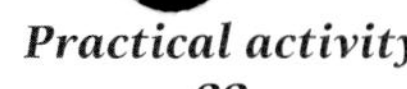

Constructing an electronic system

See 'Electronic life support' on pages 262–266, and 'Digital information' on pages 270–273 in the student book.

Background This activity gives students a guided activity, using a block diagram and a circuit diagram. They are then asked to develop their own ideas for a monitoring and controlling sytem. This practical leads to Unit 3 assessment in Assignment 12 'The design and construction of a nightlight'.

Health and safety *A risk assessment has to be carried out for each practical (see page III:2). Risks in this activity are minimal, but the power supply should be visually checked before use. Care is needed when using boiling water.*

Skills See the summary tick list on page III:3.

Materials The materials listed are for one group of students.

- 6 V power supply, mounted with 4 mm sockets
- lots of 4 mm leads in a variety of colours
- resistors (see 'Notes' below), mounted with 4 mm sockets
- standard red LED, mounted with 4 mm sockets
- thermistor (see 'Notes' below), mounted with 4 mm sockets
- transistor (see 'Notes' below), mounted with 4 mm sockets
- small test tube
- 250 cm^3 beaker
- access to boiling water

Notes

- R_1 is a 10 kΩ linear potentiometer arranged as a variable resistor. Students need to be provided with some indication of the settings for maximum and minimum resistances.
- R_2 is a 1 kΩ resistor.
- R_3 is a 100Ω resistor.
- R_4 is a 220Ω resistor.
- The thermistor is a 4.7 kΩ at room temperature general purpose ntc disc thermistor, with leads soldered to 4 mm sockets.
- The transistor needs to be a RFP2N10L MOSFET, in a plastic component box with 4 mm terminals. Label the terminals c, b and e, as shown in the diagram. Using a MOSFET instead of a BJT saves a lot of problems in the long run. MOSFETs are relatively indestructible, and matching them to the thermistor is easy.

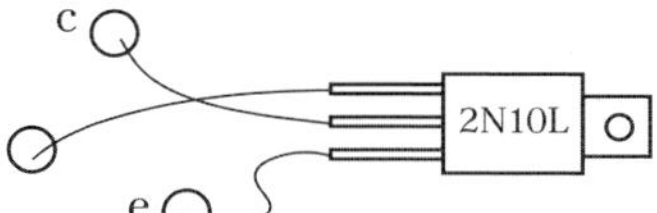

- In the diagram, the MOSFET is shown as viewed from the top, looking at the printed label.

Constructing an electronic system (continued)

Answers

Q1 Examples include:
- **a** Intensive care, monitoring of temperature.
- **b** Monitoring of greenhouse temperature, soil moisture, soil pH.
- **c** Intruder detection using light beams and LDRs.
- **d** Container fill levels can be monitored using light beams.

Q2
- **a** The two resistors share the total voltage. The voltage across a single resistor would be simply the supply voltage.
- **b** At least one resistor must change, in response to a physical change in its environment.

Investigating a lever

See 'Lifting' on pages 274–277 and 'Gears' on pages 278–281 in the student book.

Background

The activity uses the simple lever to allow students to examine issues of force ratios, distance ratios and energy ratios. As an extension activity, the same steps can be used to investigate the behaviour of a pulley system. This allows a comparison of efficiency between a simple lever and a pulley system.This practical leads to Unit 3 assessment in Assignment 11 'The construction of a lifting system'.

Health and safety

A risk assessment has to be carried out for each practical (see page III:2).
Where clamped nails or pins are used as pivots, their points must be covered by corks to prevent injury.
Clamp stands should be prevented from toppling.

Skills

See the summary tick list on page III:3.

Materials

The materials listed are for one group of students.

- metre rule to act as a lever
- pivot, with clamp stand if necessary
- a G-clamp to fix the clamp stand to the bench
- masses, for use as loads, up to 800 g
- hanger with hook or other suitable means to hang loads from the lever
- forcemeter
- two metre rules to measure distances

Notes

- Students can find it difficult to measure the input and output distances. These measurements often need two people working together.

Answers

Q1 Examples can include:
- **a** Many tools, such as spanners, as well as levers for tyre removal.
- **b** Many tools, such as scissors, tap handles.
- **c** Tools such as scissors, door handles.

Q2 Levers would take up too much space, might be more hazardous.

Q3
- **a** There is little friction in a lever, so little energy lost by heating.
- **b** Friction between moving parts.

Q4
- **a** When one increases, so does the other.
- **b** This relationship applies to all machines.

Section IV Assignments

OCR

Portfolio building – Guidance for teachers

Introduction

Units 1 and 3 are internally assessed and moderated by the awarding body. The work that you will need to set for your students is listed in the assessment evidence grids for Units 1 and 3.

Your students will need to present evidence of the following:

Unit 1:
- Health and safety in scientific workplaces
- Microscopy
- Microorganisms
- Qualitative analysis
- Quantitative analysis
- Electrical properties
- Physical properties

Unit 3
- Using science at work
- Making a chemical product, 1
- Making a chemical product, 2
- Mechanical machines
- Electrical or optical devices
- Growth/development/responses of a living organism

Setting assignments

You will need to set assessment activities or assignments to help your students to develop the evidence required. The *Folens Applied Science Teachers' File (2nd edition)* contains a full set of assignments for your awarding body. You may use these as provided, alter parts to suit your own school resources, or substitute your own choice of work.

You will wish to guide your students as to the work required in order to develop their evidence for assessment. You should be aware that the higher grades need some evidence of independent work by the students. You will use your professional judgement to decide how much direct guidance each of your students needs.

When each assignment is completed, you must assess it against the criteria set by your awarding body. The assessment criteria may change over time, so it is essential to refer back to the assessment evidence grids for your specification, provided by the awarding body. Please be aware that the criteria set by the different awarding bodies are significantly different. You need to make sure that you guide your students to produce the evidence specified by your chosen awarding body. The Folens assignments are tailored to the requirements of your awarding body, and contain specific guidance on what to look for when assessing work.

Portfolio building – Guidance for teachers (continued)

Moderation

Your students' work will be required for moderation at the end of the course. It is important that every student completes and retains work against each of the requirements. This can best be done by building a portfolio.

Your moderator will expect to find each piece of work for each student quickly and easily. You can help this to be done by ensuring that only formally assessed work is filed in the portfolio. Class notes, class work, other practicals and homework exercises should not be included unless they contribute to the assessed activities. Please discourage the inclusion of downloaded or photocopied materials, unless they have been used directly. Your moderator will not be pleased to wade through material that is not relevant to meeting the specifications. Moderation involves reading the students' work. It is worth emphasing to students it is quality not quantity that is required.

Types of evidence

The work of your students for Units 1 and 3 is subject to moderation by your awarding body. The evidence of what each student has achieved must, therefore, be recorded and presented clearly to the moderator.

The majority of the evidence required relates to practical work and how well each student was able to carry it out. The evidence of having carried out a practical exercise falls into three main categories:

- evidence of process – what the student did and the standard to which they did it;
- evidence of product – what the student produced;
- supporting evidence to show understanding of scientific principles, where required.

All three categories can be delivered through a variety of methods. Evidence for successful completion of a practical assignment could be as follows.

Student's practical report

It is not necessary to produce a full report in the form of introduction, plan, practical procedures, observations and measurements, data processing, conclusions and evaluation for each exercise. The report should, however, be of a form that will show accurately what was done.

The assignment briefs in the Folens *Teachers' File* contain a series of forms to guide the students to record their evidence. These forms will, ideally, be completed as the practical work progresses. This will avoid the need for lengthy 'writing up' periods at the end of each assignment. Where detailed practical procedures are provided, they could be included as an appendix to the report; it is not necessary for each student to copy out such procedures.

The report will also include evidence of the product of the work. This will often be in the form of diagrams. Examples include drawings of microscopic observations or diagrams of equipment used. In the latter case, drawings of standard equipment, such as beakers and so on are rarely informative. Note that photocopies of articles from textbooks are rarely valid evidence: these are <u>secondary evidence</u>, and the philosophy of Units 1 and 3 is that each student will produce his/her own <u>primary evidence</u>. You may wish to include photographic evidence of the process or product of practical work. Video evidence will rarely be appropriate to the types of activity required for Units 1 and 3.

The use of customised record forms, as recommended by Folens, reduces the task of reporting the practical procedures used. This should enable the students to

Portfolio building – Guidance for teachers (continued)

concentrate their thoughts and efforts on thinking about what their results mean and drawing appropriate conclusions from them. These are the higher level skills that students will need to demonstrate to access the higher grades. The teaching programme should develop these interpretative/evaluative skills to enable each student to achieve to the maximum of their potential.

Schools may wish some students to give presentations rather than a written report for some assignments. A presentation may be a valid form of evidence, but records must be provided for moderation purposes. Appropriate records might be evidence of preparation, PowerPoint sequences, handouts and so on. Some form of confirmatory material should support the student evidence. This could be an audiotape, a videotape or a witness statement. In the latter case, the statement should be sufficiently detailed to confirm which criteria have been met, and at what level.

The teachers' supporting evidence

Teacher support is required both for evidence of product and for evidence of process.

The products of the practical work, especially for the biological and chemical assignments, will not normally be required by moderators. Each awarding body will provide specific instructions on this. Teachers will normally provide a statement for each exercise confirming that the required product, for example a pure, dry sample of a chemical presented in a labelled container, has been produced. Each Folens assignment has an assessment record form for this purpose. You may wish to photograph products to enhance evidence of product.

Teacher evidence on process is fundamental to the assessment and grading processes. Many of the criteria can only be assessed by observation. Examples are 'followed instructions with guidance/some guidance/little guidance' or 'safely assembled one electrical or electronic device'. In the former case, only the teacher present during the practical work can know how much guidance each student required. In the latter case, the safety of the circuit can only be established whilst the device remains in existence.

The most effective and efficient way to provide such supporting evidence is to annotate the students' work, for example 'needed only occasional guidance – 7/11 marks'. Alternatively, the Folens assessment records can be used to indicate the levels of guidance needed and the levels of practical skills shown.

Supporting evidence of scientific understanding

Students will need to carry out guided reading and research in various parts of the programme. The need to include information from secondary sources in reports is not large. The principal areas in which secondary information may be necessary are for the safety assignment in Unit 1 and the scientific organisations assignment in Unit 3.

In all cases, information and/or data from secondary sources should only be included where it is essential to meeting criteria. Students should, in all cases, show how and where the secondary information has been used to address criteria; any information and/or data that is not clearly used should be excluded.

Similarly, class notes and homework exercises should not be included in student portfolios. These may show coverage of the 'What you need to learn' sections of the specifications, but this is not a requirement. The evidence requirements are clearly identified in the Assessment Evidence Grids; only materials which contribute to meeting the specified criteria should be included in student reports and portfolios.

Portfolio building – Guidance for teachers (continued)

Hints on portfolio building

There is a sheet for student guidance on portfolio building (page IV:6) that you may like to copy and hand out to the students.

It is best for the students to add work to their portfolios only when it is completed and you have marked it and signed it off. Portfolios are most moderator friendly when the pages are punched and secured in a ring binder. Punched plastic envelopes may be used, but work contained in them is more time-consuming to read because of the need to remove and replace the pages.

Portfolios should have an index to identify clearly where each piece of work is. The students will need to number the pages to facilitate indexation. An index template is provided for this purpose (page IV:7). It is also advisable for the student's name to be included on each page.

Experience has shown that the development of an individual portfolio provides considerable motivation for many students. The higher the quality of the work and the better the structure of the portfolio, the greater the pride.

You may find that some of your students find it difficult to start their portfolios. However, portfolio building usually develops its own momentum, which increases as the course progresses. Ultimately, building and maintaining the portfolio is the responsibility of each individual student. However, as a professional, you also will develop pride in your students' achievements as the portfolios grow.

and finally...

Good luck in your development of your course; you will find the Folens student book and support pack of immense help to both you and your students.

Building your portfolio – To the student

Some of the work you will be doing on your course will be to show that you can do what is needed to pass the course. To check how well you can do them, your teacher will set you work called **assessments** or **assignments**. Your teachers will assess this work. The awarding body that runs the course may then want to check your work to make sure that it has been assessed fairly by your teachers, and assessed to the correct standards. This checking by the awarding body is called **moderation**.

Hints

- You need to keep all your assessed work safe until the end of your course so that the awarding body can check it. The best way to do this is to file all your assessed work tidily in a file or folder called a **portfolio**.
- It is best to start your portfolio at the beginning of your course and add your work to it regularly. By doing this, you will make sure that none of your work gets lost.
- When you are doing a piece of assessed work it is not always easy to follow instructions. Try highlighting each point on the assignment sheet as you go through a procedure so you know where you are. You will be less likely to make mistakes.
- When you have finished each piece of assessed work, your teacher will collect it in to mark it. Sometimes, you may have missed out some small but important part of the work. Your teacher will give you this work back and tell you what you need to do to finish it. Other work that you hand in may be complete. Your teacher will give you a mark for each piece of work.
- Remember it is the quality of the work you have done, not how much you have written, that is important.
- Only put work that has been assessed into your portfolio. Your teachers will tell you which work this is. You should not put other class work, coursework or homework in your portfolio.
- When a piece of assessed work is completed and has been given a mark, you should number the pages and put the work into your portfolio. You can do this by punching holes and using a ring binder. Make sure that you put your name on every page.
- Record each piece of assessed work on an index page when you put it into your portfolio. The next page shows an index page that you could use. This lists all the work that you will need to do by the end of the course. Your teachers will set you assessments or assignments to help you do all of this work.

At the end of your course, your teachers will have marked all of the work in your portfolio. The awarding body will then moderate it and decide what grades you have earned. It will be easier for the awarding body to award your grades if your coursework is filed neatly and your index page is filled in properly.

The grades that you get for your coursework will be added to your external test mark to work out the two grades that you will get for the GCSE in Applied Science (Double Award).

Good luck, and enjoy your science.

Name ______________________ Date ______________

GCSE in Applied Science: Index to portfolio of work

Unit	Activity	Assignment title	Pages
1	Health and safety in scientific workplaces		
1	Microscopy		
1	Microorganisms		
1	Qualitative analysis		
1	Quantitative analysis		
1	Electrical properties		
1	Physical properties		
3	Using science at work		
3	Making a chemical product, 1		
3	Making a chemical product, 2		
3	Mechanical machines		
3	Electrical or optical devices		
3	Growth/development/responses of a living organism		

Introduction to the assignments

Teachers' notes

As Science teachers, you have a big responsibility, especially when you have groups of students doing some types of practical work. You should be aware of your obligations under the Health and Safety at Work Act, the Control of Substances Hazardous to Health (COSHH) Regulations, the Management of Health and Safety at Work Regulations, and other legislation. In this respect you should follow the requirements of your employers at all time. Some materials used in science, for example some chemicals and microorganisms, can be hazardous and it is up to you to see that unacceptable risks are not taken with them. You must consult your employer's risk assessment for each activity before you do any practical work, and consider whether modification is needed for your particular circumstances. This is a legal requirement. Keep your risk assessments from year to year and modify them in the light of experience. Although only some materials and procedures specifically require the use of eye protection, mandatory eye protection in the laboratory is recommended.

The most likely reasons for modifying your employer's risk assessments relate to laboratory discipline and conditions. If you have *any* reason to believe that the (lack of) ability or (lack of) discipline of a group renders an otherwise acceptable activity dangerous, or that class size or laboratory conditions are unsuitable, then omit the activity and devise a safer alternative.

The risk assessment should take into account the hazards associated with the materials in the form that they are to be used (for example, dilute, concentrated, powdered) and the nature of the operations to be carried out. The DfEE book 'Safety in Science Education' (published by The Stationery Office) is an excellent source of information, as are *Hazcards* and the publications of CLEAPSS (see page III:2 for more on safety publications). 'Safety in Science Education' is now available, with permission, on the Members' Section of the ASE website (www.ase.org.uk).

It is assumed that pupils have been given basic laboratory training. Tying back long hair when using flames, wearing eye protection and some sort of laboratory coat, and not leaving bags with trailing straps on the floor should be automatic.

Some operations take too long to describe to be suitable for inexperienced pupils to do 'cold' from a worksheet. For example, the teacher should demonstrate doing a 'rough' titration the first time students encounter it, otherwise they will either meticulously measure 1 cm^3 at a time from the burette (or even smaller aliquots) and the lesson will finish before the titration, or they will add such large quantities that the exercise will have no value.

When a particularly hazardous material is to be used, for example concentrated acid, the class must also be told the dangers verbally at the start of the lesson, irrespective of the risk assessment that has been carried out. It is irresponsible to imagine that every student will read, understand and remember printed information. Where they have to produce a risk assessment, the 'Student Safety Sheets' from CLEAPSS are recommended, as *Hazcards* may be too technical. The duplicated section of Tables from 'Safety in Science Education', mentioned above, may also be found to be suitable. The teacher must always check their own risk assessment before practical work starts, as the student sheets deliberately do NOT give safety information. Teachers need to check students' risk assessments before practical work is started.

Introduction to the assignments (continued)

For some assignments a lot of equipment will be needed. You could split the class and while one half is doing the assessment activities the other half could be working through other activities. This could include the corresponding topics in the student book, which provide activities and case studies that the students could usefully carry out. The related topics for each assignment are tabulated later (for Unit 1 on page IV:12 and for Unit 3 on page IV:74).

In some activities, the sheets advise students that the teacher will provide some specific information, for example comparative prices of materials. It is easiest to give the (cheapest) prices from your laboratory supplier's catalogue. It is a useful point for class discussion as to how real this is in the manufacturing world.

Useful information, addresses and website details can be found in the Teachers' File (pages I:36–41) and may be a source of useful information for some of the assignments. Other ideas for assignments are available from your awarding body. The website address and other details for your awarding body can be found on page I:36 of the Teachers' File.

Guidance on the assessment of Unit 1

Unit 1 of the GCSE in Applied Science is based on developing and assessing some of the skills that are needed to carry out scientific work, whether in employment or in further education. The skills involved include those required to carry out practical work safely, to process and analyse experimental data and to evaluate processes undertaken.

The practical work that students are required to carry out is defined in the assessment evidence grid. It includes the following:

- biological work – microscopy and handling microorganisms;
- chemical work – qualitative and quantitative analysis;
- physical work – measuring electrical and physical properties.

In addition, students need to show an appreciation of health and safety issues in laboratories and other scientific workplaces.

The activities required for assessment reflect industrial practice by using standard operating procedures, which students are required to follow accurately and safely. The implication is that each student must work individually. Teacher demonstration or extensive group work will not enable students to develop the evidence required for assessment purposes.

Students will need to be taught the various skills required for assessment purposes. Ideally, this will involve a programme of formative practical work, within which students have opportunities to develop and practice each of the required skills. This formative work may be designed to illustrate some of the theory contained in Unit 2. You will find that some of the Optional Practical Activities in Section III of this Support Pack will be of use here.

The Assessment Evidence Grid in the specification defines the criteria against which each of the activities must be assessed. In Unit 1, assessment criteria a is assessed separately from assessment criteria b, c, d and e. Assignment 1 covers assessment criteria a. Assignments 2–7 are all assessed using criteria b, c, d and e. Each assignment is assessed against the appropriate criteria to give the mark band at level 1, 2 or 3. These levels for individual assignments are then combined to give an overall mark for each of a–e. Guidance for this aggregation is provided in the OCR specification.

The *Folens Applied Science Teachers' File (2nd edition)* contains a set of assignments that address all the activities defined in the assessment evidence grids, advice on the evidence to be presented, forms for the students to present their evidence and advice on how the criteria may be customised for each activity. These assignments have been designed for use in the school laboratory and to develop all the evidence required for Unit 1. Completion of all the assignments as presented will produce the assessment evidence in total. Teachers may wish to use the assignments as presented, adapt them or substitute others of their own choice.

In general, differentiation between mark bands is strongly linked to the independence of the student in carrying out the tasks. A student may achieve level 1 by completing a given grid or results table. However, at level 3 the student would be expected to have chosen their own method of presentation and designed any results tables. At level 2, students would be expected to design and label tables with some guidance. In these

Guidance on the assessment of Unit 1 (continued)

assignments results tables are provided that are suitable for level 1. They should NOT be used by students working at levels 2 or 3.

Each assignment is set out as follows:

- Introduction;
- Standard procedure set out in discrete tasks;
- Answer sheets to record evidence;
- A list of what the learner must present for assessment (on the CD-ROM only);
- An assignment-specific assessment record form (on the CD-ROM only).

Guidelines for the Unit 1 assignments

Links

This table shows links to the student book, to the reference sheets (Section I of the Teachers' File) and to the optional practical activities (Section III of the Teachers' File) that can help students prepare for these assignments.

Unit 1 Assignments	Reference sheet	Practical activity	Links to the student book
1: Health and safety in scientific workplaces	4 Monitoring living organisms		Working safely in science (pages 1–10)
2: Microscopy	3 Working with microscopes 19 The microscope 20 Parts of a light microscope	1: Using a light microscope	The working cell (pages 25–50)
3: Investigating microorganisms	2 Presenting data 3 Working with microscopes 19 The microscope 20 Parts of a light microscope	10: Investigating the action of antibiotics	Microorganisms in action (pages 81–106)
4: Qualitative analysis	8 Structures and properties 9 Particles in reactions 10 Amounts of substance 21 Distillation		Investigating chemistry (pages 183–208)
5: Quantitative analysis	1 Using measuring instruments 10 Amounts of substance	16: Finding the concentration of an acid	The chemical industry (pages 165–182)
6: Electrical properties	1 Using measuring instruments	18: Investigating resistance	Materials for making things (pages 209–226)
7: Physical properties	13 Comparing materials 14 Composites	19: Measuring density	Materials for making things (pages 209–226)

Each practical enables the development of certain skills – see the mapping grid in the Practical activity section (page III:3).

Guidelines for the Unit 1 assignments (continued)

Teachers

Teachers need to look at the general introductory notes on page IV:8, as the comments below are specific to particular assignments and tasks.

Technicians

When handling chemical materials, technicians should familiarise themselves with any associated hazards. All the hazards that are likely to be relevant are tabulated on pp 56–107 of 'Safety in Science Education' (published by The Stationery Office). This book is an essential purchase, and there is other important information in the same section. This book is also available, with permission, on the Members' Section of the ASE website (www.ase.org.uk). *Hazcards* and 'Student Safety Sheets', both from CLEAPSS, are also helpful.

If in any doubt, the technician should consult the teacher responsible for the lesson. Full information on chemical hazards is provided with each chemical by the supplier.

It is assumed that the technician has had basic training in safety and in the preparation of solutions. Whilst the following notes provide some guidance (for the inexperienced) with regard to safety, their primary aim is to make the technician aware of the apparatus and materials required for each activity.

Assignment 1

Health and safety in scientific workplaces

Each student (or group) needs:

- the school's set of health and safety regulations
- sources of safety information
- examples of the following hazards with warning symbols:
  - toxic
  - flammable
  - corrosive
  - oxidising
  - irritant
  - microorganism
  - laboratory service hazard, for example gas or electricity

It would be useful to tackle this assignment in conjunction with Topics 1.1 and 1.2 in the student book.

Sources of information on laboratory safety include HSE publications and CLEAPSS *Hazcards* and Student Safety Sheets. Numerous websites are also available, including www.hi-litesigns.com

A display of the materials could be provided. Laboratory chemicals have appropriate symbols on the packaging. If you have a poster available showing the warning symbols this could be helpful. There are many websites showing the warning symbols, such as www.hi-litesigns.com

Students will have access to materials on basic first aid and fire procedures. In particular basic first aid methods and qualifications, and fire precautions relating to emergency fire procedures, fire doors, fire extinguishers and the use of sprinklers. These may be from the Internet, or a talk by the school nurse or first aider. The local fire service usually have schemes whereby officers can visit and talk to students.

Guidelines for the Unit 1 assignments (continued)

Assignment 2

Microscopy

Each student (or group) needs:

- eye protection (for transferring iodine solution)
- light microscope (may be fitted with eyepiece graticule)
- stage micrometer (if using method provided)
- bench lamp if microscope is not fitted with built-in illumination
- microscope slides
- coverslips
- onion (alternatives are red onion, *Elodea*)
- dilute iodine solution
- small paintbrush
- fine forceps
- dissecting scissors
- pipette
- filter paper
- prepared slides (for example, kidney or blood smear)
- cotton wool buds (if cheek cells are prepared)
- methylene blue stain (if cheek cells are prepared)
- 1% Virkon solution for disposing of temporary cheek cell slides

A full assessment of health and safety is given in Practical activity 1 'Using a light microscope' (pages III:5 and III:62). An unlabelled diagram of a microscope is provided as Reference sheet 20 'Parts of a light microscope' (page I:33), and the labelled version of this diagram is Reference sheet 19 'The microscope' (page I:32). Reference sheet 3 'Working with microscopes' (page I:8) gives some simple principles of light microscopy and could be given to the students if appropriate.

Task 3: Setting up the microscope

Prepared slides of kidney have tubule cells that are clear to see. Prepared slides of blood smears are also suitable for students proficient at working with ×40 objectives, as they can only be seen clearly at this magnification. They would need to be advised to use white blood cells for their drawing.

Task 4: Calibrating the microscope

The procedure provided only uses the stage micrometer, so the student would have to estimate the size of the cells indirectly having calibrated the field of view for each objective lens. Philip Harris sell photographs of graticules which are much cheaper than using glass or plastic eyepiece graticules. These can be used as stage micrometers by mounting on a slide. If you want to extend the practical to teach students how to calibrate the microscope for direct measurements of cells using an eyepiece graticule, the photographic scale can be mounted between two round coverslips and inserted into the eyepiece.

Task 5: Preparing and observing a slide of a plant cell

The students should find in their risk assessment that eye protection is needed when transferring iodine solution for staining. Red onion or *Elodea* can be used instead of onion. Both red onion and *Elodea* can be mounted in water without staining and the cell contents will be clearly seen.

Guidelines for the Unit 1 assignments (continued)

You will need to discuss drawing a scale bar to indicate the actual size of the cell/cells before students do the experiment. Otherwise, this would be challenging even for those working at Higher Tier.

Task 6: Preparing and observing a slide of an animal cell
If you are not permitted to allow students to make temporary slides of their own cheek cells, they are available from Philip Harris Education. Any other animal tissues can be used instead, provided that the cells are clear enough to be measured and drawn.

Assignment 3

Investigating microorganisms
Note: This is an assignment you may wish to tackle with a half of the class at a time as a lot of sterile equipment is needed.

Task 3: Estimation of number of microorganisms
Each student (or group) needs:

- sample of pasteurised milk
- boiling tubes and rack
- ready poured China blue lactose agar plates (three per student or group)
- sterile 1 cm^3 pipettes and safety fillers
- sterile L-shaped disposable plastic spreaders
- Chinagraph pencil or spirit marker pen
- sticky tape
- incubator at 30°C
- discard jar containing disinfectant (for example, Virkon)
- cling film
- 10 cm^3 measuring cylinders
- sterile distilled water

Two other media are recommended for growing/maintaining yoghurt bacteria. These are GYLA and MRS agar. GYLA (Glucose Yeast extract Lab Lemco agar) may be available from Blades Biological, which also sells the ingredients to make up this agar. It is recommended for the *Lactobacillus* bacteria supplied by Blades. MRS (de Man, Rogosa and Sharpe) agar can be purchased ready-made. Philip Harris recommends MRS for the *Lactobacillus* cultures it supplies.

It will be useful to look at the 'Health and safety' sections of Practical activity 9 'Microorganisms, milk and yoghurt' (pages III:22 and III:67) and Practical activity 10 'Investigating the action of antibiotics' (pages III:24 and III:68). Reference sheet 6 'Aseptic techniques' (page I:11) reviews safety precautions, and so would be a useful handout to discuss before starting this assignment.

Students should know that the pipette should be placed just above the surface of the water when adding the sample. The pipette used for the next transfer can be used for the mixing. Economy with pipettes when plating is possible if the most dilute is used first. The small amount of contamination for the lower dilutions will not be significant.

China blue lactose is designed to allow counts of bacteria from dairy products, in particular to distinguish lactose fermenters from non-lactose fermenters. The china blue is a pH indicator; colonies that are lactose fermenters stain blue while other colonies are colourless. China blue is therefore useful for studying bacteria from milk.

Guidelines for the Unit 1 assignments (continued)

Counting colonies that produce between 50 and 500 colonies on a plate is best – the ideal is about 300. Results can be checked using other dilutions. If other dilutions produce a discrepancy in the calculated figures it could indicate a faulty technique.

By the time they do this assignment, students should understand the benefit of repeat procedures from which a mean is calculated. They may then suggest using more than one plate for a particular dilution or pooling the class results for each dilution so that a mean for a particular dilution can be obtained for the group.

It may be helpful to work out some theoretical values for number of bacteria per cubic centimetre for various dilution factors before the students carry the practical out as an assessment. This will also ensure they understand the basis of the calculation.

Task 4: Investigation of yoghurt growth
Each student (or group) needs:

- sterile boiling tubes and rack
- UHT milk
- sterile pipettes and safety fillers or plastic syringes for measuring volumes
- sterile distilled water
- live yoghurt
- cling film
- pH paper or pH probe
- water bath set at between 40 and 43°C
- Chinagraph pencil or spirit marker pen
- discard jar containing disinfectant (for example, Virkon)
- ready poured China blue lactose agar plates (six for each plating)
- sterile L-shaped disposable plastic spreaders

Only fresh natural yoghurt should be used for Task 4.

If a pH probe is used for measuring pH it must be thoroughly washed after use.

Assignment 4

Qualitative analysis
Each student (or group) needs:

- eye protection
- test tubes in rack
- small spatula
- wash bottles (distilled water)
- Bunsen burner
- Nichrome wire and holder
- watch-glass
- bung with delivery tube for gases
- hazard labels for the samples listed below

Access is required to the following 'samples'. These should be provided as solids in small, wide-mouthed, screw-capped jars appropriately labelled:

- sodium chloride, labelled 'chloride (Cl^-) sample'
- hydrated sodium sulphate, labelled 'sulphate (SO_4^{2-}) sample'
- anhydrous sodium carbonate, labelled 'carbonate (CO_3^{2-}) sample – *irritant*'
- hydrated copper(II) sulphate, labelled 'copper (Cu^{2+}) sample – *harmful*'

Guidelines for the Unit 1 assignments (continued)

- hydrated iron(III) sulphate, labelled 'iron (Fe^{3+}) sample – *irritant*'
- sodium chloride (again), labelled 'sodium (Na^{+}) sample'
- potassium chloride, labelled 'potassium (K^{+}) sample'
- powdered (precipitated) calcium carbonate, labelled 'calcium (Ca^{2+}) sample'
- hydrated copper(II) chloride, labelled 'Salt A – *toxic*'
- potassium carbonate, labelled 'Salt B'

After class use, the screw caps should be checked. Salt A, in particular, tends to absorb moisture and also to cement on its screw cap. It might be thought worthwhile to replace the cap by a wide rubber bung. The sample material should be crushed to about the size of table salt grains if possible. Sodium sulphate and iron(III) sulphate tend to come from the suppliers in unsuitably large lumps. Some salts tend to cake between use.

Access is required to the following stock bottles:

- dilute nitric acid (0.4 mol dm^{-3} – *irritant*)
- silver nitrate solution (0.05 mol dm^{-3} – *wash off immediately* – see below)
- barium nitrate solution (0.1 mol dm^{-3} – *harmful*)
- dilute hydrochloric acid (1 mol dm^{-3})
- limewater
- ammonia solution (2 mol dm^{-3} – *choking fumes*)
- sodium hydroxide solution (0.4 mol dm^{-3} – *irritant*)
- concentrated hydrochloric acid (*corrosive, irritant vapour*)
- tissues

Insist that students use eye protection throughout this assignment. There is a risk of splashing concentrated acid and spitting from the hot wire.

The concentrated hydrochloric acid is best supplied in a small bottle with dropping pipette. These bottles can be purchased with ground glass fitting dropper. If these are used the rubber teat should be replaced frequently since it tends to harden and crack. The technician should check that the 'stopper' is free in the top of the bottle before issue. The labelling should carry some indication of danger but will depend on the size of the label.

Silver nitrate at this concentration does not pose a serious hazard but contact with the crystals (or even the solution) leaves long-lasting black stains on the hands.

Concentration of the stock reagents is not critical, but the hazard may be different if the concentration is different from that shown above. If the school uses more dilute solutions they will normally suffice. Technicians should seek advice from the chemistry teacher if in doubt.

Limewater should be tested regularly or before issue by blowing through it with a drinking straw. If it does not go cloudy it should be replaced.

Should any pupils return unwashed test tubes, the technician should be aware that a test tube might contain concentrated hydrochloric acid.

A 'spatula full' has little more quantitative precision than 'a bag full' but gives the pupils an idea. Students should realise that it is best to use a very small amount – more can

Guidelines for the Unit 1 assignments (continued)

be used if the result is uncertain. The carbonate test requires more than the others. The sheets start with this test because, for example, more able pupils may want to go on to testing mixtures of anions. Even if acid is added before the sulphate test, many inexperienced pupils tend to use quantities of the 'unknown' such that residual carbonate would give a precipitate with barium ions.

Nichrome wires should be in some sort of holder; *wooden* spring-type clothes pegs are a cheap and expendable alternative to expensive holders. Students should be encouraged to use only the tip of the (fairly long) wire for the specimen and the contaminated end can then be cut off.

Students should be warned particularly of the dangers of concentrated acid before the lesson and reminded of emergency action. They should be told how important it is to avoid contamination of one sample with another – a good topic for class discussion.

Assignment 5

Quantitative analysis

The method used in this assignment involves pipettes and pipette fillers to measure out volumes accurately. If teachers think that this technique would be too difficult for some of their students, they should refer to Practical activity 16 'Finding the concentration of an acid' (pages III:40 and III:72), which uses a measuring cylinder as an easier (but less accurate) alternative method.

Each student (or group) needs:

- eye protection
- 50 cm^3 burette
- 25 cm^3 pipette
- pipette filler
- burette stand or similar
- small (plastic) funnel to fit burette loosely
- 250 cm^3 conical flask
- wash bottle (distilled water)
- 'sodium hydroxide solution (8.0 g dm^{-3})' (so labelled), about 120 cm^3 *Wear eye protection if making up from solid. This is corrosive, 'sticky' and gives severe burns.*
- 'hydrochloric acid' (so labelled), about 0.25 mol dm^{-3}, about 100 cm^3
- two 250 cm^3 beakers (for the acid and the alkali)
- access to dispensers of methyl orange indicator

Methyl orange indicator is found difficult to use by some students. Most acid–alkali indicators (for example, screened methyl orange or methyl red) are suitable. The colours on the work cards will need to be changed for some indicators.

If this is the first time that students have met titration, then a 'rough' titration will need to be demonstrated or overcautious students will never finish and cavaliers will get a useless result. 'Swirling' may be unfamiliar vocabulary, and the distinction with 'shaking' should be explained. Ideally, pupils should swirl the flask and operate the tap simultaneously. They should be reminded how to clamp a burette safely and how to use a pipette filler.

Guidelines for the Unit 1 assignments (continued)

In the calculation, the more able students should be actively discouraged from giving their answers to silly levels of precision; three significant figures is enough. With regard to accuracy (Task 7, Question 7), the more able pupils should attempt something roughly quantitative; pupils of lesser ability who write 'Pretty accurate' should at least qualify this with, for example, 'pipettes are better than measuring cylinders'.

Assignment 6

Electrical properties
Each student (or group) needs:

- 1.5 V cell in cell holder
- digital multimeter on 2 V range, with sockets marked + and –
- digital multimeter on 200 mA range, with sockets marked + and –
- 1 m of 0.27 mm diameter constantan wire (giving a resistance of about 8 Ω)
- length of wooden rod to wrap the wire around
- two crocodile clips
- leads with 4 mm plugs
- variable resistance (0 to 25 Ω is ideal but not imperative)

Sticky labels on the multimeters can be used to block up sockets which are not required, as well as indicate the polarity of the sockets which will be used.

The replacement resistance wire should be 1 m of 0.56 mm diameter constantan wire, with a resistance of about 2 Ω.

It will be necessary to demonstrate how best to connect the resistance wire to the rest of the circuit with the crocodile clips. A good secure electrical contact is vital for the experiment to succeed. It is also important to avoid short-circuits in the resistance wire. Coiling the wire and placing it on the bench with separated coils around a wooden rod is a good strategy.

You will need to check that the meters have been inserted the correct way round. Weak students may be confused that a digital multimeter can be used as an ammeter or a voltmeter depending on its settings. The ammeter will give readings in milliamps. Students will need to know how to convert them to amps.

Assignment 7

Physical properties
<u>Task 2: Measuring tensile strength</u>
Each student (or group) needs:

- goggles
- clamp, stand and boss
- G-clamp to secure stand to the bench
- vices for securing test samples to clamp and weights
- access to scales for measuring mass
- 0.28 mm diameter copper wire
- 0.08 mm stainless steel wire
- monofilament nylon fishing line (2 kg strength)
- glass fibre
- 100 g masses and their hangers

Guidelines for the Unit 1 assignments (continued)

The length of the samples is not critical, but there must be enough for it to be secured in the vice without kinking it. The glass fibre can be teased out of glass fibre matting – a diameter of 0.5 mm will snap under a load of about 1 kg.

Eye protection (using goggles) is important for Task 2. When the sample breaks, a lot of energy can be released as kinetic energy and scratch an unprotected eyeball carelessly left in the vicinity. A G-clamp should be used to make sure that the clamp stand does not topple over.

It will be necessary to demonstrate the use of the micrometer to make a measurement in millimetres. If students could be issued with a short length of partially stripped solid-core 0.6 mm plastic coated tinned copper wire, they could all have a go at making a pair of diameter measurements at the same time.

You will also need to show students how to clamp the sample into the vice. It is important that they don't kink the wire or try to knot it as this seriously weakens it.

You will find a large variation of results from one student to the next, particularly for the non-metallic samples. Tensile strength has as much to do with the recent history of the sample as it has with the material that it is made of.

Task 3: Measuring density
Each student (or group) needs:

- plastic measuring cylinder which can accommodate the solid samples
- access to scales for measuring mass
- samples of aluminium, copper, Perspex and marble/stone

The samples need to be fairly chunky, with a volume of at least 10 cm^3. Their shape is not important, provided that they don't get jammed in the measuring cylinder. Don't use glass measuring cylinders, as they are easily broken by angular metal objects being dropped into them. Remind students that 1 ml (the usual unit of measurement for measuring cylinders) is the same as 1 cm^3.

Task 4: Comparing thermal conductivity
Each student (or group) needs:

- clamp, stand and boss
- 250 ml plastic beaker
- enough ice to half-fill the beaker
- rods of copper, iron, wood and glass
- split rubber tubing to insulate rods from the clamp

The rods need to have same length and approximately the same diameter as each other. Make sure that the students understand the need for a fair test – the length of rod in the ice/water mixture as well as the overall dimensions of the rod need to be kept the same each time. Check that the rubber insulation is in place around the rod, otherwise the heat will be drawn from the clamp rather than just the top of the rod as required.

Assessment record for Unit 1

Name ______________________ Date ______________

Assignment	Mark band (1, 2 or 3) for criteria				
	a	b	c	d	e
1 – Hazards and risks					
1 – First aid					
1 – Fire prevention					
2 – Microscopy					
3 – Microorganisms					
4 – Qualitative analysis					
5 – Quantitative analysis					
6 – Electrical properties					
7 – Physical properties					
Marks awarded					
Maximum mark	12	6	8	12	12

Overall Mark:

Health and safety in scientific workplaces

Assignment 1 provides students with the opportunity to produce assessment evidence for Unit 1 skill area a (see page IV:10).

Introduction

Many things that you do in your life can be dangerous if not carried out carefully. They are said to be hazardous.

For example, crossing the road is hazardous. The **hazard** is being hit by a car. The hazard is always there and cannot be removed. However, the **risk** of being hurt will not be very great if you use a pelican crossing or look carefully both ways before you cross the road. You can control the risks of most activities by carrying them out sensibly and taking precautions to reduce the effects of the hazards.

There are many hazards in a scientific laboratory:

- some **chemicals** are hazardous; so are the experiments when you use chemicals
- **microorganisms** are hazardous; they sometimes cause diseases
- using **electricity** is hazardous; many people are killed each year by electric shocks.

Practical work in science almost always brings you into contact with hazards. However, taking sensible precautions can reduce the risks. The most important precaution is to carry out a risk assessment for each piece of practical work before you start. A risk assessment involves:

- <u>finding out</u> what the hazards are
- considering <u>how much</u> of the hazardous substance you need to use
- considering <u>how long</u> you will be exposed to the hazardous substance for
- identifying the <u>safety equipment and procedures</u> that will be used.

A **risk assessment** will tell you what the risk of the experiment is. If you find that the risk is too great, you should not carry out the experiment. Most of the practical work that you do will have very little risk, but you need to know what the risk is before you start work.

In this assignment, you will find out about the **hazards** and **risks** involved in your practical work. One common risk in science laboratories is fire:

- you will find out how to <u>reduce the risk of fire</u> by taking precautions to prevent it
- you will find out what to do if an <u>accident does happen</u>
- you will learn about getting some <u>first aid</u> to the person affected.

The CD-ROM contains a checklist for students and an assessment record form.

Task 1: Safety procedures

Your laboratory will have a set of health and safety regulations posted on a notice board. You need to find these regulations and then complete Form 1.

Task 2: Sources of information on laboratory safety

There are many ways that you can find information on safety in the laboratory.

- The Health and Safety Executive (HSE) is the body that has overall responsibility for safety in the workplace. The HSE publishes guides about workplace safety, including scientific workplaces.
- CLEAPPS provides information on laboratory safety for schools and colleges. CLEAPPS publishes 'Hazcards' and 'Student Safety Sheets' on laboratory materials and procedures.
- Suppliers of laboratory materials provide safety information with each delivery.
- There are many commercial sources of safety information.
- You can find safety information both in published form and on the Internet.

Find some sources of safety information and list them in Form 2. Put them in order of how useful you found them. Judge their usefulness by how easy they are to find and how easy the information is to understand.

Task 3: Hazards in the laboratory

A risk assessment will have been carried out for every practical exercise you carry out in the laboratory. For every assignment in Unit 1, your first task is to read the risk assessment form and list the hazards. You should then consider the safety precautions to be taken and write down the risks in the assignment.

1. Find one example of each of the following hazards in your laboratory or the laboratory preparation room:
   - a toxic material
   - a flammable material
   - a corrosive material
   - a material that is oxidising
   - an irritant material
   - a microorganism hazard
   - a hazard from a laboratory service (water, gas, electricity).

Write down what you find on Form 3.

2. Find the <u>warning symbol</u> for each of the hazards you have found. Sketch the warning symbol on Form 3. (Not all hazards have their own symbol.)

3. Find out the safety precautions to be taken when working with each of the hazards. Write down the safety precautions on Form 3.

4. Imagine that someone has had an accident with each material. Find out what first aid must be given. Write down the first aid needed on Form 3.

5. On Form 3 you need to list your sources of information for each of the hazards.

Task 4: Hazards and risks

Write down what you understand by the terms 'hazard' and 'risk'.

Select one of the hazards you chose in Task 3. Show how the risk from the hazard is reduced by taking safety precautions.

Task 5: First aid

You should write a list of common injuries in laboratories. (You can use your list of hazards from Task 3 to give you some ideas.) For each injury you should describe the basic first aid to give and when it would be dangerous to give first aid. You can do this by completing Form 4.

Research and find out the names of organisations that give training in first aid qualifications and how to contact them.

You should list the resources you used to complete this task. Complete a copy of Form 2 for your first aid research.

Task 6: Fire prevention

Fires in laboratories can be particularly hazardous.
You should find out:

- what must be done when you hear a fire or smoke alarm
- what must be done if you find a fire
- how fire doors work
- what different types of fire extinguisher are used on different types of fire
- about the use of automatic sprinkler systems.

Present you findings in a report, a poster or a pamphlet. Complete a copy of Form 2 for your fire prevention research.

Name ______________________________ Date ______________

Form 1: Safety regulations and procedures (Task 1)

Where are the health and safety instructions kept?	
What safety clothing is available in the laboratory?	
What can you eat and drink in the laboratory?	
Where can you find out what hazard symbols mean?	
Where are risk assessments kept?	
What must you do if a fire breaks out in the laboratory?	
Where must you go if the laboratory needs to be evacuated?	
Who can provide first aid if an accident happens?	

Form 2: Sources of information for ______________________________

Source	Ease of use	Information provided and reasons for its rating
	1 – easiest	
	2	
	3	
	4	
	5	
	6	
	7	
	8 – hardest	

Name ______________________________ Date ______________

Form 3: Hazards in the laboratory (Task 3)

Hazard	Symbol	Safety precautions	First aid	Source
Toxic material				
Flammable material				
Corrosive material				
Oxidising material				
Irritant material				
Microorganism hazard				
Laboratory service				

Name ______________________ Date ______________

Form 4: Common injury in the laboratory

Injury	First aid treatment	when not to use first aid

Name ______________________ Date ______________

Form 5: First aid organisations

Name of organisation	First aid qualifications available	How to contact

Microscopy

Assignment 2 provides students with the opportunity to produce assessment evidence for Unit 1 skill areas b, c, d and e (see page IV:10).

Introduction

Light microscopes are used to examine very small objects (microscopic objects). The light microscope works by making objects look bigger – **magnifying them**. Microscopy is used widely in biology, chemistry and physics. Examples of the uses of light microscopy are:

- in biology – examination of animal cells, plant cells and bacteria
- in chemistry – examination of the shapes of crystals
- in physics – examination of faults in structures, such as hair-line fractures in the metal of an aeroplane wing.

The light microscope works by passing light through lenses. Laboratory microscopes have an eyepiece lens and an objective lens.

Many light microscopes have more than one objective lens. The objective lenses are commonly labelled ×4, ×10 and ×40. The number tells you the number of times the lens magnifies the image. A ×4 lens produces an image that is four times larger than the object, and the ×40 lens produces an image that is 40 times larger. The eyepiece lens may also magnify the image. You can calculate the total magnification of the microscope. You need to multiply the magnification of the objective lens by the magnification of the eyepiece lens.

The size of small cells can be found by using a light microscope calibrated for each magnification. A simple way this can be done is by using a **stage micrometer**. A stage micrometer is a glass slide with a very accurate scale marked on it. The scale may be 10 mm long and have 100 divisions. Each division would then be 0.1 mm. One micrometre (1 μm) is 0.001 mm. This means that each division on the stage micrometer is 100 μm.

The diameter of the field of view should be measured and recorded using the stage micrometer for *each* magnification you use.

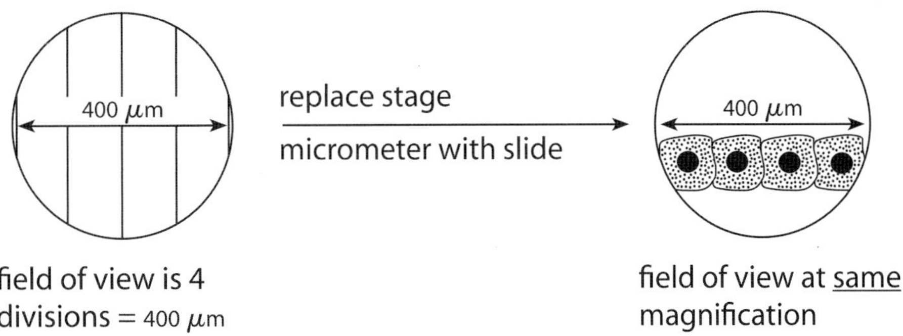

For this example, each cell is approximately 100 μm wide.

The CD-ROM contains a checklist for students and an assessment record form.

Task 1: Safety procedures

You need to carry out a risk assessment for this assignment. Write down your findings on Form 1.

Task 2: Investigating the light microscope

You will be given a diagram of a light microscope. You also need to look at an actual light microscope.

1. You need to label the following parts on your diagram:
   - eyepiece lens
   - objective lens
   - stage
   - coarse focus knob
   - fine focus knob
   - light source.

2. Write your name and the date on the diagram.

3. Write a brief description of how the light microscope works.

Task 3: Setting up the microscope

A light microscope is a very expensive piece of equipment. You must be very careful when you carry a light microscope and you must treat it with care. Light microscopes can be damaged if adjusted wrongly.

1. Position the microscope in the middle of your bench and tidy the electric lead (if it has one).
2. Plug the power lead into the mains socket and switch on your microscope. Check the bulb at the bottom is on. If your microscope does not have its own light supply, adjust a lamp and mirror to reflect light up to the sample stage.
3. Click the ×4 objective lens into place.
4. Place the tissue slide supplied onto the stage and clip it into place.
5. Move the slide so that the tissue is under the lens and the light is shining up through it. **Never focus directly on the Sun.**
6. Use the coarse focus knob to adjust the focus so that the objective lens is about 13 mm above the surface of the slide. You will need to look at the microscope from the side to do this.
7. Look through the eyepiece and adjust the coarse focus knob to lower the stage very slowly until the cells come into focus. Use the fine focus knob to obtain a sharp clear image.
8. You should not have to adjust the fine focus knob very much to focus the cells. Check the image is actually of cells by moving the slide around a little. The image should move when you move the slide.
9. Once the cells are in focus at low magnification, you can change the objective lens to the ×10 lens. You may need to use the fine focus knob to view the cells clearly.

10. Once the cells are clearly visible, make sure the ones you want to look at are in the centre of the field of view. Now you can use the highest power ×40 lens. This must be clicked into place with care because the lens will be very close to the slide and could break the cover slip. The cells should still be visible. Use ONLY the fine focus knob to focus the cells.
11. Ask your teacher to check that you have suitable cells in view to draw. If you lose focus of the cells at high power it is best to return to the lower power lens and follow steps 6 to 10 of this task again.
12. Draw the cells that you see through the microscope. Write down the type of cells you have drawn.

Task 4: Calibrating the microscope

Calibration means 'to determine true values by comparison with an accurate standard'.
When your microscope has been calibrated, you can estimate the size of what you see through it.

1. Ask your teacher what microscope standard you have in your laboratory. You might have a slide with a scale marked on it, called a stage micrometer.
2. How many objective lenses does your microscope have? Draw a circle for each different magnification.
3. Use your stage micrometer to measure the field of view for each magnification. You need to write the diameter for each field of view across each of the circles.
4. Now you can estimate the size of the cells.

Task 5: Preparing and observing a slide of a plant cell

1. Use a pair of fine forceps to peel a single layer of cells from the inner curve of a piece of onion.
2. Place the layer of cells on a white tile. Use a sharp pair of scissors to cut a small 5 mm × 5 mm square of this tissue.
3. Place one drop of iodine stain onto a microscope slide. (Care: iodine will stain your skin and clothes. Use eye protection when transferring iodine.)
4. Place the square of tissue on top of the iodine on the slide.
5. Use a paintbrush to smooth the tissue so it is flat on the slide and free of air bubbles.
6. Add one drop of iodine stain to the top of the tissue.
7. Use a mounted needle to lower a cover slip over the tissue gently, taking care not to trap any air under the cover slip.
8. Gently press the cover slip down. Remove any excess stain with a filter paper.

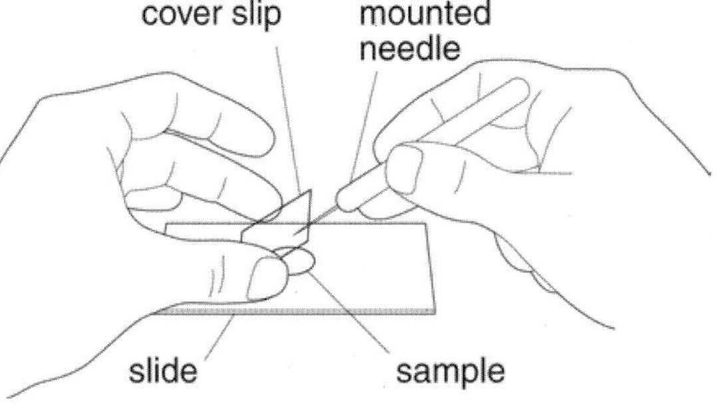

Applying a cover slip.

9. Use the procedure in Task 3 to position, focus and magnify the cells so that you can see the cells clearly.
10. Choose a suitable cell to draw.
11. Use a pencil to draw the cell outline. Make the outline big enough to fill half an A4 sheet of paper.
12. Draw the internal structures of the cell in scale with the cell outline.
13. Write the name of the cell you have drawn and the magnification at which you drew it.
14. Label on your diagram as many of the parts of the cell as you can.
15. Use the calibration of your microscope for this magnification to estimate the actual size of the plant cell.
16. Add a scale bar to your drawing to indicate the actual size of the cell.

Task 6: Preparing and observing a slide of an animal cell

Health and safety

Make sure you use only your own cheek cells. However, your teacher may give you prepared cheek cells or other animal tissue instead.

1. Use a clean cotton bud to gently wipe cells from the inside of your cheek.
2. Wipe the cotton bud across the microscope slide several times.
3. Check that cells are present by holding the slide up to the light. There should be a milky coloured liquid on the slide.
4. Dispose of the used cotton bud in 1% Virkon solution.
5. Add one drop of methylene blue stain to the cells on the slide.
6. Gently lower a cover slip over the slide. Make sure no air bubbles are trapped.
7. Press the cover slip down gently.
8. Remove any excess stain with a tissue or filter paper.
9. Follow steps 9 to 16 of Task 5 to view the slide and produce a labelled diagram of your cheek cells. Estimate the size of the cheek cells.
10. Dispose of your slide in the 1% Virkon solution.
11. Produce a table to give any differences between the plant and animal cells you have drawn.

Task 7: Evaluation of the experiments

Think about what you did in Tasks 5 and 6. Write down your answers to the following questions on Form 2.

1. What were the difficulties in setting up the microscope?
2. Which parts of the cell preparations were easy to carry out?
3. Which parts of the cell preparations were hard to carry out?
4. Which parts of the cell were difficult to see under the microscope?
5. Compare the sizes of the plant and animal cells. How did you estimate the sizes of the cells?
6. How could you improve the methods used?

Name ______________________ Date __________ Checked by ______________________ Date __________

Form 1: Risk assessment (Task 1)

Material	Hazard	What could go wrong?	Safety precautions	What to do in case of accident	Risk: low/ medium/high
Procedure					

Name ______________________________ Date ______________

Form 2: Evaluation of the experiment (Task 7)

Question	Response
1. What were the difficulties in setting up the microscope?	
2. Which parts of the cell preparations were easy to carry out?	
3. Which parts of the cell preparations were hard to carry out?	
4. Which parts of the cell were difficult to see under the microscope?	
5. Compare the sizes of the plant and animal cells. How did you estimate the sizes of the cells?	
6. How could you improve the methods used?	

Investigating microorganisms

Assignment 3 provides students with the opportunity to produce assessment evidence for Unit 1 skill areas b, c, d and e (see page IV:10).

Forms 2 and 3, as provided, are suitable for mark band 1. For mark band 2/3, students should choose their own column headings.

Introduction

What are microorganisms?

Microorganisms are any living organisms which are so small that you can only see them by using a microscope. There are many types of microorganisms. Some microorganisms are useful but others are harmful. Examples of microorganisms are bacteria, viruses and yeasts.

How can I stay safe and prevent contamination?

When working with microorganisms, it is important that you take safety precautions against the possibility of releasing bacteria grown in a laboratory, as some can be harmful, causing disease and illness. Bacteria that cause disease are called **pathogens**.

It is important not to contaminate the experimental microorganisms with other microorganisms from you or the surroundings. This risk is reduced by using **aseptic techniques**.

Are microorganisms useful?

Microorganisms are often used in the manufacture of foods. One example is the manufacture of yoghurt. Yoghurt is made by the reaction of milk with particular microorganisms under controlled conditions. In this assignment you will use standard procedures to grow microorganisms and to measure their growth.

The CD-ROM contains a checklist for students and an assessment record form.

Task 1: Safety procedures

You need to carry out a risk assessment for this assignment. Write down your findings on Form 1.

Task 2: Use of aseptic technique

It is important that you use aseptic techniques when working with microorganisms. Aseptic techniques will prevent any contamination from other sources from taking place. This would ruin the experiment. In addition to normal laboratory rules on eating and drinking, aseptic technique includes the following points.

1. Yourself: Cover any cuts or grazes on your skin with a plaster, wear a laboratory coat or other form of protective clothing.
2. Bench area: Clean the bench area using disinfectant, before and after work.
3. Equipment: Sterilise equipment before use by autoclaving or heating by flaming.
4. Keep cultures covered when you are not working on them.
5. Disposal: Dispose of all materials by autoclaving.
6. Used equipment: Collect all used equipment for autoclaving.
7. Wash your hands with soap and water.

Write one sentence on each of points 1 to 7 above, explaining why each of these precautions is necessary when working with microorganisms.

Task 3: Estimation of number of microorganisms

Microorganisms are often too small to be easily counted individually. You can estimate how many microorganisms are in a sample by allowing the individual microorganisms to grow into colonies. Colonies of microorganisms are more easily counted. Growing organisms like this is called **culturing**. Culturing is carried out in a culture medium, which feeds the organisms so they can grow. This method uses a **dilution series** and **plating**. Plating involves transfer of the bacteria on to the agar plates to let them grow. A dilution series is used because milk contains so many bacteria that it would be impossible to count all the colonies grown if it was not diluted. If we dilute the milk 10 times, 100 times and so on, we will then be able to count the number of colonies growing on some of the plates quite accurately. As we are using 0.1 cm^3, we need to multiply by 10 as well as by the dilution factor to find the number of bacteria per cm^3 of the original milk sample.

1. Ensure that all your equipment has been sterilised.
2. Take six test tubes and label them 1/10, 1/100, 1/1000, 1/10 000, 1/100 000 and 1/1 000 000.
3. Use a measuring cylinder to transfer 9 cm^3 of sterile distilled water into each tube.
4. Add 1 cm^3 of milk to the 1/10 tube using a sterile pipette. Mix the milk and water thoroughly.
5. Rinse your pipette with sterile distilled water then with the 1/10 mixture.
6. Take 1 cm^3 of the mixture from the 1/10 tube, add it to the 1/100 tube and mix thoroughly.
7. Repeat steps 5 and 6 until all the tubes have had a milk/water mixture added. Take 1 cm^3 from the 1/100 tube for the 1/1000 tube, 1 cm^3 from the 1/1000 tube for the 1/10 000 tube, 1 cm^3 from the 1/10 000 tube for the 1/100 000 tube and 1 cm^3 from the 1/100 000 tube for the 1/10 000 000 tube.

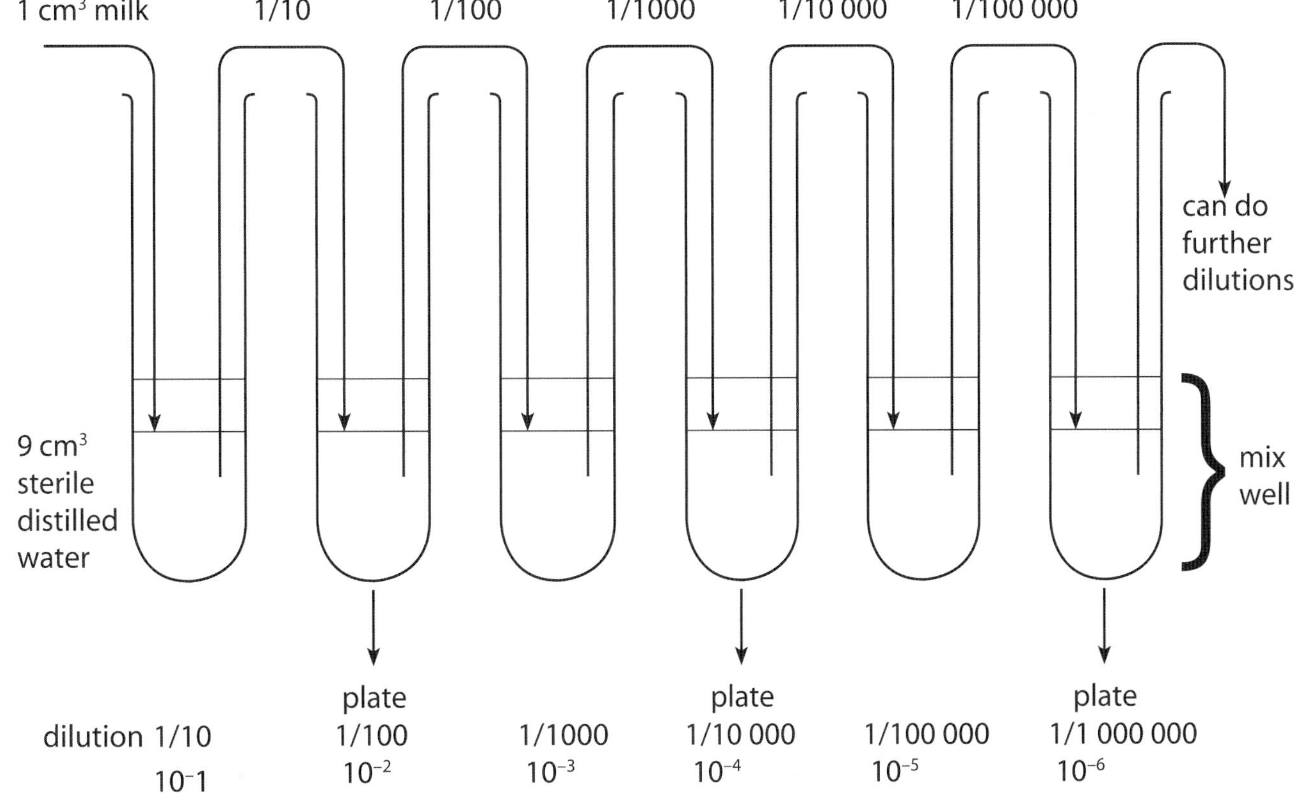

8. Take three prepared sterile agar plates, initial them and mark on the base: 1/100, 1/10 000 and 1/1 000 000.
9. Use a sterile pipette to take 0.1 cm^3 of the 1/100 mixture, remove the lid from the 1/100 plate and place the mixture on the agar. Use a sterile spreader to spread the liquid evenly over the surface of the agar. Replace the lid on the plate and secure with sticky tape.
10. Repeat step 9 for the other two plates (1/10 000 and 1/1 000 000). Once sealed, you should not open the seals on your plates.
11. Place the plates upside down in an incubator at 30°C for 24 hours.
12. Count the number of colonies on each plate. Hold the sealed plate up to the light. You may find it easier if you mask the colonies you have counted with a dot on the bottom of the agar plate. You will find that one of the plates will be the easiest to count.
13. If none of the plates have clearly visible colonies, incubate them all for a further 24 hours. Continue looking and incubating until at least one plate has clearly visible colonies.
14. Take the count from the plate with the most visible colonies and multiply by 10 and by the dilution factor to give an estimate of the number of bacteria in the original milk sample.
15. Write down your value for the number of microorganisms per cm^3 of the milk tested. Use Form 2.

Task 4: Investigation of yoghurt growth

Yoghurt is formed by action of special types of bacteria on milk. In this experiment, you will investigate the process used to make yoghurt. You will use some sterilised milk as a control to compare the progress on the yoghurt.

1. Ensure that all your equipment has been sterilised.
2. Measure 1.5 cm^3 of live yoghurt into a test tube. Add 15 cm^3 of milk and mix well. Seal the top of the tube with cling film.
3. Add 1.5 cm^3 of distilled water to a second test tube. Add 15 cm^3 of milk and mix well. Seal the top of the tube with cling film. This is your control tube.
4. Place the tubes in a water bath at 40°C.
5. After one hour, remove 3 cm^3 of the contents from each tube. Then re-seal the tubes and return them to the incubator.
6. Note the appearance and smell of the samples removed. Measure the pH using pH paper or a pH probe. Write down your observations on Form 3.
7. Make a dilution series for each sample up to 10^{-8} by using eight test tubes (rather than six) for the dilution series. Plate the 10^{-4}, 10^{-6} and 10^{-8} dilutions from each dilution series. The basic method is as in Task 3.
8. Repeat steps 5 to 7 of this task after five hours and 24 hours.
9. Use your observations to draw conclusions on the effect of the live yoghurt on the milk.

Task 5: Evaluation of your investigation into the growth of microorganisms

Think about what you have done in this assignment. Write down your answers to the following questions on Form 4.

1. Why is it necessary to use aseptic technique when working with microorganisms?
2. What were the difficulties in Task 3?
3. What were the difficulties in Task 4?
4. Why were a number of different dilutions necessary in Task 3?
5. Why did you need to make measurements in Task 4 after one, five and 24 hours?
6. Where were the possible sources of error in Tasks 3 and 4?
7. How could these errors be minimised?

Name ______________________ Date __________ Checked by ______________________ Date __________

Form 1: Risk assessment (Task 1)

Material	**Hazard**	**What could go wrong?**	**Safety precautions**	**What to do in case of accident**	**Risk:** low/ medium/high
Procedure					

Name ______________________ Date ______________

Form 2: Estimation of number of microorganisms (Task 3)

Dilution factor of plate counted	Number of colonies counted	Number of microorganisms per cm^3

Form 3: Investigation of yoghurt growth (Task 4)

Sample or control	Time/ hour	Number of microorganisms	pH	Appearance	Smell
Sample	1				
Control	1				
Sample	5				
Control	5				
Sample	24				
Control	24				

Name ______________________ Date ______________

Form 4: Evaluation of the experiment (Task 5)

Question	Response
1. Why is it necessary to use aseptic technique when working with microorganisms?	
2. What were the difficulties in Task 3?	
3. What were the difficulties in Task 4?	
4. Why were a number of different dilutions necessary in Task 3?	
5. Why did you need to make measurements in Task 4 after 1, 5 and 24 hours?	
6. Where were the possible sources of error in Tasks 3 and 4?	
7. How could these errors be minimised?	

Qualitative analysis

Assignment 4 provides students with the opportunity to produce assessment evidence for Unit 1 skill areas b, c, d and e (see page IV:10).

Forms 2, 3, 4 and 5, as provided, are suitable for mark band 1. For mark bands 2/3, students should choose their own headings or table designs.

Introduction

'**Qualitative analysis**' is used wherever it is important to know what is in a material. An example would be the identification of paint samples at the scene of a road traffic accident.

This assignment involves one of the most important types of qualitative analysis – finding out the identity of a salt. Tests are available to identify both the positive metal ions and the negative non-metal ions in a salt.

You will use two types of test in this assignment:
- chemical tests
- flame tests.

Chemical tests use simple reactions to identify the presence of **positive ions** and **negative ions**. For example, chloride ions react with silver ions to form the salt silver chloride. Silver chloride is insoluble in water, so forms a precipitate that is white in colour. If you think that a material might contain chloride ions, you add silver nitrate solution. If a white precipitate forms, you know that chloride ions are present. There are similar tests that can be carried out to identify the positive ions and negative ions which may be present in a substance.

Flame tests are carried out by putting the substance under test into a flame and looking for a colour. Many positive metal ions give out distinctive colours when they are hot. If these positive metal ions are heated in a flame, the flame becomes coloured. For example, sodium ions give a yellow colour, which you will have seen in streetlights.

The CD-ROM contains a checklist for students and an assessment record form.

Task 1: Safety procedures

You need to carry out a risk assessment for this assignment. Write down your findings on Form 1.

Task 2: Chemical tests for negative ions

You will be provided with samples containing the following negative ions:

- carbonate ions (CO_3^{2-})
- sulphate ions (SO_4^{2-})
- chloride ions (Cl^-).

Carry out the tests in the table below.

Ion	Test
Carbonate	Place a spatula full of the carbonate in a test tube. Carefully add 2 cm^3 of dilute hydrochloric acid. Hold a second test tube, containing limewater, close to the mouth of your reaction tube. You may prefer to use a delivery tube, so that the gas bubbles through the limewater.
Sulphate	Dissolve a spatula full of the sulphate in 5 cm^3 of water in a test tube. Add 2 cm^3 of dilute nitric acid. Add 2 cm^3 of barium nitrate solution.
Chloride	Dissolve a spatula full of the chloride in 5 cm^3 of water in a test tube. Add two drops of dilute nitric acid, using a dropping pipette, then four drops of silver nitrate solution.

Use Form 2 for your results. Write down what happens in the 'Observation' column. Things to look out for are precipitates and gases. Write a brief explanation for each observation. One explanation has been done for you as an example.

Task 3: Chemical tests for positive ions

You will be provided with samples containing the following positive ions:

- copper ions (Cu^{2+})
- iron ions (Fe^{3+}).

Carry out the tests in the table below.

Ion	Test
Copper	Dissolve a small spatula full of the salt containing the copper ions in 5 cm^3 of water in a test tube. Then add ammonia solution.
Iron	Dissolve a small spatula full of the salt containing the iron ions in 5 cm^3 of water in a test tube. Then add sodium hydroxide solution.

Use Form 3 for your results. Write down what happens in the 'Observation' column. Things to look out for are precipitates and changes in colour. Write a brief explanation for each observation.

Task 4: Flame tests for positive ions

You are provided with samples containing the following positive ions:

- sodium (Na^{+})
- potassium (K^{+})
- calcium (Ca^{2+})
- copper (Cu^{2+})

Carry out flame tests by following the procedure below.

1. (CARE) Put a 1 cm depth of concentrated hydrochloric acid in a test tube.
2. Dip a Nichrome wire in the acid and then place it in the upper part of a hot Bunsen flame.
3. Repeat step 2 until there is no change in the flame colour (other than a dull orange) when the wire is put into it. The wire is now clean. If you cannot clean it, see your teacher.
4. Put a few crystals of the salt on a watch-glass. Put two drops of concentrated hydrochloric acid on the watch-glass, next to the salt.
5. Move the tip of the Nichrome wire from the acid to the salt. Tap off any crystals which stick to the wire.
6. Move the tip of the wire sideways, just into the edge of the Bunsen flame. Note the colour produced. Repeat steps 5 and 6 if you are in doubt.
7. Heat the wire strongly until the colour disappears from the flame.
8. Wash the watch-glass and dry it with a clean tissue.

Write down what happens in the 'Observation' column in Form 4.

Task 5: Identification of unknown salts

You are provided with two unknown salts, A and B.

Carry out the series of tests below. Note your observations in Form 5. Use your results to identify the ions in salts A and B.

Salt A
Use chemical tests to test for:

- carbonate;
- sulphate;
- chloride;
- copper;
- iron.

Also use a flame test to test for the positive ion present.

Salt B
Use chemical tests to test for:

- carbonate;
- sulphate;
- chloride;
- copper;
- iron.

Also use a flame test to test for the positive ion present.

Task 6: Evaluation of the use of qualitative tests for negative and positive ions

Think about what you have done in Tasks 2 to 5. Write down you answers to the following questions on Form 6.

1. Which tests worked well?
2. Which tests did not work well?
3. Which observations were difficult to make?
4. Which tests in Tasks 2, 3 and 4 did not give results you expected?
5. How well do you think that the tests that you mentioned in questions 3 and 4 might work on mixtures of salts?

Name ____________ Date ________ Checked by ____________ Date ________

Form 1: Risk assessment (Task 1)

Material	**Hazard**	**What could go wrong?**	**Safety precautions**	**What to do in case of accident**	**Risk:** low/ medium/high
Procedure					
Using a dropping pipette					
Flame tests					
Disposal of waste materials					

Name ______________________ Date ______________

Form 2: Chemical tests for negative ions (Task 2)

Ion	Observation	Explanation
Carbonate		
Sulphate		
Chloride	A white precipitate	Silver chloride, AgCl, is formed

Name ______________________________ Date ______________

Form 3: Chemical tests for positive ions (Task 3)

Ion	Observation	Explanation
Copper		
Iron		

Form 4: Flame tests for positive ions (Task 4)

Positive ion	Observation
Sodium	
Potassium	
Calcium	
Copper	

Name ______________________ Date ____________

Form 5: Identification of unknown salts (Task 5)

Salt A

Test for	Observation	Absent/present?
Carbonate		
Sulphate		
Chloride		
Copper		
Iron		

Flame test

Colour produced	Positive ion present

Conclusion: **A** contains ______________ ions and ______________ ions.

Salt B

Test for	Observation	Absent/present?
Carbonate		
Sulphate		
Chloride		
Copper		
Iron		

Flame test

Colour produced	Positive ion present

Conclusion: **B** contains ______________ ions and ______________ ions.

Name ______________________ Date ______________

Form 6: Evaluation (Task 6)

Question	Response
1. Which tests worked well?	
2. Which tests did not work well?	
3. Which observations were difficult to make?	
4. Which tests in Tasks 2, 3 and 4 did not give results you expected?	
5. How well do you think that the tests that you mentioned in questions 3 and 4 might work on mixtures of salts?	

Quantitative analysis

Assignment 5 provides students with the opportunity to produce assessment evidence for Unit 1 skill areas b, c, d and e (see page IV:10).

Introduction

'**Quantitative analysis**' means finding out how much of something is present in a given sample of a substance. (You can remember this by thinking about 'quantities'.) Quantitative analysis is widely used by weights and measures inspectors, by pharmacists in making up medicines, by forensic scientists and in all types of quality control.

The method you will use in this assignment is called a '**volumetric**' method. This means that you will be measuring volumes of solutions. This assignment uses a method called '**titration**'.

The **concentration** of a solution tells you the amount of a material dissolved in a known amount of a solution. The material that is dissolved is called the **solute.** The liquid in which the solute is dissolved is called the **solvent.** In this assignment, the solvent will be distilled water.

In this assignment you will be investigating the reaction between sodium hydroxide and hydrochloric acid. They react together like this:

hydrochloric acid + sodium hydroxide → sodium chloride + water

$$HCl + NaOH \rightarrow NaCl + H_2O$$

If you know how much sodium hydroxide you have used, you can calculate the concentration of the hydrochloric acid.

You will be provided with:

- a solution of sodium hydroxide of known concentration (your teacher will tell you what the concentration is)
- dilute hydrochloric acid of unknown concentration.

The CD-ROM contains a checklist for students and an assessment record form.

Task 1: Safety procedures

You need to carry out a risk assessment for this assignment. Write down your findings on Form 1.

Task 2: Set up the equipment

You will need the following equipment:

- 25 cm^3 pipette and pipette filler
- 50 cm^3 burette
- two 250 cm^3 beakers, to hold the two solutions
- small funnel to help in filling the burette
- 250 cm^3 conical flask in which to carry out the titration

Collect these items together. Check that they are clean and not damaged. If they are not clean, wash them carefully and rinse with distilled water. If they are damaged, show them to your teacher.

Set up your burette carefully in a burette stand. Take care not to tighten the clamp too much. Make sure that your burette is held vertically in the stand.

Task 3: Preparing to titrate

A *Preparing the burette*

1. Close the tap of the burette. Place the small funnel in the neck of the burette. Use the 100 cm^3 beaker to add about 10 cm^3 of the dilute hydrochloric acid to your burette. Remove the funnel.
2. Rinse the dilute hydrochloric acid around the inside of the burette.
3. Empty the dilute hydrochloric acid from the burette into the waste container by opening the tap.
4. Replace the funnel in the neck of the burette and close the tap. Add dilute hydrochloric acid to the burette until the top of the column of liquid (the meniscus) is above the zero mark.
5. Place a sheet of white paper behind the burette so that you can see the meniscus more clearly.
6. Make sure that your eye is at exactly the same level as the burette graduation being read. Place a small beaker under the burette to catch the waste. Open the tap of the burette slowly to adjust the level to read '0.0'.

B *Using the pipette*

1. Using the pipette filler, about half-fill the pipette with sodium hydroxide solution.
2. Gently shake the solution around the inside of the pipette.
3. Empty the sodium hydroxide solution into the waste vessel.
4. Fill the pipette to just above the mark with sodium hydroxide solution.
5. Adjust the level exactly to the mark on the pipette.
6. Empty the sodium hydroxide solution into the 250 cm^3 conical flask that you will use for the titration.

Task 4: Carrying out the titration

Add two drops of methyl orange solution to the sodium hydroxide solution in the conical flask. If the solution does not go yellow, tell your teacher.

Your burette has marks (graduations) to show every 0.1 cm^3. You can read a 50 cm^3 burette to 0.05 cm^3 by estimating where, between the two marks, the meniscus is.

A *Rough titration*

1. Take the reading of the level of the dilute hydrochloric acid in your burette at the start of the rough titration. Write down the volume on Form 2.
2. Add dilute hydrochloric acid from the burette to the sodium hydroxide solution. Add 1 cm^3 at a time, closing the tap and swirling the conical flask after each addition. You will see that where the drops of acid enter the flask, the yellow colour disappears and a small amount of the solution turns red. The yellow colour returns when you swirl the flask. Carry on adding dilute hydrochloric acid a few cm^3 at a time until the red colour seems to remain for a moment when you swirl the flask. Then add about 1 cm^3 at a time.
3. Read the volume of dilute hydrochloric acid in your burette. Write down the volume on Form 2.
4. Take your starting volume away from your finishing volume to find how much dilute hydrochloric acid you added. Write down this volume on Form 2.
5. This is your rough volume. It will probably be slightly bigger than the correct volume.

B *Accurate titration*

1. Rinse out your conical flask using distilled water and add another 25.0 cm^3 of sodium hydroxide solution using the pipette and filler, as explained in Task 3B.
2. Add two drops of methyl orange solution.
3. Re-fill your burette with dilute hydrochloric acid. Read the starting volume and write down the volume on Form 2.
4. Add dilute hydrochloric acid from the burette quickly, until you have added 2 cm^3 less than the amount you added in your rough titration.
5. You are now near the end-point of the titration. Now add dilute hydrochloric acid one or two drops at a time, swirling the flask after each drop of acid has been added. When the methyl orange solution stays red, read your finishing volume. Write down this volume on Form 2.
6. Work out the volume of dilute hydrochloric acid you added. This is your first accurate volume.
7. Carry out another accurate titration. Write down the volumes on Form 2. If your volumes for titrations 1 and 2 do not agree to within 0.3 cm^3, carry out a third titration. Carry on doing this until you get two titrations to agree within 0.3 cm^3.
8. Take the two nearest volumes and calculate their average. There is space on Form 2 for you to carry out this calculation.

Task 5: Calculating the concentration of the sodium hydroxide solution

Use Form 3 for this calculation.

1. Your teacher will tell you the concentration of the sodium hydroxide solution in g dm^{-3}.
2. Use a table of relative atomic masses to calculate the relative mass of sodium hydroxide (NaOH).
3. Divide the concentration (in g dm^{-3}) by the relative mass to get the concentration in mol dm^{-3}.
4. Divide the concentration in mol dm^{-3} by 1000 to get the concentration in mol cm^{-3}.
5. You used 25.0 cm^3 of sodium hydroxide in your titration. So, if you multiply the concentration in mol cm^{-3} by 25 you will have worked out how many moles of sodium hydroxide you used.

Task 6: Calculating the concentration of the hydrochloric acid solution

The reaction that took place between the hydrochloric acid and the sodium hydroxide during your titration was:

hydrochloric acid + sodium hydroxide → sodium chloride + water

$$HCl + NaOH \rightarrow NaCl + H_2O$$

This means that one mole of sodium hydroxide reacts with one mole of hydrochloric acid. At the end-point, the number of moles of sodium hydroxide present is equal to the number of moles of hydrochloric acid added.

Use Form 4 for this calculation.

1. The equation for the titration tells you that the number of moles of hydrochloric acid is equal to the number of moles of sodium hydroxide used.
2. Divide the number of moles of hydrochloric acid by the average titration volume. This gives you the number of moles in 1 cm^3.
3. Now multiply the number of moles in 1 cm^3 by 1000 to work out the number of moles in 1 dm^3. This is the concentration of hydrochloric acid in mol dm^{-3}.

Task 7: Evaluation of the experiment to measure the concentration of hydrochloric acid (Form 5)

Think about what you have done in Tasks 2 to 6. Then answer the following questions.

1. What were the difficulties in setting up the equipment?
2. Which parts of the procedures were easy to carry out?
3. Which parts of the procedures were hard to carry out?
4. Which observations were difficult to make?
5. Which measurements do you think were not accurate?
6. Where did errors occur? How could these errors be reduced?
7. How accurate do you think your result for the concentration of hydrochloric acid was?
8. What other methods could be used to measure the concentration of hydrochloric acid?

Name ______________________ Date ____________ Checked by ______________________ Date ____________

Form 1: Risk assessment (Task 1)

Material	Hazard	What could go wrong?	Safety precautions	What to do in case of accident	**Risk:** low/ medium/high
Procedure					

Name ______________________________ Date ______________

Form 2: Titration volumes (Task 4)

	Rough	Accurate				
		1	2	3	4	5
Volume at end (cm^3)						
Volume at start (cm^3)						
Volume used (cm^3)						

$$\text{Mean titration volume} = \frac{\text{titration (}\quad\text{) + titration (}\quad\text{)}}{2}$$

$$= \frac{\boxed{} + \boxed{}}{2} \quad cm^3$$

$$= \boxed{} \ cm^3$$

Form 3: Calculating the concentration of the sodium hydroxide solution (Task 5)

Remember to add the correct units to each stage of this calculation.

Step 1: Write down the concentration of the sodium hydroxide solution: ....

Step 2: Calculate the relative mass of sodium hydroxide.

relative mass of sodium (Na) = ...

relative mass of oxygen (O) = ...

relative mass of hydrogen (H) = ...

relative mass of sodium hydroxide (NaOH) = ...

Name ______________________________ Date ____________

Form 3: continued

Step 3: concentration in mol dm^{-3} = $\frac{\text{concentration in g dm}^{-3}}{\text{relative mass of NaOH}}$

= $\frac{\ldots\ldots}{\ldots\ldots}$

= ……

Step 4: concentration in mol cm^{-3} = $\frac{\text{concentration in mol dm}^{-3}}{1000}$

= $\frac{\ldots\ldots}{1000}$

= ……

Step 5: moles sodium hydroxide used = concentration in mol cm^{-3} $\times$ 25

= …… $\times$ 25

= ……

Form 4: Calculating the concentration of the hydrochloric acid solution (Task 6)

Step 1: the number of moles hydrochloric acid used = ……

Step 2: number of moles in 1 cm^3 = $\frac{\text{number of moles hydrochloric acid}}{\text{volume of hydrochloric acid used (cm}^3\text{)}}$

= $\frac{\ldots\ldots}{\ldots\ldots}$

= ……

Step 3: concentration of hydrochloric acid = number of moles in 1 cm^3 $\times$ 1000

= …… $\times$ 1000

= …… mol dm^{-3}

Name ______________________ Date ______________

Form 5: Evaluation of the experiment (Task 7)

Question	Response
1. What were the difficulties in setting up the equipment?	
2. Which parts of the procedures were easy to carry out?	
3. Which parts of the procedures were hard to carry out?	
4. Which observations were difficult to make?	
5. Which measurements do you think were not accurate?	
6. Where did errors occur? How could these errors be reduced?	
7. How accurate do you think your result for the concentration of hydrochloric acid was?	
8. What other methods could be used to measure the concentration of hydrochloric acid?	

Electrical properties

Assignment 6 provides students with the opportunity to produce assessment evidence for Unit 1 skill areas b, c, d and e (see page IV:10).

Forms 2 and 3, as provided, are suitable for mark band 1. For mark bands 2/3, students should choose their own headings or table designs.

Introduction

Electrical circuits are used in almost every aspect of modern life. Circuits can be found in a very simple form in a torch, or in very complex devices such as a computer, hi-fi or industrial control equipment. In this assignment, you will build some simple circuits and use them to make some electrical measurements.

The CD-ROM contains a checklist for students and an assessment record form.

Task 1: Safety procedures

You need to carry out a risk assessment for this assignment. Write down your findings on Form 1.

Task 2: Assembling your circuit

You are provided with the following electrical components:

- a cell (mains voltages will not be used)
- voltmeter
- ammeter
- variable resistance
- resistance wire and crocodile clips.

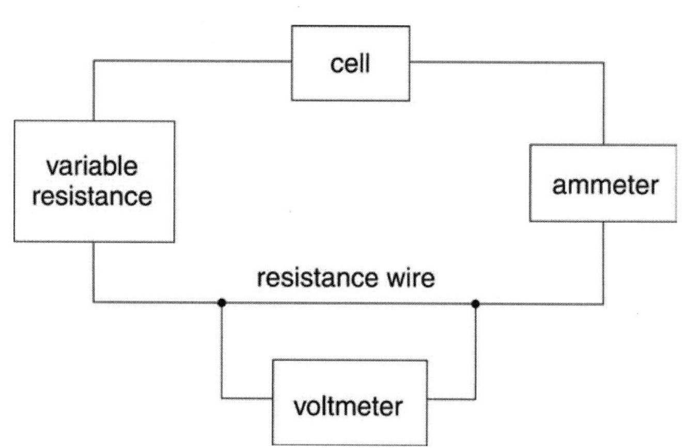

1. Use the leads provided to assemble the circuit shown in the diagram.
2. Get your teacher to check your circuit for correct assembly.
3. Draw a diagram of your circuit, using standard symbols for the components.

Task 3: Making measurements and presenting the data

1. Use the circuit you made in Task 2. Take a reading from the voltmeter and the ammeter. Write these down on Form 2.
2. Change the variable resistance in the circuit. Now take another pair of readings of voltage and current.
3. Carry on changing the variable resistance until you have six sets of readings.
4. Plot a graph of your readings. Use graph paper and axes like those on Form 2. Draw the best straight line you can using the data points.
5. Change the resistance wire. Now repeat stages 1 to 4. Write down your measurements on Form 3. Plot another graph on graph paper, using axes like those on Form 3.

Task 4: Considering your results

1. Do the graphs look the same? If not, how are they different?
2. Find out what the slopes of your graphs represent.
3. The only change you made in your circuit was changing the resistance. Find out what 'electrical resistance' means, and how it changes the current in the circuit.

Name ______________________ Date __________ Checked by ______________________ Date __________

Form 1: Risk assessment (Task 1)

Material or device	**Hazard**	**What could go wrong?**	**Safety precautions**	**What to do in case of accident**	**Risk:** low/ medium/high
Procedure					

Name ______________________________ Date ______________

Form 2: Results from wire 1 (Task 3)

Reading	Voltage (in volts)	Current (in amps)
1		
2		
3		
4		
5		
6		

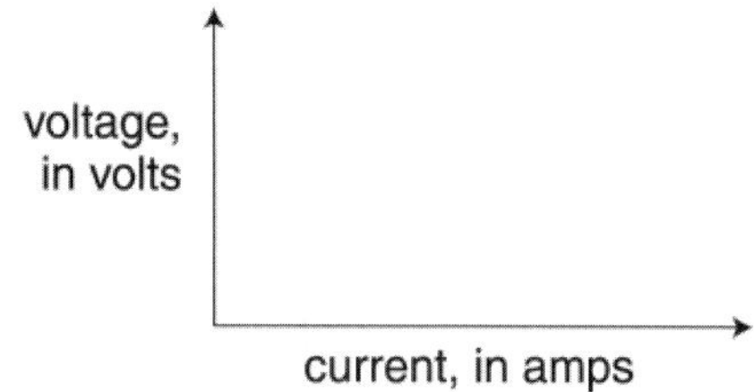

Form 3: Results from wire 2 (Task 3)

Reading	Voltage (in volts)	Current (in amps)
1		
2		
3		
4		
5		
6		

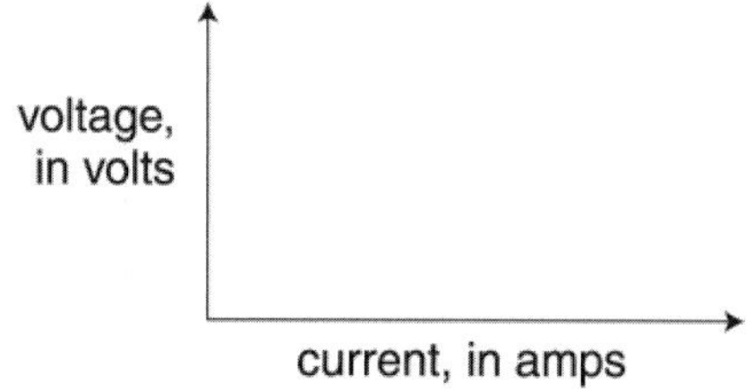

Physical properties

Assignment 7 provides students with the opportunity to produce assessment evidence for Unit 1 skill areas b, c, d and e (see page IV:10).

Forms 2, 3 and 4, as provided, are suitable for mark band 1. For mark bands 2/3, students should choose their own headings or table designs.

Introduction

The different ways a material can be used depends on its **physical properties**. These properties include strength, density, hardness, and electrical and thermal conductivity.

A material to be used in the construction of a bicycle frame needs to be light but strong. Designers used their knowledge of materials to design the bicycle built for Chris Boardman to ride in the 4000 m pursuit in the 1992 Olympic Games. Their work helped him to win the gold medal.

The design of a complex machine, such as a racing bicycle, starts with simple tests on the properties of materials. In this exercise, you will carry out some of these tests.

The CD-ROM contains a checklist for students and an assessment record form.

Task 1: Safety procedures

You need to carry out a risk assessment for this assignment. Write down your findings on Form 1.

Task 2: Measuring tensile strength

Tensile strength is the property that allows a material to resist breaking when it is being stretched.

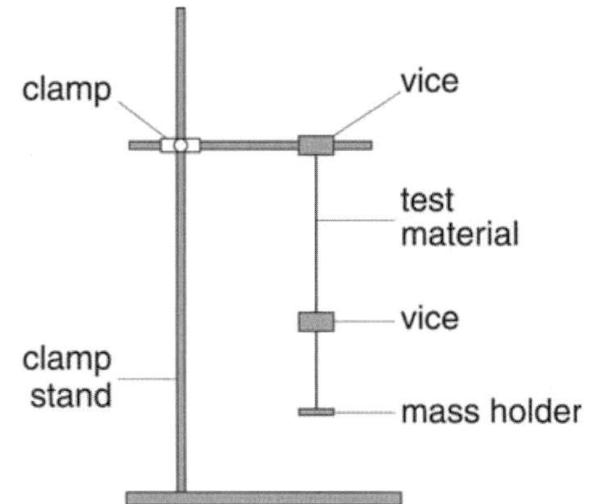

1. Set up the apparatus as shown. The material to be tested needs to be held firmly between the two vices.
2. Use a micrometer to measure the diameter of the wire.
3. Repeat your measurement of the diameter of the wire.
4. Now calculate the average value for the diameter. Use the formula: area = $\pi/4 \times (\text{diameter})^2$. Write down the average value in Form 2.
5. Add masses to the mass holder until the wire breaks.
6. Write down the mass attached to the wire at the breaking point. Include the mass of the lower vice and mass holder. Write down the value of the mass in Form 2.
7. Repeat steps 1 to 6 for three other materials (a wire made of another metal, nylon thread, fibreglass).
8. Calculate the tensile strength of each material tested. Assume that a mass of 1 kg has a weight of 10 N.
9. In Form 2, write the names of the materials tested, in order of increasing tensile strength.
10. In Form 2, write an example where the measurement of tensile strength is important to the use of a material in industry.

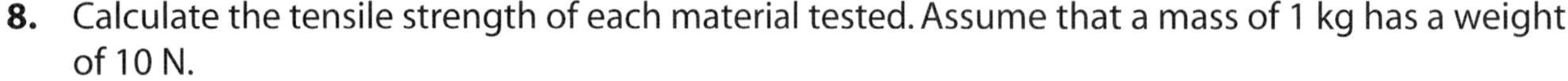

Task 3: Measuring density

Density is a useful measurement because it tells us something about the structure of materials. We can use density to compare materials even if we do not know anything about their microscopic structure.

Density is the relationship between the mass of a material and the amount (volume) of material:

$$\text{density} = \frac{\text{mass}}{\text{volume}}$$

For example, an ordinary house brick is quite heavy, but a piece of sponge that is the same size and shape as the brick will be much lighter. In this example, both materials have the same volume, but they have different masses because of the way the molecules of the materials fit together. That means they will have different densities too.

The units of density are kg m^{-3}. You may find that some references to densities are given in units of g cm^{-3}. 1000 kg m^{-3} = 1 g cm^{-3}.

1. Measure the mass of a piece of metal using a balance. Write down the mass in Form 3.
2. Pour enough water into a measuring cylinder to cover the piece of metal. Write down the volume in Form 3. Remember that 1 ml is 1 cm^3.
3. Now put the piece of metal into the water. (The water should cover the piece of metal. If it doesn't, you will need to go back to step 2 and make sure you put enough water into the measuring cylinder.) Write down the level of the top of the water, which is the total volume of the water and the piece of metal. Write down your readings in Form 3.
4. Repeat steps 2 and 3 and write down your readings in Form 3. Now you can calculate the average value for the volume of the piece of metal.
5. Repeat steps 1 to 4 for three other materials.
6. Calculate the densities of each material tested. You need to use the equation given on the previous page.
7. In Form 3, write the materials in order of increasing density.
8. In Form 3, write an example of where measuring density is useful in industry.

Task 4: Comparing thermal conductivity

Thermal conductivity is a property that tells us about the way heat can pass through a material. Thermal conductivity is not easy to measure accurately in the classroom. But there is a simple test that you can do to tell which materials are better conductors than others.

1. Set up the apparatus shown in the diagram. Clamp a piece of metal rod with its bottom end immersed in ice. The rubber insulator should be between the clamp and the rod.

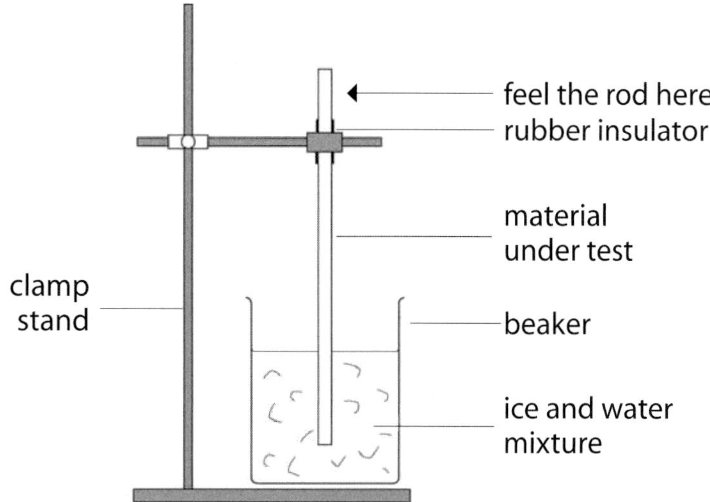

2. Feel the rod above the clamp.
3. Leave the apparatus for five minutes and then feel the rod again in the same place. In Form 4, write down how you think the rod feels now (very cold, cold, or no change in temperature).
4. Repeat steps 1 to 3 for three other materials.
5. In Form 4, write down the materials tested in order of increasing thermal conductivity.
6. Look up measured values of thermal conductivities for the materials tested. Write these 'measured values' in Form 4, and think about how these compare with your test results.
7. In Form 4, write an example where measuring thermal conductivity is important in industry.

Task 5: Choosing the right material for the job

Of all the materials you have tested, which would you choose to build the frame of a bicycle to be used for racing? Explain why you have made your choice (Form 5).

Task 6: Evaluate your experiments to measure physical properties of materials

Think about what you have done in this assignment. Write down your answers to these questions in Form 6.

1. What difficulties did you have when setting up the equipment?
2. Which parts of the procedures were easy to carry out?
3. Which parts of the procedures were difficult to carry out?
4. Which measurements were difficult to make?
5. Which measurements do you think were not accurate?
6. Where did errors occur? How could they be reduced?
7. How accurate do you think your results were for each experiment?

Name ______________________ Date __________ Checked by ______________________ Date __________

Form 1: Risk assessment (Task 1)

Material	**Hazard**	**What could go wrong?**	**Safety precautions**	**What to do in case of accident**	**Risk:** low/ medium/high
Procedure					

Name ____________________ Date ____________

Form 2: Tensile strengths (Task 2)

Material	**1:** ______	**2:** ______	**3:** ______	**4:** ______
Diameter of wire (1) (mm)				
Diameter of wire (2) (mm)				
Average diameter (mm)				
Average diameter (m)				
Cross-sectional area (m^2)				
Breaking mass (kg)				
Breaking force (N)				
Tensile strength ($N\ m^{-2}$)				

The order of strengths of the materials tested is:

1. ____________ 2. ____________

3. ____________ 4. ____________

Measurement of the tensile strength of materials is important for:

Name ______________________ Date ____________

Form 3: Densities (Task 3)

Material	**1:** ______	**2:** ______	**3:** ______	**4:** ______
Mass (g)				
Volume of water (1) (cm^3)				
Volume of water + material (1) (cm^3)				
Volume of material (1) (cm^3)				
Volume of water (2) (cm^3)				
Volume of water + material (2) (cm^3)				
Volume of material (2) (cm^3)				
Average volume of material (cm^3)				
Density (mass/volume) ($g\ cm^{-3}$)				
Density ($kg\ m^{-3}$)				

The order of densities of the materials tested is:

1. ____________ 2. ____________

3. ____________ 4. ____________

Measurement of the densities of materials is important for:

Name ______________________________ Date ______________

Form 4: Thermal conductivity (Task 4)

Material	Feel	Thermal conductivity (from reference book) ($W\ m^{-1}\ K^{-1}$)

The order of thermal conductivity of the materials tested is:

1. ____________ 2. ____________

3. ____________ 4. ____________

Measurement of the thermal conductivity of materials is important for:

Form 5: Choosing the right material for the job (Task 5)

Which material would you use to build a racing bike and why?

Unit 1, Assignment 7

Name ______________________ Date ______________

Form 6: Evaluating the experiment (Task 6)

Question	Response
1. What difficulties did you have when setting up the equipment?	
2. Which parts of the procedures were easy to carry out?	
3. Which parts of the procedures were difficult to carry out?	
4. Which measurements were difficult to make?	
5. Which measurements do you think were not accurate?	
6. Where did errors occur? How could they be reduced?	
7. How accurate do you think your results were for each experiment?	

Guidance on the assessment of Unit 3

Unit 3 of the GCSE in Applied Science is a practically based unit. It takes the practical skills developed in Unit 1 and uses them on more extensive tasks. It also challenges the students' scientific knowledge and their skills of analysis and evaluation.

The practical work that the students are required to carry out is defined in the assessment evidence grid. It includes the following:
- chemical work – preparations of pure, dry chemical products;
- physical work – constructing and testing mechanical and electrical/electronic devices;
- biological work – monitoring the development of an organism under controlled conditions.

In addition, students need to carry out research into the commercial or industrial uses of science.

The practical work in the Unit 3 assignments assumes that students have developed some degree of competence in the use of standard operating procedures during their work for Unit 1. The assignments in Unit 3 may require additional skills; these will need to be taught before the assignments are carried out. Again, the Optional Practical Activities in Section III of this Support Pack will be of use here. The practical work for Unit 3 assessment must be carried out individually in the main; group activities or demonstrations will not meet the assessment criteria.

The Assessment Evidence Grid for Unit 3 in the awarding body specifications defines the criteria against which each of the activities must be assessed. The grid also gives the marks available for each of stages 1, 2 and 3. The Unit 3 activities are divided into four parts for assessment purposes:
- the use of science in the workplace;
- making new products – two chemical preparations;
- assembling instruments and machines – mechanical and electrical/electronic;
- monitoring living organisms.

The *Folens Applied Science Teachers' File* contains a set of assignments that address all the activities defined in the assessment evidence grids, advice on the evidence to be presented, forms for the students to present their evidence and advice on how the criteria may be customised for each activity. These assignments have been designed for use in the school laboratory and to develop all the evidence required for Unit 3. Completion of all the activities as presented will produce the assessment evidence in total. Teachers may wish to use the activities as presented, adapt them or substitute others of their own choice.

Each assignment is set out as follows:
- Introduction
- Practical instructions
- Answer sheets to record evidence (suitable for mark band 1)
- A list of what the student must present for assessment (on the CD-ROM only)
- An assessment record form (on the CD-ROM only).

Guidance on the assessment of Unit 3 (continued)

Assessment record forms are included in each activity. The marks awarded are then aggregated as follows:

A The use of science in the workplace – Marks as awarded (Assignment 8)
B Making new products – Marks from the three chemical preparations are aggregated (Assignments 9, 10)
C Assembling instruments and machines – Marks from the mechanical and electrical/electronic devices are aggregated (Assignments 11, 12)
D Monitoring living organisms - Marks as awarded (Assignment 13)

An assessment record for Unit 3 is included to help to record the final mark for each student. Your awarding body will provide guidance on how to do this.

In general, differentiation between mark bands is strongly linked to the independence of the student in carrying out the tasks. A student may achieve level 1 by completing a given grid or results table. However, at level 3 the student would be expected to have chosen their own method of presentation and designed any results tables. At level 2, students would be expected to design and label tables with some guidance. **In these assignments, results tables are provided that are suitable for level 1. They should NOT be used by students working at levels 2 or 3.**

Guidelines for the Unit 3 assignments

Links

This table shows links to the student book, to the reference sheets (Section I of the Teachers' File) and to the optional practical activities (Section III of the Teachers' File) that can help students prepare for these assignments. The table also shows how the Unit 1 assignments lead on to the Unit 3 assignments.

Unit 3 Assignments	Reference sheet	Practical activity	Links to the student book	Unit 1 Assignments
8: Using science at work	11 The blast furnace 12 Fractional distillation of crude oil		Science in the workplace (pages 307–312)	Assignments 1 to 7
9: The extraction of copper from an ore	8 Structures and properties 9 Particles in reactions 10 Amounts of substance	15 Investigating rates of reaction	Investigating chemistry (pages 183–208)	1 Health and safety in scientific workplaces 4 Qualitative analysis
10: The production of a fertiliser	8 Structures and properties 9 Particles in reactions 10 Amounts of substance	15 Investigating rates of reaction 17 Making ammonium sulphate	The chemical industry (pages 165–182)	1 Health and safety in scientific workplaces 5 Quantitative analysis
11: The construction of a lifting system	15 Energy calculations	23 Investigating a lever	Devices at work (pages 261–282)	1 Health and safety in scientific workplaces
12: The design and construction of a nightlight	1 Using measuring instruments 15 Energy calculations	22 Constructing an electronic system	Devices at work (pages 261–282)	1 Health and safety in scientific workplaces 6 Electrical properties
13: The production of yoghurt from milk	5 The Mansfield Brewery 6 Aseptic techniques	9 Microorganisms, milk and yoghurt	Microorganisms in action (pages 81–106)	1 Health and safety in scientific workplaces 2 Microscopy 3 Investigating microorganisms

Each practical enables the development of certain skills – see the mapping grid in the Practical activity section (page III:3).

Guidelines for the Unit 3 assignments (continued)

Teachers

Teachers need to look at the general introductory notes on page IV:8, as the comments below are specific to particular assignments and tasks.
Note: Assignments 9 and 10 are assessed jointly for strand b.

Technicians

Technicians need to refer back to the general comments in the introductory notes to the Unit 1 Assignments (page IV:10), as the comments below are specific to particular assignments and tasks.

Assignment 8

Using science at work

The following is suggested for each student (or group):

- Dun and Bradstreet Business Directory, or similar
- Yellow Pages, or the website http://www.Yell.com/
- local information from local library, local careers office and so on
- Careers directory such as Occupations or http://www.connexions.gov.uk/occupations/
- local papers for local science jobs
- Theme 6 'Science in the workplace' in the student book would be a useful introduction before the students start the assignment.

Some of the sources of information will be detailed so it would be helpful to tell students to be selective when they are carrying out this assignment.

Assignment 9

The extraction of copper from an ore

Task 2: Making copper sulphate from malachite

Each student (or group) needs:

- eye protection
- about 10 g of basic copper carbonate (green, precipitated) labelled 'Powdered malachite – *harmful*'
- 50 cm^3 or 100 cm^3 measuring cylinder
- 250 cm^3 beaker
- glass stirring rod
- dilute sulphuric acid (1 mol dm^{-3} – *irritant*)
- funnel
- stand and clamp (or filter stand)
- Bunsen burner
- tripod and gauze
- evaporating basin
- filter paper
- watch-glass

The mineral malachite is less tractable than precipitated basic copper(II) carbonate and the latter should be used. It has the disadvantage that being a dried, precipitated powder it is slightly more hazardous to handle.

In the evaporation stage, if complete neutralisation of the acid has been achieved (unlikely) heating may cause hydrolysis to the green basic copper(II) sulphate. This can be reversed by adding a few drops of dilute sulphuric acid.

Students must not have excess acid, otherwise highly corrosive fumes will escape on evaporation.

Guidelines for the Unit 3 assignments (continued)

Task 3: Extracting copper from copper sulphate crystals

Each student (or group) needs:

- eye protection
- distilled water
- 50 cm^3 or 100 cm^3 measuring cylinder
- stand and clamp (or filter stand)
- 250 cm^3 beaker
- glass rod
- funnel
- filter paper
- about 2 g of zinc filings
- dilute hydrochloric acid (2 mol dm^{-3} – *irritant* – about 50 cm^3)

In the displacement, zinc turnings are generally best. Granulated zinc is coarse and slow; powdered zinc, if old stock, tends to be coated with a thin layer of oxide which impedes displacement.

Task 7: Commercial production of copper

This subject is covered quite well in many chemistry textbooks. A very detailed source of information is to be found on-line at:
http://www.nrcan.gc.ca/mms/ and then follow the links.

Assignment 10

The production of a fertiliser

Each student (or group) needs:

- eye protection
- 50 cm^3 burette
- 25 cm^3 pipette
- pipette filler
- 250 cm^3 conical flask
- 'potassium hydroxide solution' (so labelled, 28 g dm^{-3} – about 120 cm^3 – *corrosive, wear eye protection, if making up from solid this can be 'sticky' and gives severe burns*)
- 'nitric acid' (so labelled, *corrosive* – about 0.5 mol dm^{-3}, about 100 cm^3)
- three 250 cm^3 beakers (two are for the above solutions)
- glass rod
- evaporating basin
- Bunsen burner
- tripod and gauze
- spatula
- weighing container (watch-glass or weighing bottle)
- measuring cylinder (not bigger than 50 cm^3)

Access is required to:

- methyl orange indicator solution (in dispenser)
- Universal indicator paper (in dispenser)

The teacher should refer to the notes for Unit 1, Assignment 5 'Quantitative analysis' (page IV:18).

Guidelines for the Unit 3 assignments (continued)

In the evaporation stage, teachers will no doubt want to employ their own preferred methods. The candidates should be familiar with Universal indicator (wide range) and the pH scale, but litmus can be substituted if required. Pupils unfamiliar with the technique should be shown how to pour from a beaker down a glass rod without loss. In the final evaporation at room temperature a stiff piece of paper can be folded into a 'roof' over the evaporating dish to keep dust out but allow evaporation.

Teachers of less able groups who feel that 0.5 mol dm^{-3} potassium hydroxide is a little too concentrated are at liberty to reduce the concentration. It is advisable to reduce the corresponding concentration of acid to maintain suitable burette readings.

Task 9: The commercial importance of potassium nitrate
For information you could try http://www.chemindustry.com/ and follow suitable links.

Task 6 is required for students working at mark band 3 only.
Each student will require:

- a car jack (any common type will do)
- a load for the car jack, 4–6 kilograms should be OK
- forcemeters appropriate to the car jack and load
- meter rule
- 30 cm rule
- string.

Assignment 11

The construction of a lifting system
Each student (or group) needs:

- clamps, stand and bosses
- G-clamp to prevent stand from toppling over
- pair of single sheave pulleys
- double sheave pulley
- string
- 500 g mass on its hanger
- forcemeter (0–10 N)
- 50 cm rule

Toppling is a likely hazard with this procedure. Students should use a G-clamp to secure the base of the stand to the bench.

You will need to demonstrate how to assemble the pulley system. Start off by fixing the string to the base of the top pulley. Thread it around the bottom pulley and then over the top pulley. Finally, make a loop at the free end for the forcemeter. Use the demonstration to show how to support the rule firmly against the bench, and how to put a marker on the free end of the string with sticky tape.

Guidelines for the Unit 3 assignments (continued)

Assignment 12

The design and construction of a nightlight

Note: For mark band 3, students should select their own components from a range in tasks 2, 3, 4 and 5.

<u>Task 2: Building a circuit to test the effect of resistance on current</u>
Each student (or group) needs:

- 6 V battery
- 220 Ω linear potentiometer arranged as a variable resistor
- 6.5 V, 150 mA MES bulb in holder
- digital multimeter on 200 mA range with unused socket taped over and used sockets labelled with polarity
- four 4 mm leads

Components will need to be mounted with 4 mm sockets. Plastic component boxes are useful.

<u>Task 3: Investigating how a light-dependent resistor behaves</u>
For Task 3, each student or group will need the equipment from Task 2 and:

- LDR, for example NORP12 suitably mounted
- something to shade LDR from light, such as opaque plastic bottle top

<u>Task 4: Using a transistor to control the current in a circuit</u>
For Task 4, each student (or group) needs:

- 4.7 kΩ resistor as resistor 1
- 1 kΩ resistor as resistor 2
- 10 kΩ linear potentiometer arranged as a variable resistor, with some indication as to the settings for maximum and minimum resistances
- 6 V battery
- 6.5 V, 150 mA MES bulb in holder
- RFP2N10L MOSFET as the transistor, in a plastic component box with 4 mm terminals labelled C, B and E as shown.

Guidelines for the Unit 3 assignments (continued)

Using a MOSFET instead of a BJT saves a lot of problems in the long run – MOSFETs are relatively indestructible, and matching them to the LDR is easy. Be warned: the MOSFET is shown as viewed from the top, looking at the printed label.

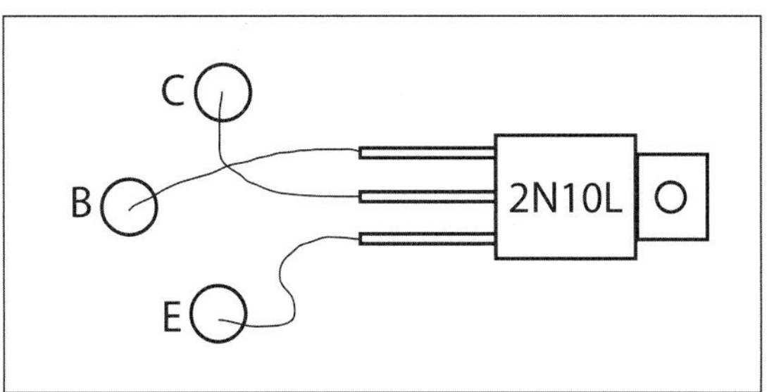

Task 5: Making your circuit light-dependent

For Task 5, each student (or group) needs the Task 4 equipment, except for the 4.7 kΩ replaced with NORP12 LDR.

You will, of course, need to check the circuits that your students assemble. Incorrect polarity of the ammeter is the most likely fault. They will need guidance about interpreting the reading of the display in milliamps.

The LDR will need a lot of light to deliver a large current – a well-lit laboratory would help. Provide some means of shading the LDR – an opaque plastic bottle top works well.

It would pay to keep the 6 V battery in your possession until you have checked their transistor circuit. It is important that students realise the importance of assembling the circuit correctly for it to be useful. You might want to demonstrate how to follow the circuit diagram before you let them have a go. In case one of the circuits contains a dead component which you can't trace, it helps to have a functioning circuit up your sleeve for the students to borrow.

Guidelines for the Unit 3 assignments (continued)

Assignment 13

The production of yoghurt from milk

Task 1: Preliminary work

Yoghurt manufacture is treated in most biology textbooks. A good industrial perspective is available at http://www.pauls.com.au/ and follows links via 'Students' to 'Yoghurt'.

Note: Exact requirements will vary depending on the factors the students decide to investigate.

Each student (or group) needs:

- UHT milk
- live yoghurt
- sterile boiling tubes and rack
- water bath set at between 40°C and 43°C
- sterile pipettes and safety fillers or plastic syringes for measuring volumes
- 10 cm^3 measuring cylinders
- sterile distilled water
- cling film
- Universal indicator solution (or pH papers, range 3 to 7, or pH probe)
- ready poured plates of China blue lactose agar
- sterile L-shaped disposable plastic spreaders
- resazurin tablets
- distilled water
- Chinagraph pencil or spirit marker pen
- sticky tape
- discard jar containing disinfectant (for example, 1% Virkon)

See the notes for Assignment 3 (page IV:15), as they also apply to this assignment.

For this investigation students will find helpful information on the National Centre for Biotechnology website (http://www.ncbe.reading.ac.uk).

Additionally:

If the students want to use resazurin, they should be aware that it is a redox indicator. Practical activity 9 (pages III:22 and III:67) gives a non-quantitative introduction to the use of this indicator. It can be made quantitative by attributing a number to the colour changes as the dye is reduced.

Grey purple 0

Purple 1

Violet 2

Violet/pink 3

Blue/pink 4

Rose pink 5

Pale pink 6

Very pale pink 7

White 8

Note that this colour number scale is not the same as that used in the dairy industry. The resazurin tablets are available from Philip Harris Education or BDH Ltd.

Assessment record for Unit 3

Name: ____________________________________

Strand a – Science in the Work Place	
	Mark band awarded
Identify careers	
Work carried out by organisation	
Location of organisation	
Job titles and qualifications	
Use of science	
Quality of report	
Mark awarded (/11)	

Strand b – Chemical Reactions		
	Mark band awarded	
	reaction	
	1	**2**
Type of reaction		
Products and reactants/equation		
Obtain product		
Calculation of yields		
Evaluation		
Energy inputs/disposal of waste		
Mark awarded (/13)		

Strand c – Electronic Device	
	Mark band awarded
Uses of electronic devices	
Assemble device	
Evaluate device	
Mark awarded (/7)	

Strand d – Mechanical Device	
	Mark band awarded
Types of mechanical devices and components	
Assemble/investigate performance	
Calculations of performance	
Mark awarded (/6)	

Strand e – Monitoring an Organism	
	Mark band awarded
Identify organism	
Produce plan/monitor organism	
Record measurements/observations	
Present and process data	
Explain findings	
Evaluate monitoring process	
Mark awarded (/13)	

Total mark (/50)	

Using science at work

Assignment 8 provides students with the opportunity to produce assessment evidence for Unit 3 skill area a (see page IV:72).

Introduction

Most people think of scientists as people who wear white coats and work in laboratories. Many scientists do work in laboratories as analysts, technicians or research workers. These scientists do important jobs such as:

- making sure that the food and water you eat and drink are safe
- testing the materials used to build cars
- developing new medicines to protect your health.

But, science is much more than an activity carried out in laboratories. Science is also used when:

- a nurse measures your blood pressure
- a farmer produces food
- a mechanic tests your car during an MOT test
- you use washing-up liquid to clean plates.

In fact, science is all around us all the time. Many people who use science do not realise that this is what they are doing. In this assignment, you will look for science wherever it is used. You will look at some of the businesses near to your school. You will ask these businesses if they use any science in their work. If the answer is yes, and it usually will be, you will then ask:

- about the people who work in the organisation
- what they do
- how they were trained to do their jobs
- what qualifications they need
- what skills they have.

At the end of this assignment, you will have a better idea of how science is used. You will have also learned about possible careers in which you can use the science you learn at school.

The CD-ROM contains a checklist for students and an assessment record form.

Task 1: Survey jobs in science

You need to work in groups. Carry out some research into jobs in science. Start by doing some brainstorming in your group. Decide which jobs use science. Each member of your group can then take one type of job and find out more about it.

For each type of job, think about:

- what the job is about (the 'content' of the job)
- what type of organisation employs people to do it
- what skills are needed to do it
- what qualifications the people need
- how they achieve their qualifications.

Write down the findings of your group in Form 1

Here are some ways of finding the information you need.

1. Careers directories.
   Your local library, careers service or careers teacher will have a copy of *Occupations*, which is published by the careers service Connexions. This lists jobs in sections, one of which is 'Sciences, mathematics and related work'. Each job is described by what the work involves, the work environment, the skills needed, entry requirements, and training and career opportunities. A search through *Occupations* will give you most of the information you need.
   - Note that *Occupations* is also available on-line. Visit www.connexions.gov.uk/occupations
   - You do not need to write down everything you find out. You could list the main qualification, for example, rather than all the possible qualifications.

2. Local paper.
   Many jobs are advertised in your local paper. You could cut out all the advertisements about jobs in science over a few weeks and sort them into types. The company advertising the job may tell you more about it. You could visit an organisation that uses science and ask the human resources or training department about all the jobs it provides.

Task 2: Identify careers in science and science related areas

Use your findings from Task 2. Draw up a summary of the careers that people who work in science may have. Examples are laboratory technician, doctor, trading standards officer, forensic scientist.

You should ask the following questions about each career you select:

- What is the name of the career?
- What do people having this as a career do?
- What qualifications do they need to enter this career?
- How do they get these qualifications?

Write down your findings in Form 2. You must list at least ten careers.

Task 3: Survey the uses of science

You need to work on your own. Carry out some research into businesses or other organisations that use science. Tasks 1 and 2 will have given you some ideas. Choose two organisations to research in more detail.

For each of the two organisations, you need to answer the following questions:

- its name
- where it is – its address
- why it is where it is (there may be scientific, economic, social and environmental reasons)
- what work does the organisation do (for example, produces frozen foods, provides health care)
- write down the job titles of some people in the organisation who have scientific jobs, what qualifications and skills do they need for the job?
- what is the type of scientific work done by the people you have chosen?

You should present your answers in the form of a report on 'Science in the workplace'.

You may need some help in finding things out. Here are some ways of finding the information you need.

1. A very good source of information is the *Dun and Bradstreet Business Directory*, which you will find in your local library. This lists businesses in your area by industry in numbered categories. For example:
   - section 0182 is food crops grown under cover
   - section 2844 is producers of perfumes, cosmetics and other toilet preparations
   - section 4941 is water supplies.

   The directory also lists how many people work for each organisation.

2. Use a copy of *Yellow Pages*. At the back is a Classification index. This gives details on how various types of organisations are listed in *Yellow Pages*. For example, 'Chemists – analytical & research' can also be found under 'Laboratory facilities' and 'Science & research consultants'.

3. You may find some local business directories in your local library. You could also try the local careers service, your careers teacher, or look on the Internet.

Name ____________________ Date __________

Form 1: Jobs in science (Task 1)

Job title	Content of job	Organisation type	Skills needed	Qualifications needed	How to achieve qualifications

Name ______________________ Date ______________

Form 2: Careers in science (Task 2)

	Career	What they do
1		
2		
3		
4		
5		
6		
7		
8		
9		
10		

The extraction of copper from an ore

Assignment 9 provides students with the opportunity to produce assessment evidence for Unit 3 skill area b (see page IV:72).

Forms 2, 3, 4 and 5, as provided, are suitable for mark band 1. For mark band 2/3, students should choose their own formats for recording results and presenting the analysis.

Introduction

Metals have been important to humans for thousands of years. In fact, two periods of human history are called the 'Iron Age' and the 'Bronze Age'.

Scientists think that the core of the Earth is formed from metals of many types. Unfortunately, we cannot get metals from the core of the Earth. At present, we get all of our metals from the crust of the Earth. The crust of the Earth is rich in metal compounds, called ores. Mining of metals was one of our earliest industries. It is still important in countries all over the world.

However, very few metals exist in a pure form in the Earth's crust. One reason for this is that metals react with the oxygen in the atmosphere and form metal compounds:

$$\text{metal} + \text{oxygen} \longrightarrow \text{metal oxide}$$

Extracting a metal element from a metal compound requires energy. This reaction is called a reduction reaction, because it takes away oxygen. Processes used to extract metals from their ores usually include one reduction reaction. What sort of reduction reaction is used depends on how reactive the metal atoms are.

The CD-ROM contains a checklist for students and an assessment record form.

Task 1: Safety precautions

You need to carry out a risk assessment for this assignment. Write down your findings on Form 1.

Task 2: Making copper sulphate from malachite

Malachite is an **ore** of copper. In this task you will convert malachite to copper sulphate.

1. Measure out about 50 cm^3 of dilute sulphuric acid using a measuring cylinder. Pour the dilute sulphuric acid into a 250 cm^3 beaker.
2. Weigh out about 10 g of malachite. Write down the exact mass on Form 2.
3. Add a small amount of the malachite to the dilute sulphuric acid. Add the malachite very slowly.
4. The mixture will fizz as the malachite reacts with the dilute sulphuric acid. Stir the mixture with a glass rod until all signs of reaction have stopped.
5. Repeat steps 3 and 4 until the mixture no longer fizzes when you add malachite to the dilute sulphuric acid.
6. Filter the solution into a clean evaporating basin. While this is filtering, weigh what remains of the malachite. Write down this mass on Form 2.
7. Place the evaporating basin on a wire gauze on a tripod.
8. Heat the solution very gently using a low Bunsen burner flame until crystals begin to form on the surface of the liquid. If the liquid goes green, add drops of dilute sulphuric acid until it goes blue.
9. Stop heating. Allow the solution to cool. When the solution is cool, move the basin to a warm place. This will complete the crystallisation of the copper sulphate. This may take a few days!
10. After a few days, pour any liquid from the copper sulphate crystals and transfer them to a dry evaporating basin or watch-glass.
11. Allow the copper sulphate crystals to dry for at least 24 hours.
12. Weigh the copper sulphate crystals. Write down the mass on Form 2.
13. Store the copper sulphate crystals in a stoppered container. Label the container with your name and the name of the contents.

Task 3: Extracting copper from copper sulphate crystals

1. Measure out about 50 cm^3 of distilled water using a measuring cylinder. Pour the distilled water into a 250 cm^3 beaker.
2. Weigh out about 5 g of the copper sulphate crystals you made in Task 2. Write down the exact mass on Form 3.
3. Add the copper sulphate crystals to the distilled water. Stir the mixture with a glass rod until all the copper sulphate dissolves. The solution should now be coloured blue.
4. Weigh out about 2 g of zinc filings or zinc powder.
5. Add the zinc to the copper sulphate solution. Stir the mixture. You will see solid copper forming.
6. After five minutes, allow the solid to settle. Then pour off as much of the colourless liquid as you can without losing the solid.
7. Carefully add about 50 cm^3 of dilute hydrochloric acid. This will dissolve any unused zinc.

8. When the mixture no longer fizzes, filter off the copper and wash it with distilled water.
9. Now allow the copper to dry for at least 24 hours.
10. Weigh the copper you have produced. Write down the mass on Form 3. Store the copper in a stoppered container. Label the container with your name and the name of the contents.

Task 4: The chemical reaction

Find out the type of chemical reaction(s) used to get the copper from the copper sulphate. Describe the type of chemical reaction and how you can tell this reaction is the same type. Write down the chemical equation for this reaction.

Task 5: Calculating the yield of copper obtained from copper sulphate

Your **actual yield** is the mass of copper you measured at the end of the experiment.

The **theoretical yield** is the mass you would expect if the reaction was complete and you were able to collect and isolate all of your product. You can calculate this using the method in Form 4 or ask your teacher for the theoretical yield.

Calculate the **percentage yield** (you may use form 5 to help).

In practice, you will always end up with the actual yield less than the theoretical yield. Give some reasons why your experiment produced less than the theoretical yield. Suggest parts of your experiment that could be improved and how the method could be improved.

Task 6: Commercial production of copper

1. Carry out some research to find out how copper is made commercially.
2. Compare your findings with the method you used in the laboratory.
3. Suggest reasons for any differences you find.
4. What are the energy inputs and waste products? What methods are used to treat the waste products?

Name ______________________ Date __________ Checked by ______________________ Date __________

Form 1: Risk assessment (Task 1)

Material	Hazard	What could go wrong?	Safety precautions	What to do in case of accident	**Risk:** low/ medium/high
Procedure					

Name ______________________________ Date ______________

Form 2: Masses from Task 2

mass of weighing vessel + malachite at start = ☐ g

mass of weighing vessel + malachite at end = ☐ g

mass of malachite = ☐ g

mass of weighing vessel + copper sulphate crystals = ☐ g

mass of weighing vessel = ☐ g

mass of copper sulphate crystals = ☐ g

Form 3: Masses from Task 3

mass of weighing vessel + copper sulphate crystals = ☐ g

mass of weighing vessel = ☐ g

mass of copper sulphate = ☐ g

mass of weighing vessel + copper = ☐ g

mass of weighing vessel = ☐ g

mass of copper = ☐ g

Form 4: Calculating the yield of copper sulphate crystals (Task 5)

Each mole of malachite, $CuCO_3Cu(OH)_2$, produces two moles of copper sulphate, $CuSO_4.5H_2O$.

1. The formula of malachite is $CuCO_3Cu(OH)_2$.
Calculate the relative mass of malachite by filling in this table:

Atom	Relative mass	Number of atoms present	Total mass
Cu			
C			
O			
H			
		relative mass of malachite =	

Name ____________________ Date ____________

2. The formula of copper sulphate is $CuSO_4.5H_2O$.
Calculate the relative mass of copper sulphate by filling in this table:

Atom	Relative mass	Number of atoms present	Total mass
Cu			
S			
O			
H			
		relative mass of copper sulphate =	

3. Calculate the theoretical yield of copper sulphate by carrying out this calculation:

$$\text{theoretical yield of copper sulphate} = \frac{2 \times \text{relative mass of copper sulphate} \times \text{mass of malachite used}}{\text{relative mass of malachite}}$$

$$= \frac{2 \times \boxed{} \times \boxed{}}{\boxed{}}$$

$$= \boxed{}$$

THIS IS A BLANK PAGE

The production of a fertiliser

Assignment 10 provides students with the opportunity to produce assessment evidence for Unit 3 skill area b (see page IV:72).

Forms 2, 3, 4, 5, 6 and 7, as provided, are suitable for mark band 1. For mark band 2/3, students should choose their own formats for recording results and presenting the analysis.

Introduction

The three most important elements for plant growth are potassium, nitrogen and phosphorus. Commercial fertilisers usually contain one or more of these elements. In this assignment, you will investigate the production of potassium nitrate in the laboratory. You will also determine whether you can make potassium nitrate more cheaply than you can buy it from your local garden centre.

Suppose that a chemical plant near to your school produces potassium hydroxide solution of unknown concentration as a by-product. The chemical plant would normally be required to dispose of this material safely and within the legal restrictions on industrial effluents. To avoid this disposal problem, the chemical plant will supply the potassium hydroxide solution free to anyone who will guarantee to use it safely. Your task is to use the potassium hydroxide solution to make solid potassium nitrate for sale as a fertiliser.

The problem is that the concentration of the potassium hydroxide solution is not known. Potassium hydroxide solution is alkaline. You will need to ensure that the fertiliser produced is neither strongly acidic nor strongly alkaline. Either would be harmful to crops.

Before you start on this assignment, make sure that you have completed Unit 1, Assignment 5. During Assignment 5, you reacted sodium hydroxide, a similar compound, with an acid (hydrochloric acid) to find the concentration of the hydrochloric acid solution.

The CD-ROM contains a checklist for students and an assessment record form.

Task 1: Safety precautions

You need to carry out a risk assessment for this assignment. Write down your findings on Form 1.

Task 2: Examining the type of reaction

You are going to make potassium nitrate by the reaction of potassium hydroxide solution with dilute nitric acid.

Consider the following questions. Write down your answers on Form 2.

1. What type of compound is potassium hydroxide?
2. What type of compound is nitric acid?
3. What type of reaction does the equation describe?
4. When all the potassium hydroxide has reacted with nitric acid, what will the solution be called?
5. Identify other industrially important uses of this type of reaction.

Task 3: Investigating the amount of nitric acid needed

You don't know the concentration of the potassium hydroxide solution. You will first have to find out how much dilute nitric acid you need to react with the potassium hydroxide solution. You also need to make sure that the product is neither strongly acidic nor alkaline.

1. Measure out 25.0 cm^3 of the potassium hydroxide solution, using a pipette and pipette filler.
2. Pour the potassium hydroxide solution into a 250 cm^3 conical flask.
3. Add two drops of methyl orange indicator. The indicator will turn the solution yellow.
4. Fill a 50 cm^3 burette to the 0.00 mark with 0.5 mol dm^{-3} nitric acid.
5. Add the dilute nitric acid from the burette to the potassium hydroxide solution, using the titration method from Unit 1, Assignment 5, until the solution just turns red.
6. Calculate the volume of dilute nitric acid you have used. Write down your burette readings in Form 3.

Task 4: Preparation of potassium nitrate solution

In Task 3, you used 25.0 cm^3 of the potassium hydroxide solution and 0.5 mol dm^{-3} nitric acid. You will use the same reaction to make potassium nitrate fertiliser. However, you will start with more potassium hydroxide solution. This means you will need to use more dilute nitric acid. You will use 50 cm^3 of potassium hydroxide solution.

How much more dilute nitric acid will you need to use? Carry out the calculation on Form 4.

1. Use a measuring cylinder to transfer 50 cm^3 of the potassium hydroxide solution to a 250 cm^3 beaker.
2. Use a measuring cylinder to add the volume of 0.5 mol dm^{-3} nitric acid that you calculated on Form 4.
3. Test the mixed solution using Universal indicator paper.
   - **a** If the solution is acidic, add more potassium hydroxide solution, drop by drop, until the indicator shows that the solution is nearly neutral (pH 6, 7 or 8).
   - **b** If the solution is alkaline, add more dilute nitric acid, drop by drop, until the indicator shows that the solution is nearly neutral (pH 6, 7 or 8).

Task 5: Isolation of potassium nitrate from your solution

Potassium nitrate is very soluble in water. To isolate it, you need to reduce the volume of water by heating.

1. Pour the contents of the beaker into the evaporating basin until it is half-full. Put the basin over a heat source (for example, a Bunsen burner and tripod) and heat gently.
2. Boil the liquid gently, periodically adding more liquid from the beaker to maintain the level until the beaker is empty.
3. When a white solid appears round the edge of the basin, carefully push it back into the liquid to re-dissolve it. Be careful not to upset the basin.
4. When the white solid no longer re-dissolves, stop heating and allow the basin to cool.
5. Place the basin where your teacher tells you, loosely protecting the contents from dust with a folded piece of paper. Leave the basin until your next lesson.
6. If any liquid remains in the dish, pour it away from the crystals.
7. Scrape out the crystals onto a dry filter paper. If the crystals have set hard, you need to wear eye protection.
8. Place the filter paper on a watch-glass and allow it to dry in the air. Do not heat the crystals because potassium nitrate will decompose if heated too strongly.
9. Store the potassium nitrate crystals in a stoppered container. Label the container with your name, the name of the contents and the yield.

Task 6: Measuring how much potassium nitrate you have prepared

1. Write down the mass of a weighing bottle on Form 5.
2. Transfer your potassium nitrate to the weighing bottle and weigh. Write down this mass on Form 5.
3. The mass of potassium nitrate that you have prepared (your yield) is the difference between these two values.
4. Calculate the yield of your preparation.

Task 7: Calculating the yield of copper obtained from copper sulphate

Your **actual yield** is the mass of copper you measured at the end of the experiment.

The **theoretical yield** is the mass you would expect if the reaction was complete and you were able to collect and isolate all of your product. You can calculate this using the method in Form 6 or ask your teacher for the theoretical yield.

Calculate the **percentage yield** (you may use Form 7 to help).

In practice, you will always end up with the actual yield less than the theoretical yield. Give some reasons why your experiment produced less than the theoretical yield. Suggest parts of your experiment that could be improved and how the method could be improved.

Task 8: Commercial production of potassium nitrate

1. Carry out research to find out how potassium nitrate is made commercially.
2. Compare your findings with the method you used in the laboratory.
3. Suggest reasons for any differences.
4. What are the energy inputs and waste products? What methods are used to treat the waste products?

Name ____________________ Date __________ Checked by ____________________ Date __________

Form 1: Risk assessment (Task 1)

Material	Hazard	What could go wrong?	Safety precautions	What to do in case of accident	**Risk:** low/ medium/high
Procedure					

Name ______________________________ Date ______________

Form 2: About the reaction (Task 2)

1. Potassium hydroxide is ______________ .
2. Nitric acid is ______________ .
3. The reaction between potassium hydroxide and nitric acid is a ______________ reaction.
4. When the potassium hydroxide has reacted completely with the nitric acid, the solution will be ______________ .
5. This type of reaction is used by industry to:

- ______________
- ______________
- ______________ .

Form 3: Titration volumes (Task 3)

Titration	1	2	3
Final burette reading (cm^3)			
Burette reading at start (cm^3)			
Volume of acid added (cm^3)			

Your titration volume, ______________ cm^3 of 0.5 mol dm^{-3} nitric acid, reacts with 25 cm^3 of the potassium hydroxide solution.

Form 4: Calculating amount of acid needed (Task 4)

In Task 3, you used 25 cm^3 of the potassium hydroxide solution.

The volume of 0.5 mol dm^{-3} nitric acid you used was [ ].

In Task 4, you will use 50 cm^3 of the potassium hydroxide solution.The volume of 0.5 mol dm^{-3} nitric acid you will need is [ ] × 2 = [ ] cm^3.

Form 5: Mass of potassium nitrate prepared (Task 6)

mass of weighing bottle + potassium nitrate = [ ] g

mass of weighing bottle = [ ] g

mass of potassium nitrate = [ ] g

Yield of potassium nitrate = [ ] g

Name ______________________________ Date ______________

Form 6: Calculating the theoretical yield (Task 7)

On Form 4, you calculated the volume of 0.5 mol dm^{-3} nitric acid you needed to add to the potassium hydroxide solution to produce potassium nitrate in Task 4.

$$\text{number of moles of nitric acid used (in } cm^3\text{)} = \frac{\text{volume of nitric acid added}}{1000} \times \text{concentration of nitric acid (in mol } dm^{-3}\text{)}$$

$$= \frac{\boxed{}}{1000} \times 0.5$$

$$= \boxed{}$$

The relative masses you need in this calculation are:
potassium hydroxide = 56 g
nitric acid = 63 g
potassium nitrate = 101 g

The number of moles of nitric acid added is the same as the number of moles of potassium nitrate obtained, theoretically.

$$\text{theoretical yield of potassium nitrate (in g)} = \text{number of moles of potassium nitrate produced} \times \text{relative mass of potassium nitrate}$$

$$= \boxed{} \times 101$$

$$= \boxed{}$$

Form 7: Calculating the percentage yield (Task 7)

$$\text{percentage yield of potassium nitrate} = \frac{\text{actual yield}}{\text{theoretical yield}} \times 100$$

$$= \frac{\boxed{}}{\boxed{}} \times 100$$

$$= \boxed{}$$

The construction of a lifting system

Assignment 11 provides students with the opportunity to produce assessment evidence for Unit 3 skill area c (see page IV:71).

Forms 2, 3 and 4, as provided, are suitable for supporting mark band 1. For mark band 2/3, students should choose their own formats for recording results. Task 6 is only required by students working at mark band 3.

Introduction

The term '**machine**' is used very generally, and often for very complicated devices. In science, a machine is anything that makes forces easier to use. The simplest example of a machine is a lever.

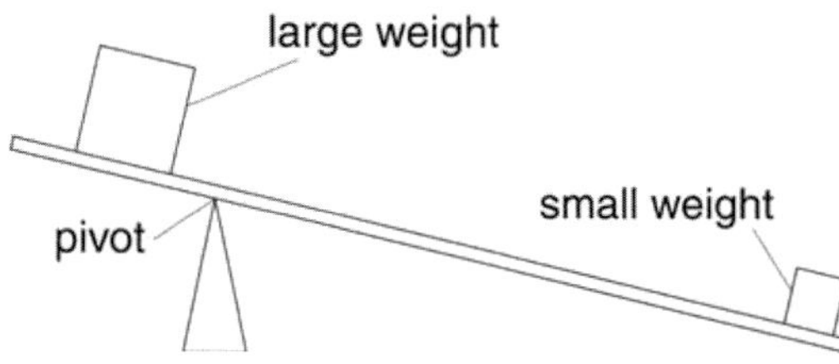

In the diagram, the large weight on the left side has been lifted by the much smaller weight on the right. The lever has multiplied the effect of the small force (the small weight). This can only happen because the small weight moved a greater distance than the large weight. Scientists say that the lever has 'magnified' the force.

Some other machines multiply movement. For example, when you ride a bicycle, you apply a force when you turn the pedals. Turning the pedals turns the wheels. But the bike's wheels travel a greater distance than your feet, so the bicycle multiplies your movement.

Work is defined as:

$$\text{work} = \text{force} \times \text{distance moved}$$

You cannot get more work out of a machine than you put into it. If the machine magnifies force, it must decrease the distance moved. If it magnifies distance moved, it must decrease force.

In practice, the work you get out of a machine is less than the work you put into it. This is because there is friction between the moving parts. Friction uses up some of the energy that is put into the machine. This means that the machine is not totally efficient.

$$\text{efficiency of a machine} = \frac{\text{work output}}{\text{work input}} \times 100$$

Efficiency is a ratio of two numbers, and it is usually written as a percentage. Mechanical advantage measures how much the force is multiplied.

$$\text{mechanical advantage} = \frac{\text{load (output force)}}{\text{effort (imput force)}}$$

The CD-ROM contains a checklist for students and an assessment record form.

Re-opening the flour mill

In this assignment, you will solve the following problem.

Some organic food enthusiasts want to re-open an old flour mill so that they can use it to make organic flour. Unfortunately, some of the original machinery in the mill is old or broken and they do not have enough money to replace it.

Originally, all the power for the mill was provided by a water wheel. The water wheel can be restored to working order to turn the millstones, but it cannot be used to provide power for other tasks.

The flour is made by grinding organically grown grain. The millstones that grind the grain are in the mill chamber, 10 m above the ground. Grain is supplied in 100 kg sacks. These sacks are too heavy for the mill workers to carry up 10 m by hand. This work used to be done by a hoist that was powered from the water wheel. The hoist cannot be repaired.

The workers see some old pulley wheels in the mill and they have plenty of rope. They also see the strong beams 20 m above the ground, where the original hoist was fastened. Your task is to design and test a model of a pulley system that will hoist a sack of grain to the mill chamber. The requirements are:

- the hoist must be able to lift 100 kg through 10 m
- one person must be able to operate the hoist without help.

You will build and test some simple pulley systems. This will give you some experience of how pulley systems work and what can be achieved. You will use your results to design and test a model system for the mill hoist. You will then recommend a design to solve the problem of lifting grain sacks to the mill chamber.

Task 1: Safety precautions

You need to carry out a risk assessment for this assignment. Write down your findings on Form 1.

Task 2: Identifying the uses of mechanical machines

Find out about some mechanical machines, what they do and what they are used for. For each of the machines, find out about some of the parts (components) used in each one. Describe the function of each of these components in the machines. Try to choose examples of machines that do different things and are built differently. You may use Form 2 to record some of your findings.

Task 3: Building and testing a two-pulley system

1. Construct the pulley system shown in the diagram.

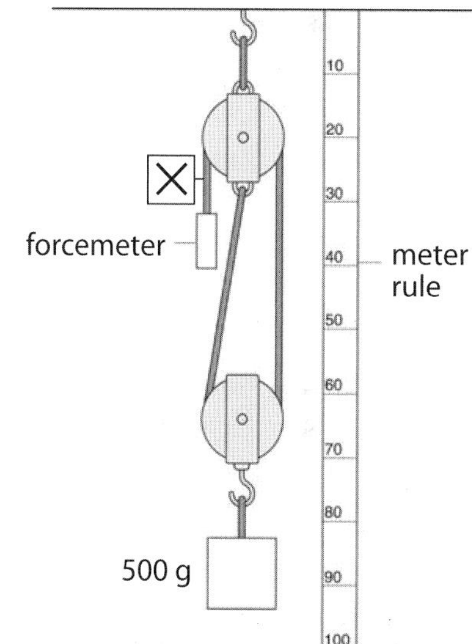

2. Attach a marker **X** to the string leaving the upper pulley.
3. Pull on the forcemeter to raise the 500 g mass a distance of 10 cm.
4. On Form 3, write down:
- the reading on the forcemeter
- the distance moved by **X**
- the distance moved by the mass.

5. Repeat steps 3 and 4, four more times, so that you have five sets of readings.
6. Use the equations on Form 4 to calculate the input force and the output force, the work input and the work output, and the efficiency of the pulley system for each set of measurements. Write your answers on Form 4.
7. Calculate the average efficiency of the pulley system.

Task 4: Building and testing a three-pulley system

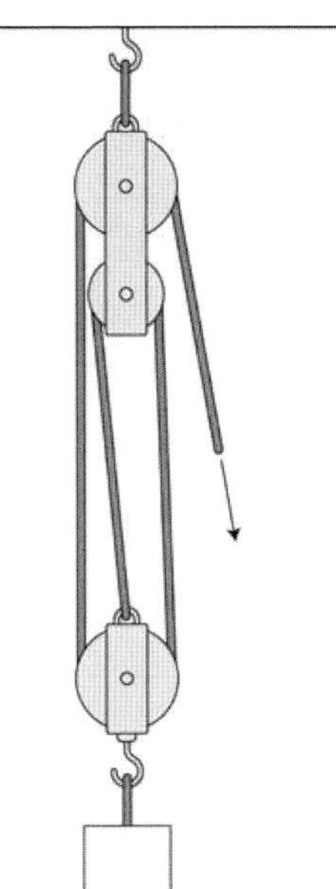

1. Construct the pulley system shown in the diagram.
2. Draw up a suitable table for your test results.
3. Test the pulley system as you did in Task 3.
4. Calculate the efficiency of the three-pulley system.
5. Write down why you think the efficiency of the three-pulley system is less than 100%.

Task 5: Designing and testing a model for the mill hoist

1. Use the ideas you have gained from Tasks 3 and 4 to design a suitable model system.
2. Show your design to your teacher, to check for safety.
3. When your teacher has agreed your design, you should build it.
4. Now test your machine. Write down your results in a table.
5. Use your conclusions to calculate:
   (a) what force will be needed to raise 100 kg through 10 m
   (b) how far the rope will need to be pulled to raise the grain to the mill chamber (you can assume that the efficiency of the working system will be the same as the efficiency of your model).
6. Identify any sources of error in your measurements or calculations. Describe how the effects of these errors could be reduced.
7. Write down some ways that your new system could be improved, either by reducing the force needed or by reducing the distance the rope must be pulled.

Task 6: Another type of lifting machine (optional)

A car jack uses a different type of machine to lift a car.

1. Design experiments to measure the forces and distances involved in using the car jack.
2. Use your results to work out the mechanical advantage, the work done and the efficiency of the car jack.
3. Write a report describing the tests you carried out and presenting you results. Include a comparison of the two lifting machines and an evaluation of their performance.

The construction of a lifting system

Name ______________________ Date __________ Checked by ______________________ Date __________

Form 1: Risk assessment (Task 1)

Procedure	**Hazard**	**What could go wrong?**	**Safety precautions**	**What to do in case of accident**	**Risk:** low/ medium/high

Name ______________________________ Date ______________

Form 2: Examples of mechanical machines (Task 2)

Machine	Uses	Parts

Form 3: Building and testing a two-pulley system (Task 3)

Experiment	Input force (N)	Distance moved by X (cm)	Distance moved by 500 g mass (cm)
1			10
2			10
3			10
4			10
5			10

Name ______________________________ Date ______________

Form 4: Calculate the efficiency of the two-pulley system (Task 3)

Stage 1

force needed to lift the load (the input force) = the reading of the force meter

= .... N

distance moved by the input force = ... m

work input = force × distance

= .... × ....

= .... J

Stage 2

mass of load = 500 g = 0.5 kg

output force = mass × 10

= 0.5 × 10

= 5 N

distance moved by the output force = 0.1m

work output = force × distance

= 5 × 0.1 J

Stage 3

efficiency of the pulley system = $\frac{\text{work output}}{\text{work input}} \times 100$

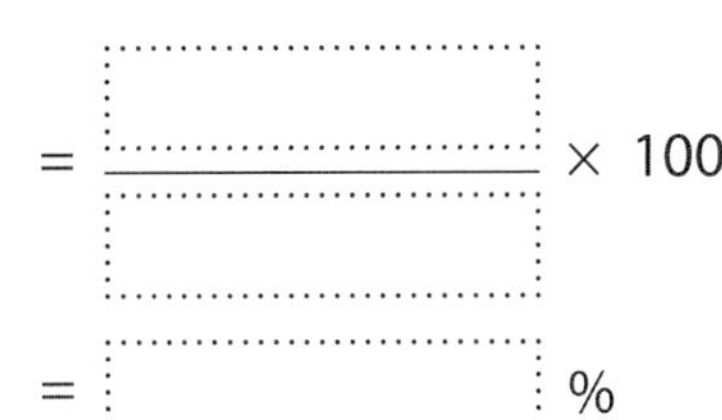

= .... %

Name ______________________________ Date ______________

Stage 4

The number of times the machine multiplies in the input force is called the mechanical advantage.

$$\text{Mechanical advantage} = \frac{\text{loud (output force)}}{\text{Effort (input force)}}$$

$$= \frac{\square}{\square}$$

$$= \square$$

Experiment	Efficiency (%)	Mechanical Advantage
1		
2		
3		
4		
5		
Average value		

The design and construction of a nightlight

Assignment 12 provides students with the opportunity to produce assessment evidence for Unit 3 skill area d (see page IV:71).

Forms 2, 3 and 4, as provided, are suitable for supporting mark band 1. For mark band 2/3, students should choose their own formats for recording results. For mark band 3, students should select their own components from a range in Tasks 2, 3, 4 and 5.

Introduction

In this exercise, you will design and build an electrical circuit for a nightlight for use in a baby's bedroom. The nightlight will provide enough light for the baby or its carer to see during the night, but must not be so bright that it prevents the baby from sleeping.

Your nightlight will need a switch to switch it on when the light level falls (in the evening) and off when the light level rises again (in the morning). In electronic circuits, switching can be carried out by transistors.

Before starting this assignment, you should have completed Unit 1, Assignment 6 on measuring electrical properties. Your nightlight will use a similar circuit to those you looked at in Assignment 6, but will use more components. The most important of these components are:

- the transistor
- the light-dependent resistor (LDR).

The resistance of the LDR changes when the brightness of the light shining on it changes. The LDR will act as a sensor in your final circuit.

The CD-ROM contains a checklist for students and an assessment record form.

Task 1: Symbols for and functions of components of electrical circuits

Form 1 shows the symbols for many common components of electrical circuits.

1. Find out what component each symbol represents. Write this down on Form 1.
2. Find out what each component does in the circuit. Write down your findings on Form 1.

Task 2: Building a circuit to test the effect of resistance on current

You are supplied with the following components:

- battery
- lamp
- variable resistor
- ammeter.

1. Connect the components in series to form the circuit shown.

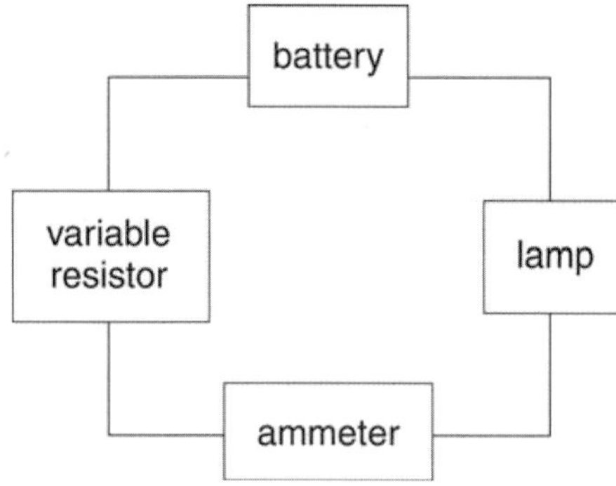

2. Vary the resistance until the lamp just lights. Read the value showing on the ammeter. This is the smallest current that will light the lamp. Write down this value on Form 2.
3. Draw a circuit diagram for your circuit on Form 2. You need to use the correct symbols for the components you have used.

Task 3: Investigating how a light-dependent resistor behaves

1. Re-use your circuit from Task 2, but with two changes. Take out the variable resistor and put the light-dependent resistor (LDR) in its place. Replace the ammeter with a milliammeter.
2. Expose the LDR fully to light from the rest of the room and read the milliammeter. Write down the value on Form 3.
3. Shield the LDR from the light and read the milliammeter again. Write down this value on Form 3.
4. Think about how these results compare to the results using the variable resistor.

Task 4: Using a transistor to control the current in a circuit

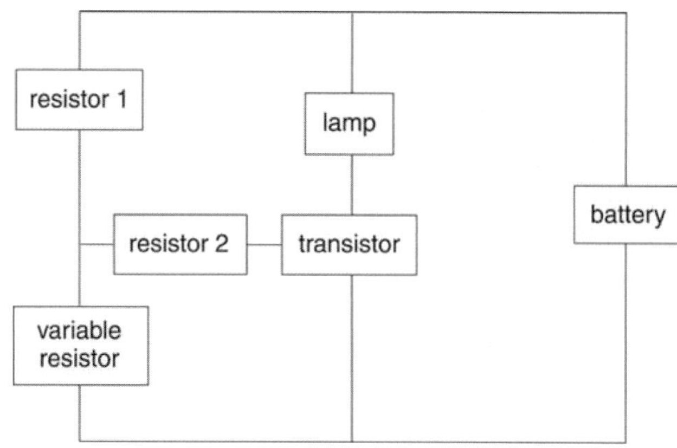

1. Assemble this circuit, but DO NOT connect the battery until your teacher has checked your circuit.
2. Vary the resistance of the variable resistor and observe the effect on the lamp. Write down your observation on Form 4.
3. Draw a circuit diagram for your circuit on Form 4. You need to use the correct symbols for the components you have used.

Task 5: Making your circuit light-dependent

1. Re-use your circuit from Task 4, but with one change. Replace the variable resistor with an LDR.
2. Expose the LDR to full light, then cover it up to shield it from light. How was the lamp affected by this?

You will now refine the circuit so that it will work as a nightlight.

3. Replace resistor 1 in your circuit by a variable resistor. You can now vary the voltage at the base of the transistor.
4. Test your circuit in light and darkness. Alter the variable resistance until the lamp lights up when the room becomes too dark to read from a book. Demonstrate your circuit to your teacher.
5. Draw a circuit diagram for your circuit. Use the correct symbols for the components you have used.
6. Write a short description of how your circuit worked. Describe how the resistances of the LDR and the variable resistor affected your circuit.

Task 6: Identifying uses of switching circuits

There are many examples of devices that switch on or off in response to changes in light, temperature, composition of air (for example, smoke) and so on. Make a list of all those you can think

Task 7: Evaluation of nightlight circuit

Your original brief was to produce an automatic nightlight for a baby's bedroom. The light should turn on automatically when the light level falls (in the evening) and turn off when the light level rises again (in the morning).

You should produce an evaluation of your circuit, which address the following:

- How well did your circuit meet the brief?
- What weaknesses does you circuit have? (If it has none explain how you know.)
- Suggest improvements that would overcome any weaknesses.

You should use the results of your tests to support what you say in your evaluation.

Name ______________________________ Date ______________

Form 1: Symbols and functions of electrical components (Task 1)

For all of the symbols shown below, your need to find out:

(i) the name of the component and

(ii) what the component does.

Name: ______________________________

Function: ______________________________

____

Name: ______________________________

Function: ______________________________

____

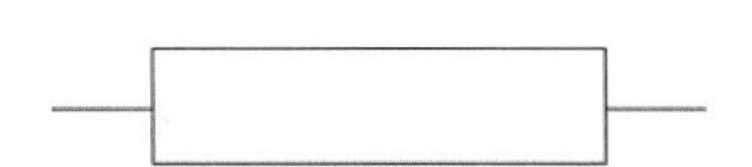

Name: ______________________________

Function: ______________________________

____

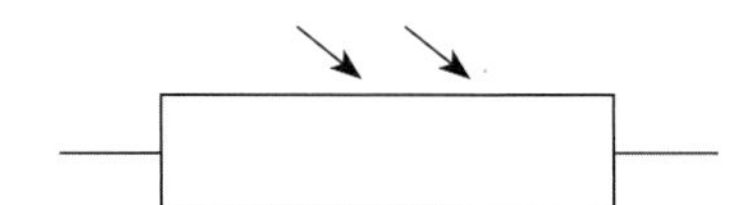

Name: ______________________________

Function: ______________________________

____

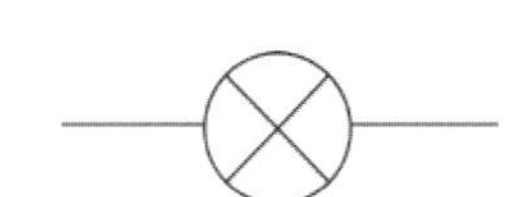

Name: ______________________________

Function: ______________________________

____

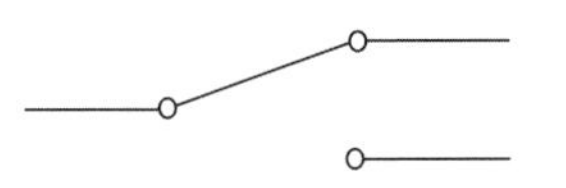

Name: ______________________________

Function: ______________________________

____

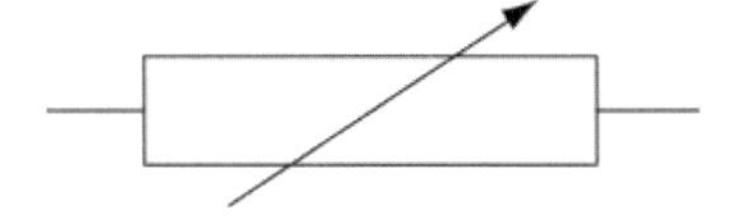

Name: ______________________________

Function: ______________________________

____

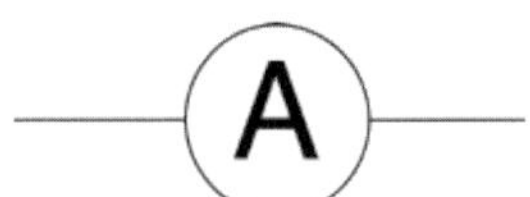

Name: ______________________________

Function: ______________________________

____

Name ______________________________ Date ______________

Form 2: Resistance and current (Task 2)

The smallest current that will light the lamp is [ ] amp.

The circuit diagram for Task 2 is:

Form 3: LDR and current (Task 3)

The current when the LDR is fully exposed to light is [ ] milliamp.

The current when the LDR is in the dark is [ ] milliamp.

The resistance of the LDR is **low**/**high** in bright light and **low**/**high** in darkness.

Form 4: Using a transistor (Task 4)

The lamp lights when the variable resistor has **low**/**high** resistance .

The value of the resistance is [ ] .

The circuit diagram for Task 4 is:

The production of yoghurt from milk

Assignment 13 provides students with the opportunity to produce assessment evidence for Unit 3 skill area d (see page IV:72).

Introduction

Milk and milk products are among our most important foods. Milk will deteriorate quickly if not kept properly. Milk turns sour as a result of the action of microorganisms. Processing of milk to form products such as butter, cheese and yoghurt is also the result of the action of microorganisms, but under controlled conditions. In this assignment, you will investigate the effect of microorganisms on milk, you will determine the best conditions for the production of yoghurt, and you will learn how to control these conditions.

Milk is converted to yoghurt by the action of bacteria such as *Lactobacillus bulgaricus* and *Streptococcus thermophilus*. The thickening of the milk during the manufacture of yoghurt is due to the production of lactic acid, which coagulates the proteins in the milk.

The dairy industry needs to make its products as effectively as possible, to make sure that it can sell them at a profit. The action of the bacteria is very dependent on the conditions used. The production of yoghurt is most effective when carried out under the best possible conditions.

In this assignment, you will carry out some preliminary tests using different conditions for the formation of yoghurt. You will use the results of these preliminary experiments to plan your investigation into the effect of the conditions used on the formation of yoghurt.

- Your plan will indicate those conditions you intend to vary, those that you will keep constant and how you intend to monitor the formation of the yoghurt.
- Your plan will describe the measurements that you will make and how you will record them.
- Your plan will identify what you intend to find out during your experiments – the aim of the work.

At the end of the experiment, you will consider whether or not your experiment was successful in identifying the best conditions for the formation of yoghurt. This is called an evaluation.

Your experiment may not be totally successful in finding the best conditions. This will not mean that your experiment was a failure. Success involves working out exactly what happened during your work, and why.

Before you start this assignment, you should have completed the Unit 1 assignment on investigating microorganisms (Assignment 3). This assignment will have developed the practical skills that you need for this assignment.

The CD-ROM contains a checklist for students and an assessment record form.

Task 1: Preliminary work

This preliminary work is needed to help you to plan your investigation. In the preliminary work, you will find out what conditions might be important for the formation of yoghurt.

You need to look at as many possible conditions as possible during this preliminary work. You can do this best by working in a group. Start by discussing the possible conditions that you could use. Allocate a different set of conditions to each member of the group to look at.

You should consider the following:

- type of milk
- type of bacteria
- temperature
- time.

Milk can be bought from the milkman or supermarket in many forms. These include full-fat, semi-skimmed, skimmed, sterilised and ultra-heat treated (UHT). Any of these could be used in your preliminary experiments.

The most common way to make yoghurt is by the joint action of the bacteria *Lactobacillus bulgaricus* and *Streptococcus thermophilus* on milk. You will use these bacteria in all your experiments. You can get them either as a starter culture or by adding some live yoghurt to the milk sample chosen.

Bacteria tend to be most active at a particular temperature. If the temperature is too low, the activity will be slow. If the temperature is too high, the bacteria might be destroyed. There will be a temperature range within which the bacteria are effective in forming yoghurt.

One of the effects of the bacteria on the milk is to thicken it by coagulating the milk proteins. This thickening takes place over a period of time. Too short a time will produce a thin yoghurt, too long a time may produce a solid product.

You also need to consider what you are going to measure, to monitor the progress of the yoghurt formation. Possibilities are:

- changes in appearance and smell of the milk
- clotting time of the milk
- the number of microorganisms
- changes in pH as lactic acid is produced.

Any or all of these factors could be used to monitor the formation of the yoghurt.

Think about the hazards of the work you are going to do before you start any practical work. The work you did on microorganisms in Unit 1, in which you used aseptic technique, will help you. Make a record of the safety precautions you are going to use. You must agree these with your teacher.

Carry out some experiments using different conditions and methods of monitoring to gain some experience of how the process is affected by conditions.

You can find some information on the effects of conditions on yoghurt formation by reading about yoghurt manufacture. This information will help you to plan your investigation.

Task 2: Plan your investigation

Gather together the results for Task 1 from all members of your group, as you now need to work on your own. You can now plan an investigation into the best conditions for the formation of yoghurt.

Your plan should include:

- what you hope to find out (your aim);
- the safety precautions to be taken;
- the types of bacteria used;
- the type or types of milk to be investigated;
- the temperature or temperatures to be used;
- the time or times to be used;
- any other conditions that you wish to vary;
- why you have chosen these conditions;
- your control to compare your investigation against;
- the equipment and materials needed;
- how you are to measure the changes;
- how you are to record your results;
- how you will decide whether your experiments have been successful.

Discuss your plan with your teacher. He or she will not tell you what you must investigate, since that is your decision. He or she will, however, advise you on whether what you have planned is a reasonable way to investigate the formation of yoghurt.

Task 3: Carry out your investigation

Follow your plan and record your observations and measurements in any appropriate way.

You may decide, after you have completed part of the work and obtained some results, that things are not working as you had hoped. You may decide to change your plan. This is a normal part of all research. Discuss any new plans with your teacher and revise your original plan (developed in Task 2). If you need to revise your plan, make sure to record how you changed it and why.

Task 4: Draw conclusions from your results

Use the results you have obtained to draw conclusions on how the conditions you used influenced the formation of the yoghurt. Decide what you think might be the best conditions to use.

Task 5: Evaluate your experiment

You need to consider if you achieved the aim set out in your plan.

You also need to consider:

- how well each part of the experiment worked
- which parts were unsatisfactory, and why
- what you did to overcome any unsatisfactory parts
- any observations or measurements that you were not happy with, and why
- what you would do differently if you were to repeat the work.

Task 6: Commercial applications of the monitoring of organisms

Carry out some research into investigations into the growth of organisms, including animals, plants and microorganisms, carried out in industry. Identify the purposes of such investigations.

Identify the methods used to monitor organisms in industry. Compare them with the methods you used, suggesting reasons for any differences.

Section V OCR
Practice papers

Introduction for the teacher

In these practice papers some of the questions have scenarios or contexts common to both the Foundation and Higher tiers.

A number of 'overlap' part questions and marks are identical in both tiers. These comprise questions testing topics and ideas deemed to be more challenging for Foundation candidates, but comparatively straightforward for Higher candidates. These are not necessarily whole questions. Some questions contain sections common to both tiers, combined with different sections, which target the specifications at an appropriate level in each paper.

Guidance on marking

The mark schemes provided give the expected answers, divided into separate marking points.

/	indicates alternative responses
;	separates individual marking points
bold words	are essential for the mark
(bracketed words)	are not essential
o.w.t.t.e.	(= or words to that effect) means accept any phrase that expresses that meaning
AO1, 2 or 3	refers to the Assessment Objectives
AO1	= knowledge and understanding
AO2	= application
AO3	= practical skills

The expected answers are not necessarily exhaustive. The marker should apply professional judgement – rewarding answers that show correct application of principles and knowledge.

Practice Paper

Surname	Initials

GCSE in Applied Science (Double Award)

Unit 2: Science for the needs of society

Foundation tier

Time 1 hour 30 minutes

You may use a calculator.

Preparing for your test

Read this front sheet carefully

- Write your name in the space above.
- Write your answers, in blue or black ink, in the spaces provided on the question paper.
- Answer **all** the questions.
- Read each question carefully, and make sure you know what you have to do before starting your answer.

Information

- The number of marks is given in brackets [ ] at the end of each question or part question.
- The total number of marks for this paper is **75**.

1. Tony and Sarah run a farm. They keep animals and also grow crops.

(a) The table below shows:

- some of their plant crops and animals
- a product obtained from each.

Complete the table, choosing products from the following list.
The first one has been done for you.

beef **cooking oil** **eggs** **flour** **sugar** **wool**

Plant crop or animal	**Product**
sunflower	cooking oil
wheat	
sheep	
cows	

[3]

(b) Many animal and plant products are used to make other things. Complete the table below to show **one** example of what each product is used for. Choose words from the following list. The first one has been done for you.

beer **bread** **cheese** **jam** **leather** **paper**

Product	**Used for making**
wood	paper
strawberries	
milk	
animal skins (cow hide)	

[3]

(c) Tony and Sarah's farm is organic.

(i) It is useful to have both animals and crops on an organic farm.
Explain how each is useful for the other.

The animals provide ____

____ **[2]**

The crops provide ____

____ **[2]**

(ii) Suggest how Tony controls weeds in his organic crops.

____ **[1]**

[Total: 11 marks]

2. (a) Samina is a vet. She helps to prevent animals catching diseases. She also tries to cure them if they do become ill.

(i) Name one animal disease that is caused by microorganisms.

____ [1]

(ii) How can Samina help to prevent animals catching such a disease?

____ [1]

(iii) One of Sarah's cows has an infection caused by bacteria. How can Samina try to cure this infection?

____ [1]

(b) Not all microorganisms are harmful. Some are very useful.

(i) Which **one** of the following is made using microorganisms? (Tick **one** box.)

butter	**cream**	**milk**	**yoghurt**
☐	☐	☐	☐

[1]

(ii) Give one use of microorganisms, apart from making foods and drinks.

____ [1]

[Total: 5 marks]

3. Some power stations can now burn straw instead of coal.

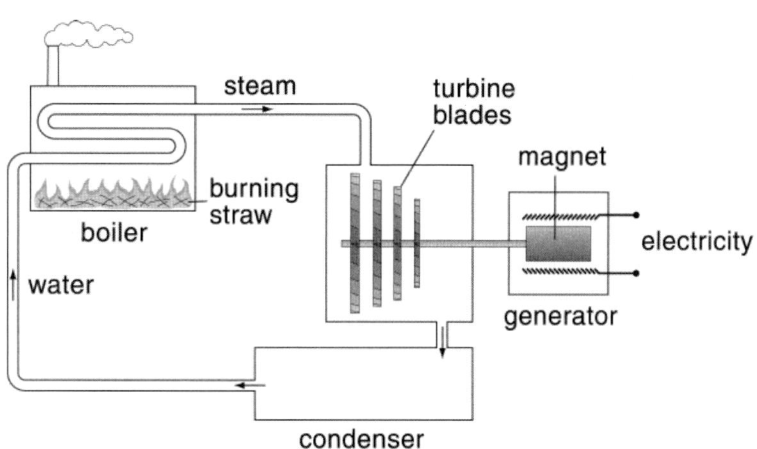

(a) The four stages of generating electricity by burning straw are given below. Put the stages in the correct order by writing 1st, 2nd, 3rd or 4th in each box.

Steam turns the turbine blades.

The spinning magnet generates electricity in the coils of wire.

Heat from burning straw boils water to make steam.

The turbine shaft spins a large magnet.

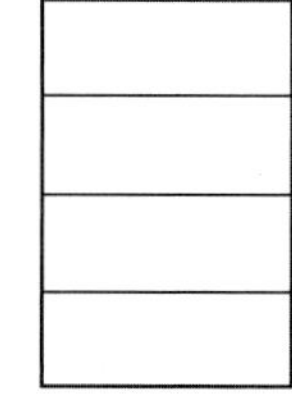

[3]

(b) Explain **one** main advantage of burning straw instead of coal. Use the following words in your answer:

fossil fuel **limited** **renewable**

___

___

___ [3]

(c) Malik uses a large electric fan heater to heat his workshop. He thinks it would be cheaper to use a straw burner.

(i) The fan heater uses a 240 V mains supply and takes a current of 25 A. Use the formula below to calculate the power of the heater in watts.

power = voltage × current

= ______ × ______

= ______ W

[1]

(ii) What is the power of the heater in kilowatts?

__________ kW [1]

(iii) Electricity costs 7p per kilowatt-hour (kWh). How much does it cost Malik to run the heater for one week (40 hours)? Show your working.

Cost = £ __________ per week [2]

(d) A simple straw burner is shown below. Air is blown through the tubes and is heated by the burning straw.

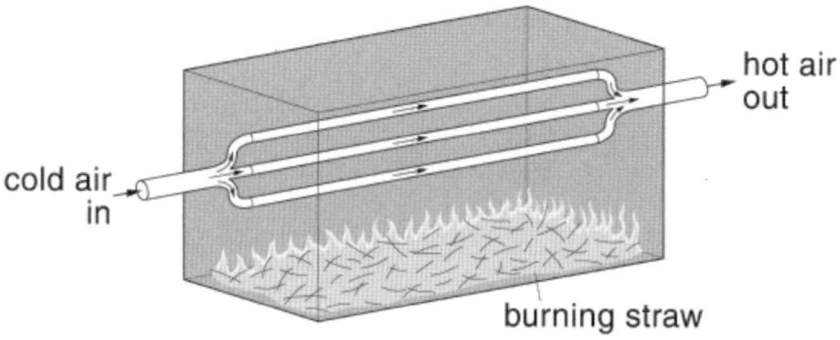

(i) Describe how the heat energy passes from the burning straw to the air inside the tubes.

____ [1]

(ii) Which is the most suitable material for these tubes? Tick **one** box.

a ceramic	☐	a metal	☐
a composite	☐	a polymer	☐

[1]

(iii) Give **one** reason for your choice of material.

____ [1]

[Total: 13 marks]

4. George is a blacksmith. He makes objects such as gates and horseshoes by hammering and bending hot strips of metal, mainly iron and steel.

(a) Which property of metals allows George to bend and hammer them into shape?

____ [1]

(b) George heats the metals in a coke fire. Coke is almost pure carbon. It burns to form carbon dioxide.

(i) What is the chemical formula for carbon dioxide?

____ [1]

(ii) Burning coke is an exothermic reaction. What does 'exothermic' mean?

____ [1]

(c) George's coke fire is in a metal tray lined with ceramic firebricks. The bricks have a very high melting point. Give **one** other property of ceramics that makes them suitable for this purpose.

____ [1]

(d) Scientists classify materials as elements (either metal or non-metal), compounds or mixtures.

Write the name of each material in the correct part of the table. Use the information below to help you. One has been done for you.

- **iron** – contains only iron; shiny; bends without breaking
- **steel** – mainly iron, with small amounts of carbon, which can vary
- **carbon** – contains only carbon; dull; brittle
- **coke** – mainly carbon, with impurities that can vary
- **carbon dioxide** – always contains the same proportions of carbon and oxygen

Metal element	Non-metal element	Compound	Mixture
iron			

[4]

[Total: 8 marks]

5. Richard grows large amounts of a plant called rape. He harvests the seeds, which will be crushed to produce rapeseed oil.

(a) Richard's rapeseed oil is turned into biodiesel. Biodiesel is a fuel that can be burned in engines instead of normal diesel.

Which **two** of the statements below describe biodiesel? Tick **two** boxes.

It is an organic material.	☐
It is a fossil fuel.	☐
It is obtained by fractional distillation of crude oil.	☐
It is a renewable energy resource.	☐
When it burns, the reaction is endothermic.	☐

[2]

(b) Richard gives his rape plants NPK fertiliser.

(i) Put rings around the **two** compounds that could be mixed together to make an NPK fertiliser.

ammonium phosphate **ammonium sulphate**

calcium carbonate **potassium nitrate**

[2]

(ii) N, P and K stand for three minerals that all plants need. Name the mineral that is needed for making proteins.

______________________________ [1]

(iii) Richard spreads the fertiliser over the soil. It dissolves in rain water and soaks into the soil. Explain briefly how the minerals get from the soil into the rape plants.

____

______________________________ [2]

(c) Richard reads a report about using fertiliser for growing rape. It includes the graph below.

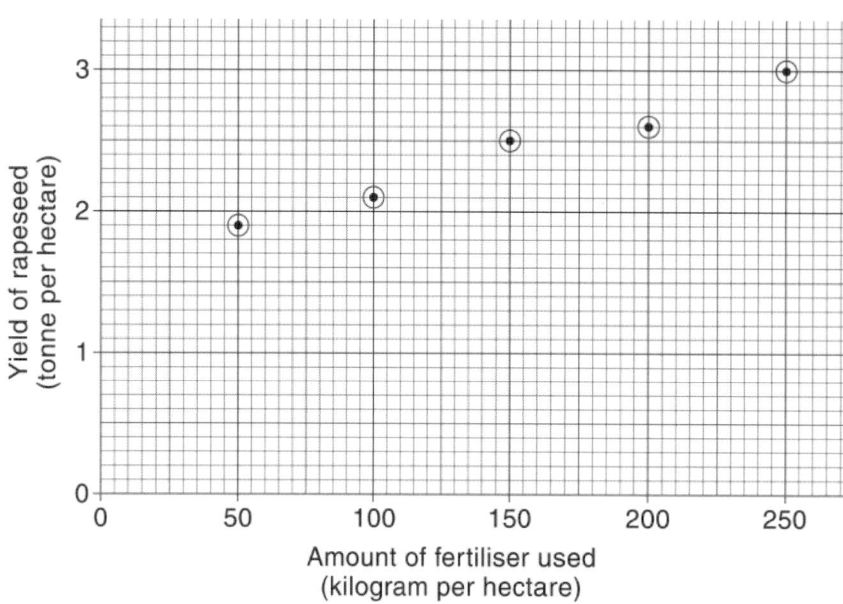

(i) What does the graph show about the effect of using fertiliser?

____ [1]

(ii) What would be the approximate yield of rapeseed if **no** fertiliser was used?
Draw a line on the graph to show how you decide your answer.

____________________ tonne per hectare [2]

(iii) Using too much fertiliser causes problems. Give **one** economic disadvantage and **one** environmental disadvantage of using too much fertiliser.

Economic ____ [1]

Environmental ____ [1]

(d) The rape plants on one part of the farm are small and less healthy than the rest. Their leaves are yellowish instead of green. Richard gave the plants NPK fertiliser, but they are short of another element.

(i) Which other element should he give to these plants to make them healthy?

____ [1]

(ii) Explain why this element helps the leaves to go green.

____ [1]

(e) Put a ring around the product that Richard uses to control weeds in his fields of rape.

fertiliser **fungicide** **herbicide** **pesticide** [1]

[Total: 15 marks]

6. Richard uses a variety of materials on his farm. Many of these consist of one substance dissolved or finely dispersed in another. Such a mixture may be:

an aerosol **an emulsion** **a foam** **a gel** **a solution** **a suspension**

(a) Complete the table below describing some of these mixtures. One has been done for you.

Example	Type of mixture	What it consists of
liquid fertiliser for plants	solution	solid dissolved in water
pesticide		oily liquid droplets in water
white paint for farmhouse walls	suspension	
weedkiller spray	aerosol	
sponge rubber cushion for tractor seat		bubbles trapped in a soft solid

[4]

(b) Tony and Sarah keep cows. Their milk is used to make dairy products.

(i) Name **two** products made from milk that are different types of emulsion.

1 ______________________________

2 ______________________________ **[2]**

(ii) Explain the difference between these two emulsions.

Emulsion 1 contains ______________ dispersed in ______________

Emulsion 2 contains ______________ dispersed in ______________ **[2]**

[Total: 8 marks]

7. Anita visits a lead mining museum to learn how lead ore was mined and how the lead metal was extracted from it. She buys samples of three minerals.

Label	Appearance
Cerussite, $PbCO_3$	dirty white
Galena, PbS	dark grey and shiny
Pyrite, FeS_2	golden and shiny

(a) From the information above, how can Anita tell that cerussite and galena contain lead but pyrite does not?

______________________________ [1]

(b) George the blacksmith shows Anita how to make some lead. They add lumps of galena to the burning coke in George's fire. Heating the galena in air converts it into lead oxide. Later they find beads of lead in the fire.

(i) Explain how the lead oxide becomes lead.

____

______________________________ [2]

(ii) Write a word equation for the reaction that converts lead oxide to lead in the fire.

______________________________ [2]

(c) Leadwort is a plant that grows near the lead mine. Lead compounds are poisonous, but leadwort has gradually developed a resistance to lead.

(i) Name the process by which plants and animals develop special characteristics over many generations.

______________________________ [1]

(ii) Anita looks through a microscope at a leadwort leaf cell. It has all the usual parts. Name the parts labelled **A**, **B** and **C** on the diagram below.

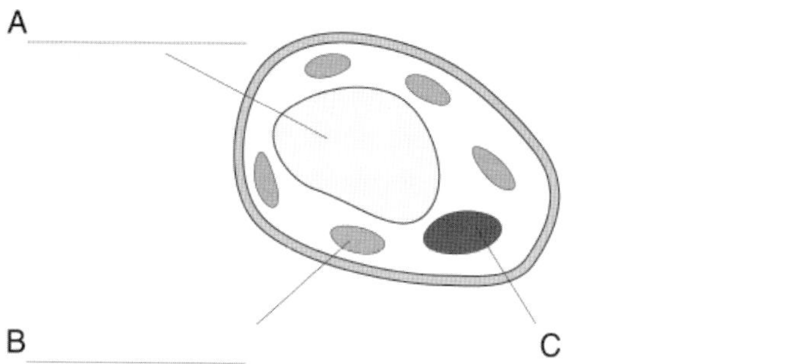

[3]

(iii) The features that make leadwort resistant to lead cannot be seen through the microscope. They are passed from one generation to the next. In which part of the cell are these features found?

____ [1]

[Total: 10 marks]

8 a) Complete the labels on the pie chart showing the gases in the atmosphere.
Use 3 gases from the list.

carbon dioxide

oxygen

ozone

nitrogen

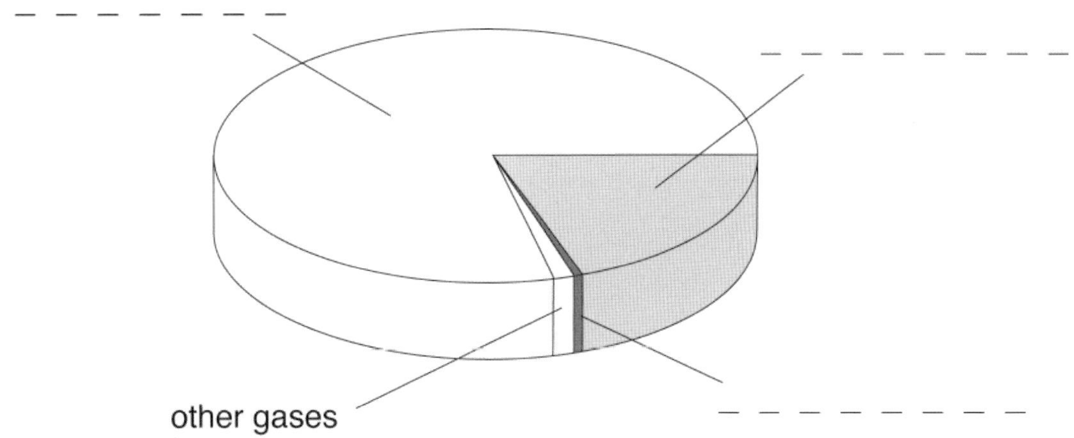

[3]

b) The surface of the Earth is made up of tectonic plates. As the plates move they cause changes on the Earths surface. Some changes are fast and some are slow.

Put the following changes into the correct columns in the table.

continents forming

earthquake

mountains forming

tsunami

Fast changes	Slow changes
volcano	continental drift

[2]

Total: 5 marks

THIS IS A BLANK PAGE

Practice Paper

Surname	Initials

GCSE in Applied Science (Double Award)

Unit 2: Science for the needs of society

Higher tier

Time 1 hour 30 minutes

You may use a calculator.

Preparing for your test

Read this front sheet carefully

- Write your name in the space above.
- Write your answers, in blue or black ink, in the spaces provided on the question paper.
- Answer **all** the questions.
- Read each question carefully, and make sure you know what you have to do before starting your answer.

Information

- The number of marks is given in brackets [ ] at the end of each question or part question.
- The total number of marks for this paper is **75**.

1. Richard runs an intensive farm. He grows large amounts of a plant called rape. He harvests the seeds, which will be crushed to produce rapeseed oil.

(a) Richard's rapeseed oil is turned into biodiesel. Biodiesel is a fuel that can be burned in engines instead of normal diesel.

Which **two** of the statements below describe biodiesel? Tick **two** boxes.

It is an organic material.	☐
It is a fossil fuel.	☐
It is obtained by fractional distillation of crude oil.	☐
It is a renewable energy resource.	☐
When it burns, the reaction is endothermic.	☐

[2]

(b) Richard gives his rape plants NPK fertiliser.

(i) Put rings around the **two** compounds that could be mixed together to make an NPK fertiliser.

ammonium phosphate **ammonium sulphate**

calcium carbonate **potassium nitrate**

[2]

(ii) N, P and K stand for three minerals that all plants need. Name the mineral that is needed for making proteins.

____ **[1]**

(iii) Richard spreads the fertiliser over the soil. It dissolves in rain water and soaks into the soil. Explain briefly how the minerals get from the soil into the rape plants.

____

____ **[2]**

(c) Richard reads a report about using fertiliser for growing rape. It includes the graph below.

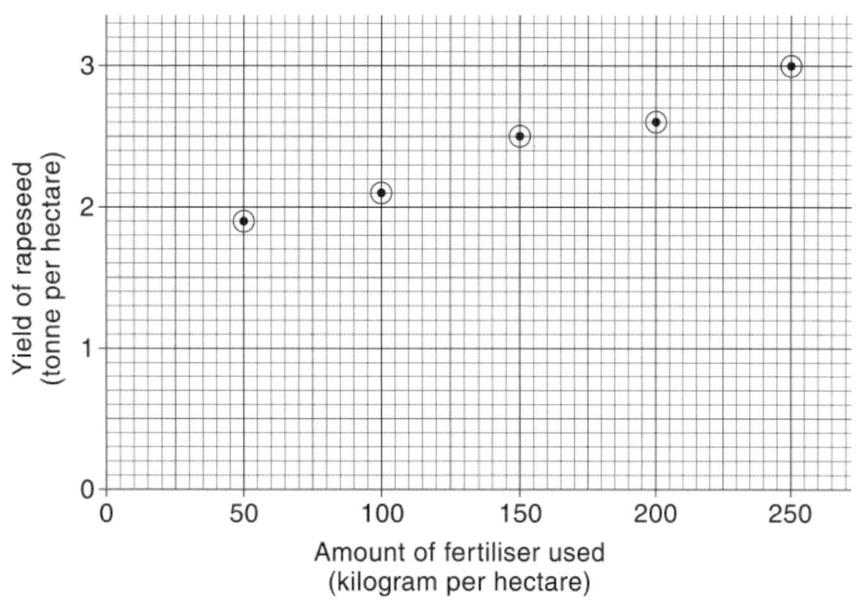

(i) What does the graph show about the effect of using fertiliser?

____ [1]

(ii) What would be the approximate yield of rapeseed if **no** fertiliser was used? Draw a line on the graph to show how you decide your answer.

____________________ tonne per hectare [2]

(iii) Using too much fertiliser causes problems. Give **one** environmental disadvantage of using too much fertiliser.

____ [1]

(d) The rape plants on one part of the farm are small and less healthy than the rest. Their leaves are yellowish. Richard gave the plants NPK fertiliser but they are short of another element.

(i) Which other element should he give to these plants to make them healthy?

____ **[1]**

(ii) Explain why this element helps the leaves to go green.

____ **[1]**

(e) Put a ring around the product that Richard uses to control weeds in his fields of rape.

fertiliser **fungicide** **herbicide** **pesticide**

[1]

[Total: 14 marks]

2. Richard uses a variety of materials on his farm. Many of these consist of one substance dissolved or finely dispersed in another. Such a mixture may be:

an aerosol **an emulsion** **a foam** **a gel** **a solution** **a suspension**

(a) Complete the table below describing some of these mixtures. One has been done for you.

Example	Type of mixture	What it consists of
liquid fertiliser for plants	solution	solid dissolved in water
pesticide		oily liquid droplets in water
white paint for farmhouse walls	suspension	
weedkiller spray	aerosol	
sponge rubber cushion for tractor seat		bubbles trapped in a soft solid

[4]

(b) Tony and Sarah keep cows. Their milk is used to make dairy products.

(i) Name **two** products made from milk that are different types of emulsion.

1 ______________________________

2 ______________________________ **[2]**

(ii) Explain the difference between these two emulsions.

Emulsion 1 contains ______________ dispersed in ______________

Emulsion 2 contains ______________ dispersed in ______________ **[2]**

[Total: 8 marks]

3. George is a blacksmith. He makes objects such as gates and horseshoes by hammering and bending hot strips of metal, mainly iron and steel.

(a) Which property of metals allows George to bend and hammer them into shape?

____ [1]

(b) Steel is an alloy. Explain the meaning of the term 'alloy'.

____

____ [2]

(c) The diagrams show the arrangement of atoms in pure iron and in steel.

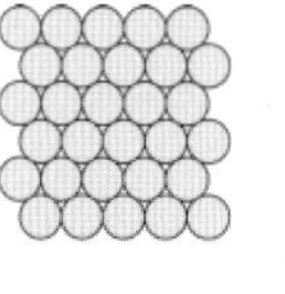

Pure iron

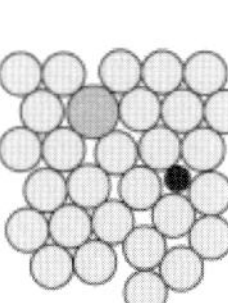

Steel

Using these diagrams, explain why:

(i) iron can bend without breaking

____

____ [2]

(ii) steel is more difficult to bend than pure iron.

____

____ **[2]**

(d) George heats the metals in a coke fire. Coke is almost pure carbon. It burns to form carbon dioxide.

(i) Draw a 'dot and cross' diagram of carbon dioxide to illustrate the equation below.

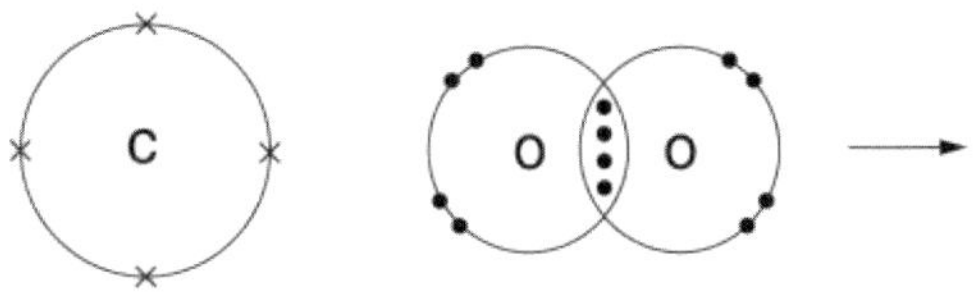

C + O_2 ⟶ CO_2 **[2]**

(ii) What type of chemical bond does the diagram show?

____ **[1]**

(iii) Each carbon atom in coke has four bonds to other carbon atoms. Oxygen atoms are bonded in pairs (O_2). Explain, in terms of bonds breaking and forming, why burning carbon is an exothermic reaction.

____

____ **[2]**

(e) George's coke fire is in a metal tray lined with ceramic firebricks. The bricks have a very high melting point.

(i) Give **one** other property of ceramics that makes them suitable for this purpose.

____ **[1]**

(ii) Firebricks are made from clay, which is a soft material that can be easily moulded into shape. Explain why clay is soft, but firebricks are hard. You may draw diagrams if you wish.

Clay is soft because________________________________

____

Brick is hard because ________________________________

____ **[4]**

[Total: 17 marks]

4 **a)** The surface of the Earth is made up of tectonic plates.
As the plates move they cause changes on the Earth's surface. Some changes are fast and some are slow.

Put the following changes into the correct columns in the table.

continents forming

earthquake

mountains forming

tsunami

Fast changes	Slow changes
volcano	continental drift

[2]

b) The following table gives some information about some astronomical objects.

Astronomical object	Size (diameter)	How observed
A	1, 000 m	reflects light
B	1, 000, 000 km	emits light
C	10, 000 km	reflects light
D	10, 000 light years	emits light

Which object is:

i) a planet? ____________________

ii) a galaxy? ____________________

iii) a star? ____________________

[3]

Total: 5 marks

5. Richard's farm produces a lot of waste straw every year. Carla, a heating engineer, designs a straw-fired boiler to produce hot water for the farm and some nearby cottages.

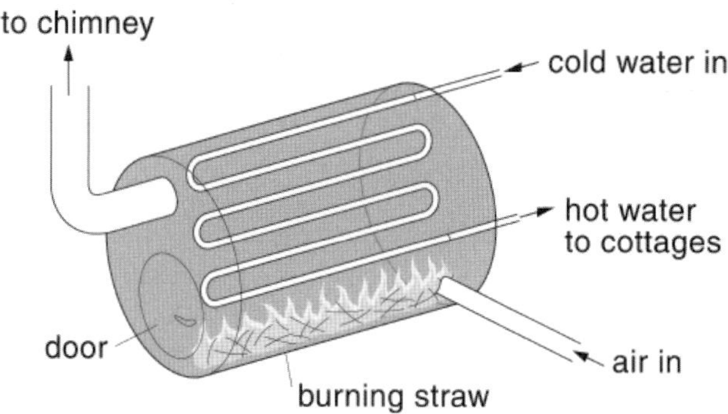

(a) Carla chooses materials with suitable properties to use for the boiler. The water pipe must be made from a metal that will not melt in the flames.
State **one** further property that this metal needs. Give a reason.

Property ________________________________

Reason ________________________________ [2]

(b) An overhead pipe carries the hot water from the boiler to cottages a few hundred metres away. Some heat energy is lost on the way.

(i) Describe **two** ways in which this heat is lost.

1 ________________________________

2 ________________________________ [2]

(ii) How can Carla make sure that this heat loss is as small as possible?

________________________________ [1]

(c) Richard blows warm air through his harvested wheat to dry it. He uses an electrical heater to warm the air.

(i) The electrical heater uses a 240 V mains supply and takes a current of 25 A.
State the formula that links voltage and current with electrical power.

________________________________ [1]

(ii) Calculate the power of the heater in watts.

_________________ W [1]

(iii) Electricity costs 7p per kilowatt-hour (kWh). Assuming the heater runs 24 hours a day, how much per day does it cost? Show your working.

Cost = _________________ per day [2]

(d) Carla suggests that Richard could use waste heat from the straw-fired boiler instead of the electrical heater. A heat exchanger is needed because the smoke would damage the wheat.

(i) Add the following labels to the diagram of the heat exchanger:

hot smoke from boiler **smoke to chimney**

cold air in **hot air to wheat**

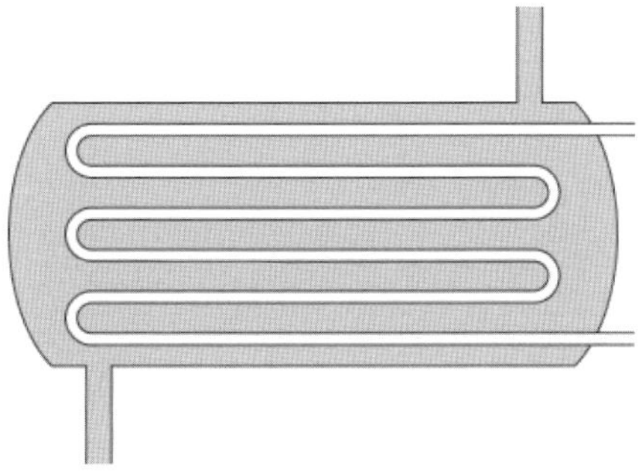

[1]

(ii) Explain how the heat exchanger works. Use the diagram to help you.

____

____

____ [3]

[Total: 13 marks]

6. Carla keeps fit by going on a cross-country run every day. She monitors her pulse and breathing rate to check that her body is working hard, but not too hard.

(a) (i) Carla starts off jogging gently. Name the process that takes place in Carla's muscle cells to provide energy.

____ [1]

(ii) The energy is released by oxidising glucose. Give the chemical formula of glucose.

____ [1]

(b) When Carla runs faster, or uphill, her pulse increases. Explain why.

____

____ [2]

(c) Towards the end of her run, Carla's muscles begin to ache because of a build-up of acid in her muscle cells.

(i) Name this acid.

____ [1]

(ii) Explain how this acid is formed in the cells.

____ [1]

(d) Even when Carla stops running, her breathing rate is still high. Explain how this helps her aching muscles to recover.

____

____ [1]

[Total: 7 marks]

7. Anita visits a lead mining museum to learn how lead ore was mined and how the lead metal was extracted from it. She buys samples of three minerals.

Label	Appearance
Cerussite, $PbCO_3$	dirty white
Galena, PbS	dark grey and shiny
Pyrite, FeS_2	golden and shiny

(a) From the information above, how can Anita tell that cerussite and galena contain lead but pyrite does not?

______________________________ [1]

(b) George the blacksmith shows Anita how to make some lead. They add lumps of galena to the burning coke in George's fire. Heating the galena in air converts it into lead oxide. Later they find beads of lead in the fire.

(i) Explain how the lead oxide becomes lead.

____

______________________________ [2]

(ii) Write a balanced equation for the conversion of lead oxide to lead in the coke fire.

______________________________ [2]

(c) Lead oxide has a high melting point.

(i) Name the type of bonding in lead oxide.

______________________________ [1]

(ii) Explain in terms of electrons how this bond is formed.

____

______________________________ [2]

(d) Lead compounds are toxic, so most plants cannot grow on soil that contains lead ores. Leadwort is one plant that can. It has developed this resistance through natural selection.

Use your knowledge of selective breeding to explain how leadwort plants developed their resistance naturally over many generations.

____

____

____

____ [3]

[Total: 11 marks]

Foundation tier – Mark scheme

Question		Suggested answer	Total mark
1	a	Flour; wool; beef	3
	b	Jam; cheese; leather	3
	c	i Animals provide manure; to use on crops instead of artificial fertilisers/ to help build up soil fertility [**or** other benefit to plants, for example carbon dioxide]. [**Reject** provide food for farmers.]	2
		Crops provide food/straw for animals; especially in winter [**Allow** second mark for specific example, for example maize, hay, silage] [**or** other benefit to animals, for example release oxygen] [**Reject** provide food for farmers]	2
		ii Mechanical weeding/mulching/black plastic [**or** other method avoiding herbicides]	1
			Total: 11
2	a	i Any suitable answer, for example foot and mouth/TB [**Accept** BSE/scrapie]	1
		ii Immunisation/inoculation/vaccination	1
		iii Give the cow antibiotics	1
	b	i Yoghurt	1
		ii Any suitable answer, for example making antibiotics/vaccines/compost	1
			Total: 5
3	a	2nd; 4th; 1st; 3rd [All four correct = three marks; two or three correct = two marks; one correct = one mark]	3
	b	Coal is a fossil fuel;	1
		so there is a limited supply;	1
		whereas straw is a renewable resource produced each year	1
	c	i $240 \times 25 = 6000$ W	1
		ii 6 kW [**Allow** error carried forward]	1
		iii $6 \times 40 \times 7$	1
		$= 1680$ p $= £16.80$ [**Allow** error carried forward. Give two marks for correct answer with or without working shown.]	1
	d	i By conduction through sides of the tube	1
		ii Metal	1
		iii **Either** good conductor of heat/high thermal conductivity; **or** high melting point/resistant to high temperatures	1
			Total: 13

Foundation tier – Mark scheme

Question		Suggested answer	Total mark
4	a	Malleability	1
	b	i CO_2	1
		ii Reaction gives out heat	1
	c	Low thermal conductivity/high thermal insulation	1
	d	**Metal element**: iron; **Non-metal element**: *carbon*; **Compound**: *carbon dioxide*; **Mixture**: *steel*, *coke* [one mark each]	2 2
			Total: 8
5	a	Organic material; renewable energy resource [Subtract one mark for each additional tick beyond two. (Min. score = 0)]	2
	b	i Ammonium phosphate; potassium nitrate. [Subtract one mark if three ringed. No marks if all four ringed.]	2
		ii Nitrate/nitrogen	1
		iii Solution is absorbed into root (hairs); by osmosis	2
	c	i Yield increases with amount of fertiliser used (o.w.t.t.e.)	1
		ii Suitable best straight line drawn; Intercept at *y*-axis read off correctly (approx. 1.6 t ha^{-1})	1 1
		iii Costs more, but gives no further increase in yield (o.w.t.t.e.) [**or** other valid disadvantage] Extra washes away, causing pollution of rivers (o.w.t.t.e.) [**or** other valid disadvantage]	1 1
	d	i Magnesium	1
		ii Needed to make chlorophyll/chlorophyll contains magnesium	1
	e	Herbicide	1
			Total: 15

Foundation tier – Mark scheme

<table>
<tr><th>Question</th><th></th><th>Suggested answer</th><th>Total mark</th></tr>
<tr><td>6</td><td>a</td><td>

Example	Type of mixture	What it consists of
pesticide	*emulsion*	oily liquid droplets in water
white paint for farmhouse walls	suspension	*solid particles in a liquid/water*
weedkiller spray	aerosol	*liquid droplets in a gas/air*
sponge rubber cushion for tractor seat	*foam*	bubbles trapped in a soft solid

[one mark each]</td><td>4</td></tr>
<tr><td></td><td>b</td><td>i Butter; cream [Accept margarine/yoghurt]</td><td>2</td></tr>
<tr><td></td><td></td><td>ii Cream/yoghurt = fat dispersed in water;
butter/margarine = water dispersed in fat</td><td>2</td></tr>
<tr><td></td><td></td><td></td><td>Total: 8</td></tr>
<tr><td>7</td><td>a</td><td>They have Pb in their formulae</td><td>1</td></tr>
<tr><td></td><td>b</td><td>i Lead oxide is reduced/oxygen is removed;
by CO/C/coke</td><td>1
1</td></tr>
<tr><td></td><td></td><td>ii Lead oxide + carbon monoxide ⟶ lead + carbon dioxide
or Lead oxide + carbon ⟶ lead + carbon oxide
[Accept carbon oxide, monoxide or dioxide in 2nd equation]
Correct reactants;
Correct products</td><td>

1
1</td></tr>
<tr><td></td><td>c</td><td>i Selective breeding/natural selection</td><td>1</td></tr>
<tr><td></td><td></td><td>ii A = vacuole; B = chloroplast; C = nucleus [one mark each]</td><td>3</td></tr>
<tr><td></td><td></td><td>iii Nucleus/chromosomes/DNA</td><td>1</td></tr>
<tr><td></td><td></td><td></td><td>Total: 10</td></tr>
<tr><td>8</td><td>a</td><td>in order: oxygen
carbon dioxide
nitrogen</td><td>1
1
1</td></tr>
<tr><td></td><td>b</td><td>fast changes: earthquake and tsunami
slow changes: continents forming and mountains forming</td><td>2 marks for 3 or 4 correct
1 mark for 1 or 2 correct</td></tr>
<tr><td></td><td></td><td></td><td>Total: 5</td></tr>
<tr><td></td><td></td><td></td><td>Total mark available: 75</td></tr>
</table>

Higher tier – Mark scheme

<table>
<tr><th>Question</th><th></th><th>Suggested answer</th><th>Total mark</th></tr>
<tr><td>1</td><td>a</td><td>Organic material; renewable energy resource. [Subtract one mark for each additional tick beyond two. (Min. score = 0)]</td><td>2</td></tr>
<tr><td></td><td>b</td><td>i Ammonium phosphate; potassium nitrate. [Subtract one mark if three ringed. No marks if all four ringed.]</td><td>2</td></tr>
<tr><td></td><td></td><td>ii Nitrate/nitrogen</td><td>1</td></tr>
<tr><td></td><td></td><td>iii Solution is absorbed into root (hairs); by osmosis</td><td>2</td></tr>
<tr><td></td><td>c</td><td>i Yield increases with amount of fertiliser used (o.w.t.t.e.)</td><td>1</td></tr>
<tr><td></td><td></td><td>ii Suitable best straight line drawn;
Intercept at y-axis read off correctly (approx. 1.6 t ha^{-1})</td><td>1
1</td></tr>
<tr><td></td><td></td><td>iii Extra washes away, causing pollution of rivers (o.w.t.t.e.)
[or other valid disadvantage]</td><td>1</td></tr>
<tr><td></td><td>d</td><td>i Magnesium</td><td>1</td></tr>
<tr><td></td><td></td><td>ii Needed to make chlorophyll/chlorophyll contains magnesium</td><td>1</td></tr>
<tr><td></td><td>e</td><td>Herbicide</td><td>1</td></tr>
<tr><td></td><td></td><td></td><td>Total: 14</td></tr>
<tr><td>2</td><td>a</td><td>
<table>
<tr><th>Example</th><th>Type of mixture</th><th>What is consists of</th></tr>
<tr><td>pesticide</td><td>emulsion</td><td>oily liquid droplets in water</td></tr>
<tr><td>white paint for farmhouse walls</td><td>suspension</td><td>solid particles in a liquid/water</td></tr>
<tr><td>weedkiller spray</td><td>aerosol</td><td>liquid droplets in a gas/air</td></tr>
<tr><td>sponge rubber cushion for tractor seat</td><td>foam</td><td>bubbles trapped in a soft solid</td></tr>
</table>
[one mark each]</td><td>4</td></tr>
<tr><td></td><td>b</td><td>i Butter; cream [Accept margarine/yoghurt]</td><td>2</td></tr>
<tr><td></td><td></td><td>ii Cream/yoghurt = fat dispersed in water;
butter/margarine = water dispersed in fat</td><td>2</td></tr>
<tr><td></td><td></td><td></td><td>Total: 8</td></tr>
</table>

Higher tier – Mark scheme

Question		Suggested answer	Total mark
3	a	Malleability	1
	b	A mixture; of metals (or a metal and non-metal, such as carbon)	1 1
	c	i The layers / planes of atoms; can slide over each other	1 1
		ii Different sized atoms; make it more difficult for layers to slide	1 1
	d	i **Four** electrons in each C–O overlap area; Correct number of other electrons shown [Four on each O, none on C]	1 1
		ii Covalent	1
		iii Energy given out by forming C=O bonds; is greater than energy put in to break bonds in C and O_2 [**or** energy in < energy out]	1 1
	e	i Low thermal conductivity/high thermal insulation	1
		ii Soft clay has water molecules between the layers (of Al silicate); allowing layers to slide over each other easily; firing the clay drives off this water; and forms cross-links between the layers	1 1 1 1
			Total: 17
4	a	fast changes: earthquake and tsunami slow changes: continents forming and mountains forming	2 marks for 3 or 4 correct 1 mark for 1 or 2 correct
	b	i C	1
		ii D	1
		iii B	1
			Total: 5

Higher tier – Mark scheme

Question		Suggested answer	Total mark
5	a	High thermal conductivity [**or** low reactivity];	1
		to transfer heat through the pipe wall into the water [**or** to prevent corrosion by water]	1
	b	i Any **two** of: conduction through pipe walls; radiation from pipe surface into the air; convection currents carrying heat away from pipe surface [**Reject** mention of water leakage] [one mark each]	2
		ii Insulate the pipe	1
	c	i Power = current × voltage (**or** amps × volts)	1
		ii 6000 W	1
		iii 6000 W = 6 kW;	1
		6 × 24 × 7 = 1008 p **or** £10.08 [**Allow** error carried forward. Give two marks for correct answer with or without working shown.]	1
	d	i Smoke in and out of shell, **and** air in and out of pipe [**Accept** vice versa]	1
		ii Heat energy in the hot waste gases/smoke from the boiler;	1
		is transferred/conducted through the pipe;	1
		into the air inside the pipe	1
			Total: 13
6	a	i **Aerobic** respiration	1
		ii $C_6H_{12}O_6$	1
	b	Any **two** of: to carry more blood to muscles; to provide more oxygen; to increase rate of respiration; to release more energy	2
	c	i Lactic acid	1
		ii Breakdown/metabolism of glucose **without oxygen/ anaerobic** respiration	1
	d	Extra oxygen breaks down/oxidises lactic acid [**or** repays oxygen debt]	1
			Total: 7

Higher tier – Mark scheme

Question		Suggested answer	Total mark
7	a	They have Pb in their formulae	1
	b	i Lead oxide is reduced/oxygen is removed;	1
		by CO/C/coke	1
		ii Correct formula, PbO;	1
		Correct completion of equation $PbO + C \longrightarrow Pb + CO$ [**or** $PbO + CO \longrightarrow Pb + CO_2$ **or** $2PbO + C \longrightarrow 2Pb + CO_2$]	1
	c	i Ionic	1
		ii Electron transfer;	1
		from lead atoms to oxygen atoms [**or** lead atoms lose electrons; oxygen atoms gain electrons]	1
	d	Award marks for concept of 'survival of the fittest', e.g. Some resistance allows better growth and more flowers;	1
		so cross-pollination with a resistant plant is more likely;	1
		so a higher proportion of next generation have resistance	1
			Total: 11
			Total mark available : 75

United Kingdom: Folens Publishers, Apex Business Centre, Boscombe Road, Dunstable, LU5 4RL.
Email: folens@folens.com
Ireland: Folens Publishers, Greenhills Road, Tallaght, Dublin 24.
Email: info@folens.ie
Poland: JUKA, ul. Renesansowa 38, Warsaw 01-905.

Editors: Tim Jackson, Melanie Thompson and Dawn Booth
Layout artists: Patricia Hollingsworth and Suzanne Ward
Illustrations: chrisorr.com and Dave Thompson
Cover design: Martin Cross and FMS

First published 2003 by Folens Limited.

Every effort has been made to contact copyright holders of material used in this publication. If any copyright holder has been overlooked, we should be pleased to make any necessary arrangements.

British Library Cataloguing in Publication Data. A catalogue record for this publication is available from the British Library.

ISBN 1 84303 973 7